Implementing IT Governance

Andere uitgaven bij Van Haren Publishing

Van Haren Publishing (VHP) is gespecialiseerd in uitgaven over Best Practices, methodes en standaarden op het gebied van de volgende domeinen:
- IT-management,
- Architecture (Enterprise en IT),
- Business management en
- Projectmanagement.

Deze uitgaven worden uitgegeven in verschillende talen in series, zoals *ITSM Library, Best Practice, IT Management Topics* en *I-Tracks.*

VHP is tevens de uitgever voor toonaangevende instellingen en bedrijven, onder andere The Open Group, PMI-NL, IPMA-NL, CA, Getronics Consulting, Pink Elephant.

Onderwerpen per domein zijn:

IT (Service) Management / IT Governance	Architecture (Enterprise en IT)	Project-, Programma- en Riskmanagement
ASL	Archimate®	A4-Projectmanagement
BiSL	TOGAF™	ICB / NCB
CATS	GEA®	MINCE®
CMMI		M_o_R®
CobiT	**Business Management**	MSP™
ISO 17799	EFQM	PMBOK®
ISO 27001	ISA-95	PRINCE2™
ISO/IEC 20000	ISO 9000	
ISPL	SixSigma	
IT Service CMM	SOX	
ITIL® V2	SqEME®	
ITIL® V3		
ITSM		
MOF		
MSF		

Voor een compleet overzicht van alle uitgaven, ga naar onze website: www.vanharen.net.

Implementing IT Governance

A Practical Guide to Global Best Practices in IT Management

Dr Gad J Selig PMP COP

Colophon

Title: Implementing IT Governance
                     A Practical Guide to Global Best Practices in IT Management

Author: Dr Gad J Selig PMP COP

Editor: Jayne Wilkinson

Publisher: Van Haren Publishing, Zaltbommel, www.vanharen.net

ISBN: 978 90 8753119 5

Edition: First edition, first impression, March 2008
                     First edition, second impression, January 2009

Design and Layout: CO2 Premedia, Amersfoort - NL

Printer: Wilco, Amersfoort - NL

Foreword

IT governance is vital to the success of the IT function within corporate enterprises on a global basis. Dr Selig's book on this very topic is a great resource for all IT practitioners, and brings together every critical aspect relating to IT governance.

This book lays out a roadmap to executing within a solid governance model. It looks at all aspects of establishing, marinating, growing and sustaining an IT ecosystem. The combination of case studies and disciplined approaches to building well structured processes, committed leaders and change agents will help the board, executive management and, most of all, CIOs and IT professionals, think through what has worked, what can work and how to deploy IT governance successfully.

Being a CIO for many years in the highly intensive technology industry, I have developed a respect for the process side of running IT like a business. There has always been a need to match governance for IT with the rapid advances in new technology. This requires effective implementation of guiding principles and controls, to ensure corporate enterprises optimize their investments.

In my experience, Information Technology and its effective management is a fundamental cornerstone of any well-run business. Insuring that this cornerstone is optimized is all about optimizing the business side of IT. Successful CIOs recognize that IT has become far more than a means of increasing efficiency and reducing costs. Rather, they see IT as a prime stimulus for, and enabler of, business innovation and transformation – and themselves as key collaborators in a process that develops business and IT strategies in concert.

The need to cultivate a holistic management model for the information technology function is critical, especially in fast growing firms. The opportunity to push a product's time to market, scale the core infrastructure and be a change agent for the firm, are all part of governing the IT activity.

Those IT practitioners, who are faced with how to scale a core delivery function and how to push innovative approaches into the business models, will especially benefit from this book's special focus on communication and building business cases.

I have known Dr Selig more than 10 years and have conducted joint teaching with him. He is a seasoned IT veteran, who has organized a set of proven, fundamental approaches for the IT professional and has a passion for sharing these approaches. In this book, Dr Selig's practical business experience and academic experience provide a great combination that represents a valuable contribution to advance the field. Whether you are a Board member, a CEO, a practicing CIO or a student of IT, this book will guide you through complex business and technological roadmaps that work and are pragmatic.

Richard Lefave
CIO
Sprint Nextel
Overland Park, KS

Dr Selig's book on IT Governance is an excellent addition to the knowledge base of the business of Information Technology.

I have spent 25 years in the IT world, going from technician to running IT groups. I am currently CEO of a company whose success is very heavily reliant on information technology. I have also taught Management Information Systems as an adjunct professor, at the MBA level for several years. Dr Selig's book is an excellent compilation of information on the governance of IT in business.

The book has many of the concepts that I have been familiar with and used over the years, as well as new ideas and information that I had not come across previously. While it is extremely comprehensive, it is written in a very business-friendly way, where the ideas are presented in a bulleted fashion, using easy to follow and find topics.

I look forward to using this book for the executives and management in my own organization, as well as using it myself to teach this course at some point. All the prep work is done – all I have to do is use the book to prepare the syllabus.

IT Governance gives you the Who, What, Where, When and How to properly organize, align and manage the IT function in any organization. Dr Selig provides a good balance between the People, Technology and Process perspectives of IT oversight.

The book reinforces the fact that IT cannot run as an independent silo. It must be aligned properly with the business and all angles of the organization. Dr Selig shows the balance, that IT is there to support the business, but also that, when properly aligned, IT can significantly help the business prosper.

Dr Selig's book is an excellent instructional text, as well as a thorough source of reference. Each topic has a very detailed list of informational details. It is a must-have for every executive or manager who deals with IT, as well as every professor teaching any business or IT course.

Michael Bodetti
President and CEO,
TNT Expense Management

Preface

There is nothing more difficult to take in hand, more perilous to conduct, or more uncertain in its success, than to take the lead in the introduction of a new order of things, because the innovator has for enemies all those who have done well under the old conditions, and lukewarm defenders in those who may do well under the new.

The Prince by Niccolò Machiavelli

IT governance has become a major concern of the Board and executive management in enterprises on a global basis. Information technology (IT) has become fundamental and critical to sustain growth, innovation and transformation, reduce and contain costs, and support the ongoing business operations of most organizations.

The author views IT governance as the focal point for more effective IT management, around which there are many important issues such as alignment, leadership, planning, execution, accountability, managing change, key performance indicators and related topics. In other words, superior IT governance represents the path to world-class IT management practices.

This pragmatic and actionable 'how to' guide is intended to integrate together current and emerging best practices, industry standards and guidelines, and draw from over twenty IT governance best practice case studies. Effective IT governance focuses on adding and sustaining value and confidence across the business to ensure optimum performance results.

Introduction

According to Susan Dallas at Gartner, *"over 75% of businesses today have ineffective or non-existent IT Governance. Most enterprises should 'blow up' their existing governance models and start from scratch."*

Effective IT governance represents a journey (not an end state in itself), which focuses on sustaining value and confidence across the business. Today, many companies start on a narrow path, or adopt a shotgun approach, and focus on the compliance component (eg Sarbanes-Oxley and others) of IT governance, without developing a more comprehensive framework, with a prioritized roadmap based on the highest value delivered to the organization.

In reviewing the current literature, completing over twenty case studies and conducting numerous private and public IT governance workshops and consulting assignments, both domestically and internationally, over the past few years (attended by thousands of executives, managers and practitioners) on IT/Business Alignment, Planning, Deployment, Program/Project Management, IT Service Management, Outsourcing, Governance and Performance Management, it is clear that much has been written and documented about the individual components of IT Governance. However, much less has been written about a comprehensive and integrated IT/Business Alignment, Planning, Execution and Governance approach; a balanced approach consisting of both a strategic top-down framework and roadmap, together with bottom-up implementation principles and practices, which address the broad range of IT issues, constraints and opportunities in a planned, co-ordinated, prioritized, cost effective and value delivery manner.

The purpose of the book is not to repeat in greater details what has been published previously, but to describe each of the major components in an overall comprehensive framework and roadmap, in sufficient detail for executives, managers and professionals. It is hoped that the book can serve as a guide for any organization in any industry, to formulate and tailor an effective approach to IT governance for its environment, and to help transition the IT organization to a higher level of maturity, effectiveness and responsiveness.

The market for the book

Many executives, managers and practitioners have expressed the need for a comprehensive, yet practical guide, based on real world experiences, on the subject of implementing IT successfully.

The book has been written by a former business and IT executive and practitioner, who has managed businesses and IT organizations, guided strategic change and advised major public and private organizations on business and IT strategy and governance; he has also completed numerous consulting assignments, and conducted private and public workshops, as well as taught graduate business and engineering courses, on the fundamentals of managing and implementing strategy, innovation, management, IT governance and change.

Our intended audiences include the following groups:

- **Directors of corporate boards** – who have overall fiduciary accountability to provide oversight for the business and key functions of the business

- **Executives** – who are primarily responsible for developing and/or approving business/IT strategy, and then overseeing its implementation and governance (the 'C' suite of Corporate Officers)

- **Managers and professionals** – who are primarily responsible for implementing and governing IT in their organizations and institutions

- **Consultants and other advisors** – who are involved in advising, planning, organizing, directing and governing IT initiatives, to help transform businesses and organizations to compete more effectively around the world

- **Academicians, graduate and upper level undergraduate students** – who must teach and master a fundamental understanding of IT, and how it impacts businesses, management, employees, the regulators and investors

The need for a comprehensive, pragmatic and actionable 'how to' guide, to help managers and practitioners plan, deploy and sustain an effective IT governance environment and culture, has been expressed by many managers and professionals in the private, public and academic sectors.

Organization of the book

The book is divided into two parts and nine chapters, which cover the three critical pillars necessary to develop, execute and sustain a robust and effective IT governance environment - leadership, people and organization, flexible and scalable processes and enabling technologies.

Part I covers the overview; business/IT alignment, strategic planning, demand management; the integrated IT governance framework and leadership, teams and organization. **Part II** covers the process and technology topics including: execution and delivery management (includes program/project management, IT Service Management with IT Infrastructure Library (ITIL) and strategic sourcing and outsourcing); performance, risk and contingency management (eg CobiT®, the Balanced Scorecard and other metrics and controls) and enabling technologies.

Part I – Leadership, people, organization and strategy

Part I of the book focuses on the chapters covering business/IT strategy, alignment, leadership, teams and organization required to develop and execute an effective IT governance environment.

Chapter 1 – Introduction to IT/business alignment, planning, execution and governance

• covers the key IT/business alignment, planning, execution, governance issues, constraints and opportunities; discusses the roles of the Board, Executive Management and Practitioners; reviews the value propositions for IT governance, provides an overview of demand management, decision rights, Balanced Scorecard metrics and how much governance is required; reviews select regulations and their compliance requirements; identifies steps in making IT governance real, and provides an assessment technique to determine the current level of IT governance maturity in an organization, and illustrates a blueprint of a future state of IT governance

Chapter 2 – Overview of a comprehensive IT governance framework and related industry current and emerging best practice frameworks

• describes and illustrates a comprehensive IT alignment, execution framework and its major components; references and brief descriptions of related current and emerging industry best practices, standards and guidelines, including maturity models are discussed such as CobiT® 4.0, Strategic Planning, Portfolio Investment Management, ISO 9001, 17799, 20000 and 27001, PMBOK, OPM3, CMMI, P-CMM, ITIL®, PRINCE2™, PMMM, ITIM, SDLC/ IDLC, Lean & 6 Sigma, eSCM, OPBOK, Baldrige, Kano, the Balanced Scorecard and AS 8000 and 8015.

Chapter 3 – Business and IT alignment, strategic/operating planning and portfolio investment management excellence (demand management)

• addresses the business and IT strategic planning cycle, executive steering groups, business/IT integration maturity model, IT planning through execution management flow, IT investment portfolio selection, prioritization and funding attributes and the customer/IT engagement (relationship building) model

Chapter 4 – Principles for managing successful organizational change, prerequisites for world-class leadership an developing high performance teams
- covers key leadership, people and soft skills and competencies required for success; it also covers the attributes of successful traditional and virtual teams in a global environment; it discusses technologies used by virtual teams located anywhere; it also reviews a framework for managing successful change in helping to transition organizations to higher levels of IT maturity and effectiveness

Part II – IT governance processes and technologies

Part II of the book covers an overview of the critical process components of IT governance, such as program and project management, IT Service Management, strategic sourcing and outsourcing, performance management and controls, select enabling technology characteristics, critical success factors and a composite checklist of required IT governance activities.

Chapter 5 – Program and project management excellence (execution management)
- program and project management is a major component of effective IT execution management; it discusses pragmatic and actionable ways to manage programs and projects within a flexible and scalable process, accommodating both fast track and complex initiatives; it provides multiple checklists, templates and metrics to help deliver programs and projects on time, within scope, within budget, with high quality and to the customer's satisfaction and/or get them back on track; it references a self-assessment maturity model that can be used to assess the current and targeted the future maturity level of an organization, and suggests a transition plan to get there

Chapter 6 – IT Service Management (ITSM) excellence (execution management)
- describes the principles and practices of IT Service Management, both versions 2 and 3, providing an overview of ITIL (IT Infrastructure Library) and its twelve process areas, including the relationships of the various processes to each other; specific objectives, benefits, and key performance indicators are covered; it illustrates a self-assessment maturity model for ITSM

Chapter 7 – Strategic sourcing, outsourcing and vendor management excellence (execution management)
- provides the fundamentals of strategic sourcing and outsourcing such as issues, concerns, opportunities, value propositions, outsourcing life cycle, the outsourcing business case, risks, modes of outsourcing (eg on-shore, rural shore, near shore, off shore, best shore, etc.), vendor selection, due diligence, contract negotiations and on-going management roles, including relationship management, metrics, escalation and disengagement considerations

Chapter 8 – IT governance performance management, management controls, risk management, business continuity and enabling technology excellence
- covers the principles and practices of achieving IT performance excellence using Balanced Scorecard metrics and linking critical success factors (CSFs) to historic and predictive key performance indicators (KPIs); it reviews CobiT; it also covers risk management, assessment

and mitigation strategies, and business and IT continuity planning and disaster recovery; finally, it describes a suite of technology tools that support and enable the key IT alignment, execution and governance functions and processes

Chapter 9 – Summary, lessons learned, critical success factors and future challenges
• summarizes the components required to anticipate and proactively (not reactively) implement IT governance effectively; it provides a summary checklist of all of the key components and critical success factors identified in each chapter, required to make IT Governance real, effective and sustainable

Acknowledgements

I gratefully acknowledge the help and support of a number of individuals, organizations and their members in the private, public and academic sectors, in conducting the research, editing the book, participating in developing the case studies, allowing me to consult for and/or teach them, and influencing, reinforcing and validating the findings, recommendations, critical success factors and lessons learned.

Select organizations include: Center for Business Information Technology (CIBT) and Center for Interdisciplinary Business, Engineering, Technology Leadership at the University of Bridgeport and its Board members, many of whom allowed me to conduct case studies or workshops at their facilities, such as ATMI, Avon, Cigna, Columbia University Graduate School of Business, EMCOR, ESPN, FujiFilm USA, Gartner, GE Asset Management, GE Real Estate, Halbrecht Lieberman, HBO, Hyperion (now Oracle), IAOP, ITsqc, IPC Corp., People's Bank, Purdue Pharma, Pitney Bowes, Sikorsky Aircraft, Sprint Nextel, TNT Expense Management, UBS Financial and Unilever. In addition, many extraordinary managers and professionals helped me from the Society of Information Management (SIM), the Project Management Institute (PMI), the Information Technology Governance Institute and its sister organization, ISACA, the International Association of Outsourcing Professionals, the CIO Group and the Advisory Council (TAC).

I would also like to thank specific people for their help, contributions and insights: Michael Pellegrino of FujiFilm USA, Jaci Coleman of Peoples United Bank, Christine Bullen at Stevens Institute of Technology, Neal Bronzo of Pepsi Bottling Company, Stuart Werner at Li and Fung, USA, Kevin Laing at ATMI, Paul Bateman at AXA, Peter Waterhouse and Debra Cattani at CA, Gabriel Michael at HBO, Charles Popper at the TechPar Group, Rebecca Brunotti, formerly of the General Services Administration – Federal Technology Services, Joann Martin at Pitney Bowes, Vito Melfi at Gevety, Joseph Puglisi at EMCOR, Len Peters at Columbia Business School, Porter Sherman at UBS, Hank Zupnick at GE Real Estate, Sigal Zarmi of GE Commercial Finance, Nicholas Willcox at Unilever, Mike Bodetti at TNT Expense Management, Tarek Sobh, Ward Thrasher and Robert Todd at the University of Bridgeport, Michael Corbett at IAOP, Jane Siegel at ITsqc, Dick Lefave at Sprint Nextel, Peter Shay at TAC, Jim Shay at Syracuse University, Erran Carmel at American University and many others.

Special thanks go to Omur Yilmaz, my graduate assistant at the University of Bridgeport, who helped me with conducting research for the book and co-ordinating the many revisions to the manuscript. I also want to thank the many executives, managers and professionals who have attended my seminars and workshop over the years, as well my students who have attended my graduate classes. All of them have contributed to my knowledge and challenged me to learn more and stay current in a rapidly changing field.

In addition, I would like to thank my publisher, Annelise Savill at Van Haren Publishing for her friendship, editorial suggestions and encouragement to complete this project, as well as my editor, Jayne Wilkinson.

I would like to dedicate this book to my wife, mate and life-long partner, Phyllis, for her love, dedication, understanding and support that she has given me throughout our time together. Our children, Camy, Dan, Gabe, our children through marriage, Beth and Andy, and our grandchildren, Jason, Jacob, and Jesse, also inspired me to finish the project, so that I could devote more time to them. I would most of all dedicate this book to my mother, Ruth, who passed away in November 2007, without whom this project would not have been possible.

Dr Gad J Selig
March 2008

About the Author

Dr Gad J Selig is the Director, Masters of Science in Technology Management and Dual Graduate Business and Engineering Degree Programs, and leads the Center for Inter-disciplinary Business, Engineering and Technology Leadership at the University of Bridgeport.

Dr Selig is also the Managing Partner of GPS Group, Inc., a consulting, research and education firm that focuses on strategic marketing and growth, business and technology transformation, IT strategy and governance, program/project management, strategic sourcing and innovation and managing change issues and opportunities, and provides:

• Marketing and Strategy Consulting Services: Business and Marketing Assessments, Plans, Processes and Strategies

• Technology Consulting Services: Information Technology Assessments, Plans, Processes and Strategies

• Education Services: Executive, Management and Professional Briefings, Seminars and Workshops, including select industry certification preparation workshops. Topics covered include: IT Governance, Business and Marketing Strategy and Plan Development, Program/Project Management, Strategic Sourcing and Outsourcing, Managing Accelerating Change and Innovation, World-Class Leadership and High Performance Teams, Strategic Marketing, Demand Creation and Growth and New Product Development and Commercialization.

Select clients include: ATMI, Air Products & Chemicals, Bank General of Luxembourg, Bridgeport Hospital, Bristol-Myers Squibb, Cendant, Cigna, Columbia University Graduate School of Business, CA (Computer Associates), Daston Corp., First Energy (GPU Telecomm.), FujiFilm USA, GE, IAOP, Intel, GSA's Federal Technology Services, JPMorganChase, Keyspan Energy (National Grid), Lehman Brothers, Object Edge, People's United Bank, Purdue Pharma, Robbins-Gioia, Syracuse University, Starwood Hotels and Resorts, TDK, Verizon and others.

Dr Selig has more than thirty years of diversified domestic/international executive, management and consulting experience, with both Fortune 500 and smaller companies in the financial services, utility, telecommunications, software and high technology, manufacturing and retail industries. His experience includes: marketing, sales, planning, operations, business development, mergers and acquisitions, general management (with full P & L responsibility), systems/network integration, strategic sourcing and outsourcing, MIS/CIO, electronic commerce, product development, project management, business process transformation, governance and entrepreneurship. Dr Selig has worked for the following companies: Marketing Corporation of America, Advanced Networks and Services, Continental Group, Contel Information Systems, NYNEX (Verizon), Standard Kollsman Industries, CBS and AT&T.

He earned degrees from City, Columbia and Pace Universities in Economics, Engineering and Business. He has authored three books and over 50 refereed articles and/or conference proceedings. He is a dynamic and popular speaker at industry conferences in the U.S. and abroad.

Dr Selig has been a board member of Telco Research, BIS Group, LTD. and AGS. He is a member of the Academy of Management, Project Management Institute, IAOP, ISACA and others. He holds a top secret clearance with the U.S. Federal Government.

Dr Gad J Selig PMP COP
Director, Technology Management & Dual Graduate Business/Engineering Degree Programs,
University of Bridgeport, Graduate Schools of Business and Engineering &
Managing Partner, GPS Group, Inc.
E-mail: HYPERLINK "mailto:gjselig@optonline.net"gjselig@optonline.net
www.gpsgroupinc.com

Table of contents

Part I – Leadership, people, organization and strategy

Part II – IT governance, its major component processes and enabling technologies

6 IT Service Management (ITSM) excellence (execution management) 149

7 Strategic sourcing, outsourcing and vendor management excellence 173

List of Figures

List of Tables

Part I – Leadership, people, organization and strategy

Part I of the book covers Chapters 1 through 4. It focuses on an overview of IT governance, alignment and strategy, planning, leadership, world class teams, organization and managing change. It also references current and emerging best practice industry frameworks, guidelines and standards that are useful and applicable to IT governance and its major components.

1 Introduction to IT/business alignment, planning, execution and governance

On Change and Innovation:

"Never be afraid to try something new.
Remember, amateurs built the Ark,
Professionals built the Titanic!"

- Anonymous

1.0 What is covered in this chapter?

This chapter contains:
- an overview and execution summary of the key IT/business alignment, planning, execution, governance issues, constraints and opportunities and processes
- discussion of the roles of the Board, and responsibilities of executive management and the CIO
- a review of the value propositions for IT governance
- an overview of IT demand management, decision rights, Balanced Scorecard metrics and how much governance is required
- identifying the steps in making IT governance real
- discussion of an assessment technique to determine the current level of IT governance maturity in an organization, and illustration of a blueprint of an ideal, future target state of IT governance

1.1 Overview

The issues, opportunities and challenges of aligning information technology more closely with an organization, and effectively governing an organization's information technology (IT) investments, resources, major initiatives and superior uninterrupted service, is becoming a major concern of the Board and executive management in enterprises on a global basis. Information technology (IT) has become a vital function in most organizations, and is fundamental to support and sustain innovation and growth.

Therefore, a comprehensive top-down approach, with bottom-up execution of IT governance, which includes all the activities of business/IT alignment, planning, execution and governance of IT, as well as the leadership of those entrusted with the task, is critical to achieve a cost effective solution. Effective 'management' includes the activities of planning, investment, integration, measurement and deployment, and providing the services required to manage a complex strategic asset.

None of this is easy, or obvious, and this pragmatic and actionable 'how to' guide is intended to draw from about 200 current and emerging best practice sources, and over 20 IT governance best practice case studies, some of which are featured in the book.

The purpose of the book is not to repeat in greater detail, what has been published previously. Instead, it aims to describe each of the major IT governance components as part of an overall comprehensive framework and roadmap, in sufficient detail for executives, managers and professionals; to serve as a guideline and starting point for any organization in any industry; to develop and tailor a workable and realistic approach to its environment, strategies, priorities, capabilities and available resources; and to transition IT organizations to a higher level of maturity, effectiveness and responsiveness.

Today's business challenges

The pace of change is accelerating on a global basis. Reducing costs, increasing speed to market, continuous improvements and innovation, greater compliance, more effective accountability, globalization, and more demanding and sophisticated customers, are some of the many pressures facing business and IT executives.

Figure 1.1 illustrates select pressures and trends that organizations must deal with, in a rapidly and dynamically changing global environment.

The pace of change is accelerating

Reduced Cycle Time and Increase Speed

Retain and Attract Key Human Resources

More Demanding/ Sophisticated Customers

Globalization of Markets & Supply Chain Economics

Rapidly Changing Technology

Improve Governance and Compliance

Cut costs & grow profits

Business Issues

Sustainability, Growth and Profits

Growing Trade Partnerships (Competition& Co-operation)

Process enabled best practices

Reduce Time–to–Market

Protect Intellectual Property

Continuous Innovation

Organizational Empowerment

Privacy, Security & Ethics

Competitive Differentiation & Value Proposition

Figure 1.1   Today's business challenges

Scope and definition of enterprise governance and its relationship to business and IT governance

According to the International Federation of Accountants (IFAC),

"enterprise governance constitutes the entire accountability framework of the organization."

- International Federation of Accountants (IFAC)

Enterprise governance is the set of responsibilities and practices exercised by the Board and executive management, with the goal of providing strategic direction, ensuring that plans and objectives are achieved, assessing that risks are proactively managed, and assuring that the enterprise's resources are used responsibly.

Enterprise governance deals with the separation of ownership and control of an organization, while business governance focuses on the direction and control of the business, and IT governance focuses on the direction and control of IT. Figure 1.2 compares and differentiates the key characteristics of enterprise versus business versus IT governance.

Enterprise Governance	Business Governance	IT Governance
Separation of Ownership & Control	Direction & Control of the Business	Direction and Control of IT
• Roles of Board and Executives • Regulatory Compliance • Shareholder Rights • Business Operations & Control • Financial Accounting & Reporting • Risk Management	• Business Strategy, Plans & Objectives • Business Processes & Activities • Innovation and Research • Intellectual Capital • Human Resource Management • Performance Metrics and Controls • Asset Management	• IT Strategy, Plans & Objectives • Alignment with Business Plans and Objectives • IT Assets and Resources • Demand Management • Value Delivery and Execution Management (PM and ITSMD) • Risk, Change & Performance Management

Figure 1.2   Enterprise governance versus business governance versus IT governance

The Board's role in IT governance

Historically, the Board of Directors of public companies has focused, through committees, on such issues as audit, executive compensation, executive succession and planning.

With the growing importance of IT in an increasing number of organizations, the Board is becoming a committee that focuses on IT strategy, investments and governance as well. Based on a report by the IT Governance Institute,

"IT governance is the responsibility of the Board of Directors and executive management. It is an integral part of enterprise governance and consists of the leadership and organizational structures and processes that ensure that the organization's IT function sustains and extends the organizations strategies and objectives."

- IT Governance Institute, 2003

Major challenges and issues faced by IT

In our research, we compiled a list of IT challenges and issues, identified by multiple independent sources. There appears to be a common thread running through these issues and therefore, we have summarized them into strategic, value enhancing and execution questions.

Board and executive questions for IT:

- Does the IT strategy align with the business strategy?
- Is the IT investment justified, based on its contributions to the business?
- How likely will IT meet or exceed its plans, objectives and initiatives?
- Is IT being managed prudently or effectively? How is it measured?
- How is IT delivering value? Is there a consistent IT business case format used for justifying IT investments?
- Is IT developing and maintaining constructive relationships with customers, vendors and others?
- Is IT delivering projects and services on time, within scope, within budget and with high quality?
- Is IT staffed adequately, with the right skills and competencies?
- Is there a standard measurement for IT investment across the firm?
- How does IT management and operations compare to other best practice organizations?
- How is IT managing and planning for contingencies, disasters, security, and back-up?
- How is IT measuring its performance? What are the key performance measures?
- How effectively is IT communicating its progress and problems to its constituents?
- What controls and documentation have been instituted in IT? Are they sufficient?
- Does the Board review and possibly approve the IT strategy?
- Is a risk management policy, assessment and mitigation practice followed for IT?
- Is IT compliant to federal, state, country (for global organizations) regulations, and to internal policies and controls?
- Are IT audit policies, procedures and processes in place and followed?
- Is there a succession plan in place for the CIO and key direct reports?

Top issues identified and ranked by over 100 CIOs in a CIO Magazine survey completed in 2006 (CIO Magazine, 2006):

1. align IT strategy with the business strategy and governance
2. meeting the business needs effectively
3. infrastructure and Service Management (reliability and scalability)
4. coping with accelerating change (and become one of the key drivers of innovation)
5. dealing with senior management and the Board (get a seat at the 'C' table)
6. managing costs, budgets and resources (internal and external)
7. keeping up with technology
8. recruiting and retaining staff
9. executing projects effectively (time, cost and resource management)
10. maintaining skills and knowledge (continuous learning)

Select issues addressed by a panel of CIOs of global organizations, such as Pepsi, GE, Ogilvy and Mather and Footstar, at a recent Society for Information Management (SIM) Chapter meeting (Selig, March 15, 2007):

- How do you align the IT strategy with the business strategy? What processes and tools are used? Who is involved? What worked? What did not?
- How, and in what areas, is IT delivering value to your organizations? How is it measured?
- How do you ensure that IT delivers on its plans and commitments, and executes effectively? Program/project management? IT Service Management and delivery? Security? Business and IT continuity? Performance metrics? Other?
- How is IT developing/sustaining constructive and positive relationships with its customer community? Executive management? Vendors?
- What IT controls, governance and compliance frameworks, processes, tools and techniques are being used? What worked? What did not?
- Has your business aligned itself with technology, innovation, the customer, and is it open to managing accelerating change?
- How is IT performance measured? What KPIs are used at CIO level? Above CIO Level? Below CIO level?
- How effective is IT in marketing and communicating its progress and performance results to its constituents? What tools and techniques are used? How often?
- How do you sustain continuous improvement initiatives to increase the level of IT maturity and effectiveness, staff development, constituent ownership and decision rights?
- How are you sustaining compliance processes and reporting?
- Does the Board/operating committee/senior business leadership, review and approve the IT strategy, priorities and funding? Major changes to plan, programs and budgets?

Summary of key strategic, value enhancing and execution questions:

Strategic questions - Are we doing the right thing?
Is the investment in IT:
- inline with our business vision and strategy?
- consistent with our business principles, plan and direction?
- contributing to our strategic objectives, sustainable competitive differentiation and business continuity support?
- providing optimum value at an acceptable level of risk?
- representing a long-term view (roadmap)
- including an architectural roadmap, based on a detailed analysis of the current state or condition of IT?

Value questions – Are we getting the benefits?
Is there:
- a clear and shared understanding and commitment to achieve the expected benefits?
- clear accountability for achieving the benefits, which should be linked to MBOs and incentive compensation schemes, for individuals and business units, or functional areas?

Are they:
- based on relevant and meaningful metrics?
- based on a consistent benefits realization process and sign-off?

Delivery and execution questions – Are we deploying well and effectively? How do we measure our results?

Metrics include:

- scalable,disciplined and consistent management, governance, delivery of quality processes
- appropriate and sufficient resources available with the right competencies, capabilities and attitudes
- a consistent set (of metrics) linked to critical success factors (CSFs) and realistic key performance indicators (KPIs)
- succession planning

Figure 1.3 summarizes the major IT challenges being addressed by a large, global software organization, as part of its IT planning and governance process.

Major IT challenges must be dealt with as part of an IT planning and governance process

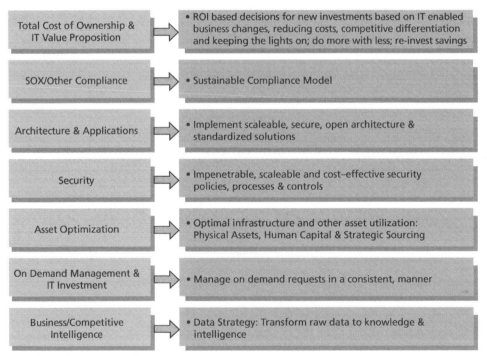

Figure 1.3   Major challenges for IT

Basically, it comes down to the need for a plan that can be executed. At the same time, the role of the CIO is also undergoing significant change. Successful CIOs recognize that IT has become far more than a means of increasing efficiency and reducing costs. Rather, they see IT as a prime stimulus for, and enabler of, business innovation – and themselves as key collaborators in a process that develops business and IT strategies in unison. Throughout the book, we address many of these challenges and issues.

1.2 Definition, purpose and scope of IT governance

Definition of IT governance:
Governance formalizes and clarifies oversight, accountability and decision rights for a wide array of IT strategy, resource and control activities. It is a collection of management, planning and performance review policies, practices and processes; with associated decision rights, which establish authority, controls and performance metrics over investments, plans, budgets, commitments, services, major changes, security, privacy, business continuity and compliance with laws and organizational policies.

Purpose of IT governance
IT governance:
- alignsIT investments and priorities more closely with the business
- manages, evaluates, prioritizes, funds, measures and monitors requests for IT services, and the resulting work and deliverables, in a more consistent and repeatable manner that optimize returns to the business
- maintainsresponsible utilization of resources and assets
- establishesand clarifies accountability and decision rights (clearly defines roles and authority)
- ensuresthat IT delivers on its plans, budgets and commitments
- managesmajor risks, threats, change and contingencies proactively
- improves IT organizational performance, compliance, maturity, staff development and outsourcing initiatives
- improves the voice of the customer (VOC), demand management and overall customer and constituent satisfaction and responsiveness
- managesand thinks globally, but acts locally
- championsinnovation within the IT function and the business

Scope of IT Governance:

Key IT governance strategy and resource decisions must address the following topics:
(Modified from Weill and Ross, 2004; Popper, 2000)

- **IT principles** – high level statements about how IT is used in the business (eg scale, simplify and integrate; reduce TCO (Total Cost of Operations) and self fund by re-investing savings; invest in customer facing systems; transform business and IT through business process transformation; strategic plan directions, PMO (project management office), sustain innovation and assure regulatory compliance, etc.)
- **IT architecture** – organizing logic for data, applications and infrastructure captured in a set of policies, relationships, processes, standards and technical choices, to achieve desired business and technical integration and standardization
- **SOA architecture** – service oriented architecture (SOA) is a business-centric IT architectural approach that supports the integration of the business as linked, repeatable business tasks or services; SOA helps users build composite applications that draw upon functionality from multiple sources within and beyond the enterprise to support business processes
- **IT infrastructure** – centrally co-ordinated, based on shared IT services that provide the foundation for the enterprise's IT capability and support

- **business application needs** – specifying the business need for purchased or internally developed IT applications
- **IT investment and prioritization** – decisions about how much and where to invest in IT (eg capital and expense), including development and maintenance projects, infrastructure, security, people, etc.
- **people (human capital) development** – decisions about how to develop and maintain global IT leadership management succession and technical skills and competencies (eg how much and where to spend on training and development, industry individual and organizational certifications, etc.)
- **IT governance policies, processes, mechanisms, tools and metrics** – decisions on composition and roles of steering groups, advisory councils, technical and architecture working committees, project teams; key performance indicators (KPIs); chargeback alternatives; performance reporting, meaningful audit process and the need to have a business owner for each project and investment

Who benefits from effective and sustainable IT governance?

Everyone in an organization benefits from effective IT governance. According to Charles Popper (Popper, January 2003), the following audiences benefit:

- What executives get
  - business improvements that result from knowledgeable participation in IT decision-making from an enterprise perspective
  - ensures that key IT investments support the business and provide optimum returns to the business
  - ensures compliance with laws and regulations
- What mid-level business managers get
  - convinces senior business managers that their combined business-IT resources are being managed effectively
  - helps to communicate with peers in IT to ensure that business services for which they are responsible will meet commitments
- What senior IT managers get
  - obtains sponsorship and support and a clear focus on important strategic and operational initiatives
  - improves customer relationships by delivering results in a more predictable and consistent manner, with the involvement of the customer
- What program/project and operations managers get
  - helps in resolving issues, reviewing progress and enabling faster decisions
- What everyone gets
  - facilitates communications about how IT contributes to the business
  - improves co-ordination, co-operation, communications and synergy across the organization
  - less stress

Value propositions from best-in-class companies on business and/or IT governance

Based on primary and secondary market research, it is possible to identify a number of benefits attributed to major organizations relating to improved governance business and/or IT structures and environments (Selig, March 15, 2006):

Effective and sustainable governance:
- lowers cost of operations by accomplishing more work consistently in less time and with fewer resources without sacrificing quality (General Motors)
- provides better control and more consistent approach to governance, prioritization, development funding and operations (Kodak)
- developsa better working relationship and communications with the customer (Nortel)
- provides for a consistent process for more effectively tracking progress, solving problems, escalating issues and gate reviews (Cigna)
- alignsinitiatives and investments more directly with business strategy (GE)
- improves governance, communications, visibility and risk mitigation for all constituents (Robbins Gioia)
- facilitates business and regulatory compliance with documentation and traceability as evidence (Purdue Pharma)
- increases our customer satisfaction by listening proactively to the customers and validating requirements on an iterative and frequent basis (Johnson and Johnson)
- reuse of consistent and repeatable processes helps to reduce time and costs and speeds up higher quality deliverables (IBM)

Successful IT governance is built on three critical pillars – leadership, organization and decision rights, scalable processes and enabling technologies

Effective IT governance is built on three critical pillars. These pillars include: leadership, organization and decision rights, flexible and scalable processes, and the use of enabling technology (Luftman, 2004; Board Effectiveness Partners, 2004; Melnicoff, 2005; Pultorak and Kerrigan, 2005):

- **Leadership, organization and decision rights** - define the organization structure, roles and responsibilities, decision rights (decision influencers and makers), a shared vision and interface/ integration touch points and champions for proactive change:
  - roles and responsibilities are well defined with respect to each of the IT governance components and processes, including the steering and review hierarchies for investment authorizations, resolution of issues and formal periodic reviews
  - clear hand-off and interface agreements and contracts exist for internal and external work and deliverables
  - motivated leaders and change champions with the right talent, drive and competencies
  - meaningful metrics
  - CIO is a change agent who links process to technology within the business, and provides the tools for enablement and innovation

- **Flexible and scalable processes** - the IT governance model places heavy emphasis on the importance of process transformation and improvement: (eg planning, project management, portfolio investment management, risk management, IT Service Management and delivery, performance management, vendor management, controls and audits, etc.):
  - processes are well defineßd, documented, measured
  - processes define interfaces between organizations and ensure that workflow spans boundaries and silos including organization, vendors, geography, technology and culture
  - processes should be flexible, scalable and consistently applied, with common sense

- **Enabling technology** - leverage leading tools and technologies that support the major IT governance components:
  - processes are supported by software tools that support the IT imperatives and components (eg planning and budgeting, portfolio investment management, project management, risk and change management, IT Service Management and delivery processes, financial, asset and performance management and scorecards, etc.)
  - tools provide governance, communications and effectiveness metrics to accelerate decisions, follow-up and management actions

If any one of the above pillars is missing or ineffective, the IT governance initiative will not be effective or sustainable. In addition, over dependence on one dimension over the others will result in sub-optimal performance.

Results of ineffective IT governance can be devastating

A number of negative impacts may result from poor IT governance. These include the following (IT Governance Institute, *The CEO's Guide to IT Value and Risk*, 2006):

- businesslosses and disruptions, damaged reputations and weakened competitive positions
  - Nike lost an estimated $200 million, while running into difficulties installing a supply chain software system
  - Hershey attempted to install SAP several years ago and at that time, was not successful; it cost the company significant money and lots of embarrassment
  - Whirlpool ran into significant trouble in attempting to implement a supply chain management system, which did not provide accurate inventory counts at various inventory stages
- schedulesnot met, higher costs, poorer quality and unsatisfied customers
- core business processes are negatively impacted (eg SAP and other enterprise resource planning systems impact many critical business processes) by poor quality of IT deliverables
  - an operational meltdown of the Southern Pacific-Union Pacific merger was traced largely to the inability to co-ordinate their IT systems
- failureof IT to demonstrate its investment benefits or value propositions

Poor regulatory compliance procedures, controls, audits and/or unethical executive business practices resulted in the demise of such companies as Enron and Andersen, and the jailing of former heads of Tyco and Worldcom. Others such as Parmalat and Global Crossing have also been impacted by compliance issues.

The simple fact is that a poorly executed IT operation will result in the business not working. In addition, business and IT continuity and resumption plans have become critical.

The implications of Sarbanes Oxley Act (SOX) and other regulations on IT governance

In general, governance should be the responsibility of the Board of Directors and executive management in organizations. In order to develop an effective compliance program, executives must understand that compliance can and does involve more than just SOXs. It can involve multiple national, international, local and industry specific regulations, as well as best practices, guidelines and frameworks.

Compliance with a growing number of regulations and laws, regarding financial disclosure, privacy, environmental conformance and others, etc. developed by the SEC, FDA, EPA, Sarbanes-Oxley, HIPPA, Basel II and specific industry-focused regulations, in banking, insurance, brokerage, healthcare, pharmaceutical and others, are creating new and greater IT reporting and systems support requirements for organizations. Much like IT governance, to achieve sustainable compliance, this complex and confusing mix can be approached most effectively as a single comprehensive compliance program that addresses people, process and technology (Sun Microsystems and Deloitte, 2006).

Regulatory, audit and management requirements generally determine the level of management and administrative controls that a company deploys. As an example, Section 302 of Sarbanes-Oxley requires CFOs and CEOs to personally certify and attest to the accuracy of their companies' financial results. Section 404 of Sarbanes-Oxley focuses on financial controls and requires IT to be able to document and trace a company's financials (eg profit and loss, balance sheet, etc.) back to the systems, software and operational processes and sources of the transactions that comprised the numbers. A company has to demonstrate a documented audit trail to be in compliance, and to further demonstrate how an organization plans to sustain that compliance effort. Within IT, the Sarbanes-Oxley Act:

- improves financial reporting/disclosures – new requirement to report on internal controls for financial statements – Section 404
- expands insider accountability – new requirements for code of ethics for executive management and protection for whistleblowers
- means that the external auditors can insist that any gaps in IT controls must be addressed before an overall opinion is reached on the effectiveness of the internal company controls
- requires a back-up for all 'financially significant files, storage of those files and periodic restoration of back-up files'
- requires IT change management tracking and documentation for financial systems
- requires the maintenance of logs for user access to financial data bases, security logs, administrative logs, problem and incident logs, as well as an independent review of the logs to detect any activities that could adversely impact financials
- requires systems documentation and verification that data is properly handed off from one system to another
- strengthens overall corporate governance

In a growing number of companies subject to SOXs, the CIO must internally certify the accuracy of the information audit trial each quarter to support the CEO/ CFO SOX certifications.

There is a growing library of books, articles and documents that provide recommendations on how to deal with these regulatory and legal requirements (Anand, 2006; Ernst and Young, 2005; Forrester Research, March 14, 2004; Protivity, December 2003), In addition, Appendix 1 provides an illustration of a template, used by a manufacturing company as a guideline to help the company track SOX compliance activities and reports.

1.3 Linking the CEO role to achieving business growth, improving profitability and creating an effective governance and compliance environment

The role of the CEO and the executive management team is complex, and requires a balance between sustaining growth and profitability while optimizing organizational effectiveness and complying with the growing and confusing number of regulatory requirements.

Executing enterprise-wide strategic initiatives and managing effective business operations is a complex undertaking that requires effective corporate and IT governance to play a growing role in how the CEO and the executive team deploy the organization's strategy.

As Michael Cinema, President and CEO of Etienne Aligner Group stated, "*The Board of Directors is well aware of its role to oversee the company's organizational strategies, structures, systems, staff, performance and standards. As President, it is my responsibility to ensure that they extend that oversight to the Company's IT as well, and with our growing reliance on IT for competitive advantage, we simply cannot afford to apply to our IT anything less that the level of commitment we apply to overall governance.*"

- IT Governance Institute, 2003

Figure 1.4 identifies the attributes that must be addressed for effective growth and profitability. Effective governance is a prominent component for both.

How much governance is required and when is enough, enough?

There are few, if any, standards or guidelines developed that identify and clearly lay out in more detail what level of governance is required for either management or regulatory compliance by an organization. Generally, it is dependent on a number of variables such as:

- investment$ (capital and expense) criticality to the organization (mission critical)
- degreeof business dependency on technology
- strategic corporate value proposition and alternatives for focus (eg growth centric, customer centric, process centric, cost centric, etc.)
- managementphilosophy and policy (eg first mover versus follower)
- program/projectand/or operational importance
- complexityscope, size and duration of initiative

Executing enterprise–wide strategic initiatives & effective business operations is a complex undertaking that requires a balance between growth, effectiveness and efficiency

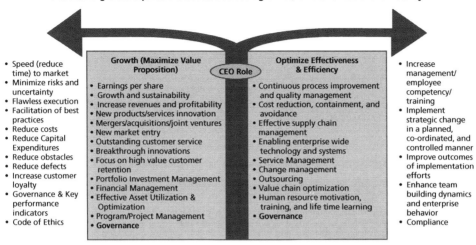

- Speed (reduce time) to market
- Minimize risks and uncertainty
- Flawless execution
- Facilitation of best practices
- Reduce costs
- Reduce Capital Expenditures
- Reduce obstacles
- Reduce defects
- Increase customer loyalty
- Governance & Key performance indicators
- Code of Ethics

Growth (Maximize Value Proposition) **CEO Role**
- Earnings per share
- Growth and sustainability
- Increase revenues and profitability
- New products/services innovation
- Mergers/acquisitions/joint ventures
- New market entry
- Outstanding customer service
- Breakthrough innovations
- Focus on high value customer retention
- Portfolio Investment Management
- Financial Management
- Effective Asset Utilization & Optimization
- Program/Project Management
- **Governance**

Optimize Effectiveness & Efficiency
- Continuous process improvement and quality management
- Cost reduction, containment, and avoidance
- Effective supply chain management
- Enabling enterprise wide technology and systems
- Service Management
- Change management
- Outsourcing
- Value chain optimization
- Human resource motivation, training, and life time learning
- **Governance**

- Increase management/ employee competency/ training
- Implement strategic change in a planned, co-ordinated, and controlled manner
- Improve outcomes of implementation efforts
- Enhance team building dynamics and enterprise behavior
- Compliance

Critical Success Enablers include: superior leadership skills and motivated change agents, flexible and scalable processes, pragmatic and realistic metrics, a clear governance policy and structure, and the use-enabling technologies.

Figure 1.4   Linking the role of the CEO to the success of strategic enterprise initiatives and governance

- numberof interfaces and integration requirements with business
- degreeof risk and potential impact (of doing or not doing)
- numberof organizations, departments, locations and resources involved
- customeror sponsor requirements
- regulatorylegal, control and compliance required
- degreeof accountability desired and required
- levelof security required or desired
- audit,documentation and traceability requirements

Chapter 2 discusses many of the current and emerging standards, guidelines and frameworks either developed or being developed, that help improve the overall IT alignment, execution, governance, control, strategic sourcing and outsourcing management and performance management processes.

1.4   Overview of the integrated IT governance framework, major components and prerequisites

Grounded in industry best practice research and required to plan, develop, deploy and sustain a cost effective approach to IT governance, the blended and integrated governance framework consists of five (5) critical IT governance imperatives (which leverage best practice models and are 'must do's') and address the following work areas:

- **business strategy, plan and objectives (demand management)** - this involves the development of the business strategy and plan which should drive the IT strategy and plan
- **IT strategy, plan and objectives (demand management)** – this should be based on the business plan and objectives, and will provide the direction and priorities of the IT functions and resources; this should also include portfolio investment management investments, a prioritization scheme and identify the decision rights (who influences decisions and who is authorized to make the decisions) on a wide variety of IT areas; in addition, the CIO is responsible for the infrastructure investments such as servers, networks, systems software and management
- **IT plan execution (execution management)** – this encompasses the processes of program and project management, IT Service Management and delivery (including ITIL – IT Infrastructure Library), risk and threat management, change management, security, contingency plans and others
- **performance management and management controls (execution management)** – this includes such areas as the Balanced Scorecard, key performance indicators, CobiT, and regulatory compliance areas; more details on these topics are provided in Chapters 2 and 8
- **vendor management and outsourcing management (execution management)** – since companies are increasing their outsourcing spending, selecting and managing the vendors and their deliverables has become critical
- **people development, continuous process improvement and learning** - it is critical to invest in people, knowledge management, and sustain continuous process improvement and innovation initiatives

For each IT governance imperative, a description of the key components are provided and further detailed in subsequent chapters. Step one for a new CIO is to assess the current IT governance environment and what shape IT is in.

Figure 1.5 illustrates each of the major work areas or components of the IT governance framework, including a short description of each component and provides select references.

Key work breakdown areas required to plan and manage an IT governance initiative

Today, many companies start on a narrow path or shot gun approach without developing a more comprehensive framework, with a prioritized roadmap based on the highest value delivery to the organization. A good place to start the IT governance initiative is to decompose it into manageable and assignable work packages - as in a work breakdown structure - and assign these work packages to champions and owners responsible for them.

Figure 1.6 illustrates such a work breakdown for the major and key work areas of IT governance, including planning, execution and performance management.

IT governance – decision rights and authority

Peter Weill and Jeane Ross (Weill and Ross, 2004) identified the concept of IT decision rights as an important component of effective IT governance. The purpose of a decision rights matrix is to identify the IT decision influencers and decision makers in an organization, to clarify the

**Identifies the major areas that must be addressed on the journey to a
higher level of IT governance maturity and effectiveness**

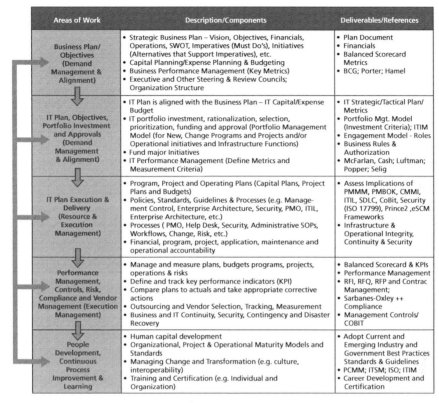

Areas of Work	Description/Components	Deliverables/References
Business Plan/ Objectives (Demand Management & Alignment)	• Strategic Business Plan – Vision, Objectives, Financials, Operations, SWOT, Imperatives (Must Do's), Initiatives (Alternatives that Support Imperatives), etc. • Capital Planning/Expense Planning & Budgeting • Business Performance Management (Key Metrics) • Executive and Other Steering & Review Councils; Organization Structure	• Plan Document • Financials • Balanced Scorecard Metrics • BCG; Porter; Hamel
IT Plan, Objectives, Portfolio Investment and Approvals (Demand Management & Alignment)	• IT Plan is aligned with the Business Plan – IT Capital/Expense Budget • IT portfolio investment, rationalization, selection, prioritization, funding and approval (Portfolio Management Model (for New, Change Programs and Projects and/or Operational initiatives and Infrastructure Functions) • Fund major Initiatives • IT Performance Management (Define Metrics and Measurement Criteria)	• IT Strategic/Tactical Plan/ Metrics • Portfolio Mgt. Model (Investment Criteria); ITIM • Engagement Model - Roles • Business Rules & Authorization • McFarlan, Cash; Luftman; Popper; Selig
IT Plan Execution & Delivery (Resource & Execution Management)	• Program, Project and Operating Plans (Capital Plans, Project Plans and Budgets) • Policies, Standards, Guidelines & Processes (e.g. Management Control, Enterprise Architecture, Security, PMO, ITIL, Enterprise Architecture, etc.) • Processes (PMO, Help Desk, Security, Administrative SOPs, Workflows, Change, Risk, etc.) • Financial, program, project, application, maintenance and operational accountability	• Assess Implications of PMMM, PMBOK, CMMI, ITIL, SDLC, CoBit, Security (ISO 17799), Prince2 ,eSCM Frameworks • Infrastructure & Operational Integrity, Continuity & Security
Performance Management, Controls, Risk, Compliance and Vendor Management (Execution Management)	• Manage and measure plans, budgets programs, projects, operations & risks • Define and track key performance indicators (KPI) • Compare plans to actuals and take appropriate corrective actions • Outsourcing and Vendor Selection, Tracking, Measurement • Business and IT Continuity, Security, Contingency and Disaster Recovery	• Balanced Scorecard & KPIs • Performance Management • RFI, RFQ, RFP and Contrac Management; • Sarbanes-Oxley ++ Compliance • Management Controls/ COBIT
People Development, Continuous Process Improvement & Learning	• Human capital development • Organizational, Project & Operational Maturity Models and Standards • Managing Change and Transformation (e.g. culture, interoperability) • Training and Certification (e.g. Individual and Organization)	• Adopt Current and Emerging Industry and Government Best Practices Standards & Guidelines • PCMM; ITSM; ISO; ITIM • Career Development and Certification

Figure 1.5   Integrated IT governance framework

**The IT Governance Initiative must be decomposed into manageable and accountable
work packages and deliverables and assigned to owners for planning, development,
execution and continuous improvement**

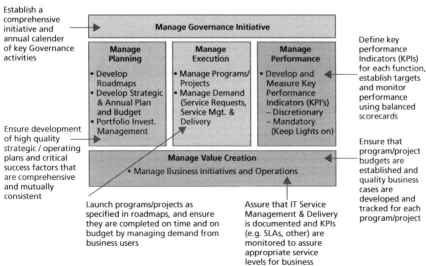

Figure 1.6   Key work breakdown areas for IT governance

decision roles and authority levels for the major IT areas. It eliminates confusion, identifies accountability and clearly defines decision roles and scope.

Figure 1.7 provides an illustrative example of a partial IT governance decision rights matrix for a financial services organization.

A decisions rights matrix identifying decision influencers and decision makers is necessary to clarify decision roles and authority levels for the major it governance components

IT Governance Component	Input to Decision	Decision Authority	Comments/Examples (Varies by Organization)
IT Principles (High value statements about how IT will be used to create business value)	Business Units	IT Senior Leadership Group & CIO; Executive Officer Group	• Scale, simplify, integrate • Reduce cost of IT & self fund • Re-engineer/consistent processes • Invest in customer facing systems • Investment $ Threshold Approvals • Key Performance Indicators/CSFs
IT Investment, Plan, Prioritization, Critical Success Factors and Key Performance Indicators (KPIs)	Business Units	IT Steering Committee (ITSC) (Business & IT Executives), Projects over $500K:	• ITSC recommends priority to CEO for any projects requiring over $500K • Identify, track and measure critical success factors and associated KPIs
Business Applications	Business Units and Corporate Functional Unit Heads	IT Steering Committee	Significant business application spend must be approved during the annual budgel process, and if over $500K, approved by ITSC
IT Infrastructure and Architecture; Outsourcing & Vendor Management; +++Others	IT Steering Committee IT Steering Committee + Business Units	IT Architecture/Technology Review Board (and Business Units (for related applications) Senior leadership (Depends on scope)	Significant infrastructure spend must be approved during the annual budget process, and if over $500K, approved by ITSC. Significant outsourcing initiative should be recommended by ITSC & approved by Executive Officer Group

Figure 1.7   IT governance decision rights (financial service organization)

IT/business steering and governance boards, working committees and roles

Many top performing companies have established multi-level and multi-disciplinary business/IT steering and governance boards and working committees, with clear roles and responsibilities, to ensure appropriate commitments, sponsorship, escalation, ownership, more effective communications and more formal visibility and commitment of the Board, executive management and other constituents.

Why are they important?

They:

- help to ensure alignment across all of the parts of an organization; it is recognized that the demand for IT resources will exceed available resources/budget, and establishing organization wide and business unit priorities is essential
- provide a forum for investment decision-making which is synchronized with the business
- build an enterprise view and help to eliminate stovepipe systems, processes, and duplication of effort across the organization

What (charter) should they focus on?

Boards should aim:

- to review and approve strategic plans, major programs/projects and establish priorities among competing requests for resources to ensure that everyone is aligned on those initiatives with highest 'value add' to the organization as a whole
- to establish and support processes where needed, to effectively fulfill the charge outlined
- to conduct formal periodic reviews of major initiatives, and operational service performance

Roles and responsibilities:

They:

- review and approve overall IT plans
- review prioritize, approve major IT investments
- conduct formal periodic project progress and performance reviews
- final escalation point for major IT/business issues resolution
- support and sponsor IT governance policy and process improvement programs impacting the Executive Steering Board membership organizations, and help deploy them in their organizations

Other steering and working committees:

- Successful IT governance requires multi-level and multi-functional participation. Many organizations establish additional business/IT working committees at the business unit level, as well as major functional areas such as supply chain management, global financials, marketing and sales, research and development, and others as necessary.
- Program and projects working groups focus on specific initiatives.

Figure 1.8 illustrates an example of the IT/business steering and governance boards and roles at multiple levels for a large organization.

IT demand management - sources and classifications

Typically, requests for IT services should be identified and accommodated for in the strategic and tactical plans and budgets. If they are not, they are classified as 'out-of-plan'. Therefore, each request should be evaluated on its own merits against consistent evaluation criteria discussed in more detail in Chapter 3.

Demand for IT services generally comes in several flavours — mandatory ('must do's' such as addressing service interruptions, standard maintenance, keeping the lights on and/or regulatory compliance) and discretionary ('could do's' if aligned, feasible, cost justified, strategic and/or

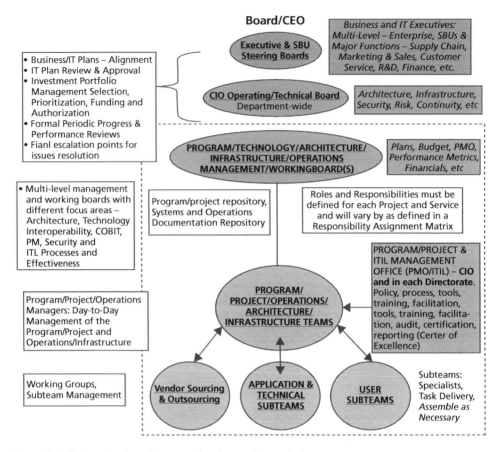

Figure 1.8   IT/business steering and governance boards, committees and roles

requested by executive management). Both mandatory and discretionary requests should be approved by the business/IT leadership in the IT strategic and operating plans, or in accordance with an organization's decision rights and approval authority guidelines established for IT.

The following considerations will further help prioritize business needs with IT:

- clearly define and relate the value (eg cost reduction, containment and avoidance; increased revenues; faster access to information; shorter time to market etc.) that IT provides in support of the business
- identify value adding activities (eg value chain and other business models/attributes) and strategies that would enhance then through IT.
- focuson listening to the voice of the customer
- ensure that all IT initiatives are evaluated using a consistent, but flexible set of investment selection, prioritization and review criteria, to assure a strong link to the business plan, project implementation and on-going operations

- develop a strategic IT plan that identifies major initiatives, technical/architecture, operational, organizational, people development and financial objectives and measurements in support of the business

Figure 1.9 illustrates a demand management chart for a major bank.

Classification	Type of Request or Demand Mgt.	Comments/Description
Mandatory or Core (Business Enablement)	**Service Interruption (Break & Fix)**	A problem caused the disruption of IT service and must be fixed and restored as soon as possible
	Maintenance	Scheduled maintenance must be performed to keep applications and infrastructure operating efficiently
	Keep the Lights On and Legal/ Regulatory	The costs and resources required to support the basic steady state operations of the business, including some components of infrastructure
Discretionary* (Require ROI)	**Major New/Change (Complex) Initiatives (Full Risk Mitigation)**	Complex new initiatives or major changes (major enhancements or modifications) to systems, processes or infrastructure that provide new or additional functionality or capacity
	Fast Track (New/Change) (Simple or Limited Scope)	Simple new initiatives and minor changes that do not required the rigor and discipline of a complex initiative and be fast tracked.
	Standard (Repetitive) Request	Describe product/ service (functions, features and price in a product/service catalogue)
Strategic	**Major initiative – Realistic ROI may not be doable – too early**	A strategic initiative may fall into several categories – first market mover (new product or service); R & D; competitive advantage, etc.

* Note: Criteria for differentiating between complex or fast track initiatives or service catalogue listings will vary for each organization.

Figure 1.9   IT demand management: classifications

IT demands generally come in several flavors – mandatory or core, discretionary and strategic – These should be identified and resourced in the IT strategic and operating plan and budgets - If they are not in the plan, each request should be evaluated on its own merits against consistent alignment, investment and service criteria. A steady state (normalized and repeatable) service could be included in a service catalogue.

Business/IT governance performance management and the Balanced Scorecard

A performance management plan must be developed for IT. The development of the performance management plan should be a collaborative effort between the business and IT. It should be based on a number of objectives, such as strategic, financials, customer, quality, process innovation, operational and service effectiveness which, in turn, support an organization's business vision, mission, plans, objectives and financials.

It is important to measure the performance of IT in terms that can be understood by the business. It is equally important to have two types of reporting systems based on critical success factors and key performance indicators: those that are developed by IT for the external (out of IT) environment, such as executive management, the Board and the business managers, and those developed for internal use by IT management.

The execution of these plans and objectives must be monitored and measured by a combination of Balanced Scorecard key performance indicators (KPIs), as well as formal and informal status review meetings and reports (eg report cards, dashboards). Figure 1.10 illustrates high level business and IT Balanced Scorecard categories and related metrics. The outcomes should link critical success factors to KPIs that are measurable, part of a standard reporting system and linked to a governance component. If one cannot measure the result, they do not count. Chapter 8 provides more details on performance management, controls, Balanced Scorecard and other metrics.

Should link Critical Success Factors (CSFs) to Key Performance Indicators (KPI's) for Business and IT (Illustrative Example)

Balanced Score Card – Key Performance Measures – Business*

- Financial (including compliance) – revenue &, profit growth, budgets/expenses, ROA, ROI, NPV, cost reduction, etc.
- Strategic/Customer – new product/service development, intellectual property, asset management , portfolio valuation, customer satisfaction, etc.
- Internal/External Processes – process and/or technology innovation and transformation in sales and marketing, productivity, regulatory compliance, human resources, operations, engineering, manufacturing, customer service, IT, purchasing, vendor management, etc.
- Learning and Growth – people development, education, training, certification, job rotation, mentoring, R+D investments, etc.

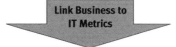

Balanced Score Card – Key Performance Indicators - Information Technology*

- Financials – revenue and profit growth, cost reduction & self funding, budgets/actuals/variances, ROI, Payback, NPV, cost per IT customer, % of IT budget to revenue
- Strategic – competitive positioning, business value, alignment, differentiation through technology, growth, etc.
- Customer (User) Satisfaction – ownership, commitment, involvement, part of team, level of service
- Employee Satisfaction/People Development – training, certification, productivity, turnover
- Program/Project Management Process* – time/schedule, budget/cost, deliverables, scope, quality, resources, number of risks, number of changes, key issues, earned value, % of rework, etc.
- Service (Operations) Process*– service levels, uptime, service delivery, reliability, redundancy, availability, problem reporting and control, scalability, back-up & disaster recovery plans, mean time to repair, response times, amount of errors and rework, etc.

* (Note: For each category, more granular metrics are available, depending what needs to be measured))

* Modified from Kaplan and Norten, 2001

Figure 1.10   Select Balanced Scorecard metrics for business and IT governance

1.5 Steps in making IT governance real

IT governance represents a journey towards continuous improvement and greater effectiveness. The journey is difficult, but can be facilitated by the following steps:

- must have a corporate mandate from the top - the Board and the executive team (including the CIO) are committed to implementing and sustaining a robust governance environment
- must have dedicated and available resources - identify executive champion and multi-disciplinary team (to focus on each IT governance component)
- do homework – educate yourself on past, current and emerging best practices
- market the IT governance value propositions and benefits to the organization - develop and conduct a communications, awareness and public relations campaign
- develop a tailored IT governance framework and roadmap for your organization based on current and emerging industry best practices
- assess the 'current state' of the level of IT governance maturity, or other frameworks that relate to specific IT governance components, such as project management maturity model (PMMM), vendor management (eSCM), performance management (Balanced Scorecard) and others, as a reference base (where are we today?), using a leading industry best practice framework such as CMMI or another framework that may apply to a specific component of IT governance
- develop a 'future state' IT governance blueprint (where you want to be) and keep it in focus
- decompose the IT governance components into well defined work packages (assign an owner and champion to each process component)
- develop an IT governance action plan, identify deliverables, establish priorities, milestones, allocate resources and measure progress
- sponsor organizational and individual certifications in the IT governance component areas, where they are available (eg PMP, ITIL, IT Security, IT Audit, BCP, Outsourcing, eSCM, COP, etc.)
- identify enabling technologies to support the IT governance initiative
- establish a 'web portal' to access IT governance policies, processes, information, communications and provide support
- market and communicate the IT 'value proposition' and celebrate wins
- plan for and sustain IT governance process improvements and link to a reward and incentive structure; create a 'continuous IT governance improvement' group to sustain the framework
- do not focus on specific ROI as a measure of success - use TCO (Total Cost of Operations) and business innovation and transformation metrics as measures of improvement

Avoiding IT governance implementation pitfalls

To avoid IT governance implementation pitfalls, key factors to remember include the following:

- treat the implementation initiative as program or project with a series of phases with timetables and deliverables
- remember that implementation requires cultural change and transformation, which requires:
  - marketing of the value proposition and overcoming resistance to change
  - managing culture change and transformation

　　　– obtaining executive management buy-in and ownership
　　　– mobilizing commitment for change at multiple organization levels
- manage expectations of all constituents – IT governance takes time and represents a series of continuous improvement processes
- demonstrate measurable and incremental improvements in the environment and communicate them to the constituents

A first step - assess current maturity level of key IT governance components

As an organization develops its IT governance strategy, IT is useful to assess the level of maturity of the IT governance. An industry standard methodology that is useful for this purpose is SEI's Capability Maturity Model Integrated (CMMI®) framework (Software Engineering Institute, 2002 and 2005). The model consists of five levels of maturity and can be used to analyze the current state of the major IT governance components, as well as to establish a targeted future state maturity level for each major IT governance component:

The framework consists of five levels of maturity:

1. **Initial level**: The IT governance processes are characterized as ad hoc and occasionally even chaotic. Few processes are defined and success depends on individual efforts.
2. **Repeatable level**: Basic IT governance processes are established. The necessary discipline is evolving to repeat earlier successes.
3. **Defined level**: The IT governance processes are documented, standardized, and integrated into the management policies and procedures. All governance processes are implemented using approved, versions as part of the IT governance policy and framework.
4. **Managed level**: Define, collect and make decisions based on each IT governance component's measurements. IT governance processes and metrics are quantitatively understood, reported and controlled on an enterprise level.
5. **Optimizing level**: Continuous process improvement is enabled by quantitative feedback from the process, from piloting innovative ideas and from adopting external industry best practices and standards.

Figure 1.11 provides an illustration of the CMMI® model levels and illustrates an insurance company's current state maturity level and its objective for a targeted future state maturity level.

Figure 1.12 was developed by Luftman suggesting an overlay framework to the CMMI model that focuses on assessing an organization's maturity based on the following six factors: communications, value, governance, partnership, architecture and skills (Luftman, 2004).

IT governance - current and future state transformation roadmap

In order to develop and/or improve the IT governance process, an organization must assess its current and future governance state and develop a transition roadmap for its IT transformation.

Figure 1.13 illustrates a roadmap for an organization to follow, as IT transitions from its current state to its desired future state or environment.

Illustrates an organization's current and future targeted state of IT governance maturity. All organizations require a roadmap and plan to move up to higher levels of maturity and effectiveness

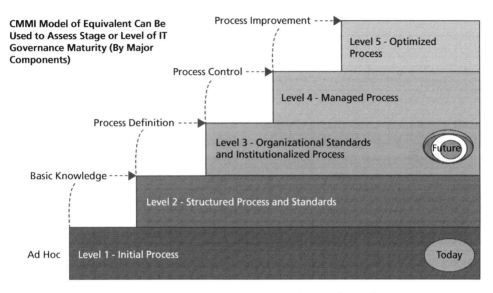

Figure 1.11   High level assessment of current state and targeted future state based on the CMMI® model

Future state of IT governance – a blueprint concept

When all is said and done, most organizations would like to have an effective IT governance process and environment. Figure 1.14 identifies a blueprint of the 'ideal' future state and the key components that are necessary for effective governance deployment and strategic planning (business/IT alignment driven), application and infrastructure development (metrics driven) programs and projects and IT service support and delivery (metrics driven). Other components that should be added include architecture, security, business continuity, back-up and disaster recovery and related areas.

Key components of managing large scale enterprise change successfully, and providing the appropriate leadership and environment

As organizations transition to a more mature and effective governance environment, a 'sea change' has to occur, either through incremental and/or radical change that could involve large scale change, depending on an organization's level of maturity, management philosophy and cultural readiness.

John Kotter, a Harvard University professor, is a recognized expert on leadership and managing change successful. According to Kotter (with some modification by the author), the four key principles for managing large scale change successfully include (Kotter, 1996):

- engage the top and lead the change
  - create the 'value proposition' and market the case for change
  - committed leadership
  - develop a plan and ensure consequence management

Relates IT/business alignment criteria to assist enterprises to evaluate their level of maturity and set a direction to improve, in six areas.

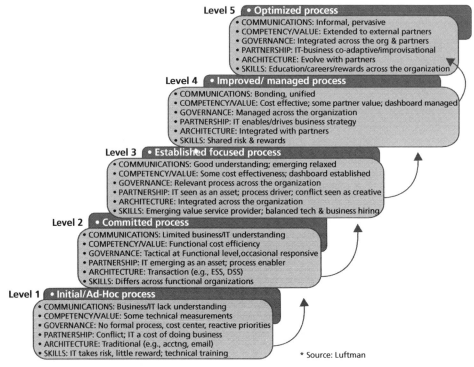

Level 5 • Optimized process
- COMMUNICATIONS: Informal, pervasive
- COMPETENCY/VALUE: Extended to external partners
- GOVERNANCE: Integrated across the org & partners
- PARTNERSHIP: IT-business co-adaptive/improvisational
- ARCHITECTURE: Evolve with partners
- SKILLS: Education/careers/rewards across the organization

Level 4 • Improved/ managed process
- COMMUNICATIONS: Bonding, unified
- COMPETENCY/VALUE: Cost effective; some partner value; dashboard managed
- GOVERNANCE: Managed across the organization
- PARTNERSHIP: IT enables/drives business strategy
- ARCHITECTURE: Integrated with partners
- SKILLS: Shared risk & rewards

Level 3 • Established focused process
- COMMUNICATIONS: Good understanding; emerging relaxed
- COMPETENCY/VALUE: Some cost effectiveness; dashboard established
- GOVERNANCE: Relevant process across the organization
- PARTNERSHIP: IT seen as an asset; process driver; conflict seen as creative
- ARCHITECTURE: Integrated across the organization
- SKILLS: Emerging value service provider; balanced tech & business hiring

Level 2 • Committed process
- COMMUNICATIONS: Limited business/IT understanding
- COMPETENCY/VALUE: Functional cost efficiency
- GOVERNANCE: Tactical at Functional level, occasional responsive
- PARTNERSHIP: IT emerging as an asset; process enabler
- ARCHITECTURE: Transaction (e.g., ESS, DSS)
- SKILLS: Differs across functional organizations

Level 1 • Initial/Ad-Hoc process
- COMMUNICATIONS: Business/IT lack understanding
- COMPETENCY/VALUE: Some technical measurements
- GOVERNANCE: No formal process, cost center, reactive priorities
- PARTNERSHIP: Conflict; IT a cost of doing business
- ARCHITECTURE: Traditional (e.g., acctng, email)
- SKILLS: IT takes risk, little reward; technical training

* Source: Luftman

Figure 1.12   IT/business alignment maturity assessment model

- cascade down and across the organization and break down barriers including silos
  - create cross-functional and global teams (where appropriate)
  - compete on 'speed'
  - ensure a performance driven approach
- mobilize the organization and create ownership
  - role out change initiative
  - measure results of change (pre-change versus post-change baselines)
  - embrace continuous learning, knowledge and best practice sharing
- attributes of effective change teams and agents
  - strong and focused leader
  - credibility and authority (charter) to lead the initiative
  - 'chutzpa', persistent and change zealots
  - ability to demonstrate and communicate 'early wins' to build the momentum
  - create a sense of urgency and avoid stagnation
  - knock obstacles out of the way, diplomatically or otherwise

By applying Kotter's principles to facilitating the transition to a successful IT governance culture and environment, the following steps can be followed:

IT Governance Process Improvement Flow - In order to develop and/or improve a governance process (business or IT), an organization must assess its current & future IT governance state and develop a plan to transform IT.

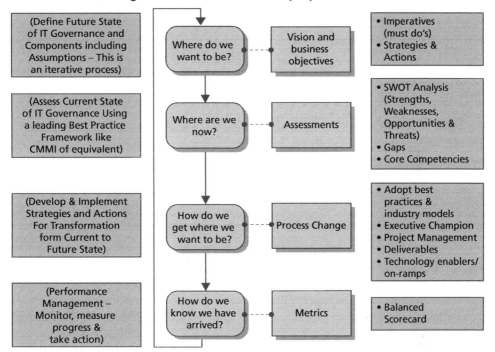

Figure 1.13   IT governance – current and future state transformation flow

- **proactively design and manage the IT governance program** – requires executive management sponsorship, an executive champion and creating a shared vision that is pragmatic, achievable, marketable, beneficial and measurable; link goals, objectives and strategies to the vision and performance evaluations
- **mobilizing commitment and provide the right incentives** – there is a strong commitment to the change from key senior managers, professionals and other relevant constituents; they are committed to make it happen, make it work and invest their attention and energy for the benefit of the enterprise as a whole; create a multi-disciplinary empowered 'Tiger Team' representing all key constituents to collaborate, develop, market and co-ordinate execution in their respective areas of influence and responsibility
- **make tradeoffs and choices and clarify escalation and exception decisions** – IT governance is complex, and requires tradeoffs and choices, which impact resources, costs, priorities, level of detail required, who approves choices, to whom are issues escalated, etc.; at the end of the day, a key question that must be answered is, 'when is enough, enough?'
- **making change last, assign ownership and accountability** – change is reinforced, supported, rewarded, communicated (the results are through the web and intranet), and recognized and championed by owners who are accountable to facilitate the change so that it endures and flourishes throughout the organization

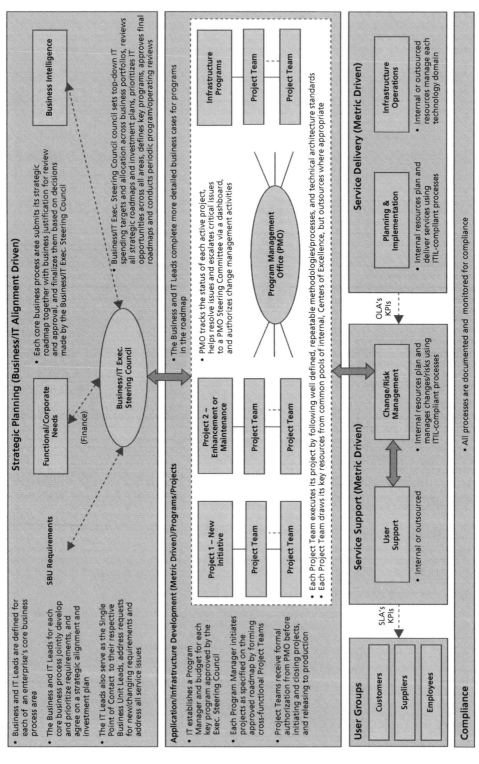

Figure 1.14   Future state IT governance: a blueprint concept

- **monitoring progress, common processes, technology and learning** – develop/ adapt common policies, practices, processes and technologies which are consistent across the IT governance landscape and enable (not hinder) progress, learning and best practice benchmarking; make IT governance an objective in the periodic performance evaluation system of key employees and reward significant progress

1.6   Case study – global consumer goods company

A number of IT governance case studies are included in the book, representing mid-size to large global organizations in a variety of industries, including consumer products, manufacturing, financial services, pharmaceuticals, entertainment and other diversified industries. The identities of the organizations have been kept confidential. The data for each of the case studies was collected through interviews with CEO's, CIOs, direct reports to the CIOs and other executives and professionals, as well as a review of appropriate plans, budgets, metrics, controls and processes and has been disguised to protect the identity of the participating organizations.

The format of the case studies is consistent with Figure 1.15, which represents an IT governance case study for a global consumer goods organization.

1.7   Summary and key take aways

Summary
IT governance is a broad and complex topic with many parts. IT governance represents a journey. It is not a one time event, and to achieve higher levels of IT maturity, IT governance should be persistently and relentlessly pursued, both from a top-down and a bottom-up perspective. Creating and sustaining a more effective IT governance environment will take time and resources, and should be focused on achieving incremental IT governance successes in priority areas, based on their value proposition or reduction of major 'pain point' to the organization.

It is critical to break down or segment the IT governance initiative into manageable, assignable and measurable components or work packages, with targeted deliverables. It is important to define clear roles for the Board, executive management and the IT governance project team, including ownership and accountability for each component and the overall initiative.

IT governance requires all three critical pillars to succeed: leadership, organization and people, scalable and flexible processes and enabling technologies.

Key take aways
The approach to IT governance must be consistent, but yet scalable, and tailored to each organization's environment and management style, key issues, opportunities, level of maturity, audit/legal requirements, available resources and cultural readiness. Remember, IT governance represents a journey, hopefully, towards higher levels of IT maturity, effectiveness and integration with the business.

Figure 1.15 – Case Study - Global Consumer Goods Organization

Environment	Approach
• Annual Revenue range – $8 – 12 Billion • Number of Employees – 40,000 – 50,000 • Number of IT Employees –1,200 – 2,000 • IT spend as a % of revenues – 2 – 3% • Very competitive industry with operations in 50 –70 countries • Brand management driven with strong focus on marketing and sales • CIO reports to CEO and is a member of the Executive Management Team & Seats at the "C" table • Company is transitioning from a decentralized environment to a more coordinated regional & global management environment to take advantage of operating synergies	• Company has been moving towards a more coordinated global and regional operating environment by establishing various steering committees that focus on the specific functional/process areas such as Supply Chain, Marketing and IT to assist in working and creating synergies across global regions • Senior IT management representatives are members of each of the key business councils • Recently, IT is establishing a strategic planning process, which will link to the portfolio investment process, capital and expense budget process and program/project execution process • IT established a global architecture group to coordinate consistent hardware and software (e.g. Operating Systems, Major Application Packages, etc.)
Issues and Challenges	
• IT strategic plan process is new & not yet linked to annual operating plan & budget • IT has many disparate applications, operating systems and hardware inherited from a historical decentralized environment that is slow and difficult to change. Global IT consistency is a challenge • Tensions of a matrix organization Regional IT Managers report into regional business heads with dotted line to CIO	• Established a strong Project Management Office, which is in the process of developing a uniform and consistent process which will be rolled out globally across all regions in a coordinated and collaborative manner • Involved the business owner to assure closer alignment between the business and IT.
Results - Alignment	**Results - IT Service Management & Delivery**
• CIO sits on the Executive Management Operating Council and is an equal peer/partner with business & assures a closer alignment of IT support for business • A 3 year financial plan is developed for IT, about 50% is dedicated to supporting the business unit applications (charged back) and 50% to infrastructure and keeping the lights on • IT portfolio investment management is a rolling process & identifies IT capital spend by geography and functions. It is prioritized based on discretionary and mandatory criteria with top down and bottom up input • Balanced scorecard and report card metrics are linked to critical success factors of business and IT(financials, cost performance, quality, etc.) • Established an customer/IT engagement (single point of contact) model to improve relationships, build trust and focus on priorities of major business functions	• A variety of metrics and tools are used to measure the efficiency, capacity and availability, utilization and service-ability of the operations and infrastructure assets and group • Elements of ITIL processes have been and are being implemented in the IT operations and infrastructure area • The IT infrastructure (Operations and Telecommunications) are centralized through the CIO organizations with strong dotted line coordination throughout the globe

Results - Program/Project Management • Established a PMO center of excellence • Developing a flexible and scalable PM process to handle fast track and complex projects • Implementing a global Portfolio/Project Management tool (Nikku)	
Results – Performance Management & Management Controls • Select IT metrics are included in the IT monthly status report (e.g. key line items designated as green, yellow and red) • An annual user satisfaction survey is conducted by IT measuring 8 areas of IT delivery: communications, responsiveness, up-time, alignment, business process transformation, IT process transformation (streamline IT process), project, relationship mgt. and application support • A monthly Serbanes Oxley report is issued & tracks a number of required categories • A narrative IT annual report is issued reporting news, strategies, etc.	**Lessons Learned** • IT governance is a journey towards continuous improvement • Cultural and organizational transformation is difficult, but necessary to survive • Involve local, regional and corporate management employees in direction setting and execution initiatives in a spirit of cooperation, communications, trust and partnership • Establish global centers of excellence (located in multiple regions) for IT and let them lead by example: Web/e-business, Core center applications, Infrastructure, PMO/SDLC, Enterprise Data Architecture, Advanced Technology, Etc.

IT Mission & Key Management Principles – Consumer Goods Organization (Illustrative Example)

IT Mission
• Enable business growth • Advance Business Transformation • Increase the productivity of associates and Sales Representatives • Support our global operating model

Growth Enablers		
Maintain a deep understanding of our business	**Achieve business alignment**	**Deliver contemporary business solutions**
• Anticipate business needs • Proactively identify how information and technology can drive the direct selling business model • Partner with the business to implement hard to do transformation • Leverage our cross-functional and cross-geography view	• IT strategy in step with business strategy • Forge strong relationships with business partners • Communicate early, frequently and simply • Ensure IT talent is aligned with growth strategies	• Champion integration and collaboration • Reduce the number of solutions while supporting business differences across markets • Provide information for business decision-making • Affordable and suitable alternatives

Operational Levers		
Lead through process discipline	**Provide the best value**	**Maintain Service Excellence**
• Comply fully with our project management and software development methodologies • Adhere to IT Governance policies and procedures • Ensure adequate controls and KPIs • Sponsor appropriate certifications	• Implement make vs buy decisions that deliver speed, competitive advantage, affordability • Leverage worldwide IT resources • Effectively manage services and assets	• Systems are reliable and available to optimize revenue and representative service • The enterprise is secure, controlled and protected • Disciplined problem, change & risk management

Figure 1.15   Case study: global consumer goods company

2 Overview of comprehensive IT governance framework and related industry best practice frameworks

2.0 What is covered in this chapter?

This chapter:
- describes an integrated IT governance framework and the related industry standards, guidelines and frameworks
- provides an overview of select examples of current and emerging industry (vendor independent) best practice frameworks, maturity models and standards and the appropriate references
- discusses the implications of these frameworks on an organization's approach to IT governance

2.1 Overview

There are a growing number of models and frameworks that address one or more aspects of IT governance. There are few that integrate the components necessary to plan, develop and deploy a comprehensive IT governance framework and roadmap to help guide organizational process improvement initiatives in this area.

- Some organizations use the COBIT® 4.0 (Control Objectives for Information and Related Technologies - IT Governance Institute, 2006) as a checklist focused primarily on the control aspects of improving IT governance.
- Others approach the problem from a security perspective and use ISO 17799 or BS 7799 as a framework.
- Meanwhile, others approach it from a project management perspective and use PMBOK® (Project Management Book of Knowledge - Project Management Institute, 2004) or PMMM® (Project Management Maturity Model – Crawford, 2002) or PRINCE2 (OGC, 1998).
- Others have embraced the IT Service Management and Delivery model based on the ITIL® framework (IT Infrastructure Library – OGC, 2002).
- Several organizations have embarked on the quality improvement route through the use of ISO 9001-2000 or Six Sigma or Lean.
- Some use frameworks such as CMMI® (Capabilities Maturity Model Integrated – Software Engineering Institute, 2002, 2006) for systems and software development and eSCM® (eSourcing Capability Model developed for Service Providers and Customers to facilitate the outsourcing process by the ITSqc {IT Services Qualification Center at Carnegie Mellon University – Hyder, 2006; Hefley, 2006}).
- The University of Amsterdam developed a generic framework for information management which is being used in Europe (Akker, 1997).

- Efforts are being made by several groups to correlate CobiT with ITIL, ISO 17799, CMMI, PRINCE2, PMBOK, eSCM, ISO 9001, ISO 27001-2005 ISMS (Information Security Management Systems), AS 8000 and 8015, and other frameworks, and to streamline the use and application of these frameworks to improve the IT governance environment.

To establish and successfully deploy an IT governance initiative effectively, it must permeate the enterprise, and can be characterized as a mix of formal systematic processes blended with behavioral science techniques and people skills. Robinson suggested a generic IT governance model, which consists of multiple layers split into categories broadly covering business drivers, internal environment and culture, entrustment network and accountability, decision model and authority, value realization and delivery, performance management and value management (Robinson, 2007). Figure 2.1 illustrates this model.

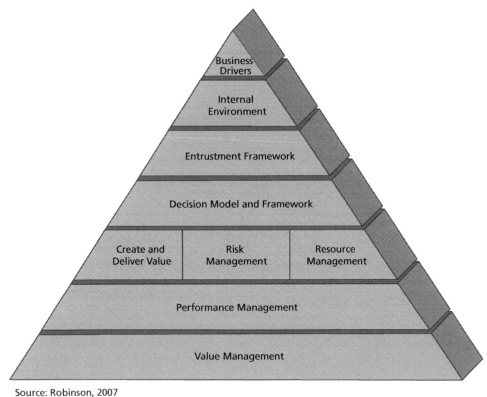

Source: Robinson, 2007

Figure 2.1   The generic IT governance model

While this model lays out a conceptual framework, it requires much more detailed policies, processes and tools for practical deployment.

Limitations of existing models, standards and frameworks

Most of the current models do not address the entire body of knowledge or life cycle of IT governance. While some provide a checklist of processes such as CobiT, most fall short by not providing the 'how to' processes, templates, checklists and tools for effective deployment and continuous improvement. Another shortcoming of many current models, with some exceptions, is that they do not readily provide methods to appraise capabilities or provide guidance for improvement of IT governance process. Some of the frameworks have structures that are either too flexible or too rigid and are not easily scalable.

A practical approach to IT governance for many organizations is to select the best of all of the models and standards, develop a blend of the best attributes of each of the frameworks, and tailor an approach that is realistic and sustainable for their respective environment.

Benefits of using a unified IT governance framework leveraging best practices models:

- grounded in industry best practice research and experience
- improve credibility and confidence
- overcomes vertical silos
- faster acceptance
- better resource utilization (reduce, contain and/or avoid costs) based on consistent standards
- improve customer satisfaction and responsiveness
- common terminology and definitions
- clear accountability
- consistent, repeatable, end-to-end measurable processes
- accelerated deployment (do not have to re- invent the wheel)

2.2   Integrated IT governance framework and roadmap

Based on our findings, many organizations start or focus the IT governance initiative on their 'pain' points and expand from there. Given that most organizations are at different levels of maturity for each of the major components of IT governance or IT governance as a whole, there appears to be no single, best approach for all organizations. Rather, each organization should tailor its approach to its environment, and consider such factors as the organization's operating and management philosophy, key issues and opportunities, its change tolerance, state of level of maturity, audit and legal compliance requirements and its cultural readiness.

At the end of the day, every organization must address each of the major components of IT governance including:

- **business strategy, plan and objectives (demand management)** - This involves the development of the business strategy and plan and this should drive the IT strategy and plan.
- **IT strategy, plan and objectives (demand management)** – This should be based on the business plan and objectives and should provide the direction and investment priorities of the IT functions and resources. This should also include portfolio investment management priorities, enterprise architecture and identify the decision rights (who influences decisions on IT and who is authorized to make the decisions on a wide variety of areas).
- **IT plan and service execution (execution management)** – This encompasses the processes required to assist in the execution of systems and services, such as program and project

management, IT Service Management (including ITIL – IT Infrastructure Library), risk management, change management, security management, business and IT continuity, contingency, disaster recovery management and others.

- **performance management, management controls and compliance (execution management)** – This would include such areas as the Balanced Scorecard, key performance indicators, CobiT and regulatory compliance areas, management controls and audits including Sarbanes - Oxley, HIPPA, BASEL II and other general or industry specific regulations.
- **vendor management and outsourcing management (execution management)** – Since organizations are increasing their outsourcing spending as a percent of their budget, selecting and managing the service providers effectively has become more critical.
- **people development, continuous IT governance process improvement and learning** – To stay at the top of one's game, it has also become critical to invest in learning and education, knowledge management and continuous process improvement.

Most of today's IT models, frameworks and standards only address one or a limited number of components that must be an integral part of a comprehensive IT governance framework. Many of the current models are being used by industry and should be understood, leveraged, integrated and/or tailored. These should be used to develop an integrated approach to IT governance.

The proposed integrated IT governance framework described in this chapter references the previously cited industry frameworks, standards and guidelines, as well as additional ones that are relevant for improving IT governance maturity and effectiveness in organizations.

Figure 2.2 provides an illustration of the integrated IT governance framework and its proposed major components, listing select references as a pragmatic approach to improving the IT governance environment. This was briefly covered in Chapter 1.

Figure 2.3 is another version of the CMMI® model related to IT governance in general. It is difficult to assess IT governance as a whole in this way. Rather, it must be broken down into as many of the components that an organization must deploy that are part of IT governance.

Figure 2.4 represents a template that integrates the major and key sub-components of IT governance (see Figure 2.2) with the CMMI® model levels, to provide a self-assessment tool to help evaluate the current level of maturity by each component. The major components and sub-components can be tailored according the needs of a particular organization to help develop a roadmap for achieving a higher level of IT maturity and effectiveness. In addition, Figure 2.4 also identifies the chapters in the book that provide an overview of the 'how to's' for each of the major and essential components of IT governance.

2.3　Select examples of current business/IT alignment and governance reference models, frameworks and standards

This section summarizes select current and emerging industry best practice models, frameworks and standards relating to IT governance and its major components.

Identifies the major areas that must be addressed on the journey to a higher level of IT governance maturity and effectiveness

Areas of Work	Description/Components	Deliverables/References
Business Plan/ Objectives (Demand Management & Alignment)	• Strategic Business Plan – Vision, Objectives, Financials, Operations, SWOT, Imperatives (Must Do's), Initiatives (Alternatives that Support Imperatives), etc. • Capital Planning/Expense Planning & Budgeting • Business Performance Management (Key Metrics) • Executive and Other Steering & Review Councils; Organization Structure	• Plan Document • Financials • Balanced Scorecard Metrics • BCG; Porter; Hamel
IT Plan, Objectives, Portfolio Investment and Approvals (Demand Management & Alignment)	• IT Plan is aligned with the Business Plan – IT Capital/Expense Budget • IT portfolio investment, rationalization, selection, prioritization, funding and approval (Portfolio Management Model (for New, Change Programs and Projects and/or Operational and Infrastructure Functions) • Fund major initiatives • IT Performance Management (Define Metrics and Measurement Criteria)	• IT Strategic/Tactical Plan/ Metrics • Portfolio Mgt. Model (Investment Criteria); ITIM • Engagement Model - Roles • Business Rules & Authorization • McFarlan, Cash; Luftman; Popper; Selig
IT Plan Execution & Delivery (Resource & Execution Management)	• Program, Project and Operating Plans (Capital Plans, Project Plans and Budgets) • Policies, Standards, Guidelines & Processes (e.g. Management Control, Enterprise Architecture, Security, PMO, ITIL, Enterprise Architecture, etc.) • Processes (PMO, Help Desk, Security, Administrative SOPs, Workflows, Change, Risk, etc.) • Financial, program, project, application, maintenance and operational accountability	• Assess Implications of PMMM, PMBOK, CMMI, ITIL, SDLC, CoBit, Security (ISO 17799), Prince2 ,eSCM Frameworks • Infrastructure & Operational Integrity, Continuity & Security
Performance Management, Controls, Risk, Compliance and Vendor Management (Execution Management)	• Manage and measure plans, budgets programs, projects, operations & risks • Define and track key performance indicators (KPI) • Compare plans to actuals and take appropriate corrective actions • Outsourcing and Vendor Selection, Tracking, Measurement • Business and IT Continuity, Security, Contingency and Disaster Recovery	• Balanced Scorecard & KPIs • Performance Management • RFI, RFQ, RFP and Contrac Management; • Sarbanes-Oxley ++ Compliance • Management Controls/ COBIT
People Development, Continuous Process Improvement & Learning	• Human capital development • Organizational, Project & Operational Maturity Models and Standards • Managing Change and Transformation (e.g. culture, interoperability) • Training and Certification (e.g. Individual and Organization)	• Adopt Current and Emerging Industry and Government Best Practices Standards & Guidelines • PCMM; OMB 300; ISO; ITIM • Career Development and Certification

Figure 2.2   Integrated IT governance framework

COSO - Committee of Sponsoring Organizations of the Treadway Commission

The COSO committee is a US private sector initiative, formed in 1985 to identify the factors that cause fraudulent financial reporting in corporations and make recommendations to reduce these incidents. COSO is sponsored and funded by several accounting associations and institutions, such as the American Institute of Certified Accountants, and the American Accounting Association.

The COSO framework defines internal control as a process, impacted by an organization's Board of Directors, management and other personnel, designed to provide reasonable assurance regarding the achievement of objectives in the following categories:
• effectivenessand efficiency of operations
• reliabilityof financial reporting
• compliancewith the applicable laws and regulations

CMMI* or An Equivalent Model can be used to self - assess the level of an enterprise's IT Governance maturity & develop a plan and strategy to achieve higher levels of maturity for each of the major and sub-components of IT Governance.

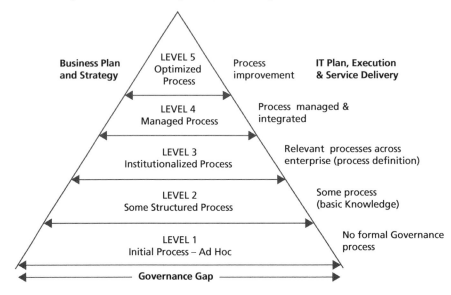

Source: Modified from Software Engineering Institute's CMMI (Capability Maturity Model Integrated)

Figure 2.3   High level IT governance maturity levels

The COSO internal control framework consists of five components:

- **control environment** – sets the tone of the organization by creating awareness of the importance of control and is the foundation for all of the other components
- **risk assessment** – sets the stage for assessing risks to achieve objectives and then managing those risks
- **control activities** – control activities are the policies, procedures and tools that help ensure that management directives are deployed
- **information and communications** – information systems play a key role in internal control systems by producing financial, operational and compliance reports and information
- **monitoring** – internal control systems need to be monitored for compliance and continuous improvement

COSO has served as a blueprint for establishing internal controls that promote efficiency, minimize risks, help ensure the reliability of financial statements and comply with laws and regulations (Institute of Internal Auditors, 2005). Many organizations are using the COSO framework to improve their business and to a lesser extent, their IT governance environments.

ITIM – IT Investment Management - stages of maturity and critical processes

The General Accounting Office (GAO), an agency of the US Federal Government, developed the IT Investment Management (ITIM) framework. It represents a maturity assessment model composed of five progressive stages of maturity and provides a method for evaluating and assessing

The template can be used to assess the level of IT Governance and its major components, process, maturity and effectiveness (1=low; 5=high). Additional IT Governance components from COBIT, ISO 17799 or others may be added across the horizontal axis as required.

Maturity	Attributes	Values
Level 5	• Optimized proces	
Level 4	• Metrics driven process improvements • Process managed and used by all	
Level 3	• Enterprise wide process and standards	
Level 2	• Basic Process • Basic Knowledge	
Level 1	• Ad hoc • No established practices or processes	

Major IT Governance Components:

Demand Management and Alignment (Chapter 3)
- Business Plan
- IT Plan
- Portfolio Investment Management
- Other

Execution Management (Chapters 5,6,7)
- Program/Project Management
- Resource Management
- Risk Management
- ITSM + ITIL
- Vendor Management
- Enterprise Architecture
- Other

Performance Management and Contols (Chapter 8)
- Critical Success Factors/CSFs
- Key Performance Indicators
- MBO's and incentives tied to CSFs
- Controls and Audit (COBIT)
- Other

People Development and Learning (Chapter 4)
- Continuous Process Improvement
- Knowledge Management
- Education, Training and Learning
- Other

Figure 2.4   IT Governance maturity self assessment framework

how well an agency is selecting, aligning the IT investment to support the agency's mission and managing its IT resources and investments.

At the Stage 1 level of maturity, an agency is selecting investments in an unstructured, ad hoc manner. Project outcomes are unpredictable and successes are not repeatable, and the agency is creating awareness of the investment process. Stage 2 processes lay the foundation for sound IT investment by helping the agency to attain successful, predictable, and repeatable investment control processes at the project level. Stage 3 represents a major step forward in maturity, in which the agency moves from project-centric processes to a portfolio approach, evaluating potential investments by how well they support the agency's missions, strategies, and goals. At Stage 4, an agency uses consistent evaluation techniques to improve its IT investment processes and its investment portfolio. It is able to plan and implement the 'de-selection' of obsolete, high-risk, or low-value IT investments. The most advanced organizations, operating at Stage 5 maturity, benchmark their IT investment processes relative to other 'best-in-class' organizations, and look for breakthrough information technologies that will enable them to change and improve their business performance (General Accounting Office, 2004).

Figure 2.5 illustrates the ITIM Framework and can be used by both private and public organizations. More details on portfolio investment management are discussed in Chapter 3.

ITIM identifies the IT investment stages, their characteristics and the levels of maturity. It also identifies criteria for IT investment oversight.

Maturity stages	Critical processes
Stage 5: Leveraging IT for strategic outcomes	– Optimizing the investment process – Using IT to drive strategic business change
Stage 4: Improving the investment process	– Improving the portfolio's performance – Managing the succession of information systems
Stage 3: Developing a complete investment portfolio	– Defining the portfolio criteria – Creating the portfolio – Evaluating the portfolio – Conducting postimplementation reviews
Stage 2: Building the investment foundation	– Instituting the investment board – Meeting business needs – Selecting an investment – Providing investment oversight – Capturing investment information
Stage 1: Creating investment awareness	– IT spending without disciplined investment processes

Source: GAO.

Figure 2.5   IT investment management maturity stages (ITIM)

PMBOK® - Project Management Book of Knowledge

PMBOK® was developed by the Project Management Institute (PMI) as a PM framework consisting of nine knowledge areas and five process areas (initiation, planning, execution, control and termination). It is the primary framework used in the Project Management Professional

(PMP) certification examination, which certifies individuals as PMPs (Project Management Institute, 2004).

As more individuals are PMP certified, the overall project management effectiveness and maturity level should improve in an organization.

Figure 2.6 illustrates PMI's nine knowledge areas and their major components.

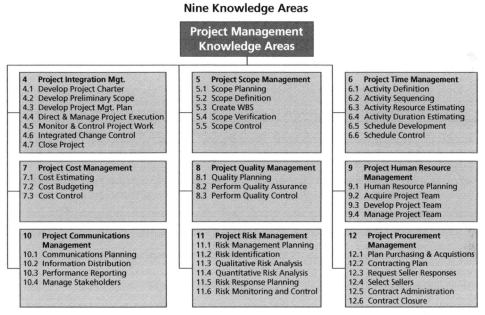

Project Management Institue, *A Guide to the Project Management Body of Knowledge (PMBOK® Guide) - Third Edition*, Proect Management Institute, Inc., 2004. Copyright and all rights reserved.

Figure 2.6   PMI's knowledge areas

OPM3® - Organizational Project Maturity Model

PMI's OPM3® is a guideline comprised of three key elements that are intended to improve the systematic management of projects, programs and portfolios, and closer align them with strategic goals and objectives of an organization:

- knowledge element – describes organization project management maturity, explains why it is important and how maturity can be recognized
- assessment element - identifies methods, processes and procedures that an organization can use to self-assess its PM maturity
- improvement element – provides a process for moving an organization from its current level of maturity to higher levels of maturity

OPM3 is not an organization certification framework, but represents a continuous improvement process. Figure 2.7 shows the OPM3 Framework and its elements.

The focus of OPM3 is to help organization reach the 'Continuous Improvement' stage for projects, programs and portfolios.

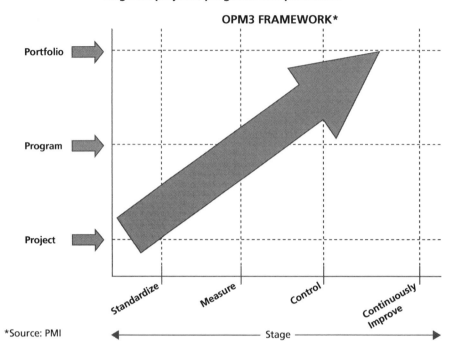

*Source: PMI

Figure 2.7   OPM3 Framework

PMMM® - Project Management Maturity Model

The PMMM® (Project Management Maturity Model) blends PMI's PMBOK® nine knowledge areas with Software Engineering Institute's (SEI) CMMI®'s five (Software Engineering Institute's Capabilities Maturity Model Integrated) levels of maturity, and enables organizations to self-assess their project management capabilities in the PMBOK areas at any given level, and focus on identified activities that would help to achieve continuous improvements up the PM maturity ladder.

PMMM identifies a well defined and easy-to-use roadmap to improve organizational PM maturity. PMMM enables an organization to assess its project management capabilities in the PMBOK knowledge areas at any given level.

Figure 2.8 depicts the PMMM Framework. It can help organizations assess their current state of project management maturity and develop a roadmap for improvement.

CMMI® - Capability Maturity Model Integrated

CMM was developed by the Software Engineering Institute (at Carnegie Mellon University) based on a government grant and is a process improvement model, originally developed, and still largely used, to manage software development efforts and provide a method for assessing the capability of contractors originally for the US Government (Ahern, 2004).

Maps PMI's 9PMBOK Knowledge Areas with SEI's 5 Level Maturity Model

Levels of Project Management Maturity	Level 1 Initial Process	Level 2 Structured Process and Standards	Level 3 Organizational Standards and Institutionalized Process	Level 4 Managed Process	Level 5 Optimized Process
Project Integration Management	No established practices, standards, or Project Office. Work performed in ad hoc fashion.	Basic, documented processes for project planning and reporting. Management only involved on high-visibility projects.	Project integration efforts institutionalized with procedures and standards. Project Office beginning to integrate project data.	Processes/ standards utilized by all projects and integrated with other corporate processes/ systems. Decisions based on performance metrics.	Project integration improvement procedures utilized. Lessons learned regularly examined and used to improve documented processes.
Project Scope Management	General statement of business requirements. Little/no scope management or documentation. Management aware of key milestones only.	Basic scope management process in place. Scope management techniques regularly applied on larger, more visible projects.	Full project management process documented and utilized by most projects. Stakeholders actively participating in scope decisions.	Project management processes used on all projects. Projects managed and evaluated in light of other projects.	Effectiveness and efficiency metrics drive project scope decisions by appropriate levels of management. Focus on high utilization of value.
Project Time Management	No established planning or scheduling standards. Lack of documentation makes it difficult to achieve repeatable project success.	Basic processes exist but not required for planning and scheduling. Standard scheduling approaches utilized for large, visible projects.	Time management processes documented and utilized by most projects. Organization wide integration includes inter-project dependencies.	Time management utilizes historical data to forecast future performance. Management decisions based on efficiency and effectiveness metrics.	Improvement procedures utilized for time management processes. Lessons learned are examined and used to improve documented processes.
Project Cost Management	No established practices or standards. Cost process documentation is ad hoc and individual project teams follow informal practices.	Processes exist for cost estimating, reporting, and performance measurement. Cost management processes are used for large, visible projects.	Cost processes are organizational standard and utilized by most projects. Costs are fully integrated into project office resource library.	Cost planning and tracking integrated with Project Office, financial, and human resources systems. Standards tied to corporate processes.	Lessons learned improve documented processes. Management actively uses efficiency and effectiveness metrics for decision-making.

Figure 2.8   PM Solutions' Project Management Maturity Model (PMMM®)

Levels of Project Management Maturity	Level 1 Initial Process	Level 2 Structured Process and Standards	Level 3 Organizational Standards and Institutionalized Process	Level 4 Managed Process	Level 5 Optimized Process
Project Quality Management	No established project quality practices or standards. Management is considering how they should define 'quality.'	Basic organizational project quality policy has been adopted. Management encourages quality policy application on large, visible projects.	Quality process is well documented and an organizational standard. Management involved in quality oversight for most projects.	All projects required to use quality planning standard processes. The Project Office co-ordinates quality standards and assurance.	The quality process includes guidelines for feeding improvements back into the process. Metrics are key to product quality decisions.
Project Human Resource Management	No repeatable process applied to planning and staffing projects. Project teams are ad hoc. Human resource time and cost is not measured.	Repeatable process in place that defines how to plan and manage the human resources. Resource tracking for highly visible projects only.	Most projects follow established resource management process. Professional development program establishes project management career path.	Resource forecasts used for project planning and prioritization. Project team performance measured and integrated with career development.	Process engages teams to document project lessons learned. Improvements are incorporated into human resources management process.
Project Communications Management	There is an ad hoc communications process in place whereby projects are expected to provide informal status to management.	Basic process is established. Large, highly visible projects follow the process and provide progress reporting for triple constraints.	Active involvement by management for project performance reviews. Most projects are executing a formal project communications plan.	Communications management plan is required for all projects. Communications plans are integrated into corporate communications structure.	An improvement process is in place to continuously improve project communications management. Lessons learned are captured and incorporated.
Project Risk Management	No established practices or standards in place. Documentation is minimal and results are not shared. Risk response is reactive.	Processes are documented and utilized for large projects. Management consistently involved with risks on large, visible projects.	Risk management processes are utilized for most projects. Metrics are used to support risk decisions at the project and the program levels.	Management is actively engaged in organization-wide risk management. Risk systems are fully integrated with time, cost, and resource systems.	Improvement processes are utilized to ensure projects are continually measured and managed against value-based performance metrics.

Figure 2.8   PM Solutions' Project Management Maturity Model (PMMM®) (cont'd)

Levels of Project Management Maturity	Level 1 Initial Process	Level 2 Structured Process and Standards	Level 3 Organizational Standards and Institutionalized Process	Level 4 Managed Process	Level 5 Optimized Process
Project Procurement/ Vendor Management	No project procurement process in place. Methods are ad hoc. Contracts managed at a final delivery level.	Basic process documented for procurement of goods and services. Procurement process mostly utilized by large or highly visible projects.	Process an organizational standard and used by most projects. Project team and purchasing department integrated in the procurement process.	Make/buy decisions are made with an organizational perspective. Vendor is integrated into the organization's project management mechanisms.	Procurement process reviewed periodically. On-going process improvements focus on procurement efficiency and effective metrics.

© Project Management Solutions, Inc.

Figure 2.8   PM Solutions' Project Management Maturity Model (PMMM®) (cont'd)

CMMI, the successor to CMM, focuses on the disciplines of software, systems and hardware process improvements that provide a set of practices that address productivity, performance, costs and overall customer satisfaction, and is being applied to a broader range of initiatives (software development, systems engineering, product development, etc.). The CMMI roadmap consists of three cycles:

- **entry/re-entry cycle** – specifies the actions required to evaluate, adopt and adapt processes for continuous improvement and reduction of defects
- **implementation cycle** – specifies the action required to create an environment and the infrastructure needed for improvement
- **process cycle** – specifies the actions required to execute and monitor the processes

The purpose of CMMI is to provide guidance for improving an organization's processes and its ability to manage the development, acquisition and maintenance of products and services. CMMI provides a structure that helps an organization to assess its organizational maturity and process area capability, establish priorities for improvement and guide the implementation of these improvements. CMMI process areas consist of five maturity levels as illustrated in Figure 2.9.

In addition, there are four process areas defined by CMMI: namely process management, project management, engineering and support. CMMI certification is performed by licensed third party independent organizations. The CMMI certification usually applies to an organization as a whole or to parts of an organization. Since obtaining the CMMI certification is not cheap, some organizations use the CMMI framework as a self assessment tool for improving their processes, rather than applying for certification. Frequently, the companies that obtain certification are the service providers and outsourcing vendors in the IT space, who use the certification for both continuous process improvement and market positioning purposes.

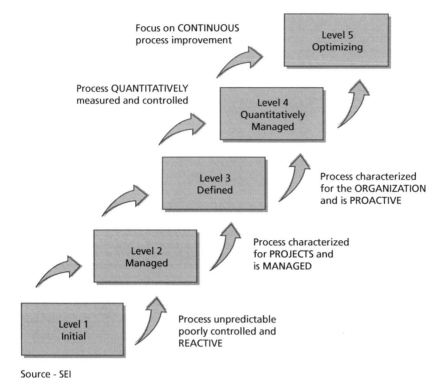

Source - SEI

Figure 2.9   CMM/CMMI process areas by maturity level

People Capability Maturity Model (P-CMM®)

The People Capability Maturity Model (People CMM) framework maintained by the Carnegie Mellon's SEI helps organizations in developing their workforce maturity and in addressing their critical people issues. Based on the best practices in fields such as human resources, knowledge management, and organizational development, P-CMM guides organizations in improving their processes for managing and developing their workforces. P-CMM helps organizations to characterize the maturity of their workforce practices, establish a program of continuous workforce development, set priorities for improvement actions, integrate workforce development with process improvement, and establish a culture of excellence.

P-CMM provides a roadmap for implementing workforce practices that continuously improve the capability of an organization's workforce.

The philosophy underlying P-CMM is based on ten principles:

- Inmature organizations, workforce capability is directly related to business performance.
- Workforcccapability is a competitive issue and a source of strategic advantage.
- Workforce capability must be defined in relation to the organization's strategic business objectives.
- Knowledge-intensework shifts the focus from job elements to workforce competencies.
- Capability can be measured and improved at multiple levels, including individuals, workgroups (teams), workforce competencies and the organization.

- An organization should invest in improving the capability of those workforce competencies that are critical to its core competency as a business.
- Operational management is responsible for the capability of the workforce.
- The improvement of workforce capability can be pursued as a process composed from proven practices and procedures.
- The organization is responsible for providing improvement opportunities, while individuals are responsible for taking advantage of them.
- Since technologies and organizational forms evolve rapidly, organizations must continually evolve their workforce practices and develop new workforce competencies.

The P-CMM consists of five maturity levels that establish successive foundations for continuously improving individual competencies, developing effective teams, motivating improved performance, and shaping the workforce that the organization needs to accomplish its future business plans. Each maturity level is a well-defined evolutionary plateau that institutionalizes new capabilities for developing the organization's workforce. By following the maturity framework, an organization can avoid introducing workforce practices that its employees are unprepared to implement effectively.

The five stages of the P-CMM framework are:

1. **P-CMM - initial level** – Characteristics include: inconsistency in performing practices, unclear rules and responsibility, and emotionally detached workforce.
2. **P-CMM - managed level** – characteristics include: work overload, environmental distractions, unclear performance objectives or feedback, lack of relevant knowledge, or skill, poor communication, and low morale
3. **P-CMM - defined level** - although basic workforce practices are performed, there is inconsistency in how these practices are performed across units and little synergy across the organization; the organization misses opportunities to standardize workforce practices because the common knowledge and skills needed for conducting its business activities have not been identified
4. **P-CMM - predictable level** - the organization manages and exploits the capability created by its framework of workforce competencies; the organization is now able to manage its capability and performance quantitatively; the organization is able to predict its capability for performing work because it can quantify the capability of its workforce and of the competency-based processes they use in performing their assignments
5. **P-CMM - optimizing level** - the entire organization is focused on continual improvement; these improvements are made to the capability of individuals and workgroups, to the performance of competency-based processes, and to workforce practices and activities; maturity level 5 organizations treat change management as an ordinary business process to be performed in an orderly way on a regular basis

The P-CMM includes practices in the areas of:
- staffing (includes recruiting, selection and planning)
- managing performance
- training
- compensation

- work environment
- career development
- organizational and individual competence
- mentoring and coaching
- team and culture development

The ultimate motivation for the P-CMM is to improve the ability of organizations to attract, develop, motivate, organize and retain the talent needed to steadily improve systems and software and other organizational development capability.

PRINCE2 – Projects in Controlled Environments

PRINCE2, an enhancement to PRINCE, was established by CCTA (Central Computer Telecommunications Agency, part of the UK Government, now known as OGC – Office of Government Commerce). It has become a de facto standard used extensively by the UK Government and its vendors to manage IT projects and is widely utilized in the private and public sectors, both in the UK and internationally. Although PRINCE was originally developed for IT projects, the methodology has also been used on non-IT projects (CCTA now OGC, 1998).

Key features of PRINCE2:

- focuses on business justification
- identifies a defined organization structure and processes for the project management team
- product (deliverable) based planning approach
- emphasis on dividing (work breakdown) the project into manageable and controllable stages or packages
- flexibility to be applied at a level appropriate to the project
- management by exception
- used as a standard for UK Government systems projects

PRINCE2 is a process-based approach for project management, and provides a tailored and scalable method for the management of all types of projects. Each process is defined with its key inputs and outputs, together with the specific objectives to be achieved and the activities to be implemented. Figure 2.10 illustrates the PRINCE2 process model.

ISO® 9001–2000 - quality and process improvement

ISO 9001 focuses on quality improvements and reduction of defects, and applies to an organization's overall operations. It strives to satisfy customers by continuing to improve the quality of an organization's processes and operations.

ISO certification is performed by licensed independent third parties and is recognized globally. It usually applies to an entire organization for certification purposes, as opposed to individual certifications such as PMP, PRINCE2 and ITIL.

The ISO 9001 framework is primarily concerned with 'quality management', and consists of eight quality management principles:

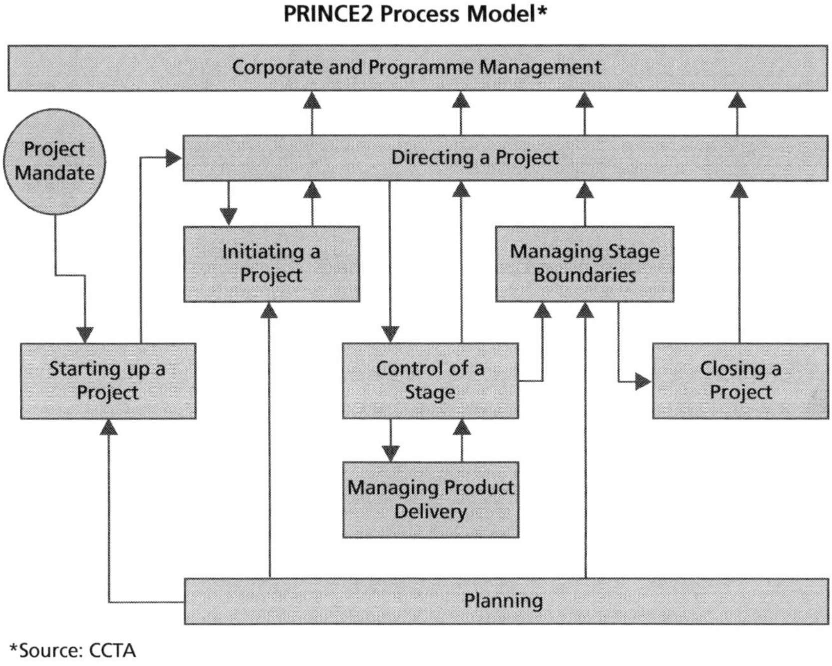

PRINCE2 Process Model*

*Source: CCTA

Figure 2.10   PRINCE2 process model

- focuson your customer – needs, requirements and expectations
- provideleadership – set the direction and sponsor related initiatives
- involveyour people – empower, educate, challenge and develop
- usea process approach – consistent, flexible and repeatable
- takea systems approach – treat inter-related processes as a system
- encouragecontinual improvement – sustain improved performance
- getthe facts before you decide – decisions based on facts *(and experience)*
- workwith your suppliers – develop a win-win relationship

Six Sigma® and Lean – quality, process and VOC (voice of the customer) improvement

Six Sigma has evolved from quality improvement practices (developed in Japan by Deming and others), and was popularized first by Motorola and then by GE in the United States. Six Sigma is an attitude and a frame of mind, not just a methodology. To be successful, the Six Sigma initiative and scope must be enterprise wide.

Organizationally, Six Sigma represents a managerial methodology for continuous process and product improvement throughout an organization, identified by process improvement techniques, and measured quantitatively through process variance statistics. If performance is measured and graphically illustrated, so that the most frequently occurring value is in the middle of the range and other probabilities tail off symmetrically in both directions, this is known as a normal distribution or a Bell Curve. The Sigma measure represents the standard deviation. Six Sigma means six times sigma, indicating 3.4 defects per million opportunities.

Six Sigma represents an individual versus an organizational certification. Individuals are certified as black belts (and other colored belts) in the public domain by the Association of Systems Quality (ASQ) and various corporations like Motorola and GE, who sponsor certification programs for their employees and in some cases, their vendors.

Six Sigma is an organizational initiative or discipline that measures statistical variances and determines what pieces of a process must be improved by: measuring the inputs, efficiency and outputs; mapping them against requirements; identifying improvements areas and resetting benchmarks at higher levels. There are eight suggested steps required to achieve positive results (GE, 2002):

- identify strategic business objectives
- identify core, key sub and enabling processes
- identify process owners
- identify key metrics and dashboards (KPIs- key performance Indicators)
- collect data from KPIs and analyze
- select process improvement criteria
- prioritize process improvement projects
- continual management of processes

GE uses two processes as part of its Six Sigma process improvement methodology:

- Improved Control – _DMAIC_ – Define, Measure, Analyze, Improve, Control *(on average, the process is great – the issues lie with the variation)*
- Process Redesign – _DMADV_ – Define, Measure, Analyze, Re-Design, Verify *(structural problem with the process)*

To be successful, Six Sigma requires a radical change in the way that an organization works.

According to GE, customers and shareholders love it. It drives customer-centricity or tends to optimize the voice of the customer (VOC), reduces costs and improves product, service and systems capability and performance.

In recent years, the concept of Lean Manufacturing or Lean has become more popular. Lean is a management philosophy focused on reducing waste (eg overproduction, waiting time, transportation, processing, inventory, motion and scrap), initially in manufactured products, and it is now spreading to other areas of business. Lean is all about getting the right things, to the right place, at the right time, in the right quantity, while minimizing waste and being flexible and open to change. The seminal book, *Lean Thinking*, by Womack and Jones, suggested five core concepts: (Womack and Jones, 1996)

- specify value in the eyes of the customer
- identify the value stream and eliminate waste
- make value flow at the pull of the customer
- involve and empower employees
- continuously improve in the pursuit of perfection

ISO/ IEC 20000 – ITSM (IT Service Management) Standard

The Standard was originally developed and published in 2000 as BS15000, by a committee of the British Standards Institution, which comprised of IT Service Managers from vendor and user groups, including the ITSMF, OGC and others. Version 2 of the standard was developed in 2002. The formal certification scheme for organizations wishing to demonstrate their conformance to the requirements of ISO/ IEC 20000 is currently owned and administered by ITSMF.

ISO/ IEC 20000 applies to IT Service Management users and providers. The Standard comprises two parts:

- Part 1 – Specification: This is the documented requirements that an organization must comply with to achieve formal certification for ISO/ EIC 20000.
- Part2 – Code of Practice: Expansion and explanation of the requirements in section 1.

Both parts share a common structure including the following parts:
- scope
- terms and definitions
- requirements for a management system
- planning and implementing Service Management
- planning and implementing new or changed services
- service delivery processes
- relationship processes
- resolution processes
- control processes
- release processes

There are five key process areas: service delivery, relationship management, resolution management, control and release.

The service delivery process consists of: service level management, service reporting, service continuity and availability management, budgeting and accounting for IT services, capacity management and information security management.

The relationship processes are: business relationship management and supplier management.

The resolution processes are: incident management and problem management.

The control processes are: configuration management and change management.

The release process is defined as a standalone process.

The ISO/ IEC 20000 Standard is concerned with IT Service Management, and primarily represents a measure of process conformance to be achieved by an organization. The relationship between ISO/ IEC 20000 and ITIL is synergistic, where the Standard addresses the questions relating to IT Service Management as to the 'why and what', ITIL addresses the question of 'how' by providing the process definitions and additional details. Therefore, ITIL is aligned with ISO/ IEC 20000. More information on IT Service Management and ITIL is provided in Chapter 6.

ITIL – IT Infrastructure Library

IT Service Management and delivery is about maximizing the ability of IT to provide services that are cost effective, and meet or exceed the needs and expectations of the business to:

- reduce the costs of operations
- improve service quality
- improve customer satisfaction
- improve compliance

The ITIL framework provides an effective foundation for higher quality IT Service Management, and delivery processes and disciplines. It aligns with ISO/ IEC 20000 (until recently known as BS 15000). It is owned and maintained by OGC (Office of Government Commerce in the UK) and was developed in recognition of the increasing dependence of organizations on IT services to support organizational needs. ITIL v2 consists of twelve repeatable, consistent documented processes for improving IT Service Management and delivery, segmented into two main areas:

- Service Delivery Processes – focus on management control to improve the quality, stability and IT cost structure.
- Service Support Processes – focus on operational aspects of IT to detect and correct problems, and ensure appropriate change, configuration and release management, authorization and documentation.

ITIL primarily focuses on IT operations and infrastructure services. It represents a standardized approach that should be applied consistently, but flexibly, with the use of common terminology:

- focuses on IT services that business/IT alignment and value propositions
- standardization of processes and key performance indicators
- provides the quality assurance foundation for ISO 9001
- industry-supported software and tools
- supports Sarbanes-Oxley
- ITIL aligns with the ISO standard (ISO/ IEC 20000)

ITIL v2 provides for three levels of individual certifications: ITIL Foundation (basic), ITIL Service Manager & ITIL Practitioner (most advanced). These are administered by EXIN (European Examination Institute for Information Science, in Holland) and by ISEB (Information Systems Examination Board, in the UK) and are licensed to other organizations in North America and other parts of the globe.

The latest version of ITIL, version 3, was released in 2007, and is more strategic and IT governance oriented. It uses a life cycle approaching to ITIL. It also recognizes that the practice of IT has matured, and shifts its emphasis from enhancing the performance of IT processes to serving the customer. More details on ITIL v3 are provided in Chapter 6.

A framework consisting of twelve repeatable, documented processes and/or functions for improving **IT Service Management** to reduce costs and improve customer satisfaction, service and compliance. IT Service Delivery Processes - focus on management control to improve the quality, stability and IT cost structure. IT Service Support Processes – focus on operational aspects to detect and correct problems, and ensure appropriate change, configuration and release management authorization and documentation.

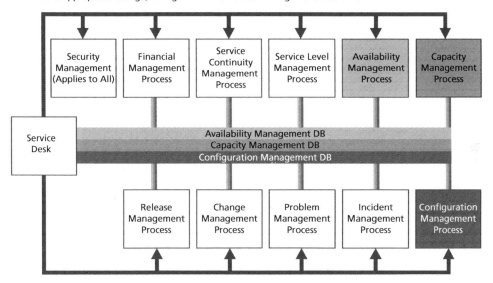

Figure 2.11   Overview of ITIL (IT Infrastructure Library) processes

CobiT® – Control Objectives for Information and Related Technology

Developed by the IT Governance Institute (ITGI®) and its affiliated organization, the Information Systems Audit and Control Association (ISACA®), CobiT,   provides a control framework linking thirty-four IT processes to four domains – planning and organization; acquisition and implementation; delivery and support and monitoring, all of which are related to specific IT resources and metrics.

CobiT defines high level business control and audit objectives for the processes, linked to business objectives, and supports these with detailed control objectives to provide management assurance and/or advice for improvement. The control objectives are further supported by audit guidelines, which enable auditors and managers to review specific IT processes, to help assure management where control is sufficient or to recommend changes.

CobiT does not provide detailed policies and procedures as to how to develop the content, or what content needs to be included in the processes on the checklist. That is the responsibility of each organization. Chapters 4 through 8 provide more details on the content of 'how to's' for each of the major components of IT governance based on a blend of best practices.

The Information Systems Audit and Control Association (ISACA®) works closely with ITGI and provides several individual certifications covering IT auditors and IT security such as the: Certified Information Systems Auditor™ (CISA®) and Certified Information Security Manager (CISM®). CobiT 4.0, the latest version of CobiT, was released in late 2005.

Figure 2.12 provides a table of the four CobiT domains and their related IT processes. The author has identified other best practice frameworks next to the appropriate CobiT processes.

Domain Process ▼————————►	Planning & Organization	Acquistion & Implementation	Delivery & Support	Monitoring
Po1-Strategic IT Plan	X			
Po2-Information Architecture	X			
Po3-Determine Technology Direction	X			
Po4-IT Organization	X			
Po5-Manage IT Investment (Portfolio Investment Management)(ITIM)	X			
Po6- Communicate Direction	X			
Po7-Manage Human Resources	X			
Po8-Ensure External Compliance (SOX ++)	X			
Po9-Assess Risks	X			
P10-Manage Project (PMMM, PMBOK, Prince2, CMMI, OPM3, etc.)	X			
A11-Identify Automated Solutions		X		
A12-Buy/Maintain Application Software		X		
A13-Acquire/Maintain Technology Infrastructure (ITIL/ISO 20000)		X		
A14-Enable Operations & Use (ITIL/ISO 20000)		X		
A15-Procure IT Resources (eSCM; OPBOK)		X		
A16-Manage Change (ITIL & PM)		X		
A17- Install & Accredit Solutions		X		
DS1-Define & Manage Service Levels (ITIL)			X	
DS2-Manage Third Party Services (eSCM; OPBOK)			X	
DS3-Manage Performance & Capacity (ITIL; Balanced Scorecard)			X	
DS4-Ensure Continuous Service (ITIL)			X	
DS5-Ensure Systems Security (ISO 17799 & ITIL)			X	
DS6-Identify/Allocate costs			X	
DS7-Educate/Train Users			X	
DS8-Manage Service Desk & Incidence (ITIL)			X	
DS9-Manage the Configuration (ITIL)			X	
DS10-Manage Problems (ITIL)			X	
DS11-Manage Data			X	
DS12-Manage Facilities & Physical Environment			X	
DS13-Manage Operations (ITIL)			X	
ME1-Monitor & Evaluate IT Performance (Balanced Scorecard)				X
ME2-Monitor & Evaluate Internal Controls				X
ME3-Ensure Regulatory Compliance				X
ME4-Provide IT Governance				X

Source: Modified from IT Governance Institute

Figure 2.12   COBIT domains, processes and related best practice frameworks

ISO 17799 and ISO/IEC 27001- 2005 IT Security Management

ISO/IEC 27001-2005 – ITSM (IT Service Management) Standard
ISO/ IEC 27001 is an information security management standard. It defines a set of information security management requirements.

The purpose of ISO/ IEC 27001 is to help organizations establish and maintain an information security management system (ISMS). It is designed to be used for certification purposes.

ISO/ IEC 27001 suggests that an organization structure's every IT Management System (ITMS) process, using the Plan-Do-Check-Act (PDCA) model. This means that every process should be:

- planned(PLAN)
- implemented,operated, and maintained (DO)
- monitored,measured, audited, and reviewed (CHECK)
- improved(ACT)

The PDCA model is woven into every aspect of the ISO/ IEC 27001 Standard. The Standard recommends that the PDCA model be used to structure every ITMS process (Praxiom, 2007).

While ISO/ IEC 27001 lists a set of control objectives and controls, which came from ISO/ IEC 17799, ISO 17799 also provides implementation guidance. ISO/ IEC 27001 is aligned with ISO 17799. Many organizations use both standards to develop and improve their information security management environment, policies, processes and controls.

ISO 17799 – ITSM Standard
The IT security Standard is very detailed. The Standard establishes an enterprise security architecture (ESA) based on two key concepts, domains and security levels. There are eleven security policy domains which are used to develop security strategy, execute plans track progress and improve security controls:

- informationsecurity organization
- riskassessment and asset classification
- operatingand architectural controls
- personnelsecurity
- physicaland environmental
- accesscontrol
- systemsdevelopment and maintenance
- monitoringcompliance
- businesscontinuity
- wirelesscommunications
- securityincident management

There are six security levels which are used to develop policies, procedures and documentation:

- information security policy statement
- information security policies
- general IT standards
- minimum security guidelines, security procedures and security guidelines
- supporting documents, templates and forms
- security awareness (marketing) material and training

Those companies that use this Standard, tailor it to fit their environment.

eSCM® – The eSourcing Capability Models for Service Providers and Client Organizations

The IT Services Qualification Center (ITsqc) at Carnegie Mellon University created two capability models and qualification methods to improve sourcing relationships in the internet-enabled economy. ITsqc developed the eSourcing Capability Model for both service providers (eSCM-SP v2) and client organizations (eSCM –CL v1).

The eSCM-SP model represents an approach to certifying service provider organizations. The purpose of the service provider model (Hyder, 2002):

- It helps IT - enabled sourcing service providers appraise and improve their ability to provide high quality sourcing services.
- It gives them a way to differentiate themselves from the competition.
- Prospective clients can evaluate service providers based on their eSCM-SP level of certification and practice satisfaction profile.

The purpose of the eSCM-CL client organization model is (Hefley, 2006):

- to give client organizations guidance that will help them improve their capability across the sourcing life cycle
- to provide client organizations with an objective means of evaluating their sourcing capability and maturity

eSCM-SP – Structure for Service Providers:

It consists of 84 practices that address the capabilities needed by IT enables service providers. Each practice has three dimensions:

- sourcing life cycle
  - on-going (spans entire life cycle)
  - initiation (negotiation, agreement, deployment)
  - delivery (delivery of service)
  - completion (transferring responsibility back to client)

- capability area – there are six on-going capability areas (eg knowledge management, people management, performance management, relationship management, technology management and threat management); in addition, there are four capability areas (eg contracting, service design and deployment, service delivery and service transfer) which are associated with one or more phases

- capability level – the third dimension of the eSCM-SP is capability levels; the five capability levels (similar but not identical to the CMMI maturity levels) describe a continuous improvement path that clients should expect service providers to achieve and they include:

  - level 1 - providing services
  - level 2 - consistently meeting requirements
  - level 3 - managing organizational performance
  - level 4 - proactively enhancing value
  - level 5 - sustaining excellence

eSCM- Structure for Client Organizations:

It consists of 95 practices that address the capabilities needed by IT service providers. Each practice has three dimensions: sourcing life cycle (eg with five phases - on-going, analysis, initiation, delivery and completion), capability areas (including nine on-going capability areas, such as sourcing strategy management, governance management, relationship management, etc.) and eight which are temporal and associated with a single phase of the sourcing life cycle, such as in the analysis phases.

There are two capability areas (sourcing opportunity and sourcing approach) and five capability levels (eg performing sourcing, consistently managing sourcing, managing organizational sourcing performance, proactively enhancing value and sustaining excellence).

Uses of eSCM:

The uses of the eSCM frameworks for customers and service providers include:

- customersof service providers
  - use eSCM evaluations to determine provider capabilities
  - rvaluate multiple potential providers
  - reduce risks in sourcing relationships

- serviceproviders
  - systematically assess their existing capabilities and implement improvement efforts
  - use results to set priorities for improvement efforts
  - implement in conjunction with other quality initiatives
  - improve their relationships with clients
  - demonstrate their capability to clients through certification

Outsourcing Professional Body of Knowledge (OPBOK®)

The International Association of Outsourcing Professionals (IAOP) is a global standard-setting organization and advocate for the outsourcing profession. The IAOP developed the Outsourcing Professional Body of Knowledge (OPBOK) as the generally accepted set of knowledge and best practices applicable to the successful design, implementation and management of outsourcing contracts. Version 6 was released in 2006. It provides:

- a framework for understanding what outsourcing is and how it fits within contemporary business operations
- the knowledge and practice areas generally accepted as critical to outsourcing success
- a glossary of terms commonly used within the field

There are nine knowledge areas and standards in OPBOK as follows:

- defining and communications outsourcing as a management practice
- developing and managing an organization's end-to-end process for outsourcing
- integrating outsourcing into an organization's business strategy and operations
- creating, leading and sustaining high performance outsourcing project teams
- developing and communicating outsourcing business requirements
- selecting outsourcing service providers
- developing the outsourcing financial case and pricing
- contracting and negotiating for outsourcing
- managing the transition to an outsourced environment
- outsourcing governance

IAOP developed and offers an individual outsourcing certification called the Certified Outsourcing Professional (COP). It focuses on three stakeholder groups – clients, service providers and advisors or consultants.

National Baldrige Quality Award

This award is named after Malcolm Baldrige, who was US Secretary of Commerce from 1981 until 1987. Baldrige was a proponent of quality management as a key to US prosperity and long-term strength. In recognition of his contributions, Congress named the award in his honor. The Baldrige Award is given by the President of the United States to businesses - manufacturing and service, small and large - and to education, health care and non-profit organizations that apply and are judged to be outstanding in seven areas: leadership; strategic planning; customer and market focus; measurement, analysis, and knowledge management; human resource focus; process management; and results.

The US Congress established the award program in 1987 to recognize US organizations for their achievements in quality and performance, and to raise awareness about the importance of quality and performance excellence as a competitive edge. Three awards may be given annually in each of these categories: manufacturing, service, small business, education, health care and non-profit. The US Commerce Department's National Institute of Standards and Technology (NIST) manages the Baldrige National Quality Program in close co-operation with the private sector.

The Baldrige performance excellence criteria are applicable to any organization. Seven categories make up the award criteria:

- Leadership - examines how senior executives guide the organization and how the organization addresses its responsibilities to the public and practices good citizenship.
- Strategic planning - examines how the organization sets strategic directions and how it determines key action plans.
- Customer and market focus – examines how the organization determines requirements and expectations of customers and markets; builds relationships with customers; and acquires, satisfies, and retains customers.
- Measurement, analysis, and knowledge management - examines the management, effective use, analysis and improvement of data and information, to support key organization processes and the organization's performance management system.
- Human resource focus – examines how the organization enables its workforce to develop its full potential and how the workforce is aligned with the organization's objectives.
- Process management - examines aspects of how key production/delivery and support processes are designed, managed, and improved.
- Business results - examines the organization's performance and improvement in its key business areas: customer satisfaction, financial and marketplace performance, human resources, supplier and partner performance, operational performance, governance and social responsibility. The category also examines how the organization performs relative to competitors.

For many organizations, using the criteria resulted in better employee relations, higher productivity, greater customer satisfaction, increased market share and improved profitability. According to a report by the Conference Board, a business membership organization,

"A majority of large US firms have used the criteria of the Malcolm Baldrige National Quality Award for self-improvement, and the evidence suggests a long-term link between use of the Baldrige criteria and improved business performance."

The Generic Framework for Information Management

The University of Amsterdam Generic Framework for Information Management is a reinterpretation of the Strategic Alignment Model originally developed by Henderson and Venkatraman. The Generic Framework for Information Management is a model for inter-relating the different components of information management. It is used in the area of business-IT alignment and sourcing. It can be useful to consider IT governance issues as well. It is a high-level view of the entire field of information management; its main application is in the analysis of organizational and responsibility issues.

The framework is used to support strategic discussions in the three different ways:
- **descriptive, orientation** – the framework offers a map of the entire information management domain, to be used for positioning specific information management issues that are being discussed in the organization
- **specification, design** – the framework is used to re-organize the information management organization, eg specifying the role of the Chief Information Officer (CIO), or determining the responsibility of an outsourcing service provider

- **prescriptive, normative** – the map is used as a diagnostic instrument to find gaps in an organization's information management, specifically aimed at identifying missing interrelationships between the various components of the framework

The framework primarily provides a reference base for the positioning of information management issues at organization and/or business unit levels. From a normative point of view, the framework states that each of the nine areas and their mutual relations should be addressed. The central axes of the framework are core to information management.

The strength of the Generic Framework for Information Management is that it is very helpful in discussing information management at an enterprise level, illustrating how different aspects of an organization interrelate.

The weakness of the Generic Information Management Model is that it is too conceptual and does not provide specific solutions and requires more detailed frameworks, to support any implementation. Figure 2.13 represents the framework.

The framework extends the Strategic Alignment Model developed by Henderson and Venkatraman from a 2×2 matrix to a 3×3 matrix focusing on interactions and relations of strategy, structure and operations represented by the business, information/communications and technology components.

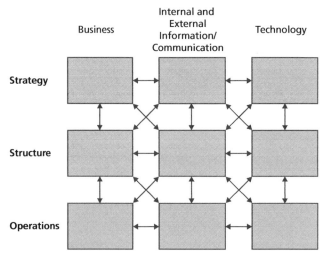

Source: University of Amsterdam

Figure 2.13   The Generic Framework for Information Management

Kano Model

The Kano Model was developed by Professor Noriaki Kano at the Tokyo Rika University to evaluate customer satisfaction relating to new products and is useful for:
- widely divergent user populations
- adding market analysis dimension
- leveraging market data for targeting marketing and promotional messages

The Kano framework represents a technique for assessing customer satisfaction by classifying product attributes into three classifications: threshold (basic/musts), one dimensional (performance/linear) and attractive (Exciters/Delighters). It helps to determine how they are perceived by the customer, and their impact on customer satisfaction. These classifications are useful for guiding design decisions, in that they indicate when good is good enough and when more is better.

Product characteristics are classified as:
- **threshold/basic attributes** – attributes which must be present in order for the product to be successful; this can be viewed as the 'price of the entry'
- **one dimensional attributes (performance/linear)** – these attributes are directly correlated to customer satisfaction (eg increased functionality will result in increased customer satisfaction)
- **attractive attributes (exciters/delighters)** - customers can get great satisfaction from a feature and may be willing to pay a premium price; these are often difficult to identify up front and therefore are called latent or unknown needs

The Kano Model can also be adopted to assess IT customer satisfaction by changing some of the questions used in the Kano framework.

Figure 2.14 illustrates the Kano framework, where the focus should be on the gradient with the happy face.

Represents a technique for assessing customer satisfaction by classifying product or systems into three classifications: threshold (basic or musts), one dimensional (linear) and attractive (exiters and delighters)

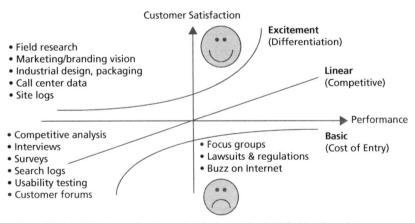

Source: Kano Model – http://www.betterproductdesign.net/tools/definition/kano/htm

Figure 2.14   The Kano Framework

The Balanced Scorecard

The Balanced Scorecard system, developed by Drs. Kaplan and Norton in the early 1990s, is a management system that provides a clear prescription as to what companies should 'measure' to clarify their vision and strategy, and translate them into actions with respect to four areas:

- Financial – to succeed financially, how should we appear to our customer and what should we measure? These are primarily historic performance measures.
- Customer – this area focuses on customer satisfaction, loyalty, retention and exceptional customer service. These metrics can be used as future predictors of success by monitoring the level of customer satisfaction.
- Internal Business Process – this area focuses on business process and how they can be improved. The original Balanced Scorecard concentrated on internal processes. This has since been modified to include both internal and external processes based on the growing network of interdependent suppliers, providers and customers. This area can also be used as part of a corporate report card for future success based on the improvements in quality, lower perfect rates, increasing process cycle times and others.
- Learning and Growth – addresses the issues and actions regarding of managing change, growth, innovation and organizational learning. This area can also be used as an indicator of future success, by comparing such areas as research and development and people development, and against best practice organizations.

To translate their vision and plans into actions for each of the above areas, organizations should identify the following elements: objectives, measures, targets, initiatives and accountability. It is important to note that all of the Balanced Scorecard areas must be used to evaluate the current performance, and project the future performance of organization. More information on the Balanced Scorecard is provided in Chapter 8.

Enterprise technology architecture domains

As identified in Chapter 1, Enterprise Technology Architecture (ETA) is also a vital component of IT Governance. Figure 2.15 identifies twelve ETA domains including client and server platforms, network architecture, business application components, enterprise applications, application development tools, web management systems management, information management and others.

The architecture domains are used to help define a consistent approach to identifying each of the domains and their respective processes, tools, preferred vendors or solutions packages, standards and other characteristics.

AS 8000 (Corporate Governance) and AS 8015 (Corporate Governance for Information and Communication Technology)

In 2003, Standards Australia became the first standards body to publish national consensus-based guidelines on Corporate Governance (AS 8000). This was recently followed by AS 8015, which is the first in a series of Standards and related publications being developed to provide guidelines for the effective, efficient and acceptable use of Information and Communication Technology (ICT) within organizations.

Client Platforms	Enterprise Applications	Application Development
Client Hardware, Operating System, Productivity, Application, Communication, Hardware Maintenance Contracts, Software Tech. Support, Upgrade Agreements	Define For Each Application: Application (Directory) Description, Owner & Key Process Flow & Maps (Input/Output Flow for Applications), Language, Package, Age, etc.	Development Tools, Languages, Compilers, Utilities, Repositories, Frameworks, Testing, Modeling, Object Reuse, Integrated Development Environment (IDE), Aging, Obsolescence, Retirement
Server Platforms	Network Infrastructure	Business Components
Mini Computers, Mainframe, Hardware, Operating System, Storage, SAN, Hardware Maintenance Contracts, Software Tech. Support, Upgrade Agreements	Data and Voice Networks, Wireless, Mobile, Cabling, Protocols, Switches, Routers, NCC, Back-Up, Mail, SAN, Routing Table	Application Systems, 3rd Party Packages, New Common functions/Services
System Management	Middleware	Collaboration
Monitoring, Configuration, Change, Release/Version Control, Asset, Problem, Disaster Recovery, Capacity Planning, Documentation, Integration	Directory, Data Hub, Message Queuing, Business Rule Engine, EAI, EDI, Translation Software	Workflow, Knowledge, Content, Email, Document, Groupware, Personalization, Video Conferencing, Issue Tracking
Security	Information Mgmt.	Web Management
Encryption, Authentication, Authorization, Administration, Intrusion Detection, Virus, Access (Remote & Local), Physical Security	RDBMS, Data Admin., Modeling, Warehousing, Analysis, Mining, Reporting, Data Retention	Web Development, Content Management, Analytics, Search Engine, Portal, SOA, Data Base Interaction, Presentation Language (HTML,AJAX, Flash, etc.)

Figure 2.15   Enterprise technology architecture

The new AS 8015 Standard combines six principles of governance with the three primary tasks of directors (of firms), to form a list of tasks for the control of ICT as follows:

- establish clearly understood responsibilities for ICT
- plan ICT to best support the needs of the organization
- acquire ICT validly
- ensure ICT performs well whenever required
- ensure ICT conforms to all external regulations and internal policies
- ensure ICT respects human factors and privacy

The three primary tasks of directors are to evaluate the use of ICT, direct the preparation and implementation of plans and policies, and monitor conformance to policies and performance against the plans.

2.4   Summary, implications and key take aways

Summary and implications

The growing number of current and emerging best practice frameworks, guidelines and/or standards covering some aspects of IT governance, imply that there is still no one, single, best way for all organizations to improve the effectiveness and efficiency of their IT assets.

- There are a growing number of continuous improvement frameworks and models that apply to IT governance and one or more of its major components.
- All of them focus on helping either individuals and/or organizations improve their effectiveness, competencies and maturity levels in one or more areas of IT governance.
- Most of the current practices do not provide the details of 'how to do' IT governance from a strategic top-down and pragmatic bottom-up perspective.
- An organization should leverage, adopt and tailor those models, frameworks and/or standards that address those issues, opportunities, pain points and threats most critical to the organization and create an IT governance roadmap with clearly defined the roles and responsibilities for IT governance development, process ownership and continuous improvement.

Figure 2.16 provides a summary of the key frameworks, their general use and source.

MODEL	GENERAL USE	SOURCE(S)
COBIT®	IT Control Objectives	ITGI (IT Governance Institute)
ITIM	IT Investment Management	GSA (General Services Administration)
Kano	Customer Needs and Requirements	Kano
CMMI®	Systems and Software Development and Systems Integration	SEI (Software Engineering Institute)
Balanced Scorecard	Corporation Measurement Scheme	Kaplan and Norton
e-Sourcing Capability Model	Sourcing (for both Service Providers and Customers)	ITsqc (IT Services Qualification Center)
People - CMM® (P-CMM)	Human Asset Management	SEI
ISO® 9001:2000	Quality Management	ISO (International Standards Organizations)
Six Sigma®	Quality Management and Process Improvement	Motorola
ISO® / IEC 17799 and 27001	Information Security Management	ISO
ISO® 20000/ BS 15000 / ITIL®	IT Infrastructure, Service and Operations Management	ISO / British Standards Organization / ITSMF (IT Service Management Forum)
PMBOK® / OPM3® / PMMM / PRINCE2®	Program and Project Management	PMI (Project Management Institute) / Project Management Solutions, Inc./ CCTA (OGC – Office of Government Commerce)
OPBOK®	Outsourcing	IAOP (International Association of Outsourcing Professionals)
Generic Framework for IT Management	IT Management	University of Amsterdam and Henderson and Venkatraman

CMMI® and People–CMMI® are registered trademarks of Carnegie Mellon University. COBIT® is a registered trademark of the IT Governance Institute (ITGI). ISO® is a registered trademark of the International Organization for Standardization. ITIL® is a registered trademark of the U.K. Office of Government Commerce. Six Sigma® is a trademark of Motorola, Inc.

Figure 2.16   Summary of current and emerging frameworks that enable IT governance and continuous improvement

Key take aways

The selection of a particular framework or combination of frameworks is largely dependent on the strategic objectives, available resources of an organization and their desired outcomes. All of the frameworks require the management of change and cultural transformation.

The unified IT governance framework model provides a comprehensive framework, based on a minimum set of required components that should provide an appropriate baseline to develop roadmap to steer a more effective journey towards a higher level of IT maturity for organization. However, each organization must tailor its approach to address its environment, current level of maturity, pain points and other factors.

3   Business and IT alignment, strategic/ operating planning and portfolio investment management excellence (demand management)

"Business and IT alignment and planning is a journey, not a destination. It takes many small things to make it a success and not one big thing."
- Selig & Waterhouse, 2006

3.0   What is covered in this chapter?

This chapter:
- identifies the principles for effectively aligning IT to the business
- illustrates business and IT strategy and plan development frameworks
- provides a high level process flow of business/IT planning through execution
- describes the enablers and inhibitors of alignment
- discusses investment portfolio management and consistent criteria for analysis, selection, prioritization and funding of IT initiatives
- describes the business and IT engagement and relationship model to establish and sustain solid relationships, communications, trust and collaboration

3.1   Overview

According to Craig Symons at Forrester Research, *"Aligning IT strategy with business strategy has been one of the top issues confronting IT and business executives for more than 20 years. Why is alignment so elusive, and when can enterprises ever expect to attain it?"* He goes on to state, *"IT and business alignment begins and ends with good IT governance. Alignment of IT strategy and business strategy is the by-product of strong IT governance structures and processes that have matured to the point of being part of an organization's culture. IT governance is about optimizing investments in information technology, and optimization implies that these investments are aligned with overall business unit strategies. More importantly, strategy alignment must be monitored and measured, and management must be held accountable for results "* (Symons, 2005).

As business and technology have become increasingly intertwined, the strategic alignment of the two has emerged as a major corporate issue. Co-operation and collaboration is becoming increasingly important in the modern business environment. The resulting emergence of new forms of relationships is challenging managers to understand fundamental dynamics of co-operation, in order to evaluate and restructure their relationships.

Alignment focuses on activities that IT and business executives within an organization should do, to work jointly to meet the business goals and to make the organization more effective. *"CIO's who achieve alignment typically do so by establishing a set of well-planned process improvement programs that systematically address obstacles and go beyond executive level conversation to permeate the entire IT organization and its culture"* (Clemons, Rowe and Redi, 1992).

Successful business/IT alignment means developing and sustaining a mutually symbiotic relationship between IT and business – a relationship that benefits both parties. This requires that IT executives be recognized as essential to the development of credible business strategies and operations, and business executives be considered equally essential to the development of credible IT strategies and operations.

Key questions to address in improving business and IT alignment include:
- How can organizations align their businesses more effectively?
- How can organizations assess and measure alignment?
- How can organizations improve their alignment?
- How can organizations achieve higher levels of alignment maturity?
- Do your processes and related measurements recognize and take into account the strong co-dependencies between the business and IT people, processes and technology?
- What information is critical to support the strategic business plan initiatives and objectives?
- What changes in business direction (and priorities) are planned or anticipated for the plan period?
- What are the current/projected major business/functional opportunities, issues, risks, threats and constraints?
- What strategic or tactical value does IT provide to your business or function?
- How can IT add more strategic value to the business (eg revenue growth; cost reduction/containment/avoidance, reduce speed to market, business process transformation, business/competitive intelligence, etc.)?
- Is IT developing and maintaining superior and constructive relationships with customers, vendors and others? How can they be improved?
- How effectively is IT communicating its progress and problems to its constituents? Is a relationship and engagement model used?
- What governance processes and controls have been instituted in IT?
- Does the Board/operating committee/senior business leadership review and approve the IT strategy, priorities and funding?

Forrester Research developed a template for helping organizations to assess the level of IT and business alignment maturity. Figure 3.1 represents the alignment maturity assessment model that can be used by organizations to assess where they are today, and also as a base line to develop a plan for achieving a higher level of alignment maturity in the future.

The role of the Board and executive management
The Board and executive management must play an increasingly important role in facilitating the alignment of the business and IT. This should include the following activities:
- Assess that the IT strategy and plan are aligned with the organization's strategy and plan.

Level	Phase	Description
5	Optimized Process	There is advanced understanding of IT and business strategy alignment. Processes have been refined to a level of external best practices, based on results of continuous improvement and maturity modeling with other organizations. External experts are leveraged, and benchmarks are used for guidance. Monitoring, self-assessment, and communication about alignment expectations are pervasive.
4	Defined and Managed Process	The need for IT and business strategy alignment is understood and accepted. A baseline set of processes is defined, documented, and integrated into strategic and operational planning. Measurement criteria are developed, and activity is monitored. Overall accountability is clear, and management is rewarded based on results.
3	Repeatable Processes	There is awareness of alignment issues across the enterprise. Alignment activities are under development, which include processes, structures, and educational activities. Some strategy alignment takes place in some business units but not across the entire enterprise. Some attempts are made to measure and quantify the benefits.
2	Initial Processes	There is evidence that the organization recognizes the need to align IT and business strategy. However, there are no standard processes. There are fragmented attempts, often on a case-by-case basis within individual business units.
1	Ad hoc	There is a complete lack of any effort to align IT and business strategy. IT functions in a purely support role.

Source: Modified from Forrester Research, Inc.

Figure 3.1   IT/Business Alignment Maturity Assessment Template

- Evaluate whether IT is delivering against the strategy through clear objectives, expectations and key performance indicators (KPIs).
- Direct IT strategy by determining the level of IT investments, balancing the investments between growing the enterprise and supporting the on-going operations of the enterprise.
- Ensure an open and collaborative culture between IT and the business.

The changing role of the CIO

In the past, many organizations have practiced a reactive agenda for IT, by defining the CIO's priorities by what had to be done – taking cost out, ensuring the continuity of the business, maintaining the integrity, security and privacy of data, etc., as well as keeping pace with the changing demands of the business.

World class enterprises have recognized the enormous impact that IT can make – not only on growth and responsiveness, but also on innovation and business transformation. In these organizations, IT is a business enabler. These organizations recognize that information technology can provide business leverage and be a driver of top-line growth. They look to their CIO for the ability to drive this growth. They are using technology to render more efficiency across the business and to enable the business to integrate and exploit new requirements more readily. They are also using technology to provide new distribution channels, understand different ways to segment markets and develop profound new customer and market insights. Superior alignment of the business with IT represents a key success factor and represents a 'win-win' environment for both the business and IT.

Components of effective alignment

According to Luftman, Papp and Brier, *"Achieving alignment is evolutionary and dynamic. It requires strong support from senior management, good working relationships, strong leadership, appropriate prioritization, trust, and effective communications, as well as thorough understanding of the business environment"* (Luftman, Papp and Brier, 1999).

Henderson and Venkatraman first developed a strategic alignment model in 1990 which was modified by Luftman, Papp and Brier in 1999, based on a study of over 500 firms representing 15 industries. The model consists of twelve components and it is the relationship and the processes linking each of the components that define business-IT alignment (Henderson and Venkatraman, 1990; Luftman, Papp and Brier, 1999).

The components of the model, which have been further modified by the author, are:

Business strategy:

- **business scope** – includes the industry, markets, products, services, customers, regulations and locations where an enterprise competes as well as the competitors, suppliers and other constituents that affect the competitive business environment
- **distinctive competencies** – the critical success factors and core competencies that provide a firm with a potential competitive edge; this includes brand and marketing, research and development, manufacturing and/or operations and new product development, innovation (eg product, process and/or technology), cost and pricing structure, and sales and distribution channels, logistics and supply chain management and culture
- **business governance** – this involves how companies set the relationship among management, stockholders and the board of directors; also included is how the companies are affected by government regulations, and how the firm manages its relationships and alliances with strategic partners; finally, the performance management, measurements and controls are included

Organization processes and infrastructure:

- **administration structure** – the way the firm organizes and structures its business and defines the decision rights, authority and accountability; examples include centralized, decentralized, matrix, horizontal, vertical, geographic, federal, and functional organizations
- **processes** - how the firm's business activities (the work performed by employees) operate or flow; major issues include value added activities, process improvement and integration and interface points between functions, departments or business units and external forces
- **skills** – people considerations such as how to hire/fire, motivate, train/educate, incentivize, manage change and culture

IT strategy:

- **technology scope** - the important information applications, data management and technologies
- **systematic competencies** - those capabilities (eg access to information that is important to the creation/achievement of a company's strategies) that distinguish the IT services
- **IT governance** - how the authority for resources, risk, and responsibility for IT is shared between business partners, IT management and service providers; program and project selection, prioritization and approval issues are included here

IT processes and infrastructure
- **architecture** -the technology priorities, policies, and choices that allow applications, software, networks, hardware, and data management to be integrated into a cohesive platform
- **processes** - those practices and activities carried out to develop synergistic plans with business, develop and maintain applications, manage IT infrastructure and institutionalize consistent IT governance processes
- **skills** - IT human resource considerations such as how to hire/fire, motivate, train/educate, incentivize, change and culture

Enablers of business/IT alignment
According to a study by IBM's Advanced Business Institute, the key enablers to business and IT alignment include: (IBM, 1999)
- senior executive support for IT
- IT involved in business strategy development
- IT understands the business
- business– IT partnership
- well-prioritized IT projects
- IT demonstrates leadership

Both the IT and business executives and professionals should co-operate to build up a comprehensive strategy that will lead to formulating a process of continuous improvement for more effective alignment. For example, one firm that successfully used cross-functional teams for strategy development includes Bristol-Myers Squibb. At Bristol-Myers Squibb, an IT Review Board composed of IT and business executives lead the strategy and planning processes, identify opportunities, and defines priorities for IT. It also tracks projects and uses the concept of an IT–business liaison to maintain and ensure closer collaboration.

Inhibitors of business/IT alignment
The alignment inhibitors are:
- IT and the business lack close relationships and may not have common goals
- IT does not prioritize projects well and in a timely manner
- IT fails to meet its commitments
- IT does not understand the core business or mission of the organization
- senior executives do not understand the value of IT, and therefore are not committed
- IT management lacks dynamic business oriented leadership

The inhibitors of alignment are the reverse of the enablers. The first inhibitor is the lack of a close relationship between the business and the IT function. In some organizations, IT executives do not participate in any strategy formulation meetings, nor have a seat at the 'C' suite. One other indicator is where the CIO reports to the CFO. This represents a constraint and handicap to more effective alignment. If these initiatives are not well defined and prioritized, then the IT department could be spending time and resources on projects that are not as important to the business. Only business executives (as sponsors or champions or owners) can drive and validate the realization of value from IT related projects. It is critical to have a strong partnership to ensure better collaboration and bonding. The vehicles for this governance process include collaborative steering committees, IT and business liaisons, budget and human resource allocation processes, value assessments and a seat for the IT executive at the executive ('C') table.

Overcoming alignment obstacles and constraints

There are a number of obstacles and constraints that must be overcome if an organization is to improve its IT and business alignment. In a study of over 100 organizations, Giga Research identified and compared characteristics of aligned and unaligned IT organizations. It seems that while IT management may have fallen short in some areas of alignment, there are conditions out of IT's control that make alignment difficult in some cases. The Giga Research results are given in the following table (Leganza, 2003):

Table 3.1   Attributes of aligned and unaligned organizations

Attributes	Not Aligned	Aligned
Reporting Structure	IT reports into the CFO or an operational executive with significant non-IT responsibilities.	IT reports into an executive that understands the strategic potential of IT and the various IT-related units report into an executive whose sole responsibility is IT. CIO also has a seat at the 'C' table.
Cultural Attitude towards IT	IT is treated as a utility.	IT is perceived as having contributed significantly to strategic business success.
Perception of IT service	IT has a recent history of unsatisfactory service, at least the perception of disorder, and/or high cost.	IT has previously worked long and hard to overcome perceptions of poor service and is proactive in monitoring dashboards that monitor service levels.
IT access to business goals and strategy	IT leadership is not aware of business goals or the business strategy at a meaningful level of detail.	IT leadership is in the loop regarding business planning at a detailed level and keeps pace with frequent changes. In many cases, the IT organization includes relationship managers that keep in close contact with internal business partners.
IT planning and project prioritization	There is no process for prioritizing projects or tasks within IT based on business priorities.	The IT organization has dynamic and pragmatic planning processes that parallel the business partners.
Business project prioritization	There is no enterprise wide or cross-silo prioritization process for business initiatives.	There are structures and processes for setting enterprise-wide priorities across business units.
Communication regarding the role of IT	The business is unaware of the role of IT in any strategic endeavors.	IT leadership has actively communicated the successes of IT with business executives and business partners.
Communication style	IT leadership and middle management communicate more effectively with technical staff than business people.	IT leadership and middle management speak in business terms and communicate effectively with business people.
Strategic role of IT	IT is not 'at the table'.	IT is 'at the table' or 'C' suite."

Others reasons why business and IT do not achieve good alignment include:
- Political reasons – Traditionally, business executives and leaders have been from non-IT fields. However, that trend is changing in more progressive organizations
- Absence of a clear business strategy and plan
- Conflicting organizational entities

Select alignment metrics

The business and IT department need to collaborate and develop accurate metrics that are linked to the business objectives, priorities and performance. Below are some examples of alignment metrics:

- revenue growth
- return on investment
- decrease in total cost of ownership (TCO)
- increase in employee productivity
- business process cost and time reduction
- speed to market
- customer satisfaction
- increase quality of products and services
- number of IT and business strategic planning and operational review meetings
- development and use of a business and IT engagement and relationship partnership model

Business and IT alignment and demand management

Demands for IT services are either planned or unplanned, and generally come in several flavors – mandatory or core ('must do's' such as service interruptions, standard maintenance, keeping the lights on and/or regulatory compliance) and discretionary ('could do's' if aligned, feasible, cost justified and/or strategic). In an ideal world, both mandatory and discretionary requests should be approved by the business/IT leadership if they have been identified in the IT strategic and operating plans, in accordance with the organization's decision rights and approval authority guidelines. The following considerations will further help align business needs with IT:

- Clearly define and relate the value (eg cost reduction, containment and avoidance; increased revenues; faster access to information; shorter time to market etc.) that IT provides in support of the business. Identify value adding activities (eg value chain and other business models/attributes) and strategies that would enhance them through IT.
- Focus on listening to the voice of the customer and develop a business/IT engagement and relationship building model.
- Ensure that all IT initiatives are evaluated using a consistent, but flexible set of investment selection, prioritization and approval criteria to assure a strong link to the business plan, deployment and integrated into the on-going operations. (See Figure 3.2 – IT/business alignment, project selection and portfolio investment management triangle). The figure identifies key selection criteria such as new/incremental revenues, strategic fit, ROI, intellectual capital, cost reduction, business transformation and other criteria.
- Develop a strategic IT plan that identifies major initiatives, technical/architecture, operational, organizational, people development and financial objectives and measurements in support of the business. This is discussed in more detail in Sections 3.3 and 3.4 of this chapter.

Figure 3.3 illustrates an example of IT investment spend alternatives and the percent of investments in each category for a technology organization. These should be driven by business needs and priorities, and will vary by organization and from year to year, based on the organization's business strategy and objectives. It is interesting to note that for this particular organization, the projected spend is segmented into three major 'buckets' or investment portfolios:

- <u>Portfolio 1 – revenue growth projects</u> – focus IT projects on such areas as new product development, customer relationship management, customer interface systems, distribution systems, marketing and e-commerce and others.

Business Plan/Portfolio/Project/SDLC/IDLC/PDLC - Imperatives must be identified in the business plan, compete for funding (Portfolio Management), must be decomposed into programs/projects and with the application of life cycle methodologies, facilitate quality deployment and on-going IT Service Management and delivery

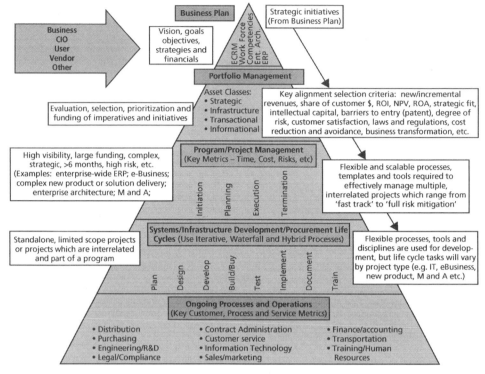

Figure 3.2   IT/business alignment, project selection and portfolio investment management triangle

- <u>Portfolio 2 – cost reduction, avoidance and containment projects</u> – focus on business transformation, innovation, quality, supply chain, ERP systems, etc.
- <u>Portfolio 3 – business enablement projects</u> – contain several areas such as infrastructure, service delivery, compliance, employee development and governance. Others can also be added.

Based on the business strategy and plan of an organization, the percent spend should change from year to year, and will also vary by organization and industry.

A global insurance company example of a world class IT alignment governance process

AXA Equitable is a New York-based, wholly owned subsidiary of the giant financial services firm AXA, which is headquartered in Paris. AXA Equitable has about 10,000 employees in the US, with about 500 in the IT organization. In 1999, AXA US decided to increase its investment in IT significantly. As a result, there was a proliferation of projects that seemed to be chosen based on qualitative analysis alone.

Since alignment represented the front end of the IT governance framework and it was a 'big pain point' for the company that had to be corrected, the company's IT governance improvement initiative started there. The VP of AXA-Technology Services Strategic Management Office, was tasked with establishing a fair and accepted means of choosing among a large array of prospective

Subportfolios ?

IT Investment Management Portfolio Alternatives Consist of Discretionary (Optional), Strategic and Mandatory (Keep the Lights On) Requirements and the Amount of Investment % in Each Portfolio Should be Driven by Business Needs and Will Change from Year to Year and Organization to Organization

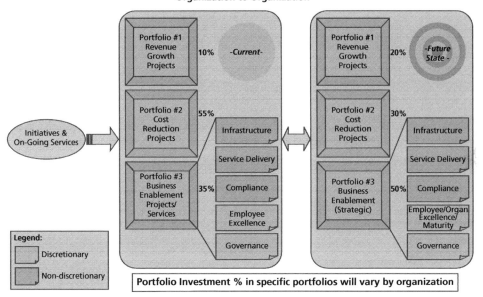

Figure 3.3   Strategic IT investment spend alternatives

IT investments – that is, develop a governance process – based on business analysis and a sound economic model that aligned IT investments much more objectively and closely, with the business.

The business and IT alignment and governance component was designed with the following elements:

- **Executive top-down governance direction** – A business/IT governance committee was formed consisting of the CEO and his direct reports, which included the CIO and business unit heads, to determine IT spend levels on IT initiatives for the company. Each initiative had to undergo two filters, one focused on the alignment of business objectives with IT initiatives first, and the second focused on cost/benefit analysis.
- **Filter 1 – Business and IT strategy alignment** – The first filter involved the identification and weighting of key business strategy objectives (eg increase revenue by 25%; reduce expense base by 30%; improve customer satisfaction by 15%, etc.) These objectives were plotted on an X-Y chart with corresponding IT projects, which were ranked by five levels of potential impact (eg extreme, strong, moderate, low and none). To help focus on the most important business objectives, all projects classified by the executive governance committee as having extreme, strong and medium impact on the business were identified in a 'Strategic Alignment Master List', which represented preliminary approval for further consideration and provided the input document for Filter 2. Concurrently, a 'total pool of money' was allocated for IT projects for the coming plan year, which was further segmented into two parts, the business-as-usual part (funds to keep the operation going and the lights on) and the discretionary portion (where the

investment choices had to be made). In addition, separate 'buckets' of budget allocations were established for corporate and business unit projects.

- **Filter 2 – IT project business case** – For the top ranked projects identified in Filter 1, IT, with the business developed a business case to determine the costs and benefits (eg ROI, NPV, payback, risks, etc.). Based on a combination of Filter 1 and 2 ranking, a priority list of projects was developed. The 'pool of IT project money' was allocated to the priority project list until the funds were fully allocated. The remaining unfunded projects were postponed, recycled or cancelled.

- **PMO handoff** – Those projects that were approved at the executive governance committee meeting were assigned to the project management office for assignments to the appropriate department, for development and deployment through the project management life cycle process.

The case was published and summarized by Gartner. The results of the AXA IT investment governance process were very positive. There was a strong sense of direction and rationality regarding how the business is using IT to advance its position. The methodology has been applied outside of IT, but within other AXA organizations.

The benefits realized are attractive:
- executive-awareness of the importance of a well-defined, repeatable project evaluation, prioritization, approval and governance system
- organizational commitment for deployment of an enterprise investment management framework
- increased knowledge and understanding of the business alignment process and how it improves organizational performance and buy-in
- identification and prioritization of key business objectives that provided an explicit rationale for investment decisions
- creation of a common and consistent way to assess project value across the enterprise
- a prioritized list of proposed projects for each business area approved and owned by that business area

This model has been implemented as a continuous improvement process that links strategy, governance and budget. Enterprises must determine the strategic direction they want to take, decide on the best investments for maximizing progress in that direction, and then allocate the budget and time for implementation. As projects proceed and the environment changes, it is necessary to track and modify the program in a seamless fashion. In essence, the insurance company used a two-tier weighted scoring model to align IT projects more closely with the business, and it is working for them.

Table 3.2 illustrates a generic IT project screening matrix originally developed by Grey and Larson and modified by the author (Grey and Larson, 2008). By multiplying the weights of the project criteria by the values assigned to each project, a weighted score is calculated for each project, and those with the highest scores are selected, until the funding is exhausted.

In summary, for IT investments to be aligned with the business more closely, they must be prioritized, both by their impact on helping the business to achieve its objectives, and by the

Project Filter Criteria	Strong Champion	Aligned to Business Strategy/Objective	Priority	Cost Benefit	Competitive Advantage	Regulatory Requirement	Weight Total
Weight	3.0	5.0	3.0	4.0	2.0	4.0	
Project 1 Value	5	5	2	0	1	4	
Project 2 Value	2	3	3	1	5	1	
Project 3 Value	4	4	2	3	3	3	

Table 3.2   IT project screening matrix

result of a business case analysis. It is also critical that this 'approved master list of aligned projects' is allocated the right resources to complete the projects.

3.2   Principles of aligning IT to the business more effectively

Based on the research (including a review of best practice organizations such as GE, Sun, IBM, Starwood Hotels, Unilever, Avon, United Technologies and others), there are several strategic planning, management control and supplementary principles and practices, which when deployed well, will improve the business and IT alignment environment. They include, but are not limited to the following:

Strategic Planning Practices:
This should be a formal process developed as a partnership and contract (in the loose definition of the word) between the business and IT. It should clearly focus on defining and relating the value that IT provides in support of the business. Specific planning principles and practices should be deployed such as (Selig, 1983):

- **Strategic planning program and processes** - Develop a strategic IT plan that is an integral part of the strategic business plan. The plan framework, format and process should be consistent, repeatable and similar, allowing for functional differences between the business units, and between functions and IT, to facilitate alignment and integration.
- **Executive steering committee(s)** – This involves top management in the IT/ business planning process, to establish overall IT direction, investment levels and approval of major initiatives across the enterprise. Each business unit and corporate staff function should have an equivalent body, to focus on their respective areas, to establish priorities and formalize periodic reviews.
- **Investment portfolio management, capital and expense planning and budgeting** – This ensures that all IT investments are evaluated, prioritized, funded, approved and monitored, using a consistent, but flexible process, and a common set of evaluation criteria, that are linked to the strategic and annual operating plans and budgets, both capital and expense, at multiple organizational levels.
- **Performance management and measurement** – This monitors strategic plan outcomes based on specific Balanced Scorecard and service level measurement categories and metrics,

and establishes organizational and functional accountability linked to MBO (management by objectives) performance criteria and reviews.

- **Planning guidelines and requisites** – A set of general instructions describing the format, content and timing of the business and IT plans; these are general in nature, as opposed to specific standards, and should provide the business units with some latitude and flexibility to accommodate local conditions.

Management Control Practices:

These management control practices focus on the tactical and operating plans and programs, and on the day-to-day operational environment.

- **Formalize multi-level IT/business functional/operations/technology steering and governance boards** with specific roles and decision rights in the day-to-day implementation and Service Management of the tactical IT plans, programs and services.
- **Tactical/operating plans and resource allocation** establishes annual and near-term IT objectives, programs, projects and the resources to accomplish the objectives (eg application development plan, infrastructure refresh plan, etc.).
- **Budget/accounting/charge-back** establishes budgets, and monitors expenditures; charges IT costs back to the business or functional users to ensure more effective involvement and ownership by the business.
- **Performance management and measurement** collects, analyzes and reports on performance of results against objectives at a more detailed and operational level than at the strategic plan level (see Chapter 8 - Performance Management). In addition, formal periodic monthly and quarterly review meetings should be held to review the status of major initiatives and the on-going performance of IT.

Supplementary Practices:

These programs will vary by organization, and can result in improving alignment:

- **IT/customer engagement and relationship model** - establishes a customer-focused relationship model to facilitate interfaces, decisions, resolution of issues, collaborative plan development and better communications, and build trust between IT and the business.
- **Program management office (PMO)** – establishes the processes, tools and IT/business unit roles and responsibilities for program and project management. Initially, PMOs were established by IT to help manage IT programs and projects. As organizations recognize the increased benefits that a PMO brings to an environment, PMOs are being established at the executive level by a growing number of organizations, to ensure that major corporate business initiatives utilize the same discipline and structure as IT initiatives, to implement them within scope, on-time, within budget and to the customer's satisfaction.
- **Marketing, public relations and communications program for IT** – given that most IT departments are particularly bad at promoting and marketing their accomplishments and value, this function creates awareness and promotes executive, management and employee education and commitment, to the value of IT in support of the business, through newsletters, websites, press releases, testimonials and other marketing and public relation events.
- **IT charter** – promotes effective and definitive interaction and links between IT and the business/functional groups they support. A charter can provide information on scope, roles and responsibilities, and provide specific program or project authority and limit to that authority.
- **Standards and guidelines** – adopt and maintain best practice standards and flexible guidelines

to describe and document IT alignment, investment and planning processes, policies and procedures for IT governance and other areas within IT. A financial services organization developed a simple guideline for its customers entitled, '*How to Request IT Services and Get Them Approved*', which was a major success.

- **Organizational and people development, skills and competencies** – develop a proactive learning environment by encouraging and rewarding education, training and certification (where appropriate).
- **Annual/semi-annual IT management meeting** – conduct periodic IT/business management meetings to share best practices, develop stronger relationships, and address organization-wide issues and opportunities.

3.3   Setting a direction for improved alignment through planning related processes

"Few of the things we want most are attainable by means that appear possible.
It is the function of planning to make the impossible possible."

- Russell Ackoff

The strategic, annual and project plans of an organization must be linked to corresponding business plans for effective alignment. To ensure that the IT organization is focusing on the appropriate investments, and providing the level of service necessary in support of business operations and transformation, each significant IT objective must be linked to a specific business objective with a business owner, who is accountable for evaluating the performance towards that objective. In a large US manufacturing company, individual IT units submit lists of proposed projects and budgets. A corporate group assembles these lists and helps business executives evaluate and approve the investments. In a survey conducted by CIO Magazine, '*plan reviews and project prioritization was rated as the most effective practice to establish IT and business alignment*'. (CIO Magazine, May, 2004)

The importance of business and IT planning has been identified by many individual and corporate researchers over the years, such as McLean, Soden, Porter, Hamel, Luftman, Wetherbe, Selig, IBM, GE, GAO, Davenport, Kaplan, T Henderson, Hitt, McFarlan, Cash, Prahalahad, Treacy, Rockart, Nolan, Norton and many others. The importance of planning is suggested by the following factors:

- identify and focus on critical issues, opportunities, objectives, scope and deliverables in a phased and structured manner
- minimize risks, obstacles and constraints
- provide a roadmap and process for action
- obtain better understanding of the alternatives
- provide a baseline for monitoring and controlling work and progress
- establish a foundation for more effective communications, commitment, buy-in and consensus building

- better anticipation and planning for change
- better management of expectations of all constituents

Many businesses and IT planning processes and techniques have been documented in previous research, such as IBM's *Business Systems Planning*, Richard Nolan's *Stages of Growth*, John Rockart's *Critical Success Factors*, John Porter's *Value Chain Analysis and Competitive Forces Model* and many others. Some of these are very complex and detailed, while others are more streamlined.

Key principles for effective business/IT strategic plan alignment

IT plans should be developed iteratively with the business and updated as necessary. Additional principles to strengthen plan alignment include:

- **ownership** - CIO with involvement of IT leadership and of the executive officers and business unit leadership
- **frequency** – IT strategic plan is written/revised/refreshed annually, although major changes may cause the plan to be updated more frequently
- **time horizon** – IT strategic plan usually covers a three year period, with annual operating plans identifying capital and expense budget levels for the first year of the plan cycle
- **plan process** – IT reviews the business strategic plan major objectives, themes and priorities with the business units and corporate services
- **IT interviews** the business units - to align and map IT objectives, initiatives and priorities with the business, using the key plan questions and discussion topics
- **IT identifies** major new or enhancement business application or service support initiatives - as well as significant technology refresh requirements (eg replace obsolete technology; support anticipated growth and new infrastructure requirements) using the business/IT strategic plan initiative alignment template (See Figure 3.14)
- The **business-driven initiatives and the infrastructure initiatives** - are combined in the IT strategic plan (which includes a rough estimate of capital funding needs) and presented to the executive operating committee and SBU heads for approval
- **Communication of the IT strategic plan** – a short version (highlights) of the approved plan is posted on the IT web intranet and reviewed with the IT department and appropriate business constituents
- **Link to annual operating plan and budget plan** – the annual capital and expense budget are approved by the Executive Team for the initiatives identified in the plan; often, new or break-fix initiatives come up during the year (which are not in original plan) that require prioritization, funding and resources; a formal portfolio investment management approval process is followed for that purpose
- **Link to portfolio of projects for annual operating plan** – once the annual operating plan and budget have been approved, a project list and related business cases are prepared, prioritized and reviewed; projects charters are developed for approved projects, and the appropriate implementation resources are allocated and/or committed
- **Link to annual MBOs (management by objectives), performance measurements, KPIs and rewards/incentives** – both the strategic plan and annual operating plan must be driven by measurable outcomes (eg cost, time, profit, volume, customer satisfaction, strategic competitive value, etc.) and appropriate management actions taken according to positive or negative results

Another good example of a well publicized alignment turnaround case is Toyota Motor, USA. In 2002, the Toyota business units and IT were not aligned, and the IT organization lost their credibility with the business due to late projects, high costs, poor perceived business value and physical isolation of key IT liaison managers from the business.

Recognizing this fact, the CIO took the following steps to regain IT's credibility and improve its alignment with the business (Wailgum, April 15, 2005):

- **Established the Toyota Value Action Program** - A team of eight staffers were established and responsible for translating the CIO's vision into actionable items. The team identified 18 business-driven initiatives, including increasing employee training and development, gaining cost savings, making process improvements, resolving inefficiencies and implementing a metrics program. Each initiative got a project owner and a team. The CIO insisted that each initiative have one or more metrics to check its success.
- **Established the office of the CIO** - This most significant initiative called for improved alignment with the business side. At the heart of this new effort would be a revamped 'office of the CIO' structure, with new roles, reporting lines and responsibilities for business and IT executives.
- **Implemented a business/IT engagement model** - As part of the overhaul, the CIO took top-flight personnel out of the IT building and embedded them as divisional information officers, or DIOs, in all of the business unit locations. These DIOs were accountable for IT strategy, development and services, and they sat on the management committees headed by top business executives. The DIOs' goal is to forge relationships with tier-one and tier-two execs (VP and senior director levels). *'I still believe in managing IT centrally, but it was incumbent on us to physically distribute IT into the businesses'*, commented the CIO. *'They could provide more local attention while keeping the enterprise vision alive'*. The difference between the previous relationship managers and the new DIOs is that DIOs have complete accountability and responsibility for the business area they serve, together with their business counterparts.
- **'Town hall' meeting** - Similarly, IT senior management held 'town hall' meetings to announce the changes and deal with questions.
- **Pay for performance** – For the first time, the CIO also tied part of the senior IT managers' bonuses to their success in meeting the goals of each of their annual plans. These managers are judged on 10 areas and on how well they meet the objectives in those areas; for example, meeting project-based goals (whether the project was done on time, and on budget) and operational goals (implementing new governance and portfolio management processes).
- **Executive steering committee** - To further strengthen the IT-business bond, the CIO chartered the executive steering committee, or ESC, to approve all major IT projects. The executive steering committee controls all of the project funds in one pool of cash, and it releases funds for each project as each phase of the project's goals are achieved. Everyone in the company can look at what money was (and was not) going to be spent. The pool's administrators can sweep unused funds out, and other projects can go after those funds.

The CIO said that the organizational structure today is *'almost unrecognizable'* to the IT employees she inherited. One key element of success was rotating IT people into other parts of the company and bringing business people into IT.

High level flow – business/IT planning, investment approval, execution and evaluation

Figure 3.4 illustrates a high level flow linking the business plan to the IT plan and subsequent selection of initiatives, and deployment and evaluation of initiatives. It includes setting priorities, identifying project selection and approval criteria discussed in more detail in Chapter 5, managing and controlling initiatives and evaluating their results.

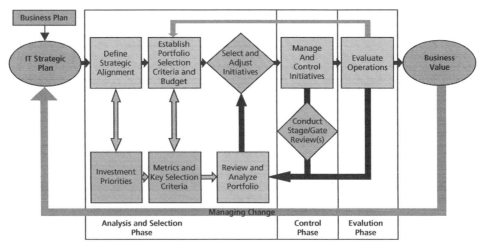

Figure 3.4   High level flow: business/IT planning, investment approval and execution

Business and IT strategy and plan development frameworks

As mentioned previously, a pragmatic business and IT planning process used successfully in industry is called 'pressure point analysis', and it can be used to develop both business and IT plans. It is primarily based on analyzing internal and external pressures and trends, and addressing six basic questions:

- **Where are we?** This question establishes the base line or current state reference base for either the business or IT plans. It considers internal factors, such the strengths, weaknesses, opportunities and threats. It also identifies core competencies and any gaps in the strategy. External trends and pressures such as industry, competition, globalization, life style, regulations, technology, economics and environmental factors are evaluated, as well as customer and prospect input.

- **Why change?** Since change is inevitable and rapid, these are the assumptions on which the current base line, plan and strategy will change. As Hamel stated, 'if organizations are to survive and prosper, they must continuously reinvent themselves' (Hamel, 2000). This question identifies the reasons and motivations for change, and examines high level alternatives for the business or IT to consider.

- **What could we do?** If there were no constraints based on an organization, this question helps them to contemplate what could be done'

- **What should we do?** This question narrows the strategic choices based on a company's vision, objectives and direction, and any constraints such as capital, people resources, time, intellectual property, existing knowledge and experience, and the risk of the initiative. It addresses the question of why that vision and its related goals, objectives and strategies are possible and what should be done.

- **How do we get there?** Any business or IT plan should have 'mandatory' strategies if an organization is to grow and prosper. These mandatory strategy classifications are called imperatives. For a business plan, select imperatives can include continual growth, maximizing customer intimacy, maximizing shareholder value, achieving operational excellence and integrating technology into the organization seamlessly. How this is done will vary by organization, and Figure 3.5 suggests some choices.
  On the IT front, the imperatives can include such factors as enterprise and information architecture, maximizing customer intimacy, new applications in support of the business, effective IT service and infrastructure management and finally, people and process development and improvement. For each business or IT imperatives, multiple actions can be pursued. Examples of select alternative strategies are provided in Figure 3.5 and Figure 3.6, which illustrate the business and IT strategy and plan development frameworks respectively.

- **Did we get there?** This question deals with performance metrics and management controls to ensure that the plan goals and objectives are met.

Figure 3.7 illustrates an IT plan template that can be used to present a high level summary of key plan elements, and maps them to the six plan questions previously described.

Business and IT plan outlines

Business and IT plan outlines and contents vary widely from company to company. However, to put a stake in the ground, a generic business plan outline for a manufacturing company is outlined in Figure 3.8. By applying the six questions previously described to the outline, a plan can be generated.

Figures 3.9, 3.10 and 3.11 provide sample IT plan outlines for a financial services company and a major university, plus a generic format which can be tailored to any organization.

Business and IT strategic planning cycle and alignment

The IT planning cycle should closely parallels the business planning cycle. IT plans should be developed iteratively with the business. Figure 3.12 describes the phases and steps involved in developing a strategic IT plan.

Figure 3.13 illustrates a manufacturing company's strategic planning process and timetable. It identifies the roles of the business and IT leaders, starting in the first quarter of the plan year and culminating in approved projects and initiatives in the last quarter of the plan year, which

Can be used as a template to develop a business plan in conjunction with a business plan detailed table of contents.

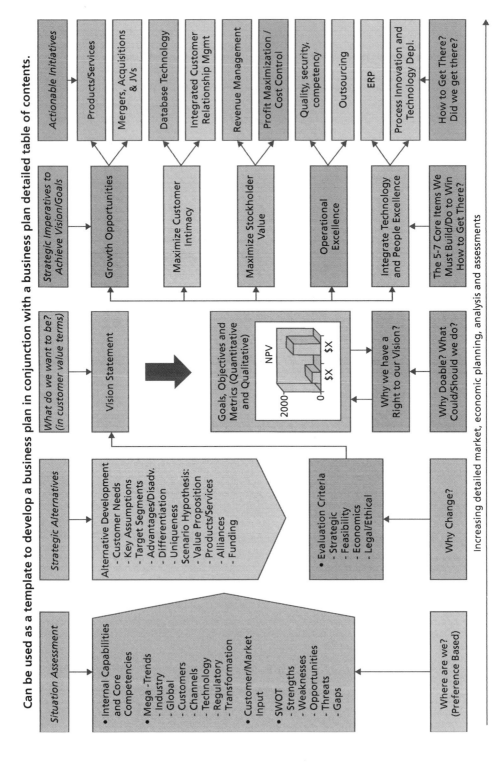

Figure 3-5   Business Strategy and plan development framework

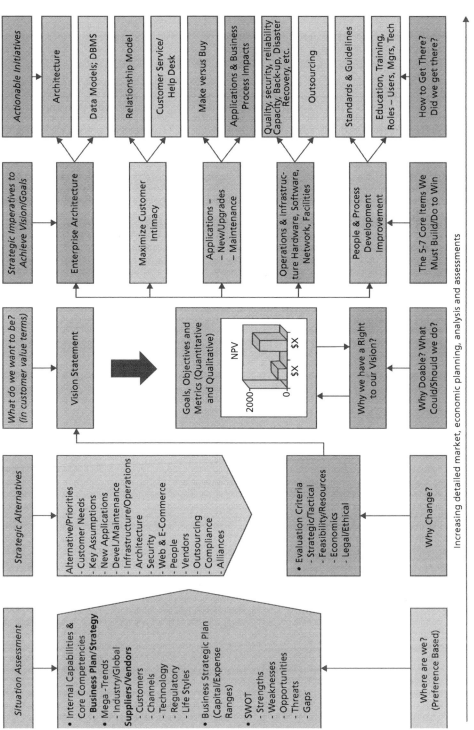

Figure 3.6 IT strategy and plan development framework

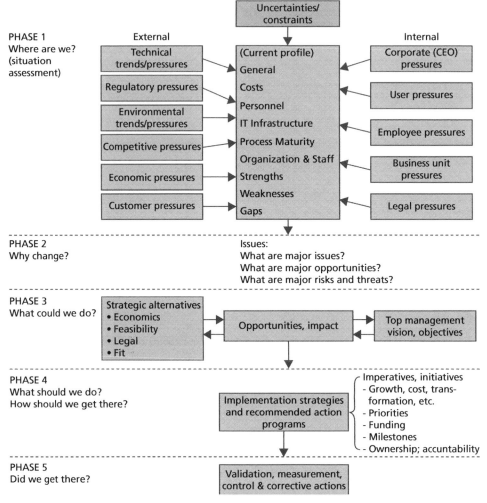

Figure 3.7   IT plan presentation template

becomes the tactical or operating master project plan for the following year. Figure 3.14 illustrates a business and IT alignment template used by the same organization.

3.4   Strategic IT investment portfolio alternatives

Figure 3.2 identified a number of IT investment evaluation criteria to help filter the IT investment choices, and make the appropriate decisions based on the strategic question: are we doing the right thing and are we getting the appropriate value delivered:

- inline with our business vision?
- consistent with our business principles, plan and direction?
- contributing to our strategic objectives and sustainable competitive differentiation?
- providing optimum value at an acceptable level of risk?

Section	Section

1. Executive Summary
  • Business Proposition
  • Current status of Enterprise
  • Market Need being met
  • Enterprise's Product/Service Advantage(s)
  • Management Expertise
  • Financials
	4. Operations or Manufacturing Plan
	  • Facilities
	  • Make versus Buy Decisions
	  • Capital Items
	  • Product Support
	  • Quality Control and Assurance
	  • Logistics and Control
	  • Supply Chain Management

2. Vision and Mission Statement	5. Human Resources Plan
	  • Management Team Background &
	    Requirements
	  • Positions/Employee skills
	  • Training and special people issues
	  • Succession Planning

3. Marketing Plan
  • Market/Industry Analysis
  • Product/Service Offerings and Development
  • Competitive Situation
  • Pricing
  • Channels of Distribution
  • Promotional Plan
  • Customer Service
  • Positioning Strategy
	6. Risk Analysis and Contingenecies
	  • Business Risks and Contingenecies
	  • Economic Risks and Contingenecies
	  • Business Continuity Risks and
	    Contingenecies
	  • Other RisksandContingenecies

	7. Financial Plan
	  • Income Statements (Actual and Pro Forma)
	  • Balance Sheet (Actual and Pro Forma)
	  • Cash Flow Statement (Actual and Pro Forma)
	  • Capital Budget (Actual and Pro Forma)
	  • Sources and Uses of Funds

*Source: Modified from Connecticut Innovations

Figure 3.8   Business plan organizational elements

1. Objectives of Document
2. Executive Summary
3. Previous IT Plan Strategies, Accomplishments and Status (including a SWOT and Gap Analysis)
4. Corporate Strategy Map and Major Business Initiatives
5. Business Unit Strategies (all include Current and Target State) (New and Revisions to IT Applications
    are Identified)
    – Retail Banking
    – Commercial Banking
    – Real Estate
    – Shared Services
      Human Resource
      Finance
      Legal
      M & A and Planning
      Bank Operations
6. IT Infrastructure Strategies (Technology Refresh and New Requirements)
7. Principles of IT
8. IT Financials (mostly capital requirements as well as multi-year project budgets)

Figure 3.9   IT plan outline: financial services company

1. Executive Summary
2. IT Vision and Mission
3. Where we are today: The Scope of the Challenge
4. Competitive Challenge (Comparison to Other Best Practice Organizations on Multiple Levels
5. Aligning IT with University's Strategic Goals
6. Strategic Goals and Initiatives
   Strategic Programs
   IT Governance
   Customer Relationship Management
   Courseware
   Alumni
   Process Excellence
7. Financials (High Level) – (These are linked to first year of the annual operating plan and budget)
8. Appendices
   Competitive Analysis
   SWOT Analysis
   Major Risks and Risk Mitigation
   IT Governance – Roles, Responsibilities and Ownership
   IT Guiding Principles
   Decision Rights

Figure 3.10   IT plan outline: major university

1. **Executive Summary**
2. **Introduction and Background**
   – Purpose & Objectives
   – Plan Methodology and Team
   – Business Vision, Objectives and Strategies
   – IT Vision, Objectives and Strategies
3. **Situation Assessment**
   (Where are we? – Reference Base)
   – External Trends – Technology, Environment,
     Economic, Life-Style, Markets & Customers,
     Regulatory, Competition, etc.
   – Internal Pressures – CEO, Business Units,
     Functional Departments, Employees, Unions, etc.
   – IT Organization Profile – Organization, Staffing
     and skills;
   User Needs and Satisfaction; Level of Maturity;
   Revenue/expense profile; Infrastructure profile;
   application profile; Core Competencies; Strengths
   & Weaknesses
4. **Major Business/IT Gaps, Needs, Opportunities and**
   Alternatives (Why Change? What Could We Do?)
   – **Macro Assessment of Needs** (Discretionary
     and non-Discretionary) and Opportunities by
     Company, Business Units and Key Functional
     Areas
   – **Macro Assessment of Costs, Benefits, Value,**
     Risk (of doing and not doing) and Priorities (by
     Company, SBUs and Key Functions)

4. Cont'd
   – Infrastructure Alternatives
   – Architecture Alternatives
   – Application Alternatives
   – Organization/Control/Administration
   – People Development
   – Business IT Continuity, Security and Backup
   – Build versus buy (Outsourcing)
   – Funding levels and prioritization
   – Standards and Compliance
   – Governance policy and process
5. **Strategies and Actions (What Should We Do?**
   How Do We Get There?)
   – New/ Enhancement Applications
   – Maintenance
   – Discretionary projects
   – Non-Discretionary support activities
   – Architecture Direction
   – Infrastructure Direction
   – Resource requirements
   – Contingency, Security, Risk & Disaster
     Recovery
   – Governance & Compliance
6. **Financials**
   – Capital and expense
   – Headcount
7. **Plan Execution (Did We Get There?)**
   – Critical Success Factors
   – Key Performance Indicators and Report Cards

Figure 3.11   IT plan outline: generic

Planning Preparation	Vision & Guiding Principles	Planning Assumptions	Goals & Strategies	Plan Completion	Plan Implementation	Ongoing Evaluation
Steps	**Steps**	**Steps**	**Steps**	**Steps**	**Steps**	**Steps**
Preplanning Preparations Determine readiness to plan Raise awareness of technology challenges Identify Executive Sponsor Identify planning team Identify information needed for planning Determine planning logistics Determine how best to communicate planning effort Review business/organization plan and direction Determine how to best align IT Plan with Business Plan (Executive Steering Council, etc.)	**Session 1** Conduct visioning session Develop a draft IT vision statement Develop a draft set of IT guiding principles Seek input from and communicate with constituencies	**Session 2** Identify internal and external factors that describe the current and near future (3 years) environment Develop assumptions Seek input from and communicate with constituencies	**Sessions 3** Identify goals, objectives and strategies to meet future needs Identify key performance indicators to measure objectives Seek input from and communicate with constituencies	**Sessions 4** Validate alignment of all plan elements with organization goals, objectives and initiatives Write draft of plan Submit draft to Steering Council for review Incorporate Council comments and edit plan Submit final plan Approve plan	**Organization** Develop annual operating and tactical plan(s) and budgets based on strategic plan Seek feedback from and communicate with constituencies	**Organization** Assess progress semi-annually Identify accomplishments Identify areas for improvement
Outcomes	**Outcomes**	**Outcomes**	**Outcomes**	**Outcomes**	**Outcomes**	**Outcomes**
Agreement on: – Readiness to plan – Plan logistics – Team members – Executive sponsor – Organizational expectations – Communication strategy	Draft IT Vision Statement Draft IT Guiding Principles Communication Plan	Set of planning assumptions and constraints that are the basis for goals, objectives and strategies	Agreement on future goals and specific objectives Three-year Implementation grid	IT Strategic plan	Annual operating plan(s) & Budgets (e.g. Capital & Expense)	Continual Assessment Plan update

Figure 3.12   IT strategic planning cycle: steps and outcomes

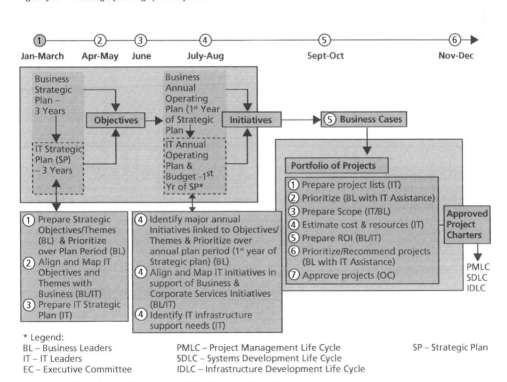

Figure 3.13   Strategic planning process and timetable: manufacturing company

Category	Business Unit 'A'	Business Unit 'B'	Corporate Service/ Function	Information Technology
Business Initiative				
Business Owner				
Business Lead				
Critical Success Factors, Metrics and KPIs				
High Level Benefits/ Measures				
High Level Requirements				
IT Issue/Opportunity				
High Level Deliverables				
Phases/Milestones				
Priority				

Figure 3.14   Business/IT plan initiatives alignment template: manufacturing company

In addition, the following prerequisites should precede any investments decisions:

Portfolio investment management
- define investment criteria to evaluate, prioritize and authorize investments
- manage, monitor and govern the overall portfolio performance
- analyze the alternatives
- assign clear accountability, ownership and decision rights

Business case development
- opportunity or problem drivers
- objectives and scope
- assumptions and constraints
- costs/benefits
- deliverables
- risk, financial returns, strategic fit, compliance and other factors

The five stages of IT investment management maturity

As previously described in Figure 2.5 of Chapter 2, the IT investment management (ITIM) developed by the General Accounting Office of the US Federal Government describes the IT investment maturity stages and related processes. This can be used to develop a plan to improve this component of IT governance for an organization.

3.5   IT engagement and relationship model and roles

IT must become more customer-centric and marketing-oriented in order to develop closer and more collaborative relationships with the business. A growing number of enterprises have instituted a business and IT engagement and relationship model.

The goals of the model are to develop a strong and sustainable partnership between the business and IT. Key elements of the model include:

- **Single point or limited points of contact** – establish a single point, or limited points of contact between IT and the business, to build a better partnership, collaboration and trust between IT and the business
- **Rules of engagement** – define standard, enterprise-wide rules of engagement for acquiring IT services
- **Accountability** – clarify roles, responsibilities and accountabilities for plans, budgets, work requests and issues resolution, escalation and performance reviews within IT, and between IT and business
- **Consistent process** – improve service delivery through a consistent process for engaging the right people at the right time using a consistent set of people, process and technology

Figure 3.15 illustrates a business and IT engagement and relationship model, which can be tailored for an organization and identifies the roles of the key constituents that should be involved.

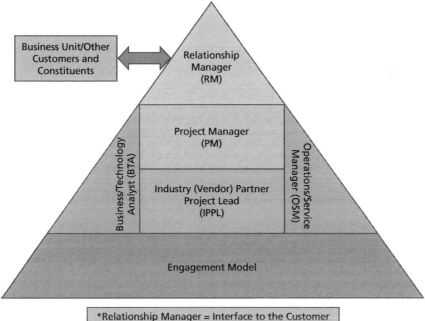

Figure 3.15   Business/IT engagements and relationship model

3.6   Case study – financial services organization

Figure 3.16 illustrates an IT governance case study for a financial services organization.

Environment	Approach
• Asset range - $15 – 25 bn • Number of Employees – 3,000 – 5,000 • Number of IT Employees – 150 – 300 • Very competitive industry with many mergers and consolidation • Conservative management (risk averse) • High use of technology for product delivery and to business unit support • CIO reports into President and CEO and is a member of the Executive Management Team	• Adopted COBIT as the general framework to guide IT process improvements for development and operations. • Identified 12- 14 COBIT IT process areas and assigned each process to one or more IT managers to develop, implement and own. • Adopted ISO 17,799 framework for IT security • Executive Capital Committee approves major investment funding • IT Steering Committee (business and IT) establishes IT priorities, reviews progress and approves major changes
Issues and Challenges	**Approach (Cont'd)**
• Align IT more closely with the business • Increase profitability and growth • Make IT more customer facing and focused • Facilitate and sustain compliance requirements	• Issued general IT principles or vision which guide how IT is managed (e.g. trust, flexibility, speed, transparency [IT is transparent to business]) • Established decision authority over major IT decisions with definitive parameters, roles and responsibilities for such items as funding approvals, architecture, security, projects • Established a strong Project Management Office
Results - Alignment	**Results -IT Service Management & Delivery**
• Capital budgeting process is linked to strategic and annual operating plan for IT and business • IT Steering Committee assures a closer alignment of IT support for business • Balanced Scorecard and report card metrics are linked to critical success factors of business and IT (speed, financials, cost, performance, quality, etc.) • Established a customer/IT engagement (single point of contact) model to improve relationships, build trust and focus on priorities • Closer alignment is being improved continuously	• A variety of metrics and tools are used to measure the efficiency, capacity and availability, utilization and service-ability of the operations and infrastructure assets and group
Results - Program/Project Management	**Results - Performance Management & Management Controls**
• Established a PMO center of excellence staffed with certified PMPs • Developed a flexible and scalable PM process to handle fast track and complex projects • Educated and trained both IT and user community on PM best practices • Created a booklet on, "How to Get Your IT Projects Approved" • Significant improvement in delivering projects on time and within budget (20-30%)	• COBIT & ISO 17799 are used as the frameworks to define, develop and deploy the IT management controls • Select IT metrics are included in the company's Balanced Scorecard: financial (e.g. Keep lights on spend; IT spend versus company revenues; IT spend per employee); non-financial (e.g. turnover; quality; risk mitigation index, etc.) • Quarterly IT report card (financial; projects; production operations, etc.
Critical Success Factors	
• Executive sponsorship is critical • CIO and executive team must be proactive and provide oversight • IT governance must be decomposed and assigned to process owners with schedules , budgets and deliverables • Metrics should be linked to business and IT critical success factors	
Lessons Learned	
• IT governance is a journey towards continuous improvement • It is harder than you think and takes longer than you estimated • The improvements in time, speed, flexible discipline, cost reduction, alignment and compliance are beneficial	

Figure 3.16   Case study - financial services organization

3.7   Summary and key take aways

Summary

IT/business alignment is complex, multi-dimensional and never complete. However, there are IT/business alignment principles (eg planning, investment portfolio management, relationship model, steering and governance boards, etc.) that, if implemented, will help to achieve a more effective and collaborative alignment.

Therefore, it is important not only to focus on measurements based on value realization (eg quantitative), but also to take into account the enterprise's performance and process improvements in creating the value.

Improving IT and business alignment can be achieved by implementing formal IT governance processes and mechanisms. Improving alignment maturity, like governance, is a journey based on a dynamic process that should be continuously improved. For organizations that are at the high end of the maturity model (level 4 or 5), IT and business strategy and operational alignment is an integral part of their culture. They constantly monitor alignment through key performance metrics and other techniques on a continuous basis.

Business and IT alignment will remain a major issue in some organizations, until they realize that they both need each other in order to sustain the growth and prosperity of the enterprise.

Business and IT executives should:
- improve the relationship between the business and IT functional areas
- work hard towards mutual co-operation, respect, understanding and participation in strategy development
- communicate more frequently and honestly
- work towards minimizing activities that inhibit alignment

Key take aways
- Ensure that IT supports the strategies of the business by developing a strategic and operating IT plan as a full partner with the business, based on similar processes.
- Establish a practical and realistic framework for measurement and reporting the results.
- Identify value adding business activities (eg value chain and other models/attributes) and strategies that would enhance them through IT; deploy incremental deliverable and communicate the benefits achieved.
- Ensure appropriate commitment and participation of executive management and the senior management team, through steering boards and formal reviews, and link alignment objectives to performance objectives, performance evaluations and rewards.
- Establish a public relations/marketing function in IT to create awareness of the value and benefits created by IT for the organization, and to improve communications.
- A successful allocation of IT resources occurs only if multiple perspectives are evaluated and the decision is not based solely on the passion of the advocate. Enterprises need to evaluate the financial perspective, the risk level and – most importantly – whether the project contributes to the achievement of the business objectives.

4 Principles for managing successful organizational change, prerequisites for world class leadership and developing high performance teams

"It is no use saying we are doing our best. You have got to succeed in doing what is necessary."

- Winston Churchill, former British Prime Minister

4.1 What is covered in this chapter?

This chapter:
- describes a framework for managing successful change in helping to transition organizations to higher levels of IT governance maturity
- reviews key leadership, people and soft skills and competencies required for success
- identifies the attributes of high performance teams

4.2 Overview

"You miss 100% of the shots you never take."

- Wayne Gretsky, Hockey Great

As previously discussed, effective IT governance is built on three critical pillars. One of these pillars focuses on effective and motivated leadership and change agents, building high performance teams and managing organizational change successfully.

Based on the large amount of research completed in these areas by individuals and institutions such as the Center for Creative Leadership, American Management Association, Burn and Moran, Peter Drucker, Beth Cohen, Katzenback and Smith, Peter Senge, David McClellan, John Kotter and many others, the author has adopted and modified several principles and practices in each of the areas covered in this chapter, to make them pragmatic and actionable in helping organizations transform themselves to higher levels of IT governance maturity.

Coping with the realities of change
"When you win, nothing hurts,"

- Joe Namath, Football Great

Formalizing and institutionalizing IT governance may require significant change in an organization, depending on its current level of maturity, culture, management philosophy, available funding and resources, time constraints, business strategy, priorities and other factors. There are a number of realities of change that organizations must take into considerations when embarking on new or major change initiatives, such as IT governance. They include:

- Change has no conscience, plays no favorites, takes no prisoners and ruthlessly destroys organizations with non-adaptive or non-innovative cultures.
- A common response to change is caution. This is wrong today. Picking up speed protects you better in today's world, to cope with constant and accelerating change. One major global organization, which uses 'lean' processes, focuses its change efforts on 'cycle time reduction'.
- Success comes from cool-headed thinking, clear focus and well aimed action. So create a culture that is steady under fire.
- Initiative must always come from individuals and not just from the company, so create a shared vision and mobilize commitment.
- Inertia is more crippling than mistakes (you should learn from mistakes). Inaction is the most costly error.
- Innovate, bust out of old routines and be willing to make radical changes to improve.
- Be willing to bend and learn because in a rapidly changing world, new competencies are required.

Major impediments to successful change

According to Norman Augustine, former Chairman and CEO of Lockheed Martin Corp., '*it is better to be 70% correct and take advantage of an opportunity rather than 100% correct after the opportunity has passed*'.

The following constraints to implementing successful change must be overcome to improve IT governance:

- no champion
- low risk tolerance
- inflexible processes
- procrastination and uncertainty
- unclear objectives, fuzzy scope and ambiguous accountability
- no reward, recognition or celebration mechanisms
- poor execution
- weak leader and change agents
- lack of decisiveness

The nature of organizational change

Large scale organizational change is represented by any substantive modification to some part of the organization (eg mergers and acquisitions, new leadership, new technology, major process transformation, formalized governance, etc.). The forces for change come from either external forces influencing the organization's environment, that compel the organization to alter the way in which it competes, such as competitors, regulators, globalization, technology, economy, life styles and customers, and/or internal forces inside the organization that cause it to change its strategy and structure.

Generally there are two types of change:

- **Planned (proactive) change** - change that is designed and implemented in an orderly and timely fashion in anticipation of future events and projected results; IT governance should be a planned, proactive initiative if it is to be accomplished in a cost effective and least disruptive manner

- **Reactive change** - change that is a piecemeal or an unanticipated response to events and circumstances as they develop, or are forced on organizations due to regulatory, customer, competitive and other conditions

Change should be thought of as a continuous process, not an event, which utilizes a wide range of tools, processes and technologies. One has to consider how to deal with and accommodate resistance to change, and the psychological and social aspects of change.

David McCelland identified key components of managing large scale change successfully (McCelland, 1995):

- Engage the top and lead the change
  - create the 'value proposition' and market the case for change
  - identify committed leadership
  - develop a plan and ensure consequence management

- Cascade down and across the organization and break down barriers/silos
  - create cross-functional and global teams (where appropriate)
  - compete on 'speed'
  - ensure a performance-driven approach

- Mobilize the organization and create ownership
  - roll out change initiative
  - measure results of change (compare current state versus future state baselines)
  - embrace continuous learning, knowledge and best practice sharing

- Attributes of effective change teams and agents
  - strong and focused leader
  - credibility and authority (charter) to lead the initiative
  - ability to demonstrate and communicate 'early wins' to build the momentum
  - create a sense of urgency and avoid stagnation
  - knock obstacles out of the way, diplomatically or otherwise

These components should become integrated into any IT governance initiative.

4.3   Framework for managing accelerating change

A framework for change should be a practical and useable roadmap for managing the change that assures the conditions of the change are met well, accepted by the organization in general, and integrated into the operations and culture of the organization.

According to John Kotter, there are two necessary conditions for accelerating change successfully:
- leadership for change and changing systems, processes, structures, technologies
- capabilities that are weaved into the fabric of the organization

Kotter goes on to suggest that there are five essential elements of change:
- creating a shared need
- shaping a vision
- mobilizing commitment
- making change last
- monitor progress and continuous learning

Successful change requires strong committed leadership and a respected champion throughout the entire initiative, and also to sustain a continuous improvement effort that should be reinforced by specific actions such as:

- Let people know that the change is not an option.
- Communicate clearly that performance measures and rewards are linked to measurable improvements as a result of the change initiative.
- Make space for 'grieving' based on the old environment, but encourage 'moving on' to the new environment.
- Ensure that the change process 'conditions' and 'elements' are fulfilled.
- Lead by example, with passion, energy and the right attitude.
- Leadership cannot do it alone and in isolation - other motivated change agents must be enlisted at all levels of the organization.
- Change requires work and attention – planning, management and governance.
- Change requires supporting systems, structures, tools and training.

Figure 4.1 illustrates a framework and the respective phases necessary for managing major change, used by a large financial service and insurance organization. It can be adopted and tailored for IT governance and its components, either individually or as a whole. Furthermore, Figure 4.1 also identified specific questions that should be addressed for key change elements. Appendix 3 provides an example of a change framework, segmented into people and organization elements, process elements and technology elements.

4.4   Organizing for the IT governance initiative

An effective IT governance environment represented by level 3 or higher on the CMMI maturity model is difficult to achieve. It takes time, resources and the right skills and attitudes. The journey

| Used to Help Organization Transition from the Current Environment to a Future Environment |

Leading Change:
– Is there a strong change leadership team (CLT) and champion? Knowledgeable in the model and tools?
– Is the CLT actively involved in leading and driving the change process and initiatives?
– Are CLT members monitoring all 'essential elements' and 'necessary conditions'?

A Framework for Managing Change

Creating Shared Need:	Shaping Vision:	Making Commitment:	Making Change Endure:	Monitoring Progress & Learning:
– Is the reason to change, whether driven by threat or opportunity, instilled within organization? – Is it widely shared through data, demonstration, demand or diagnosis? – Does the need for change exceed its resistance?	– Is the desired outcome of change clear, and legitimate? – Is the outcome expressed in simple terms? – Is it widely understood and shared?	– Is there a strong commitment from all key constituents to invest in the change, make it work, and demand and receive management attention?	– Once the change is started, can we implement it on a sustained basis? – Are the results transferred throughout the organization?	– Do we know our real progress? – Have benchmarks and metrics been set to guarantee accountability? – Has organization feedback and learning been captured?

Changing Systems, Structures & Capabilities:
– Is change woven into the very fabric of the organization?
– Are management practices used to complement and reinforce change?
– How have we addressed issues of: staffing & development, measurements & rewards?
– Is there a communication strategy?
– Do we know how the organizational structure must be changed?

Figure 4.1   Framework for managing change and related questions

can be less arduous by following a modified version of Kotter's eight stage process for leading change:

- **Establish a sense of urgency** – motivated by a threat or an opportunity
- **Create the guiding coalition** – identify the group and individuals that lead the change, encourage change agents to solicit broad based support, and facilitate the execution through empowerment
- **Develop a vision and strategy** – ensuring a realistic vision and supporting strategies
- **Communicate the vision and strategy** – over-communicating is good
- **Empower a broad based action** – encouraging risk-taking and overcome and/or neutralize obstacles
- **Generate short-term wins** – completing wins that are communicated to the constituents and are very effective for gaining support and sustaining the change direction
- **Consolidate gains and produce more change** – leverage increased credibility from successes, which facilitates and stimulates the introduction of more change
- **Anchor new approaches in the culture** – institutionalize the process, adapt enabling technology and tools, and link progress to performance

A growing number of organizations have recognized the benefits of improving the IT governance environment in their organizations, and have established IT governance functions in their IT organizations. Figures 4.2 and 4.3 represent two examples, of IT organization structures of companies in the food and manufacturing industries respectively. Clearly, these structures will vary from organization to organization based on size, management orientation (eg centralized, de-centralized, federated, etc.), geographic presence, home country versus global orientation, credibility and influence of the CIO, and other factors.

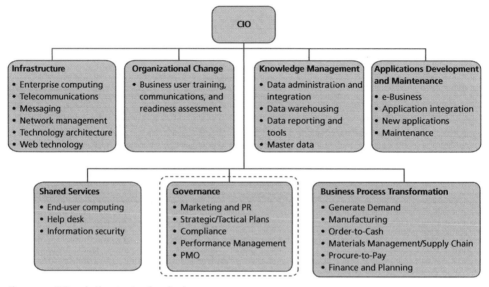

Figure 4.2   IT Organization structure for a food company

In either case, the following activities will further help to organize a successful IT governance initiative:

- identify executive champion and multi-disciplinary team (to focus on each major IT governance component)
- do your homework – get up-to-date on current and emerging best practices
- market and communicate the IT governance value proposition
- develop a tailored IT governance framework and roadmap for your organization based on current and emerging industry best practices
- decompose the IT governance components into well defined work packages (assign an owner and champion to each process component)
- assess the 'current state' of the level of IT governance maturity
- develop a 'future state' IT governance blueprint (where you want to be) and keep it in focus
- develop an IT governance action plan, identify deliverables, establish priorities, milestones and allocate resources
- identify enabling technologies to support the IT governance initiative

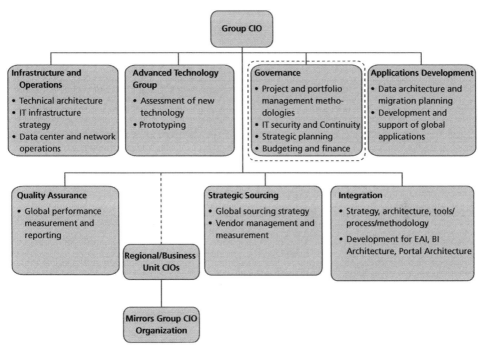

Figure 4.3   IT Organization structure for a manufacturing company

4.5   World class leadership principles and practices

According to the Chinese philosopher, Loa-tsu, a great leader has the following tendencies:

- *To lead people, walk beside them.*
- *As for the best leaders, the people do not notice their existence.*
- *The next best, the people honor and praise.*
- *The next, the people fear; and the next, the people hate.*
- ***When the best leader's work is done, the people say, 'We did it ourselves!'***

Key leadership and people skills and competencies required for success
The success of major enterprise initiatives like IT governance is more often determined by people or 'soft' skills, such as leadership communications, integrity, persistence, judgment, managing expectations, inter-personal, team building and managing change and innovation skills, performed well, rather than by 'hard' skills, such as plans, procedures, processes and technologies.

Figure 4.4 identifies select people and hard skills required to execute IT governance and other initiatives effectively. Most of the soft skills are below the water line, and are invisible and less obvious than the visible tip of the iceberg, which is represented by the hard skills. Both are necessary to achieve success.

The success and advancement of professionals up the organizational ladder is more often determined by leadership, people, team building and managing change and innovation skills well than by hard skills such as developing and/or applying policies, procedures, processes and technologies

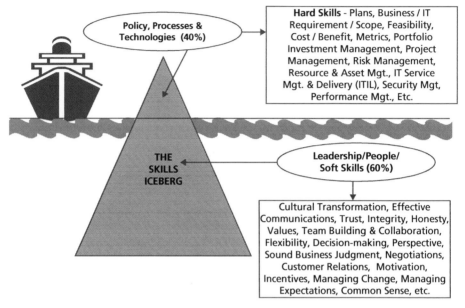

Figure 4.4   The IT governance skills iceberg

Most world class organizations develop leadership and management succession plans that are based on a specific set of skills and competencies. Figure 4.5 represents a blend of the major skills and competencies required for leadership positions in these companies. They are broken into five areas:
- leadership
- marketing and customer focus
- critical thinking
- achieving results and effective execution
- functional expertise

These can apply to IT governance as well as to many other enterprise initiatives.

Leadership profiles for winning
David McCleland, the former Harvard University psychologist, developed the concept of leadership profiles for winning (McCleland, 1995). The key actions of outstanding leaders identified in his research can be applied to developing and sustaining an organization-wide IT governance initiative.

- **Passion for winning** – asks big questions about what is possible, and takes major entrepreneurial action over time to deliver sustainable profitable business

The Leadership Competency Model represents a blend of models developed by select leading edge organizations such as Verizon, Motorola, Proctor and Gamble, GE and Others

Figure 4.5   The leadership competency model

- **Breakthrough thinking** – uses their insights into complex situations to break existing business paradigms and create new major opportunities by reinventing the organization
- **Political acumen** – understands the influences (decision-making and power structures, climate, culture and politics) which shape how organizations work; they adapt their approach to optimize results
- **Seizing the future** – gets to the future first by taking decisive action today (requires speed and first mover) to create new markets for tomorrow
- **Change catalyst** – energizes others towards new, better ways of operating and generating success, communicates vision and knocks obstacles out of the way
- **Developing others** – invests time, money and energy in developing others to build the organization's capability for the future, as well as coaches and mentors future leaders
- **Holding people accountable** – holds people and teams accountable for delivering agreed objectives, and consistently measures and rewards results or changes performance for the better
- **Empowering others** – creates commitment by empowering others to act and streamlining organizational decision-making and approval processes (eg decision rights)
- **Strategic influencing** – builds commitment by influencing others positively, without using hierarchical power to adopt a specific course of action to orchestrate change
- **Team commitment** – works co-operatively with others across the organization, to achieve shared goals, places high value on being part of a team and acts to further the interests of the team above their own
- **Team leadership** – adjusts their leadership styles to optimize team outputs, and inspires others to higher standards of performance by setting examples and energizing the team

One CIO's rules for IT service and governance

Many CIOs today have created their own set of leadership and management rules, written them down, distributed them to their organization and integrated them into the daily life of the organization. Some lists are very specific, covering such areas as governance, alignment, compliance and capital expenditures, while others relate to actionable principles.

Bill Godfrey, CIO of Dow Jones, developed a set of rules that, ' … *in one form or another are there to sustain, protect and foster alignment …* ' (Wailgum, 2005).

Godfrey's fourteen big rules for IT service and governance are:

Rule 1 – Strategic planning
* All technology divisions will have a documented technology plan.
* All technology divisions will have published goals and objectives.

Rule 2 – Production prioritization
* Production problems classified as 'severity one' production problems take resource precedent over all else. Management and staff will work on 'severity one' problems immediately and continually until resolved.

Rule 3 – Enterprise architecture
* All technology divisions will have a documented high level architecture.
* All technology divisions will adhere to infrastructure standards or seek exception approval.
* All technology projects costing more than $250,000 in total must be approved through an 'early look' screening process prior to capital approval submission.

Rule 4 – Project management
* There will be 100% adherence to the project management process for all non-trivial development projects (projects estimated to take more than two weeks of staff time).
* All development projects will have a specifically identified business sponsor, and a specifically identified IT project leader prior to initiation.
* All development projects requiring infrastructure support will directly involve infrastructure support staff during project initiation, giving the infrastructure staff an opportunity to directly participate in the design of systems solutions.

Rule 5 – Time management
* All staff time will be appropriately entered into the IT time reporting system on a weekly basis.

Rule 6 – Technology business management
* As represented in approved budgets, technology costs will not exceed plan unless explicit approval is granted by the CIO.
* Technology contracts will be managed and approved through business management services or purchasing.

- All third-party contractors and consultants will sign non-disclosure agreements, managed under the non-employee security policy, and managed through the company's preferred vendor program.

Rule 7 – Capital approval management
- All projects will adhere to corporate expenditure authorization processes.
- All projects are required to have appropriate IT senior leadership team sign-offs prior to business line submission.
- For all projects requiring CIO approval, all staff work and IT senior leadership team approvals will be complete prior to seeking CIO approval.
- Any project with a total cost of more than $250,000 will be submitted to finance for formal business case review.

Rule 8 – Requesting proposals from third parties
- All requests for proposals from third parties will be reviewed and approved by the CIO prior to execution.
- All requests for proposals from third parties which could have infrastructure implications will be reviewed and approved by IT infrastructure services prior to execution.

Rule 9 – Relationship management
- Business technology directors are 100% accountable for all technology, direct and indirect, in support of their assigned business lines.
- Business technology directors 'own' all business application vendor relationships.
- Enterprise technology directors 'own' all infrastructure vendor relationships.

Rule 10 – Infrastructure management
- Enterprise infrastructure services is 100% accountable for the global infrastructure.
- Enterprise infrastructure services is the only organization that makes infrastructure decisions.
- Enterprise infrastructure services owns and manages all infrastructure capital.

Rule 11 – Compliance with audit, regulatory and legal requirements
- Information technology services will comply will all audit, regulatory and legal requirements.
- The IT senior leadership team is accountable for compliance.

Rule 12 – Operations procedural compliance
- There will be 100% compliance with [the] enterprise change control policy and procedure.
- All production applications will be supported by a service level agreement between IT and the business.

Rule 13 – Information security
- All technology staff will comply with the company's information security policy.
- Information security approval must be secured prior to implementing new technology or making major enhancements to existing technology. This review and approval is to take place before any informal or formal obligations are made between the company and a supplier.
- All access to a financially significant application will be managed and controlled through information security.

Rule 14 – Sarbanes-Oxley compliance
- Therewill be 100% compliance to all Sarbanes-Oxley controls.
- All IT leaders will be thoroughly familiar with the IT general control policies regarding governance, project management, operations, access control and data management.
- All IT leaders, supervisor and above, are responsible and accountable for Sarbanes-Oxley compliance across their respective areas of control.

SMART (specific, measurable, assignable, realistic and time related)
Doran developed a simple device called 'SMART' to help leaders and organizations formulate objectives based on easily remembered attributes. Table 4.1 represents an adoption of Doran's attributes to IT governance. (Doran, 1981)

Attribute	Description	IT Governance Example
S = Specific	Be specific in targeting an objective.	Achieve CMMI level 3 maturity for three major IT governance components.
M = Measurable	Establish a measurable indicator(s) of progress.	Improve customer satisfaction; reduce costs; etc.
A = Assignable	Make the objective assignable to one person for completion.	Assign an IT manager as owner.
R = Realistic	State what can realistically be done with available resources.	Improve one (1) level of maturity per year across the organization.
T = Time related	State when the objective can be achieved.	Achieve specific objective (see above) within two years on an enterprise-wide scale.

Table 4.1   Doran's attributes adopted for IT governance (illustrative example)

What management expects from an IT governance project manager
The following attributes are essential attributes of a successful project manager:

- developa realistic and pragmatic IT governance plan and program
- focus on deliverables and results (as opposed to stringent process adherence – use common sense and good judgement)
- workwith customers/ constituents to define requirements and scope
- effectivestatus reporting ('theory of no surprises')
- goodmotivator, mentor and coach
- abilityto handle inter-personal problems
- self-startercommitted, driven, persistent and lead by example
- trustworthyloyal and credible
- listenswell and is open minded
- tolerantof diversity
- confident
- ethicaland honest
- negotiationskills
- professionalbehavior
- greatcommunicator

4.6   Principles for creating and sustaining high performance teams

"Always tell people the truth, because they know it already."

Jack Welsh, Former Chairman and CEO, GE

"Always do the right thing, you will gratify some people and astonish the rest."

- Mark Twain, Author

Many companies, such as Haliburton, Quaker Oats, TRW and General Mills, who have established effective team environments and culture, reported a 20-40% gain in productivity after 12–18 months (Johnson, 2002).

Organizations are developing increasingly complex team-based organizational structures to (Snyder, 2003; Katzenback and Smith, 2001; Lohr, 2007):

- address constantly changing business needs, that compel organizational structures to be fluid and where team members can be moved to where their expertise is required
- build a successful organization of the future (which is now); a few guiding principles should guide that effort:
  - organize for continuous change; stability is out and 'organizational whitewater' is in
  - develop and support knowledge workers; the person(s) whose intellectual capital will fuel future innovation
  - harvest global brains; national boundaries are no longer barriers to innovation; global 'centers of excellence', focusing on different IT competencies, have and are being set up by companies such as IBM, Toyota, Cisco, Tata and others
  - enable networks of cross-specialization experts; silos and smokestacks are dying; future success will depend on how efficiently a company links its 'centers of excellence' to create value and share learnings, independent of location

According to Snyder, the characteristics of world class team members include (Snyder, 2003):

- represent inter-disciplinary and cross-functional business units
- either serve in a full-time assignment reporting directly to a team leader, or report part-time to team leaders and part-time to their functional bosses, as in a matrix organization
- can be co-located or work at different locations, virtually
- are knowledge workers

For enterprise governance to improve the bottom line, well-lead multi-disciplinary and cross-functional teams must be established with wide representation from the business and IT. A team represents a collection of people who rely on group collaboration, such that each of the team members experiences an optimum level of success, achieving both personal and team-based goals and objectives.

A team chartered to develop an IT governance initiative and plan should include the CIO (as the champion), his or her direct reports, and have representation from both key business units and corporate staff functions (such as finance, audit, operations, legal and the executive office). The various working committee(s), responsible for developing and deploying the key IT governance components, should be composed of staff from areas such as alignment, planning, program and project management, IT Service Management, strategic sourcing, performance management and controls and audit.

Problems and issues with teams

The traditional problems and issues with teams should be identified, prioritized and overcome. They include:

- insufficient commitment to the team
- tolerance of mediocre participation and contribution
- 'groupthink'– tends to minimize individual creativity and motivation
- conflicting personal agendas of team members, and the resultant mistrust
- poor or inappropriate team leadership
- unclear scope and objectives
- lack of role clarity, communication and rules of operation
- lack of ability to work through differences of opinions
- a closed climate that prevents members from expressing honestly how they feel about issues
- emphasis on process versus results
- poor management of constituent expectations
- performance appraisals and compensation systems that are more aligned to individual versus team performance
- individual 'star' contributors who value their independence and do not really want to play the interdependent 'team game'

If teams are to be successful, the organization's culture needs to be supportive of them. To change the culture, requires a change in behavior and rewards, to provide people with a new set of (hopefully positive) experiences.

A 'win-win' team attitude

If a company wants to receive the maximum benefits from its teams, it must develop a positive 'win-win' attitude using the following tips suggested by McDermott, Brawley and Waite and supplemented by the author (McDermott, Brawley and Waite, 1998):

- focus on the benefits of working on a team
- seek the good in people around you
- seek the good in your workplace
- learn to forgive (everyone learns from mistakes)
- find humor in everyday occurrences
- let your positive attitude in one area spill over into another
- talk positively with yourself and others
- avoid attitude downers – you are in control of your attitude, not others
- take responsibility and be accountable

- standup, and speak up for what you believe in
- beflexible and willing to compromise
- createteam charters and boundaries to clarify missions, roles and responsibilities
- createownership at every organization level where teams operate
- aformal team governance process with meaningful metrics and actions is necessary
- deliver short-term incremental deliverables that work (decompose complex programs or projects) to establish team credibility and visibility
- recognizeand reward exceptional team performance

Building blocks for team development and effectiveness

Teams represent a form of organization. Most organizations function with some form of structure, rules and processes. Effective world class teams also require building blocks and guidelines to work smartly. These include some of the following:

- **Goals** – are clear to all, challenging, yet realistic; each individual's work relates to overall team goals and objectives.
- **Roles** – are mutually understood; everyone knows why they are on the team; authority and responsibilities are consistent.
- **Boundaries** – describe the scope and parameters of what the team is empowered to do, and what is off-limits.
- **Processes** exist - with key processes in place to support the work of the team:

  - problem-solving and issue identification
  - planning, decision-making and authority
  - handling conflict, resolution or escalation
  - managing expectations of constituents
  - contents, format and frequent of communications
  - meeting management – agendas, minutes, follow-up actions
  - resource management and allocation
  - team training and new team member absorption
  - evaluation of team effectiveness and performance
  - team dissolution and reassignment of team members
  - interactions with other teams and organizations

- **Relationships** - team members communicate openly and demonstrate trust for one another; the team establishes relationships beyond itself (external touch points), as needed in the organization.

The first critical step in developing high performance teams is to 'set them up for success'. Senior management and other key stakeholders (or the team itself, if it a self-directed team) should hold planning discussions to reach consensus on such issues as:

- theteam's purpose, charter, boundaries, scope and expected outcomes
- theteam's structure, team leader (individual or shared or self directed) and team members
- strategiesfor management commitment, support, resource allocation and issues escalation
- the team's measures of success, key performance indicators and their links to MBO (management by objectives), compensation and incentives

- the team's rules and processes for communications, progress reporting, meetings, conflict-resolution, problem and issues workouts, self-assessment, managing expectations of stakeholders, etc.

Figure 4.6 summarizes a list of operating characteristics generally present in effective high performance teams.

Clear Purpose	The vision, mission, goal or task of the team has been defined and is now accepted by everyone. There is an action plan.
Informality	The climate tends to be informal, comfortable, and relaxed. There are no obvious tensions or signs of boredom.
Participation	There is much discussion and everyone is encouraged to participate.
Listening	The members use effective listening techniques such as questioning, paraphrasing and summarizing to get ideas out.
Civilized Disagreement	There is disagreement, but the team is comfortable with this and shows no signs of avoiding, smoothing over, or suppressing conflict.
Consensus and Fast Decisions	For important decisions, the goal is substantial but not necessarily unanimous agreement through open discussion of everyone's ideas, avoidance of formal voting, or easy compromises. It is also important to avoid or minimize 'groupthink' which often limits individual creativity and may sub-optimize the team's actions.
Open communication	Team members feel free to express their feelings on the tasks as well as on the group's operation. There are few hidden agendas. Communication takes place outside of meetings.
Clear Roles and Work Assignments	There are clear expectations about roles played by each team member. When action is taken, clear assignments are made, accepted and carried out. Work is fairly distributed among members.
Shared Leadership	While the team has a formal leader, leadership functions shift from time to time depending upon the circumstances, the needs of the group, and the skills of the members. The former leader models the appropriate behavior and helps establish positive norms.
External Relations	The team spends time developing key outside relationships, mobilizing resources, and building credibility with important players in other parts of the organization.
Style and Cultural Diversity	The team has a broad spectrum of team-player types representing different cultures including members who emphasize attention to task, goal setting, focus on process and questions about how the team is functioning.
Self-Assessment	Periodically, the team steps back to examine how well it is functioning, examines what may be interfering with its effectiveness and takes corrective actions.
Use of Technology	Organizations are creating 'global centers of excellence' to take advantage of global brains. This has accelerated the use of technology to save time, costs and facilitate collaboration amongst multi-location team members.

Figure 4.6   Summary of operating characteristics present in world class teams

Select technologies for teams

As organizations become more global, they are establishing 'centers of excellence' in many parts of the world, to take advantage of global brains, reduced labor rates, unique and specialized skills, rare resources and, perhaps, more lax regulatory environments than exist in their home base.

Technologies used by teams generally improve communications and collaboration, increase decision-making speed and time to market, reduce costs and take advantage of a twenty-four hour work day. In addition, as organizations increase their outsourcing expenditures, technology is playing a growing and increasing important role in connecting the customers with their service providers and suppliers. Figure 4.7 provides examples of select technologies used by traditional and virtual teams, based in the same or different geographic locations and/or time zones.

Technologies used by teams generally improve communications and collaboration, increase decision-making speed and reduce costs.

Technologies for Teams:

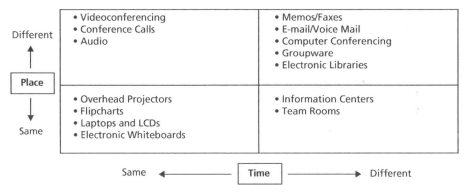

Figure 4.7   Select technologies for teams

4.7   Summary and key take aways

Summary – checklist for managing accelerating change

- define the change – create a common understanding of the change
- build company capacity – change management skills, resources and roles (champion, sponsors, agents, targets)
- assess the climate – implementation history and stress levels
- generate sponsorship – construct , cascade and sponsor role
- get the right talent - with the right skills and attitudes

Environment & Drivers	Approach
• Annual revenue range -2004 - $3.0 to $6.0 bn • Number of IT personnel range – 500-800 • Major compliance issues with former executive management team (replaced by new executive management team focused on transformation and re-invigorating growth) • Former IT organization was reactive, lethargic and slow to address business needs • Lack of formalized IT policies, practices and disciplines • New CIO reports to CEO and is part of the senior executive management team • Fragmented business processes	• New executive management team hired a new CIO, who brought in a new senior leadership team in IT • Reconstituted Business/IT Executive Steering Group which developed a strategy & priorities focused on: business growth, creating a performance based culture that rewards achievement of goals, accountability and innovation and building strong customer partnerships • CIO developed a transformation plan which was approved by executive management team • IT reorganized with following major functions: • IT Strategy and Governance (includes PMO, PR/Marketing & People Development) • Application Development • IT Operations & Infrastructure • Enterprise Architecture
Issues and/or Opportunities	**Approach (cont'd)**
• Poor IT governance, reporting and inadequate business intelligence –requires a cultural change • Poor IT customer satisfaction and unmet business needs caused business units to ramp up their own systems development functions • Inadequate and inappropriate IT skills, competencies and leadership • Challenge – Drive business process transform business for growth and greater profitability using IT • Self fund (through cost reduction programs) IT budget growth for new initiatives & keeping the lights on • Lack of business intelligence (multiple sources of inaccurate business information)	• IT hired a consulting firm to assist in developing a blueprint for IT governance framework and process. • Company is moving towards a two year realistic strategic plan (from a three year plan) linked to an annual operating plan • With new IT management team in place for only six month, many initiatives are in process and key results are not yet clearly visible or measurable (they are definitely going in the right direction, but the jury is still out)
Results – Alignment	**Results - IT Service Management & Delivery**
• Business/IT Executive Steering Committee (consisting of 'C' level executives) are closely co-ordinate strategy, direction, priorities, investments and periodically review progress on major IT/business transformation initiatives • Business strategic and operating plans drive IT plans • IT is in process of developing and deploying a pragmatic strategy and governance policy and process for the organization and re-centralizing IT development based on an improved relationships service with the business units	• ITIL is being deployed on a phased basis to improve customer service, satisfaction and related metrics (eg SLA, response and repair time to reported problems and outages, etc.)

Figure 4.8   Case study: leading software company

- determine change approach - commitment or compliance
- develop target readiness – identify and manage resistance to change at all levels and determine how to overcome it
- develop communications plan – communicate in terms of frame of reference

Results - Program/Project Management	Results - Performance Management
• An IT PMO is being established using the Nikku software tool for Portfolio Management, Project Management, Time Reporting and Resource Management • Folks being hired into the IT PMO Center of Excellence are or will be certified via Six Sigma and/or PMI's PMP • Demand Management (IT Requests for Service) will be reviewed in a consistent and uniform manner based select critical success factors and associated metrics in two categories – Discretionary and Non-Discretionary (Mandatory)	• IT is in the process of identifying key performance indicators to measure its effectiveness and progress
Critical Success Factors	
• To transform a culture and use IT to enable that transformation mandates the sponsorship and commitment of the CEO and the executive management team • Hire select competent business and IT leaders who bring in external experiences and success and who are not part of the old guard	
Lessons Learned	
• Conduct an assessment of current state of IT maturity against best practice companies and industry standards • Develop a plan and roadmap for transformation to a desired future state • Assign adequate resource to deploy a successful transition • Make sure that you have the right talent to do the job	

Figure 4.8   Case study: leading software company

- develop reinforcement strategy – align rewards and efforts required to achieve IT governance objectives, and measure results
- create cultural fit – identify conflicts and unwritten rules
- prioritize action – a project plan
- evaluate the change process
- reward significant progress – link incentive pay and other rewards to quantifiable objectives

Summary – checklist for leadership and effective teams
- clear purpose, common vision and accountability
- obsession with external customer
- participation and well defined roles
- civilized disagreement and style diversity – allow for workout meetings and discussions
- encourage open communications – silence is consent – voice your ideas
- encourage flexible discipline and even expulsion of non-productive team members
- blend of informality and formality
- focus on both process and end results; however, remember that results are more important than process
- acknowledgement of the need for change

- strongrespect and trust between members and leaders
- single point of contact for official team progress and communications (do not feed rumour-mill)
- self-assessmentof team members and adjustment
- noideas are bad ideas; encourage 'no blame game'
- useautomated tools to increase speed and communications

Key take aways

Steven Covey identified the **seven habits of highly effective people**. These not only impact on how well individuals perform, but also on how well organizations and teams perform.

These habits represent 'superior take aways' from this chapter (Covey, 1989):

- **be proactive** – take the initiative; act or be acted upon
- **begin with the end in mind** – vision, mission, scope, deliverables and boundaries
- **put first things first** – time bounds; time management (A,B,C); prioritize
- **think and act 'win-win'** – everyone wins if the team wins – individuals, team members, leaders and organization
- **seek first to understand, then to be understood** – active listening; diagnose before you prescribe
- **synergize** – creative collaboration and innovation; value differences
- **'sharpen the saw'** – continuous learning and renewal; adopt best practices; create a knowledge management database of lessons learned (good and bad) – enable easy access to them

"As a general rule, leaders have become leaders because they have done more, been better, worked harder and somehow differentiated themselves in some ways. They've accomplished this more or less on their own all along the way."

- Gregg Miller, President, RACOM Corporation

Part II – IT governance, its major component processes and enabling technologies

Part II of the book covers Chapters 5 through 9. This includes an overview of the critical process components of IT governance, such as program and project management, IT Service Management, strategic sourcing and outsourcing, performance management and controls, select enabling technology characteristics, critical success factors and a composite checklist of required IT governance activities.

Well documented processes that are consistent, repeatable and technology-enabled are one of the single biggest contributors to improved reliability, and therefore quality, in both product and service delivery.

The following identifies and groups the benefits that can be achieved through the use of consistent process implementation and improvement:

- cost– reduction, avoidance and containment
- efficiency and effectiveness – automation, reliability, consistency, speed and easier to train personnel
- governance– compliance, auditable, alignment, measurable and effectiveness
- quality – improved quality can help reduce costs, minimize rework and defects and improve customer satisfaction

5 Program and project management excellence (execution management)

"But in science, the credit goes to the man who convinces the world, not the man to whom the idea first occurs."

- Sir Francis Darwin, 1914

5.1 What is covered in this chapter?

This chapter:
- provides an overview of the key principles, issues, concepts and processes, for effectively managing enterprise-wide and limited scope programs and projects
- identifies the driving forces, value propositions and key principles and practices, for achieving excellence in program and project management as part of IT governance
- reviews the self-assessment project management (PM) maturity level assessment techniques
- links the IT plan to programs and projects that support the business
- shows how to use the program/project type-scale matrix, to determine which PM methodology – light (fast track) or complex - to use as part of a scalable and flexible framework
- explains the mandatory and discretionary key performance indicators and metrics necessary to manage programs and projects effectively

5.2 Overview

Program and project management is a major component of effective IT governance that focuses on execution management. Significant research has been conducted in the area of program and project management, resulting in many publications, as is demonstrated by the references provided in this book.

It is not the intention of this chapter to rehash what has already been published, but rather to provide a blend of frameworks, checklists, tools, templates, techniques and metrics to help deliver programs and projects on time, within scope, within budget, with high quality and to the customer's satisfaction, get them back on track and/or cancel disasters about to happened. It references several self-assessment maturity models, which can be used to assess the current maturity level of an organization, and suggests a transition plan to improve PM practices. It also suggests a scalable and flexible PM life cycle framework, based on a blend of best practices that are tailor-made to handle different project types (eg simple, moderate and complex), and that can be institutionalized in various organizational environments.

Key definitions
So that the reader is on the same map as the author, Figure 5.1 provides a working definition of key terms, such as programs, projects, tasks and processes. In addition, the extensive glossary provided includes many more project management and other IT governance terms and definitions.

Term	Definition	Examples
Program	Consists of multiple interrelated projects that are integrated and is usually large, complex and with high visibility , high $ value & high risk	An Enterprise Resource Planning System such as SAP or Oracle
Project	A discrete, one-time event that consists of such attributes as time, cost, resources, risk, deliverables, etc.	Sap Module - Purchasing
Task	A discrete element of work	Order equipment
Process	A continuous work effort to support a business or IT function	Service Management; Service Desk; Sales Order Process

Figure 5.1   Key program and project management definitions

Trends in program and project management

According to the Project Management Institute, the profession of project management has undergone tremendous growth in the past few years. With this growth, significant changes to the field of project management have evolved, with the use of more sophisticated processes, tools, knowledge management and technologies. Table 5.1 identifies the past, present and future trends in project management

Past	Future
few projects	many projects
authoritarian management style	participative management
simple projects	complex projects
employees easy to manage	employees more difficult to manage
few opportunities	more opportunities
few tools available	more tools available
no user involvement	increasing user involvement
unique management/project	standard management for all projects
manual project management processes	automated project management processes
individual project status reporting	multi-project status reporting
little management support/understanding	more management sponsorship
limited project integration	more complex and integrated enterprise-wide systems

Table 5.1   Trends in project management

Project management skills and competencies

As the complexity of projects increase, the project manager and team must have a broad range of skills and competencies to be effective. Figure 5.2 identifies the skills and competencies required in the complex and fast paced project environments of the future.

How much program and project management is required?

Many organizations have been challenged by the question of *'how much project program and project management is required in our organizational and project environment?'*

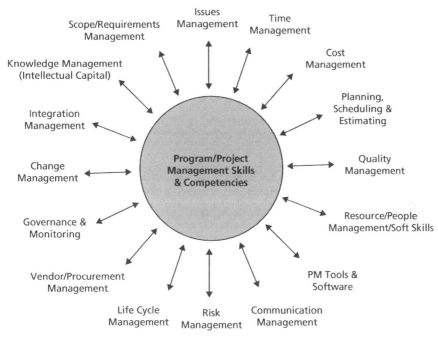

Figure 5.2   Project management is complex and requires multiple skills and competencies

There is no simple or straightforward answer to this question. The answer depends on many factors relating to the program or project such as:

- degree of visibility and strategic value of the initiative
- financial value (one time and recurring costs)
- strategic value and visibility
- complexity scope and size
- duration
- number of interfaces and integration requirements with other systems
- degree of risk
- speed of required implementation
- senior management and project manager's management style, philosophy and level of organizational project management maturity
- number of organizations, departments, locations and resources involved
- executive management and/or customer requirements
- degree of outsourcing; on shore and off shore sourcing
- regulatory and compliance requirements

For a growing number of organizations, a light or fast track project management process, which addresses, at a minimum, the project's sponsor and owner, requirements, objectives, scope, risks and contingencies, constraints, schedule, budget and deliverables is often sufficient. This is covered in greater detail in Section 5.5.

Why is program/project management important?

The objective of project management is to make the most effective use of multiple resources by delivering projects on time, on budget, within scope, with high quality, to the customer's satisfaction, with a minimum of or no rework, and the mitigation of the major risks. The resources include personnel, equipment, facilities, materials, capital, technology, external resources (eg suppliers and service providers), intellectual property and other assets.

As all kinds of programs and projects become more pervasive in organizations, to manage a wide range of initiatives (such as new product development, mergers and acquisitions, new enterprise-wide information systems, new building and facilities construction and others), both private and public sector leaders have recognized that project management is a strategic imperative. Project management provides organizations and people with a powerful set of processes, tools and technologies that improve their ability to plan, implement, integrate and manage activities to meet business objectives. Project management is a results-oriented management discipline that places a high value on building collaborative relationships among a diverse set of people located anywhere to complete specific deliverables.

The five 'W's and 2 'H's of project management

Early on, it is important to establish the basic questions that will help to define the parameters of a program or project. The fundamental questions that help to scope a project include:

- **Why** … are we doing this? Are we solving a newly discovered problem, fixing an existing problem, pursuing an opportunity, cutting costs, increasing revenues, or increasing productivity? Everyone, from top to bottom, must know the answer, and the answer must be on this list.

- **Who** … wants this done? Is it an executive sponsor, project task force/project manager and team, owner(s) of deliverables, customers or outside stakeholders? Has that person/team sold the 'why' and assumed responsibility and commitment from key people?

- **What** … are the details? Is the project feasible? Is it linked to the organization's vision and plan? Are all the resources (human, financial, material, facilities, etc.) available and committed? Have the project's scope and objectives been approved and sold to all? Have risks been evaluated and contingencies planned for? Have interface and integration concerns been addressed?

- **How** … will we do this? How much will be built? How much bought? How much will be outsourced? How will we audit outsourced progress/quality? How will problems be addressed and escalated?

- **When** … are deliverables required? Are deadlines, schedules, milestones and critical path tasks identified, and are all involved aware of them?

- **Where** … will this be done and where are the affected stakeholders? Where are the departments, functions, locations, countries and people?

- **How much** … is the budget? How much has been budgeted, committed, allocated and spent? How will we measure the performance and key metrics? How will any variances between budgets, actuals and baselines be addressed?

5.3 Project management is complex, but has significant value

According to Barkley, "Projects must be internally and externally integrated; internal integration means that project work packages, deliverables and systems are connected; external integration means that the project interfaces with customer systems and produces value for the customer, the market and the industry as a whole" (Barkley, 2006).

In addition to customers, select projects are also linked with supplier systems, government systems (eg financial reporting, taxes, etc.) and outsourcing service providers. Therefore, as programs and projects become more integrated, their complexity rises.

Major causes of program/project failures and challenges
There are many reasons for program and project failures and challenges. Major reasons include:

- lack of, or poor, business case
- lack of executive commitment, visibility and accountability
- poorly defined requirements, scope, objectives and deliverables
- poor communications
- failure to treat projects as a start-up initiative
- unrealistic expectations
- limited constituent involvement and ownership
- lack of, or insufficient, and the right kind of, resources
- lack of, or poor integration within the, organization (and to other systems)
- no plan, no risk assessment and mitigation, no contingency plan alternatives
- lack of measurable controls and metrics
- ineffective implementation strategy
- underestimation of project complexity, costs and time
- poor or unreliable vendor deliverables
- lack of training for either the project team, or those constituents who are impacted by the project
- inflexible, limited or no project management process
- poor use or over-reliance on the use of project management tools and software

The cost of program and project management failure
Both the Standish Group and Gartner have conducted periodic annual surveys on the state of project management in the USA. These surveys divide programs and projects into three classifications – failed, challenged and successful.

- **Failed:** The first class represents failed projects that have been started, but never finished for a variety of reasons – the sponsor resigned, the need went away, poor requirements definition, avoiding a disaster about to happen and scope creep.
- **Challenged:** The second class represents challenged projects, which have been implemented, but with one or more significant challenges, such as over budget, over schedule, under scoped and rework due to changing requirements.
- **Successful:** The third class represents successful projects that have been implemented, generally on time, within budget, within scope, with reasonable quality and to the customer's satisfaction.

According to a blend of Standish and Gartner surveys, the estimated annual cost range of failed and challenged projects in the USA is $100 to 150 billion. Figure 5.3 illustrates these numbers for small, medium and large organizations.

Nearly ³/₄ of all projects fail on run into trouble

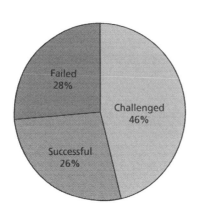

An estimated **$100 -150 bn per year is spent on failed and challenged projects in USA (out of a total estimated spend of $250 bn)**

Successful (S) = completed on-time, on-budget and within scope

Challenged (C) = completed, but with time and/or budget overruns and fewer features than originally specified

Failed (F) = cancelled before completion

Company Size	S	C	F
Large	9%	62%	29%
Medium	16%	47%	37%
Small	28%	50%	22%

Source: Blend of surveys by the Standish Group and Gartner

Figure 5.3   The cost of project management failure

Questions that the author asks senior executives of companies regarding their project environments include:

- Howmuch of these costs are contributed by your organization?
- Doyou really have a good grasp of this kind of information?
- How effective are your organization's project management governance policies, frameworks, standards, processes, tools, disciplines and training programs?

More often than not, senior executives do not have readily available answers to these questions. That is part of the problem, and can also become part of the solution. This information, or lack thereof, can be used to ignite specific actions in organizations, by creating greater awareness of the impact on lower profitability due to poor project management practices, and rallying the troops to a call-to-action, to improve the effectiveness of the project and organization environment.

Actions to overcome project management obstacles

For every obstacle found in project management, there is an action that will help to eliminate, neutralize and avoid the obstacle. Figure 5.4 describes key obstacles and suggested actions to minimize the impact of the obstacles.

Obstacles	Actions
Resistance to PM due to time investment	Create flexible and scalable PM processes with mandatory and discretionary components (eg 'fast track' vs. 'full risk mitigation')
Lack of PM value proposition awareness	• Quantify PM benefits (time savings, quality improvements, cost reductions, customer satisfaction and create/ maintain a scorecard) • Create PM advocacy groups that share information, follow uniform process and document PM value lessons learned • Market and communicate value of PM to multiple constituencies
Limited support from the top	• Identify proactive PM executive champions and use them to persuade others • Demonstrate benefits of PM by using key metrics (eg improved customer satisfaction, reduced cycle time) to gain supports
Insufficient dedicated qualified PM resources	• Continuous training of relevant constituencies • Reward and recognition of certification • Career path options – professionalize PM • Funding and support of 'PM Centers of Excellence'

Figure 5.4   Select actions to overcome major project management obstacles

Value propositions of project management from leading organizations

Based on primary and secondary research, and consulting assignment observations conducted by the author, the following leading organizations summarized the value of **applying best practice project management principles and practices** in their environments (Selig, September 2004):

- 'provided better control of scope changes, and ensured efficient use of project dollars' **(Cisco)**
- 'use of consistent and repeatable project management processes on a global basis reduced project time, and costs, sped up project deliverables, facilitated training and improved the effectiveness of global project teams' **(IBM)**
- 'developed a better working relationship and communications with the customer and other project constituents' **(Nortel)**
- 'aligned project initiatives and investments more effectively with the business and customer needs, reduced rework and cycle time, and helped to improve the voice of the customer' **(GE)**
- 'improved IT project accountability and documentation' **(Purdue Pharma)**
- 'increased our customer satisfaction by demonstrating our commitment to on-time product delivery schedules' **(Lucent)**
- 'project management education and certification resulted in more cost effective and timely program/project performance and vendor (outsourcing) management' **(US Federal Government Agency)**

Several companies such as AT&T, IBM, Cisco, a major pharmaceutical company and a global telecommunications company provided similar key drivers as reasons for supporting formalized project management in their environments:

- 'improved customer satisfaction and service'
- 'reduced costs and improved our investment portfolio management prioritization and alignment'
- 'reduced cycle time for new product development and commercialization'
- 'improved quality'
- 'improved business process efficiencies and increased speed to market'
- 'increased our ability to manage and mitigate risks more prudently'

A telecom company used its expertise in project management as a marketing and sales tool for its customers. It developed a series of project management brochures and booklets, prepared for both internal company constituents, such as executives, project management professionals, employees and customers. Figure 5.5 identifies the purpose of each of the documentation guides and brochures.

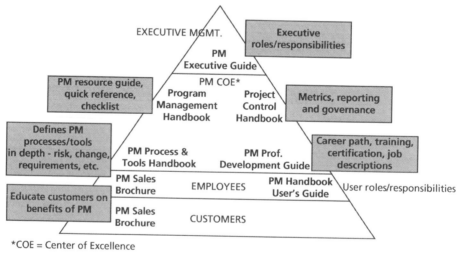

A Telecom company strongly supported project management disciplines and developed a series of PM documentation for different constituents. A PM sales brochure was developed for its customers that promoted the idea that by implementing a PM best practices, the customer's benefited in many ways, including on time delivery of products.

*COE = Center of Excellence

Figure 5.5   Project management expertise used as a marketing tool with customers

Assessing the level of project management maturity in organizations

There are several self-assessment techniques available for organizations to evaluate the current state of their project management policy, process, environment and capabilities, determine their maturity level and develop a plan to improve the project management environment as part of an overall plan to improve the IT governance environment.

These techniques were described in Chapter 2. They include the Project Management Maturity Assessment Model (PMMM®), which plots SEI's Capability Maturity Model Integrated (CMMI®) with PMI's nine knowledge areas and describes forty-five (45) separate cells with their attributes. This is illustrated in Figure 2.8 and can be used as a tool for the self-assessment. Another technique for self-assessment is PMI's Organizational Project Maturity Model (OPM3®), which utilizes three elements in the organizational maturity assessment process – knowledge, assessment and improvement. It is described in Chapter 2 and illustrated in Figure 2.7.

Yet another technique is usually administered by an external and objective project management expert, and is based on a series of interviews, which use a common set of questions to analyze and evaluate all aspects of the project management environment, culture, processes, tools, capabilities and attitudes, and help to develop an action plan for improvement. Obviously, the outcome of any of the assessments should be an actionable improvement plan.

5.4   Principles for achieving excellence in program/project management

Key attributes of successful program- and project-based organizational cultures and environments

Based on many of the case studies analyzed, a review of the literature and numerous consulting assignments, it is clear that organizations continue to struggle with establishing and enforcing a formal program/project management policy and process that is sustainable. In addition, a number of key project management principles and practices were identified and consistently applied, for the most part, by leading-edge, successful organizations (Selig, September 2004).

These principles and practices can represent a checklist for helping companies achieve improvements, and higher levels of project management maturity and effectiveness, in their environments. They have been organized into logical categories to facilitate their use.

Program/project management excellence and visibility:
- Top management must prioritize projects based on consistent and repeatable evaluation and selection processes.
- Customers must approve and set priorities among projects.
- Implement projects successfully (eg on-time, on-budget, within scope, with high quality and to the customers satisfaction).
- The CEO (eg CIO; CFO; CMO; COO; etc.) is committed to implementing project management as a core competency to manage all types of projects.
- Conduct formal periodic project management assessments and reviews with senior management.
- Projects must be limited to a size that can be fully understood by the project manager.

- Successful project management must be a joint effort between customers and the project teams. But the final responsibility for success or failure lies with the customer.
- Market and communicate the benefits and positive results of good fundamental project management disciplines through newsletters, websites, word of mouth, customer testimonials and other promotion vehicles.
- Develop a business case for major complex and moderate projects (defined later in this chapter).
- An essential element of every project is a complete project plan based on a work break down structure, with assignable work packages, task identification, estimating, budgeting and scheduling.
- Planning is everything and ongoing – detailed, systematic and team-involved.
- What is not documented has not been said or does not exist.
- The more ridiculous the deadline, the more it costs to try to meet it.
- Project sponsors and constituents must be active participants – this builds relationships, communications and commitment.
- Use industry standards and guidelines to guide your project management direction - CMMI, PMMM, ISO 9000, PRINCE2, Six Sigma, Baldrige and others.

Sponsorship, accountability and leadership:
- All programs/projects must have a sponsor and/or owner and an overall program/project manager.
- Key roles and responsibilities must be formally agreed to upfront, and communicated to all of the constituencies where individuals are assigned specific actions in the form of a **RACI** matrix (**R**esponsible, **A**pprove, **C**onsult, **I**nform) which becomes part of the project documentation.
- Program/project scope, requirements and deliverables should be approved upfront by the sponsor.
- Program/project costs and benefits (including non-financial benefits) should be quantified and approved by the sponsor and charged back to the sponsor or owner.
- Fast projects have strong leaders who create a sense of urgency and speed.
- Professionalize project management, reward certification and celebrate successes.
- Program/project scope, requirements and deliverables (as in a charter) should be approved upfront by the sponsor and monitored throughout the life cycle phases.
- The creation of a program management office (PMO) is important, to act as a 'center of excellence' to develop and maintain project management processes, co-ordinate training and certification, manage or consult on select large projects or those projects in trouble and facilitate project planning, status reporting and periodic formal reviews.
- Project Managers must focus on five dimensions of project success – on time, within budget, within scope, with acceptable quality and to the customer's satisfaction.
- Project life cycle with 'go/no go' gates allows for mid-course project reviews and adjustments and/or cancellations.
- A project manager's most valuable and least used word is 'no'.
- The same work under the same conditions will be estimated differently by five different estimators or by one estimator five different times.
- Project manager responsibility must be matched by equivalent authority.
- Projects management must be sold and resold via the value propositions.

- Project team members deserve a clear, written charter and guidelines as to the tasks they must perform and the time available to perform them.
- Questions generated by the project team deserve direct answers from the customer.
- Great project managers do not encourage burnout.
- Establish project review panels, consisting of key constituents, and conduct formal reviews with follow-up actions, dates and assigned responsibility.
- Use outside subject matter project management experts as needed.

Program/project management (PM) governance policy, change control and escalation

Key practices for successful and sustainable superior project management best practices include the following:

- A formal project management governance policy should be established, defining the components of the policy, and identify what is mandatory and discretionary, and who has decision authority for approval, resource allocation, escalation and change authorization.
- A formal governance calendar should be published, which identifies formal project reviews, status reports (eg weekly, bi-weekly, monthly, quarterly), funding reviews, etc.
- A flexible and scalable project management process should be established and continuously improved to accommodate different project types.
- A project management 'center of excellence' (PMO) should be established to develop criteria for project management competencies, encourage project management training and certification, provide expert project management help, act as project management advocates and conduct periodic health checks on select programs/projects.
- Establish a reward and recognition system to recognize project management excellence and encourage certification.
- Supply short-term incremental project deliverables that work to establish credibility and visibility (decompose complex programs and projects into no more than 80 hour work packages with targeted deliverables, formal project reviews, etc.). Shorter work packages based on 40 hours or less are also acceptable for priority projects.
- Incorporate project management objectives into annual performance reviews.
- Consistent program and project metrics should be instituted, based on time, cost, resources, quality and customer satisfaction (including earned value, where applicable). There are a number of tools that can help with estimating, resource allocation, level loading and resource utilization.
- The ability to compare planned to actual results or base lines is essential for effective project management.
- Management must be provided meaningful visibility into projects if suspicion and distrust are to be minimized.
- The key to good project management is effective and honest communications.
- A formal escalation process, with clear accountability and roles should be established to resolve key program/project issues, risks and approve changes.
- A consistent methodology must be developed and applied to report the **RAG** (eg **R**ed, **A**mber or **G**reen status of programs, projects or other major tasks: Red = significant trouble; Amber = emerging trouble; Green = everything is on target).

- Reporting must be produced on a consistent basis (eg weekly, bi-weekly, monthly, other) using a consistent format (eg with allowances made for the audience of the report).
- Aformal time tracking system should be in place to record how time is spent on projects.
- A formal link, including rework to the change management process, must be established to manage and monitor significant changes to budgets, schedules, versions and/or documentation.

Resource optimization, availability and commitment:
- Sponsors and program/project managers should have access to the right resources, based on the project phase, task requirements and competencies needed.
- The availability and commitment of the resources should be guaranteed by senior management once the program/project is approved and resourced.

Program/project repository and lessons learned:
- Lessons learned should be developed and made available to all constituencies who require them, with consideration given to security and access policies.
- Currentand evolving best practice benchmarking should be tracked and adopted.
- Maintain a project management knowledge management system, of lessons learned and lessons to be changed.
- Desirablework must be rewarded; undesirable work must be changed.

Project management life cycle phases and key components
Programs and projects are, by definition, one time events, with a start and end date. Therefore, all projects have a life cycle. Life cycles may vary by project. For example, the life cycle of a new product development project is somewhat different to a project life cycle for an information system or merger and acquisition. In addition, PMI's PMBOK® identifies five project phases:

- initiation
- planning
- execution
- control
- terminationor closure

Other project life cycles may have more or less phases. As a practical matter, the actual number of life cycle phases that a company uses is of less importance than ensuring that there is agreement that a project life cycle process, with specific phases and components, is used on a consistent, but scalable basis.

To keep things simple, Figure 5.3 represents a project management life cycle, based on four phases – initiation, planning, execution and termination. Like many other project management professionals, the author believes that 'control' is not really a separate phase in the life cycle, but rather, is an integral part of all of the life cycle phases. The actual number of phases is not as important as ensuring that a project life cycle being adopted and consistently applied, and that the value of the life cycle itself is recognized in an organization. The benefits of a project life cycle include:

- creates visibility and a roadmap through phase approvals
- establishes uniform and consistent phases
- disciplines and structures the process
- forces incremental 'go/no go' decisions at gate reviews
- forces early attention to details
- has a beginning and an end
- establishes project planning and control mechanisms
- accommodates change and risk
- creates a framework for improved communications, commitment, buy-in and visibility
- facilitates the integration of the program/project results and deliverables into the organization's core businesses, related systems, infrastructure and culture

Figure 5.6 also identifies the key components of each of the phases. Not every component must or should be used for every project, but it provides a checklist that can be applied to either light or complex projects, which are discussed in more detail in Section 5.5. The author believes that a number of the above elements are critical to help organizations develop superior project management environments and, therefore, deserve more in depth coverage.

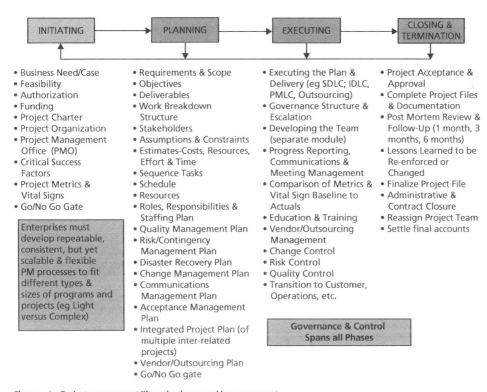

Figure 5.6   Project management life cycle phases and key components

Basic project management mechanics

Most projects, with a few exceptions, should include certain basic fundamental mechanics. These include:

- **Project definition and charter** – objectives, organization, scope and boundaries, funding and assumptions; this may also include a business case, depending on the project
- **Planning** – work breakdown, tasks and/or activities including dependencies, durations, assignable work packages, estimated (elapsed time and effort time to perform work), base line budgets and costs and a quality management plan
- **Scheduling** – allocation of resources, milestones, critical path, logic dependencies and networks and float/slack tasks and activities
- **Governance, control and progress reporting** – schedule, cost, resources, deliverables, scope, communications and status reporting, and other metrics such as cost performance index and schedule performance index, managing expectations, variance analysis, quality control, risk analysis and contingencies, escalation, change authorization and disaster planning and recovery
- **Final review, acceptance and 'operationalization'** - customer approval and acceptance, final documentation, lessons learned, transition into operations and post-mortem reviews

The business case:

Not all projects require a business case. There are many factors that should determine whether a potential program or project requires a business case. Key criteria can include such elements as:

- size and complexity
- investment amount required
- degree of risk
- degree of impact on the organization
- competitive advantage or survival
- organizational scope and geographic coverage
- degree of visibility

Figure 5.7 provides a composite project business case outline used by several organizations.

Project management plan (PMP)

A project management plan is unique to each project. It provides all stakeholders engaged in project activities with a uniform baseline of project understanding within its operating and performance environment, including requirements, schedule, resources, risks, constraints and outcomes. It also serves as a communications tool, a roadmap, and commitment to stakeholders across the project phases. It needs to be thorough, justifiable, flexible, public and realistic.

In developing a realistic and pragmatic plan, it is important to recognize that every project has a customer and, often, IT has to help the customer to define what they want and what their role is in a project, by getting the right people involved in each phase.

Contents of a PMP

Project management plans should be prepared for projects in accordance with the organizations project management policies and guidelines. Each PMP can include the following components:

1. **Executive Summary (Synopsis of Business Case Assessment):** Purpose, Objectives, Strategy and Scope Description of Opportunity, Value and Alignment Dependencies, Assumptions, Constraints Sponsor and Management Team Costs/Benefits/Risks/Issues 2. **Assessment of Current Environment (Reference Base – Where are we today?):** Current Processes, Functions and Technology Current Costs, Resources, Volumes, Locations Major Issues, Constraints and Sensitivities 3. **Change Analysis (Why Change?)** Value Proposition Analysis Financial Analysis (description and quantification; full economic life cycle; best case, worse case, most likely case; cash flow (cash in and cash out); costs/savings) Non-Financial benefits Risk Analysis & Mitigation	4. **Proposed Solutions (What Could We Do?)** Proposed Requirements, Processes, Functions and Technology Proposed Cost/Benefit Analysis Major Issues, Constraints and Sensitivities Impact on the Organization, Resources, People, Technology Pros/Cons of each solution 5. **Recommended Approach (What Should We Do and How Do We Get There?** Macro Plan, Milestones and Schedule Critical Success Factors Macro Plan, Milestones and Schedule Conversion, Transition Plan and Team Quality and Test Plan Key Performance Indicators 6. **Appendices** Detailed Project Plan Detailed Cost Benefit Analysis Detailed Risk Management Plan Detailed Contingency and Backup Plan Detailed Communications Plan Critical Success Factors

Figure 5.7   Generic project business case outline

- requirements and objectives
- work scope and deliverables
- work breakdown structure and tasks
- project organization
- roles and responsibility assignment matrix – 'who does what?'
- schedule – including start date, end date, major milestones and deliverables
- budgets, funding and resource requirements and allocation
- integration and interface plan
- quality plan
- security plan
- risk, contingency and disaster recovery plan
- monitoring, communications, control and reporting plan
- escalation policy
- operation and maintenance plan
- change management and authorization plan
- training, testing and documentation
- key contacts
- glossary of terms
- appendix

5.5   Making the choice – program and project management light or complex

IT request and demand management gate review

Chapter 3 discussed the business and IT alignment, and strategic planning processes. Once a program or project is approved as part of a plan, or sometimes even outside of a plan, it should undergo a business case review before it receives final approval and funding, to further validate that the project is aligned with the business, and contributes its share of benefits to the organization. Figure 5.8 illustrates an IT project request gate review and approval process flow. Each project must pass each 'go/no go' gate to be approved and resourced. Once a project is approved, it is then commissioned and resourced, and the project management life cycle begins. In some organizations, a number of these activities are conducted in parallel, and not always sequentially.

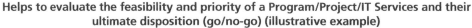

Helps to evaluate the feasibility and priority of a Program/Project/IT Services and their ultimate disposition (go/no-go) (illustrative example)

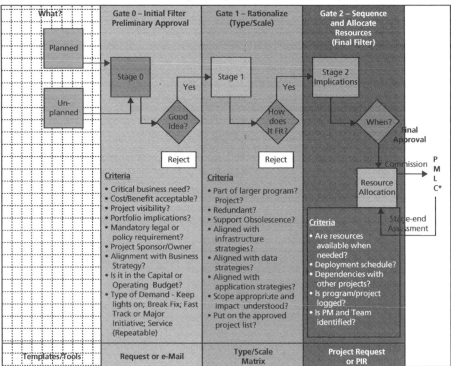

*PMLC = Project Management Life Cycle

Figure 5.8   IT project request gate approval process flow

Figure 5.9 provides a checklist of business, technical, financial and other business case factors that are part of the project approval process.

Select Criteria used to Help Evaluate an IT Request and/or Business Case

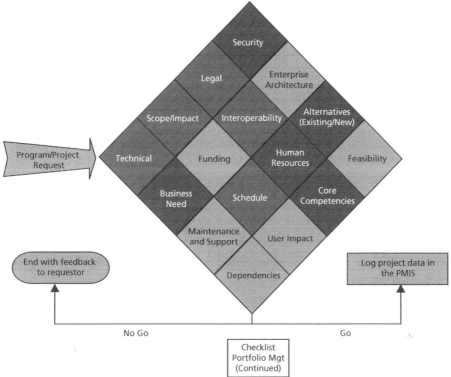

Figure 5.9a   Business/technical/financial business case checklist

---

(To be used as a guideline to assist in evaluating New or Changes in Scope Requests for IT Services)

Scope, Impact, Business Need and Feasibility
What is the scope and impact of the request? Enterprise wide? Geography? Number of People?
Is it solution technically feasible? Economically feasible? Legally feasible?
Is the request identified in the strategic and/or operating plan and budget?
What is the impact of the proposed solution on the user community? High? Medium? Low?
What business need will be satisfied by approving this request? High Impact? Low Impact? Mandatory? Strategic? Discretionary?

Technical/Interoperability/Enterprise Architecture
Is this a new technology? Has it been tested?
Is it an extension or replacement of an existing technology?
Does the proposed solution impact the approved enterprise architecture and approved infrastructure components?
Does the solution represent a standard solution? A proprietary solution?
Is the proposed solution independent or is it dependent on other infrastructure components?
Does it comply with the interoperability standards and guidelines?
Does the solution require back-up, redundancy and contingency plans?
What degree of risk does the proposed solution pose? High? Medium? Low?
Is the capacity of the proposed solution expandable to accommodate growth in volume? Locations? Employees? Etc.?

Figure 5.9b   Business/technical/financial business case checklist

Legal, Regulatory and Security
Is the request legal?
Is this request ethical?
Does this request comply with current regulatory policies and guidelines?
Does the request comply with published security regulations and guidelines?
As a result of this request, are new or modifications required to security regulations and guidelines?

Core Competencies and Human Resources
Do we have the core competencies to design and implement the proposed solution?
Do we have sufficient and the right kind of human resources to implement the solution?
Do we have to outsource the solution to an industry partner? Other?

Alternatives Considered
What alternative solutions have been analyzed?
Why was the recommended alternative selected?

Funding and Financials
Is this request a funded (budgeted) requirement defined as part of the annual budget process?
  – Defined/explicit?
  – Realignment/reallocation?
Is this an unplanned and unfunded request?
Does this request impact the enterprise architecture and/or infrastructure integrity?
Does the request require a reallocation of previously approved funding?
Is the requested completion date acceptable? Doable?

Schedule and Time Frame
Is the requested schedule doable with the resources available?

Figure 5.9b   Business/technical/financial business case checklist (cont'd)

Program/project type/scale matrix

Once a program or project is approved, a favorite question asked by many is, *'how much project management process and documentation is required for this project and what project management path should be used?'*

Best practice companies, like IBM, GE, Boeing, Bechtel and others, have developed very detailed, robust and scalable project management methodologies, that are repeatable and can be consistently applied to a wide variety of projects on a global basis.

Since all programs and projects are not equal, organizations are increasingly implementing a flexible and scalable program and project management life cycle, consisting of multiple paths, such as fast track or light versus complex process, with the associated checklists and supporting tools. A growing number of organizations have developed the equivalent of a 'Chinese menu' ('choose from either column A and/or B'), to provide more choices within a broad framework of project management best practices, where the project manager and the team either get to pick the project management process, within an overall framework established by the organization, or are required to adhere to a particular path because of contractual or compliance requirements. This is how the term 'fast track or light' versus complex project management evolved, and it also helped to overcome the often-heard complaint that project management requires substantial documentation.

One method, which provides a consistent way to help select the appropriate project management process path for organizations to follow in managing their projects, is to create a project type-scale matrix. Figure 5.10 illustrates the project type-scale matrix. It provides a structured approach to determine the appropriate project management templates (and documentation) to use, to plan, manage, monitor and control a program or project throughout its life cycle phases. In essence, the project-type-scale matrix identifies the level of project management documentation required for three types of projects – simple, moderate and complex. It has been designed as a guideline to help organizations provide flexibility and choice, but within a consistent and repeatable framework.

Figure 5.10 identifies eleven complexity factors on the vertical axis and accommodates three value ratings, ranging from a low of 1 to a high of 5. Each of the eleven elements is ranked, and the total numeric value is summarized. At the bottom of the matrix, there is a point guide as to which projects are classified as simple, moderate or complex. It suggests the templates that should be used for each of the project types, and the appropriate approval levels required, based on the numeric value of each project. The matrix can be tailored to different environments by changing the complexity factors, their values and respective weights.

Project management life cycle phases and related templates

The project type-scale matrix must be used in conjunction with Figure 5.11, which illustrates the project management life cycle phases, and defines the associated templates that represent the documentation required for different types of projects. The matrix identifies the recommended templates that should be used by project type. The templates are all web-based, and vary in size from one page to over ten pages. Each template also contains mandatory and discretionary information that must be completed for each project. In this way, the *'light'* (or low risk) project management process can be used for *'simple'* and *'some moderate projects'* and only require the use of two templates, while *'complex'* (or high risk) projects, such as a SAP installation, would require the use of all or most of the project templates.

A key question that organizations ask is *'where do we start?'* Should we apply these templates to all active projects or just to some projects? The most practical answer is to conduct a ranking of currently active programs or projects in a company, by using the project type-scale matrix. Figure 5.12 illustrates the results of such an evaluation for a service organization in terms of the 80/20 rule, where a small number of projects consume a majority of the IT project resources. Therefore, in this particular organization, the starting point should be complex projects, followed by moderate projects.

5.6   Program and project governance excellence

Prerequisites for effective project management execution and governance

For each project phase or activity, the project manager should:

- reviewthe project plan, as a reminder of the desired results of that phase or activity
- conduct a kick-off meeting, to clarify the phase deliverables, reinforce roles and responsibilities of project team members, create a shared sense of responsibility, gain commitment from the

[Insert PROJECT # - NAME]

The Project Type/Scale Matrix provides a structured and consistent approach to determine the appropriate PM Template(s) for managing/monitoring/controlling a program/project.

PROJECT TYPE/SCALE ASSESSMENT

Directions: Calculate the matrix score by subjectively using the guidelines below to assign a number between 1 and 5 to each of the 11 factors.

	COMPLEXITY FACTOR	LOW=1	MED=3	HIGH=5	NOTES	ENTER SCORE (1,3 or 5)
1	Project Type	UPGRADE Involves a change in capacity of existing technology or service. Usually additional capacity or additional location	NEW ADDITION Involves the addition of a new technology or service with no replacement of existing technology or service	REPLACEMENT Involves the replacement of old technology or service with a new technology or service	Degree of difficulty influenced by new technology and whether it replaces older technology or is simply added to the environment	
2	Technology	Established company standard	A standard in the industry, but new to FTS	A new technology, not necessarily a standard, no internal expertise.	Open standards should be encouraged	
3	Scope	Involves only one location and one function	Involves only one region and up to four functions	Involves all regions (locations) and cross-functional	The wider the geographic scope the more complex the project	
4	End User Impact	Completely transparent to end users	Minimal amount of communication necessary to inform end users of planned changes. No training required	Changes require frequent communication and some degree of end user training		
5	Implementation technique	Can be implemented without disturbing existing service, users can migrate to new environment	New technology/service is installed in parallel and users are migrated in segments.	'Flash cut' requires new technology/service to replace old with no overlap.		
6	Capital Required (Life Cycle)	Relatively small capital (<$50k)	Medium capital required ($50k - $2.5 million)	Large capital required (>$2.5 mil)		

Figure 5.10   Program/project type-scale matrix

	Small operating costs (< $100k/yr)	Medium operating cost ($100k-$999k/yr)	Large operating cost ($>1.0 mil/yr)	Includes depreciation, equipment lease, maintenance, etc.	
7	'Operating Costs (Annual)'				
8	Vendor relationship	No new vendors involved, upgrade using existing vendor product	No new vendor involved, using a new product from existing vendor.	New vendor with no prior business relationship	Established vendors are easier to do business with
9	Resource Requirements	Can be completed with use of only internal FTS resources (and industry partners)	Requires minimal resource dependency outside FTS (e.g. Phone Bridge)	Requires significant resource requirement from outside FTS and/or vendor (eg Enterprise Architecture, participation on project)	
10	Project Duration	<3 months	3-12 months	>12 months	
11	Other			Legal requirement and/or critical to business	
				TOTAL PROJECT Type/ Scale SCORE	0

TOTAL POINTS RANGE   11 to 55 Points

DEFINITIONS				
TYPE	Key Attributes	# of points	Recommended Template	Approvals
Simple	Low Complexity	Less than 20 Pts	Template - PR, PCR*	Director or Delegate
Moderate	Medium complexity	Between 20 and 35 Points	Template - PR, PIR, DTD, PCR (Others Optional)	CIO or Delegate
Complex	High visibility; AC directed; Multiple organizations affected	Greater than 35 Points	Template - All for tech. projects, otherwise TAD, IITQR, RFI opt.	ITRB or Delegate

*Assumes informal planning (additional templates are optional)

Figure 5.10   Program/project type-scale matrix (cont'd)

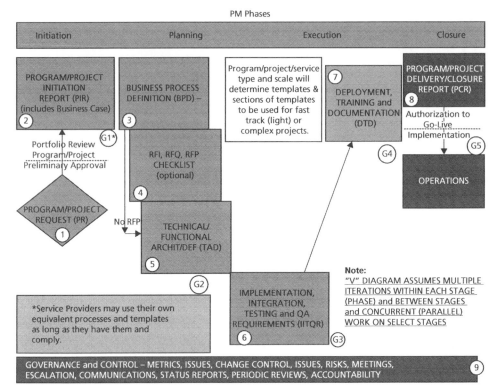

* G1-5: Go/No Go Gate Reviews

Phase(s)	Template(s)	Purpose/Description
Initiation	0. Program/Project Request (PR)	Obtains customer or other constituent authorization to request IT services
	1. Program/Project Initiation Report (PIR)	Provides sufficient high-level information on a program or project to either approve or reject the request (e.g. scope, requirements, etc.)
Planning	2. Business Project Definition (BPD)	Describes the major business objectives that the system, component or deliverable will satisfy and/or impact
	3. RFI, RFQ, RFP Checklists	Identifies the contents of a solicitation to vendors in the form of: Request for Information, Request for Quote and/or Request for Proposal
	4. Technical/Functional Architecture Definition (TAD)	Describes the complete system and/or component from a functional, technical and operational aspect
Execution**	5. Implementation, Integration, Testing and QA Requirements (IITQR)	Describes how the system and/or components is to be implemented integrated, tested and transitioned to the customer, operations and other environments
	6. Deployment, Training and Documentation (DTD)	Describes the actual installation and cutover of the system or components and identifies the training and documentation requirements
Closure	7. Program/Project Delivery/Closure Report (PCR)	Verifies and evaluates that the program/project objectives, costs, benefits and deliverables have been satisfactorily implemented and documents lessons learned

Figure 5.11   Project management life cycle phases and related templates

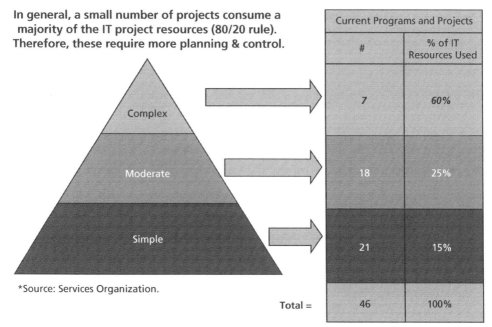

In general, a small number of projects consume a majority of the IT project resources (80/20 rule). Therefore, these require more planning & control.

| Current Programs and Projects | |
#	% of IT Resources Used
7	60%
18	25%
21	15%
46	100%

Complex

Moderate

Simple

*Source: Services Organization.

Total =

Figure 5.12   Project type-scale matrix ranking of IT projects

project team members, and ensure that all project team members have whatever they need to be successful in their roles
- provide authorization to project team members to start work on their activities
- conduct regular status meetings and/or provide regular status reports based on a maximum time reporting period of 80 hours (or less)
- if needed, provide training or other interventions to team members
- distribute progress reports according to a communications plan
- develop a governance and control policy, and communicate it to all project constituents

The project manager has the responsibility, during the execution phase, to compare and analyze a project's implementation progress against the baseline, and take actions to correct all significant issues and variances. This includes:

- schedule
- cost, benefits and budgets
- quality
- key deliverables
- human resources
- resource and asset allocation
- technology
- vendor deliverables

In the implementation phase, the project manager must constantly balance the monitoring, control and governance process that provides a disciplined framework to administer, monitor and control work, including:

- resources(budget)
- time(start and completion dates; critical path)
- product(deliverables)
- quality
- managingexpectations
- what,when and to whom to communicate

From time to time, the project manager needs help in resolving issues with difficult customers, non-supportive constituents or troublesome service providers. A formal project governance and escalation hierarchy, with clear roles and handoffs, is required. Figure 5.13 depicts such an organization.

Program management office (PMO) – roles and areas of focus
The role of the PMO is to champion project management benefit awareness, help develop project management expertise and provide administrative support (processes, tools, techniques, training, help desks) to sustain a vibrant and effective project environment in organizations. Specific PMO roles and responsibilities will vary from company to company, but can include the following:

- act as a 'center of excellence' and focal point for project management skills, competencies, methodologies, benefits and advocacy
- develop, maintain and administer all project management processes, techniques, templates and tools, to ensure effective project management implementation
- co-ordinateproject management education, training and co-ordination
- establish a 'project data base repository' to enable project managers, sponsors and other constituents to plan and track the progress of all projects
- definecommon project management metrics and vital signs, and ensure that they are applied

A formal program/project review process should be established and followed with clearly defined roles and responsibilities

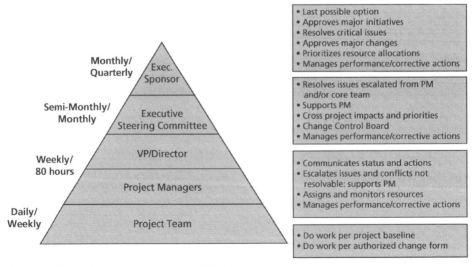

Figure 5.13   Program/project governance and escalation hierarchy

- assist project managers, team members and other project constituencies to resolve project management issues, concerns and questions
- conduct select project assessment reviews
- assist with 'troubled' projects

The discipline of the 'eighty hour' rule

Figure 5.14 illustrates a generic project management office. The '80 hour' rule facilitates project planning, scheduling, monitoring, reporting and project governance. It eliminates elastic yardsticks and subjective criteria as to monitoring project progress or lack of positive progress. There is no activity, task or event in any project which cannot be broken down into '80 hours' or less, vis-à-vis incremental deliverables, formalized project reviews and meetings, and formal status reports. There is no magic to the rule. It requires discipline, planning, thought and the ability to think in terms of decomposing projects into manageable and assignable work packages. It should be applied in the planning phase, when the work breakdown structure, schedule, budget and deliverables are developed.

The advantages of the '80 hour' rule forces the project manager and team to:

- focus fast, and reduces or eliminates scope creep
- get down to details early, and facilitates planning, budgeting and scheduling
- identify incremental deliverables (think product, not process)
- facilitate status reviews, communications and reporting
- overcome project drifting
- identify roles, responsibility and ownership early

Mandatory and discretionary project management key performance indicators

Project management metrics and key performance indicators (KPIs) should be easily captured, as normal output of transaction-based systems within an organization (such as an accounting and/or project management time reporting tracking and purchasing system). The KPIs should communicate the health of a program or project, a task, phase and/or deliverable, and should be determined by each organization in terms of whether it is mandatory or discretionary. The KPIs should also link business objectives to projects as part of IT governance, and should measure progress against a baseline for possible corrective actions. Most organizations will not support, or have difficulty supporting, multiple unsynchronized project data collection and reporting systems that are not an integral part of their operational or financial performance reporting and review processes.

The characteristics of KPIs should be quantifiable, trackable, measurable, comparable and actionable. Each organization must decide which project KPIs are mandatory and which are discretionary. Some suggestions follow for each category:

Suggested mandatory metrics:
- time and schedule
- costs – actual versus budgeted costs
- status of critical path (are we on target based on date?)
- deliverable hit ratio – number of planned versus completed deliverables (schedule)

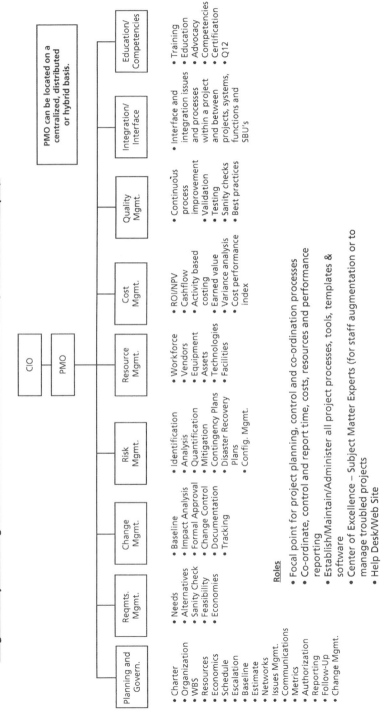

Figure 5.14   "Project Management Office"

- top issues – number of open issues should be minimized
- top risks of the project (should always be in focus) – with contingency plans
- customer satisfaction

Suggested discretionary metrics:
- milestone hit ratio – number of planned versus actual milestones achieved on targeted period
- actual versus budgeted resources (number of people)
- number of program/project changes
- % of rework and number of changes requested (including costs of change and rework)
- cost performance index (CPI)
- schedule performance index (SPI)
- earned value – requires a time reporting system in place

Sample project management 'center of excellence' organization and roles – major multi-national organization

Organizations are setting up project management 'centers of excellence'. Some make the PMO the 'center of excellence'. Others establish separate organizations to be the project management 'center of excellence', and the PMO with specific and non-overlapping roles. Figure 5.15 depicts the organizational planning of a project management 'center of excellence' for a large global product and service organization.

PM CoE's are regionalized, work closely together and support the geographic regions and business units in those regions.

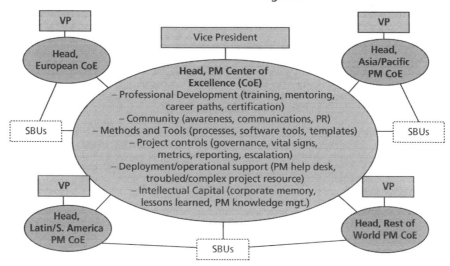

Figure 5.15   Project management 'center of excellence' organizational roles

5.7   Case study – US Federal Government Agency

Figure 5.16 describes a US Federal Government Agency case study. It illustrates a high level work break down structure of the four separate phases of the initiative, starting with one PMO in one IT function, which grew into an overall PMO for the entire IT organization.

5.8   Summary and key take aways

Summary
Critical success factors for achieving program and project management excellence include:

Create the right environment and culture:
– establish the appropriate organizational mindset, culture and environment
– obtain executive sponsorship, commitment and multi-level management buy-in
– obtain customer/other stakeholder/project team commitments and ownership
– success depends on creating a sustainable foundation (eg policy, process, metrics) for managing programs and projects, and integrating results and methodologies into the culture of the organization
– define roles and get the right people involved in every program/project phase
– market and re-enforce (eg training, rewards, mentors, tools, flexible processes) the value and benefits of good project management practices
– adopt a flexible and scalable project management process (phases, templates, repository and tools, and tailor when required) to accommodate different program and project types, based on current and emerging industry best practices

Develop program/project plans (based on a flexible and scalable process):
– define the project's scope, objectives, requirements and deliverables
– establish well-defined phases/tasks, 'go/no go' gates and milestones (break the job down into manageable work packages – '80 hour' rule) with realistic baselines (costs, time, resources and contingencies) based on short term incremental and visible deliverables
– define a responsibility assignment matrix – responsible, inform, consult and/or approve
– establish formal change management and risk management processes

Ensure governance and excellent communications:
– establish a governance, control, reporting and escalation policy and process
– manage expectations of all stakeholders proactively
– identify, measure and track mandatory and discretionary vital signs, metrics and key issues, and take necessary actions quickly – knock obstacles out of the way
– establish frequent and open communications with stakeholders (both formal and informal review meetings) on a daily, weekly, monthly and quarterly basis, depending on the project's importance and closeness to being implemented
– ensure accurate, timely and meaningful monitoring and progress reporting

Figure 5.16 – Case Study – US Federal Government Agency

Environment & Drivers	Approach
• Federal government is focusing on reducing costs and becoming more efficient through automation performance management • This agency provides IT systems and infrastructure support for several other agencies • Key areas of focus on government professionals and executives are greater accountability and improving their IT organizational and individual skills, competencies and maturity levels	• Completed assessment of one function within the IT organization and identified gaps and a plan to fill gaps • Sponsored by CIO • Three levels of steering were established: – Business/IT Steering Committee – senior managers who focused on prioritizing initiatives and funding – IT Technology Steering Committee –concerned with architecture, interoperability standards and compatibility issues – IT PMO – established to develop consistent and scalable PM policies and processes
Issues and/or Opportunities	**Approach (Cont'd)**
• Improve CMMI level of maturity from the low end of Level 1 to Level 3 within a three year period, initially in the PM area and then in other IT governance areas • Due to significant outsourcing, government employees had to be trained in more formal PM • Ad hoc and inconsistent PM and operational policies and processes throughout IT organization	• Formed an IT Governance Tiger Team, with representation of all IT departments and facilities by an external consultant to develop, review and deploy the IT governance framework and phased plan (see next slide) with the following priorities: – Program/Project Management and PMO – IT work Flows, Decision Rules and Authority Levels – IT Operations and Infrastructure – Performance Management & Management Controls
Results – Alignment	**Results - IT Service Management & Delivery**
• Business/IT Steering Group focuses on alignment and major investment priorities • Capital budgeting is part of but precedes the IT Strategic Plan • IT Annual Operating plan represents the budget authority and authorized spend levels	• Implementing the ITIL processes in the IT Operations and Infrastructure area • Improved the compliance reporting and documentation process and facilitated adherence to government regulations
Results - Program/Project Management	**Results - Performance Management**
• All agency government employees had to attend mandatory PM training • A consistent, but scalable Pm policy and process was deployed and resulted in significant reduction in rework and improved productivity through flexible discipline	• Project Management metrics for critical projects were more tightly controlled than for smaller projects • IT Operations and Infrastructure used daily, weekly. Monthly and quarterly metrics to measure customer satisfaction and service level performance, which is improving consistently
Critical Success Factors • CIO must sponsor and support • All functions must be represented in the initiative to develop trust, better communications and more effective alignment	
Lessons Learned • It always takes longer to implement process changes that anticipated • Must constantly market the value proposition of IT governance and process disciplines • Celebrate and communicate wins	

IT Governance Plan and Phases

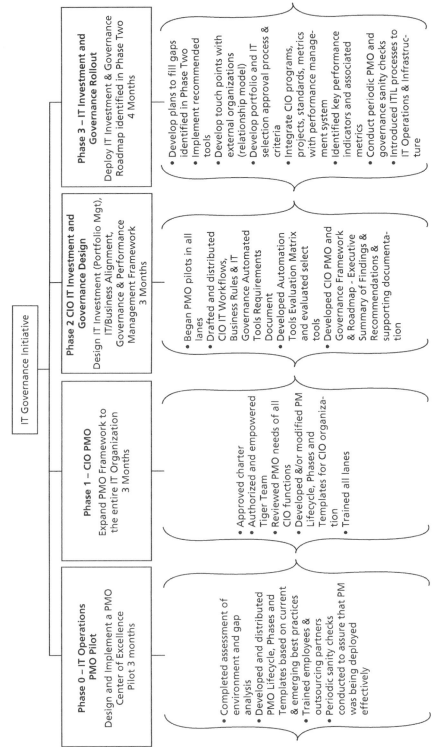

IT Governance Initiative

Phase 0 – IT Operations PMO Pilot

Design and Implement a PMO Center of Excellence Pilot 3 months

- Completed assessment of environment and gap analysis
- Developed and distributed PMO Lifecycle, Phases and Templates based on current & emerging best practices
- Trained employees & outsourcing partners
- Periodic sanity checks conducted to assure that PM was being deployed effectively

Phase 1 – CIO PMO

Expand PMO Framework to the entire IT Organization 3 Months

- Approved charter
- Authorized and empowered Tiger Team
- Reviewed PMO needs of all CIO functions
- Developed &/or modified PM Lifecycle, Phases and Templates for CIO organization
- Trained all lanes

Phase 2 CIO IT Investment and Governance Design

Design IT Investment (Portfolio Mgt), IT/Business Alignment, Governance & Performance Management Framework 3 Months

- Began PMO pilots in all lanes
- Drafted and distributed CIO IT Workflows, Business Rules & IT Governance Automated Tools Requirements Document
- Developed Automation Tools Evaluation Matrix and evaluated select tools
- Developed CIO PMO and Governance Framework & Roadmap - Executive Summary of Findings & Recommendations & supporting documentation

Phase 3 – IT Investment and Governance Rollout

Deploy IT Investment & Governance Roadmap identified in Phase Two 4 Months

- Develop plans to fill gaps identified in Phase Two
- Implement recommended tools
- Develop touch points with external organizations (relationship model)
- Develop portfolio and IT selection approval process & criteria
- Integrate CIO programs, projects, standards, metrics with performance management system
- Identified key performance indicators and associated metrics
- Conduct periodic PMO and governance sanity checks
- Introduced ITIL processes to IT Operations & Infrastructure

Figure 5.16   Case Study – US Federal Government Agency

Institutionalize a project management policy with flexible and scalable processes

– create project management 'centers of excellence' (eg advocacy center, help desk, education, training, subject matter expert help, process development, project tracking, certification requirements, etc.)
– create a reward and/or recognition policy to re-enforce and sustain
– conduct formal program/project reviews
– develop and use consistent, flexible and scalable project management processes (eg fast track or light versus complex projects) and automate processes and tools (web-based)
– capture and apply lessons learned, and focus on continuous improvement

Key take aways

Project management is a key component of IT governance. Key take aways for effective project management include:

- Executive sponsorship, management buy-in and customer ownership is critical.
- Planning is vital – scope, requirements and schedule.
- Project leadership and team building is essential - the team must be empowered to make decisions.
- A flexible and scalable process is crucial.
- A formal governance and escalation process with meaningful metrics (measurable, traceable, comparable and accurate) with consequential actions is essential.
- Effective, frequent, honest and open communications is essential.
- Risk management and change management are imperative.
- The focus should be on frequent delivery of products.
- Decomposing complex projects via WBS (Work Breakdown Structure) into manageable work packages is essential.
- Get the right people involved and committed during each phase.
- Establish project acceptance criteria between customer and project manager
- Competing on speed is doable and sustainable.
- Establish clear and unambiguous accountability (roles and responsibilities).
- Let the business and project dictate the level of project management detail required; however, establish a minimum set of project management processes.
- Do project management well and fast (automate as much as possible).
- Make project management an integral part of the corporate and IT governance policy, process and culture.
- Provide and mandate project management education and training for all levels of the organization.
- Know where you are going, and know when you have gotten there.

Remember, the keys to success are managing the expectations of all constituents and delivering what you promise to maintain credibility; execute as flawlessly as possible and create value for the customer and organization through **flexible discipline.**

6 IT Service Management (ITSM) excellence (execution management)

6.1 What is covered in this chapter?

This chapter:
- explains and reviews the best practice principles and practices for achieving and sustaining IT Service Management (ITSM) excellence
- describes the benefits and drawbacks of ITIL (IT Infrastructure Library)
- reviews the IT Infrastructure Library (ITIL), both versions 2 (v2) and 3 (v3)
- defines how to deploy an ITIL framework in an organization

6.2 Overview

This chapter describes the principles and practices of IT Service Management. It provides an overview of ITIL (IT Infrastructure Library) and the eleven process areas and one function, including the relationships of the various processes to each other, as described in version 2 (v2) of ITIL. Specific objectives, benefits and key performance indicators are covered. It also describes the newest version of ITIL – version 3 (v3) 'IT Service Lifecycle', which was released in 2007. It illustrates a self-assessment maturity model that can be used to assess the current and target the future maturity level of an organization, and suggests a transition plan to get there.

IT Service Management is about maximizing the ability of IT to provide services that are cost effective, and meet or exceed the needs and expectations of the business to:
- reduce the costs of operations
- improve service quality
- improve customer satisfaction
- improve compliance

Figure 6.1 illustrates the benefits of a well executed IT Service Management strategy.

6.3 Principles for achieving IT Service Management excellence

Top concerns of CIOs

A CIO Magazine survey completed in 2006, identified the infrastructure and Service Management as one of the top ten issues CIOs are dealing with (www.cio.com/state):

1. aligning IT strategy with business strategy and governance
2. meeting business and user needs
3. infrastructure and Service Management

Well executed IT Service Management is about optimizing the ability of IT to provide services that are cost-effective and meet the needs of the business.

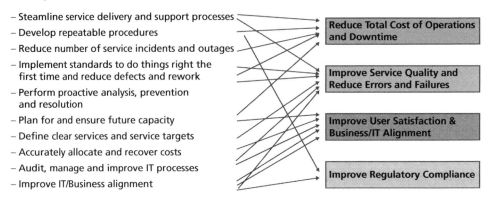

Figure 6.1   Benefits map of IT Service Management

4.   coping with accelerating change
5.   dealing with senior management
6.   managing costs, budgets and resources
7.   keeping up with technology
8.   recruiting and retaining staff
9.   executing projects effectively (time and resource management)
10. maintaining skills and knowledge

Select best practices for achieving superior IT Service Management

Based on a review of best practice companies, a number of consistent practices seem to be prevalent in these organizations regarding superior IT Service Management. They include:

- All steady-state operations (eg PBX, Data Center, Help Desk, Network Management, etc.) must have a primary owner and secondary (backup) owner.
- The overall ITSM budget should be divided into a set of defined products and services, so that all IT costs can be mapped to supportable business processes, either directly or indirectly.
- All IT services should consistently achieve the desired level of efficiency, productivity, reliability and availability, as measured by the appropriate key performance indicators (eg service level agreements, customer satisfaction, costs, etc.).
- Most IT services should be described as processes that are well documented, consistently performed and repeatable to maximize their efficiency.
- Most ITSM services should be charged back to the user or customer organization to achieve a greater level of accountability. This requires an established asset management system, a service level management process and a service catalogue.
- The use of an IT service catalogue that can define, price and provide estimated installation time for repetitive productized IT services (install a new computer or network connection) is growing in use, and can benefit the customer by providing an easy way to select, order and communicate to IT the required services desired by the customer. The service catalogue is only partially applied to complex, one time initiatives that are not repetitive (ie it can be used to quantity associated maintenance costs).

- A formal ITSM governance, reporting and escalation process should be established to resolve key operational issues and risks, and conduct periodic reviews. All steady-state operations have business continuity, back-up (including one or more off-site locations), disaster recovery and security policies and procedures.
- All ITSM related processes should be documented in a consistent, repeatable and standard framework, consisting of life cycles, processes and metrics, such as ITIL (IT Infrastructure Library) or ISO/IEC 20000, and continuously improved.
- Optimizing the utilization of IT assets and resources is critical.

ISO/ IEC 20000 – ITSM standard overview

The standard was originally developed and published in 2000 as BS15000 by a committee of the BSI (British Standards Institution), which comprised of IT service managers from vendor and user groups, including the ITSMF, OGC and others. Version 2 of the standard was developed in 2002. The formal certification scheme for organizations wishing to demonstrate their conformance to the requirements of ISO/ IEC 20000 is currently owned and administered by ITSMF.

ISO/ IEC 20000 applies to IT Service Management users and providers. The standard comprises two parts:

- Part 1 – Specification: This is the documented requirements that an organization must comply with to achieve formal certification against ISO/ EIC 20000.
- Part 2 – Code of Practice: Expansion and explanation of the requirements in Part 1.

Both parts share a common structure which includes the following sections:
- scope
- terms and definitions
- requirements for a management system
- planning and implementing Service Management
- planning and implementing new or changed services
- service delivery processes
- relationship processes
- resolution processes
- control processes
- release processes

There are four kinds of process areas that are all related to the fifth process area, the control processes.

The service delivery processes consist of:
- service level management
- service reporting
- service continuity
- availability management
- budgeting and accounting for IT services
- capacity management
- information security management

The relationship processes are:
- businessrelationship management
- suppliermanagement

The resolution processes are
- incidentmanagement
- problemmanagement

The control processes are:
- configurationmanagement
- changemanagement

The release process is defined as a standalone process.

Each of these process areas are defined in more detail in the ITIL sections of this chapter.

In addition to the formal demonstration of compliance, many organizations use ISO/ EIC 20000 internally, to identify targets of performance to measure themselves against. In this case, although compliance to all elements within the standard is not yet achieved, nonetheless improvements in compliance can be measured, either internally or by use of external consultants, and can also demonstrate period-on-period improvement.

The ISO/ IEC 20000 standard is concerned with IT Service Management and primarily represents a measure of process conformance to be achieved by an organization. In other words, ISO/ IEC 20000 is a corporate standard and its certification applies to organizations, while ITIL focuses on individual certifications.

The relationship between ISO/ IEC 20000 and ITIL is synergistic. The standard addresses the questions relating to IT Service Management as the *'why and what?'* ITIL, on the other hand, complements the standard by addressing the question of *'how?'* and providing the process definitions and other details. Key industry experts have indicated that both ITIL v2 and v3 are consistent with the requirements of ISO/ IEC 20000.

6.4   What is ITIL and why is it different?

History and key elements of ITIL (IT Infrastructure Library)
Initiated by CCTA (the UK Government's Central Computing and Telecommunications Agency – now the OGC – Office of Government Commerce), ITIL represents a systematic approach to the management and delivery of quality IT services. ITIL is vendor neutral, flexible and scalable, and focuses on best practices that can be utilized in different ways, depending on the needs and maturity level of organizations. Major elements of ITIL include:

- The ITIL framework provides an effective foundation for higher quality IT Service Management.

- ITIL consists of repeatable, documented best practice life cycle phases, and key processes based on common terminology essential for more effectively managing and improving IT Service Management. It includes checklists, tasks, procedures and responsibilities.
- ITILaligns with an ISO standard (ISO/ IEC 20000).
- The APM Group (APMG) – In 2006, OGC contracted the management of ITIL rights, the certification of ITIL exams and accreditation criteria to APMG, a commercial organization. APMG defines the certification and accreditation for the ITIL exams, and published the new ITIL version 3 (v3) certification system. In addition, ITIL v3 has been documented as five books. Each book focuses on one of the five phases of the new ITIL v3 IT Service Lifecycle.
- The itSMF (Information Technology Service Management Forum) – was originally established in the UK and the Netherlands in the early 1990s, and has since expanded into over forty-five country chapters, loosely co-ordinated under the umbrella organization, itSMF International (itSMF-I). The organization promotes the IT Service Management profession, and shares information amongst the chapters. itSMF-I promotes the use of ITIL, ISO/ EIC 20000 and other relevant frameworks.
- EXIN (Dutch) and ISEB (UK) are licensed by OGC; EXIN and ISEB co-operate in the development and provisioning of ITIL v2 certifications and other certifications. Both organizations are also contracted by APMG to administer ITIL exams for the ITIL v3 certification.
- Standardizedapproach and terminology
  - standardization of processes and key performance indicators
  - provides the quality assurance foundation for ISO 9001
  - industry supported software and tools
  - supports Sarbanes-Oxley and other regulations

ITIL value proposition – select leading company examples
A growing number of global organizations claimed to have achieved significant benefits with the use of IT (Shaw, 11/7/01, Gartner, 2005):

- **Proctor & Gamble** – started using ITIL about three years ago and realized a 6-8% reduction in IT total cost of operations (TCO).
- **Ontario Justice Enterprise** – embraced ITIL 2.5 years ago and created a virtual help desk that cut support costs by 40%.
- **Caterpillar** – embarked on an ITIL initiative 18 months ago. After applying ITIL principles, the rate of reaching the target response time for incident management on web-related services jumped from 60% to more than 90%.
- **Large global manufacturing company** – due to long problem resolution times and costs, and extended service outages, this organization established an ITSM initiative with an owner who was given the power to enforce. The result was a savings of $30 million over a three year period.
- **Petro Canada** –outsourced its IT infrastructure to multiple outsourcing vendors using ITIL process definitions and terminology. Vendors were required to perform the work on-site and integrate into the in-house process flows (ITIL based). Petro-Canada was better able to manage inter-vendor relationships, co-operation and measurement of service levels and other key performance indicators.

- **Major global consumer goods company** – conducted an external assessment of ITSM maturity and decided to deploy ITIL on a global basis to clarify roles and accountability, standardize the use of processes and tools, and improve compliance.
- **A major beverage company and a major home products company**: ITIL was used as a precursor to get their IT organizations in order, to facilitate the outsourcing of selective IT processes.

Advantages of ITIL to customers, constituents and the IT organization

Using ITIL as part of ITSM provides advantages to the customer, business and the IT organization.

Advantages of ITIL to customer and business

- provision of IT services becomes more customer-focused, and agreements about service quality and adherence to SLAs improve the relationship
- the services are described better, in customer language, and in more appropriate detail (as in an IT Service Catalogue)
- the quality and cost of the services are managed better and more effectively.
- communication with the IT organization is improved, by agreeing to limited points of contact
- provides 'cost' visibility to the customer and a better understanding of TCO (Total Cost of Operations)

Advantages of ITIL to the IT organization

- IT organization develops a clearer structure, improves accountability and documentation; it provides a standardized approach to managing and controlling IT
- change, problem and release management is formalized, authorized and traceable; it facilitates the control of increased scale and complexity of the modern IT organization
- facilitates decisions to outsource select services
- encourages the cultural change and migration towards a more effective and more mature organization
- facilitates SOX and other compliance regulations

Potential issues with ITIL

As with all things, where there are advantages, there are also issues or limitations. These include the following:

- Introduction of ITIL is lengthy and represents a significant cost and resource commitment. IT requires prioritization and agreement on key processes, check lists and accountability for implementation and continuous process improvement.
- Improvement in the provision of services and cost reductions are insufficiently visible and poorly communicated to the customer and the business. Immediate ROI cannot always be demonstrated.
- A successful implementation requires the involvement and commitment of personnel at all levels in the organization
- ITIL v2 and v3 do not represent a framework designed as one coherent model, which most organizations would prefer. Rather, it appears to be a continuum of life cycle phases, processes

and checklists, which represent a guideline of customizable best practices, rather than a prescriptive approach.

6.5   ITIL frameworks, certifications and qualifications

Background

In 2007, the APMG launched a new certification framework for ITIL, based on ITIL version 3 (v3). ITIL version 2 is to be maintained for a transition period, and is to be continued until 2008.

ITIL v3 represents a major revision to ITIL v2. ITIL v3 approaches IT Service Management from a life cycle perspective, and the way in which the various phases and processes are linked and interrelated. In ITIL v2, there are twelve (12) process components of ITIL, segmented into two major areas, namely service delivery and service support. Some of these processes have been retained in v3, others eliminated or combined, while new ones have been added.

ITIL version 3 Service Lifecycle, processes and related activities

The new IT Service Lifecycle consists of five phases (Office of Government Commerce, 2007). These phases are:

- **Service Strategy** – This phase includes the design, development and implementation planning of Service Management as a strategic resource from a macro-perspective. It also monitors the effect of strategies, standards, policy and design decisions.

- **Service Design** - This phase includes the design phase for IT services, including such areas as architecture, processes, policy, suggested metrics, check lists and other documentation. It includes the major processes of service catalogue management, service level management, capacity management, availability management, IT service continuity management, security management and supplier management.

- **Service Transition** – This phase involves the transition of newly developed or acquired hardware, software, network components or other services from development (or acquisition) to operations or a production environment. One of the first things one notices is that service asset and configuration replaces configuration, and release and deployment management seems to replace release management. There are four new Service Transition processes: transition planning and support, service validation and testing, evaluation and knowledge management (Kuhn, 2007). This seems like a significant improvement over the ITIL v2 processes, and in particular, focuses on several key areas of vulnerability for many organizations that have not done a good job of transitioning work from systems development to operations.

- **Service Operation** – This is the phase of achieving effectiveness and efficiency in providing and supporting services, in order to ensure value for the customer and the service provider. Major processes within Service Operation include: event management, incident management, problem management, request fulfillment, access management and monitoring and control of IT operations.

- **Continual Service Improvement** – the phase of creating and maintaining the value for the customer by design improvement, and service introduction and operation

Figure 6.2 shows the ITIL v3 Service Lifecycle. Figure 6.3 maps the relevant ITIL v3 processes and related activities to each of the Lifecycle phases. Many of the processes are also part of ITIL v2 and will be defined in more detail in this chapter.

ITIL Version 3 consists of five(5) phases – Service Strategy, Service Design, Service Transition, Service Operation and Continual Service Improvement. Each Phase consists of Numerous Processes, Functions and Related Activities.

OGC contracted the management of ITIL rights, the certification of ITIL exams and accreditation to APMG. APMG defines the certification and accreditation for the ITIL exams and published the new ITIL Version 3 (v3) certification system.

ITIL v3 has been documented as five books. Each book focuses on one of the five phases of the new v3 IT Service Lifecycle.

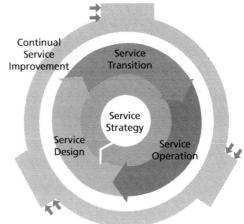

Source: APMG

Figure 6.2   IT Service Management Lifecycle (ITILv3)

ITIL v2 and v3 certification and qualifications

ITIL version 2 has three levels of certification:
- **Foundation Level** - Certificate in IT Service Management
- **Practitioner Level** - Certificate in IT Service Management. There are Practitioner Certificates for various processes or functions from ITIL version 2 (Service Level Management, Capacity Management, etc.) and Practitioner Certificates for clusters of the functions and processes (four clusters: Release & Control, Support & Restore, Agree & Define and Plan & Improve)
- **Manager Level** - Certificate in IT Service Management

For ITIL version 3, a completely new system of qualification was set up. There are four qualification levels:

- **Foundation level** – This level is aimed at basic knowledge of, and insight into, the core principles and processes of ITIL version 3. At this level the qualification remains very similar to the old ITIL version 2 Foundation.

Service Strategy	Service Design*	Service Transition*	Service Operation*	Continual Service Improvement
• Defining the Market – Understand customers – Understand opportunity • Develop Business Case • Develop the Service Plan	• Service Catalogue Management (New in v3) • Service Level Management • Capacity Management • Availability Management • IT Service Continuity Management (ITSCM) • Information Security Management • Supplier Management (New in v3)	• Transition Planning and Support (New in v3) • Change Management • Service Asset and Configuration Management** (Revised for v3) • Release and Deployment Management** (Revised for v3) • Service Validation and Testing Evaluation (New in v3) • Service Knowledge Management (New in v3) • Pilots	• Event Management (New in v3) • Incident Management • Problem Management • Request Fulfillment (Service Desk) (Revised for v3) • Access Management (New in v3) • Monitoring and Control IT Operations (New in v3)	• Defining Cycle: – Plan – Do – Check – Act • Report (Metrics)

*   NOTE: All processes in System Design, Service Transition and Service Operations are the same for v2 and v3, except where it is noted as new for v3.
**   Service Asset and Configuration Management, Release and Deployment Management have been transitioned and enhanced from v2 to v3 with additional processes.

Figure 6.3 – ITIL v3 Service Lifecycle, related processes and select activities

- **Intermediate level**:
  - **Intermediate level 1** – The first middle level is aimed at the Service Lifecycle and is built up around the five core books of ITIL version 3: Service Strategy, Service Design, Service Transition, Service Operation and Continual Service Improvement.
  - **Intermediate level 2** – The second middle level is aimed at capabilities and is built up around four clusters: service portfolio & relationship management, service design & optimization, service monitoring & control and service operation & support.
  - The two middle levels are aimed at an insight into, and application of, the knowledge of ITIL version 3. These levels replace the Practitioner and Manager levels of ITIL version 2.
- **Advanced level** – This level was still under development when this book was being written. It is anticipated that this will test the ability to apply ITIL version 3 principles in a real life situation.

For every element in the scheme, a number of credits can be obtained. Credits are also awarded for the certifications from ITIL v2. Various 'bridge exams' are offered in order to connect version 2 certificates to the version 3 exams.

Figure 6.4 presents the new certification framework and components. The number of credits for each component was not yet finalized when this section was written.

The ITIL version 3 certification framework has been significantly revised to reflect the service lifecycle approach. The new scheme recognizes the value of existing v2 qualifications and introduces a system that enables an individual to gain credits for both ITIL v2 and v3 courses. The ITIL v3 certification will be based on the following structure which will culminate in the award of the ITIL diploma in IT Service Management.

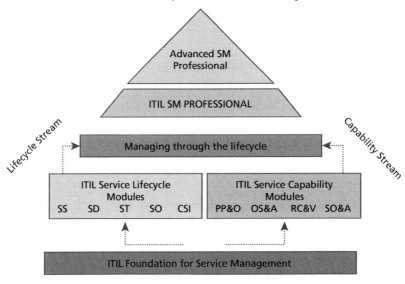

LEGEND

CSI = Continual Service Improvement
PP&O = Planning Protection and Optimization
OS&A = Operational Support and Analysis
RC&V = Release, control and Validation
SD = Service Design

SO = Service Organization
SO&A = Service Offerings and Agreements
SS = Service Strategy
ST = Service Transition

Source: OGC/ APMG

Figure 6.4 – ITIL v3 – qualification and certifications

6.6   Major ITIL processes and functions

Summary of ITIL Service Management processes – v2

There are twelve processes and/or functions defined in ITIL v2. Figure 6.5 identifies these processes and segments them into two groupings – IT service delivery and IT service support. More details of each process or function is provided below, in terms of definition, key benefits, key implications from an IT Service Management perspective and select key performance indicators (KPIs). Most of these processes apply to ITIL v3. Some of them have been combined with others and expanded in scope, while others have been renamed, and others still have been created as new processes.

IT Service Support processes and functions

These processes focus on operational aspects to detect and correct incidents problems, and ensure appropriate change, configuration and release management authorization and documentation.

IT Service Delivery Processes – focus on management control to improve the quality, stability, availability, continuity and IT financial management and cost structure.
IT Service Support Processes – focus on operational aspects to detect and correct problems, and ensure appropriate change, configuration and release management authorization and documentation.

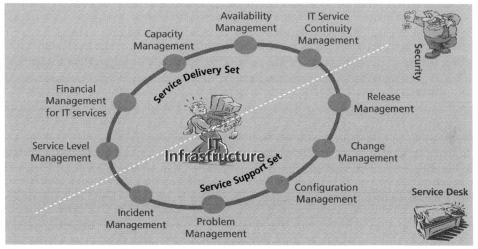

Figure 6.5 – ITIL v2-Service Management processes and functions

Service Desk (Function)

(Part of Request Fulfillment in Service Operations Phase in ITIL v3)

Definition: The Service Desk represents a function and acts as the single point of contact for the management of incidents and problem resolution, and restoration co-ordination to normal operational services with minimal business impact on the customer (inside or outside of the company), within agreed or contracted service levels and business priorities.

Key Benefits:
provides a single point of contact for customer service requests
focuses on service support and reporting of incidents
provides a single point to manage and coordinate incident and problem resolution, co-ordination and communications
maintains a log and record of reported incidents, problems and their resolution in a database
can produce cost reduction through efficient use of resources
promotes customer retention and satisfaction

Key implication: The ITIL based Service Desk becomes the primary source of communication to the end users for service, operational and infrastructure related issues.

Select KPIs: Number of Incidents Reported by Type; Number of Calls Handled per Worker or Workstation; Average Time to Resolve Incidents; Number of Priority Incidents and Response Time; Number of Incidents or Problems Routed to 1st, 2nd or 3rd level of Support; Speed to Respond to Customer and Keep Customer Current on Status of Problem and Its Resolution; etc.

Incident Management

(Part of the Service Operations Phase)

Definition: Defines process for logging, recording and resolving incidents. Restores normal service operation as quickly as possible, and minimizes the adverse impact on business operations, thus ensuring that the best possible levels of service quality and availability are maintained.

Key benefits:
- ensures that incidents are detected and that their impact on the business is known
- ensures the best use of resources to support the business during service failures or disruptions
- works to minimize the time to restore service, and the negative effect on business operations

Key implication:
Incident Management is about doing whatever is necessary to restore service to users when a disruption occurs in order to minimize business impact.

Select KPIs: Total Number of Incidents Reported and Resolved by Type and/or Priority; Average Time to Incident Resolution; Average Cost per Incident; Percent of Closed Incidents.

Problem Management

(Part of the Service Operations Phase)

Definition: A problem is either an unknown underlying cause of one or more incidents, or a known error and for which a work-around has been identified. Problem Management supports Incident Management by providing work arounds and quick fixes, but does not have the responsibility for resolving the incidents

Key benefits:
- places primary focus on root cause analysis and error prevention; not just on service restoration
- ensures better utilization of technical subject matter experts, by enabling them to avoid routine event handling and resolution activities
- supports Fault Management and Service Desk via population of knowledgebase and development of fault/incident work-around procedures

Key implication:
Problem Management should be proactive and focused on prevention, rather than fire-fighting.

Select KPIs: Number of Problems Reported and Resolved by Time and/or Type; Amount of Time/Cost Spent to Fix; Percent of Recurring Problems; Number of Closed Problems by Type of Fix – Permanent, Workaround or Quick Fix; etc.

Configuration Management

(Under Service Knowledge Management Systems that includes Configuration Management Systems that integrate CMDB(s) and Service Assets in the Service Transition Phase)

Definition: Accounts for all of the IT assets (infrastructure) and configuration items (CIs) within the organization and its services, by maintaining, documenting and verifying the configurations and their versions. It provides a sound basis for enabling Incident Management, Problem Management, Change Management and Release Management to be managed effectively.

Key benefits:
- identifiesand records the information required to manage IT services
- ensures that a central repository of configuration information is up-to-date, and accurately reflects the actual infrastructure
- documentsrelationships of IT components to IT services
- improvesthe economic and effective delivery of IT services

Key implication:
Most IT organizations do not have a good understanding of how their infrastructure devices/ components are interrelated or how they support key business processes and functions.

Select KPIs: Incidents/problems traced back to improperly made changes; Cycle time to approve and implement changes; Unauthorized IT components in Infrastructure; Number of Planned versus of Unplanned Changes; Average Cost or Time to Make Change by Type (eg Mandatory, Discretionary, etc.).

Change Management

(Part of the Service Transition Phase)

Definition: The process of controlling changes to improve infrastructure and service with minimum disruption. Ensures that a consistent and repeatable process with the appropriate decision criteria are used to review, fund, prioritize, document and authorize all changes, in order to minimize the impact of change related incidences on service quality, and consequently improve the operational and infrastructure aspects in support of the business.

Key benefits:
- provides governance as to how IT changes are requested, funded, prioritized, assessed, authorized, documented and implemented
- minimizes the number of unauthorized changes, and allows for introduction of change based on business needs

- minimizes risk and disruption caused by failed changes via performance of impact assessments, development of back-out plans, etc.

Key implication:
An effective Change Management process is critical for minimizing IT service disruptions and service level violations caused by unauthorized, unco-ordinated changes to the IT production environment. Scope includes hardware, network, systems, software and 'live' application software.

Select KPIs: Number of Requested Changes; Number of Successful Changes; Number of Pending Changes; Time or Cost of Changes per Change Type.

Release Management

(Combined with Release and Deployment Management in v3 and part of Service Transition Phase)

Definition: Ensures that all technical and non-technical aspects of an authorized release (eg hardware, software, network, application rollouts) and roll-outs are managed in a co-ordinated manner with the appropriate checklists and sign-offs between the appropriate constituents (eg development, architecture, operations, maintenance, vendors, etc.). Release types include: major, minor and emergency fixes.

Key benefits:
- provides a consistent, customer-focused approach to deploying large releases into production
- bundles similar changes together to decrease impact on the business and the workload on IT
- better control on installed hardware and software, leading to reduced costs in licensing and maintenance

Key implication:
Release Management works to bridge the gap between development and operations by ensuring that new/updated services are not just 'thrown over the fence' and formalizes the transfer process from development to production.

Select KPIs: Number of major, minor and emergency releases; Problems attributed to type of release - new, changed or deleted objects.

IT Service Delivery processes
These processes focus on management control to improve the quality, stability, availability, continuity and IT financial management, and cost structure.

Service Level Management

(Part of the Service Design Phase)

Definition: Improves and maintains IT service quality and performance, through a continuous cycle of a monitoring and reporting on IT service key performance indicators and results.

Institutes corrective actions, to eliminate poor service and support business continuity and operating improvements. In ITIL v3, process supports the Service Catalogue Management, by providing information and trends regarding customer satisfaction.

Key benefits:
- ensures customer requirements are known and that services are designed to meet these requirements
- sets forth defined service targets that all IT groups can work towards
- places a focus on service monitoring and improvement to identify and resolve issues
- ensures that IT is focused on the most important areas

Key implication:
Service Level Management should manage through a defined Service Level Agreement or contract that describes what services and corresponding SLAs are available to IT customers, with corresponding rewards and penalties if they are met or missed respectively. Service catalogues list all services, and summarize each service and its key attributes.

Select KPIs: SLAs (depends on what is critical to measure that should be related to CSFs of organization; customer satisfaction surveys; etc.).

Capacity Management

(Part of the Service Design Phase)

Definition: Ensures that all of the current and future infrastructure and operational capacity (eg storage, bandwidth, hardware, etc.) aspects, to satisfy the business requirements is scalable, backed-up and provided in a cost effective manner. It deals with service capacity management in general and the component capacity management.

Key benefits:
- ensures that the existing infrastructure is optimized in terms of capacity when compared to the agreed service targets
- understands the way in which the infrastructure is currently being used and will be used in the future
- works to ensure that future capacity exists to meet business requirements and that it is provided in a cost effective basis

Key implication:
Capacity Management is concerned with both optimizing the current environment and planning for future business requirements.

Select KPIs: Capacity, Volume and Speed Metrics.

Availability Management

(Part of the Service Design Phase)

Definition: Optimizes the capability of the IT infrastructure, services and supporting organization, to deliver a cost effective and sustained level of availability that enables the business to achieve its business objectives.

Key benefits:
- services can be designed to meet target service levels instead of defining the target and then hoping it is possible
- providesa formal way to measure availability of IT services from a user perspective
- over time, can reduce the number and impact of incidents by increasing resilience and reliability

Key implication:
It is a proactive process that strives to ensure that availability targets are reasonable and achievable, and that IT services are designed with this number in mind.

Select KPIs: Rate of availability; Overall uptime and downtime; Number of faults; Mean time to repair; Reasons, duration and impact on business of downtime due to unavailability of appropriate resources.

IT Service Continuity (ITSCM) Management

(Part of the Service Design Phase)

Definition: Supports the overall Business Continuity Management process by ensuring that the required IT technical and service facilities (eg computer systems, networks, applications, technical support and Service Desk) can be recovered within the required and approved timeframes. This also requires the development and maintenance of a back-up, contingency and disaster recovery plan and facilities.

Key benefits:
- decreasesthe cost and impact to the business when a crisis occurs
- improvesthe relationship between IT and the business
- potentiallylower insurance premiums
- abilityto adhere to regulatory requirements
- competitiveadvantage when securing business partners

Key implication:
The IT Service Continuity Plan is a part of the overall Business Continuity Plan, and is focused on the continuity of business critical IT services. ITSCM is focused on technical and operational aspects, and interacts with other ITIL processes (eg Service Level, Availability, Configuration, Capacity and Change Management).

Select KPIs: Lower insurance premiums; Impact and costs of major disruptions and discontinuity.

IT Financial Management

(Part of Service Knowledge Management Systems that include Configuration Management Systems with Service Asset Management and CMDB (Configuration Management Data Base) in v3 and part of the Service Transition Phase)

Definition: Provides cost-effective oversight of the IT assets and resources used in providing IT services, including budgeting, accounting and charging of services.

Key benefits:
- provides accurate cost information to support IT investments
- provides a budget of expected IT costs
- collects and defines the true cost of providing IT services, and allows for accurate accounting of these cost by IT customers
- allows for recovery of costs via charge-back of IT services to customers, and helps in focusing on IT/client priorities

Key implication:
IT organizations are being driven to operate as an Internal Service Provider. This demands that they have mature financial management capabilities and can accurately convey and recover costs for IT services.

Select KPIs: Cost tracking; budgeting; charge backs; asset tracking, value, utilization and retirement.

Information Security Management

(Part of the Service Design Phase)

Definition: Ensures a high (whatever is necessary) level of security, so that the IT infrastructure and services, as well as the business functions they support, are not compromised. ISO 17,799 provides a standard framework for IT security.

Key benefits:
- provides secure policies and procedures to protect infrastructure components
- creates awareness to protect and secure IT resources throughout the organization

Key implication:
IT organizations are being driven to become more secure and protect the information, infrastructure and people resources working in their environments. Security is not really a step in the Lifecycle. Information security is a continual process and is an integral component of all of the services.

Select KPIs: Number of security breaches; Impact/cost of security violations.

Summary of new or modified ITIL Service Management processes in v3

Service Catalogue Management

(Part of Service Design Phase)

Definition: The Service Catalogue Management includes description details and the status of all existing services and business processes they support, as well as those in development. There are two components of the Service Catalogue: 1) The Business Service Catalogue contains the details delivered to the customer. It represents the customer's view and 2) The Technical Service Catalogue expands the Business Service Catalogue with relationships to the supporting services, shared services, components and CIs (configuration items) necessary to support the provision of the service to business (it is not viewable by the customer).

Key benefits:
- simplifies the ordering of IT services from a customer's viewpoint
- provides a consistent description of IT services that can simplify pricing, scheduling and service fulfillment
- sustains a more proactive service level management process and function

Key implication:

It helps customers to interface and request well defined services from IT, in a consistent and effective manner.

Select KPIs: Number of services included in the service catalogue; Number of repetitive services ordered by customers from the catalogue, etc.

Supplier Management

(Part of Service Design Phase)

Definition: Involves the selection, contract management and on-going management of third party service providers.

Key benefits:
- provides a consistent process for dealing with service providers and outsourcing vendors

Key implication: This is a relatively new process within the ITIL suite. Other organizations, such as the International Association of Outsourcing Professionals and Carnegie Mellon's IT Services Qualification Center, already have developed life cycle phases, processes and certification programs for individuals and organizations, respectively.

Select KPIs: SLAs, etc.

Transition Planning and Support

(Part of Service Transition Phase)

This process focuses on plans and co-ordinates the resources to move a new or changed service into production within the projected cost, quality and time estimates. This is not really a new process, since both Release and Change Management, incorporated sections of these activities in their scope. However, the renaming of the process to Transition Planning and Support brings more visibility to an area that has suffered from poor or inadequate management and co-ordination for a long time in IT, namely transitioning either internally or vendor developed systems into IT operations, without the appropriate tests, pilots, documentation, training and acceptance processes.

Service Asset and Configuration Management – (SACM)

(Part of Service Transition Phase)

This new process assumes responsibility for maintaining all secure libraries and stores, such as the Definitive Software Library (DSL) and Definitive Hardware Store (DHS) that Release Management previously maintained.

Release and Deployment Management

(Part of Service Transition Phase)

This process has been renamed from elease management to Release and Deployment Management in v3. It now focuses on the activities of managing releases and deployments into the operational infrastructure. It also introduces the concept of early life support (ELS), which provides additional support to the users and support teams on the release of changes.

Service Validation and Testing

(Part of Service Transition Phase)

Service Validation and Testing represents quality assurance was described in ITIL v2, but was never really addressed. The new process describes the progression of testing and quality control in terms of incremental contributions to business value.

Evaluation

(Part of Service Transition Planning)

ITIT v3 is much more specific than ITIL v2 with this process. It defines how to plan, guide and execute the evaluation process, including such assessment factors as service provider capability, organizational philosophy and management style, resources, modeling, metrics, purpose and use.

Service Knowledge Management Systems (SKMS)

(Part of Service Transition Phase)

Knowledge Management is new in v3, and is important in presenting and using a wealth of knowledge stored and shared in a data base of IT Service Management. Knowledge Management addresses planning the knowledge management strategy, transferring and sharing knowledge throughout the organization, managing information and using Knowledge Management in a service environment. SKMS is supported by configuration management systems and CMDB(s) integrated with asset management.

Event Management and Request Fulfillment

(Includes the Service Desk from v2 and both are part of Service Operations Phase)

These two processes encompass the Service Desk from v2 and expand to include providing support for managing events and IT service requests from the initial request to the completion or resolution of the event or request.

Access Management

(Part of Service Operations Phase)
Access data is now incorporated into the CMDB at the information integration layer of the Service Knowledge Management System. This incorporates some of the security considerations from v2, and expands the security guidelines regarding access to specific information and data bases.

Monitoring and Control IT Operations

(Part of Service Operations Phase)

This new process focuses on the day-to-day management of IT services, including plans, policies, procedures, processes, metrics and status reporting.

Overall, v3 appears to be a substantive improvement over v2, by filling significant gaps with useful and pragmatic content, and much improved emphasis on services (Holub, Junes, 2007). It will be up to each organization to tailor a blend of both v2 and v3 into a best practice for its environment, level of maturity, pain points and other factors.

6.7 Steps in making ITIL real and effective

As with other IT governance improvement initiatives, making ITIL real and sustainable requires a number of steps:

- must have corporate mandate from the top
- must have dedicated and available resources
- identify executive champion and multi-disciplinary team
- do your homework, and educate yourself on current and emerging best practices and trends
- conduct an IT Service Management maturity assessment, using a leading best practice process such as CMMI, to assess and define current and target-state base lines for each ITIL process and function; use these baselines to gauge progress and eventually to support implementation success through process improvement
- analyze assessment results and establish a roadmap to achieve a higher level of ITIL maturity
- must recognize that 90% of an ITSM initiative is a 'culture change', and prepare accordingly for a lengthy and involved period of adjustment
- develop and prioritize a program roadmap – process refinement sequence, benefits realization, timetable, and priorities, etc.
- assign an owner to one or more process areas
- encourage and sponsor ITIL certification for key individuals
- develop and conduct a communication and awareness campaign
- establish a 'web Portal' to communicate progress and disseminate information
- plan for and sustain process improvements, and link to a reward and incentive structure; create a 'Continuous Service Improvement' group to sustain the framework
- do not focus on specific ROI as a gauge of success; use TCO (Total Cost of Operation) as a measure of improvement

ITIL process area maturity level ranking matrix

Figure 6.6 provides an illustration of an ITIL v2 process maturity ranking matrix. It should be used as part of a self-assessment by organizations to determine their level of maturity and expertise in each of the respective ITIL process areas. Once completed, this could suggest where organizations should start or focus in their quest for providing more effective IT services to the organization.

To design and help implement each of the process areas, the following templates or documents should be completed:

- process roles, responsibilities and ownership
- policies
- process workflow
- process activities and work instructions
- templates and report design
- prioritization and escalation attributes and procedures
- closure procedures
- monitoring and control procedures

A framework consisting of twelve repeatable, documented processes for improving IT Service Management and Delivery to reduce costs and improve customer satisfaction, service and compliance

ITIL Process Areas		Existing		Revised/In-Process/Planned	
		Policies and Procedures	Workflow/Processes/Technologies	Policies and Procedures	Workflow/Processes/Technologies
IT Service Support:	Problem Management				
	Release Management				
	Incident Management				
	Service Desk Function				
	Change Management				
	Configuration Management				
IT Service Delivery:	Capacity Management				
	Service Level Management				
	Availability Management				
	Financial (Asset) Management				
	IT Service Continuity Management				
Security Management (Security is part of all processes and functions)					

Note – Matrix may be used to assess level of maturity of ITIL processes (Ranking: 1= Ad Hoc; 5 = Optimized Process)

Figure 6.6   ITIL v2 Process areas: maturity level ranking matrix

- verificationstrategy and audit schedule
- keymetrics
- communicationsplan and notifications

6.8   Case study – global manufacturing company

Figure 6.7 depicts a case study of a large global manufacturing organization, with headquarters outside the United States. They have achieved significant success by deploying ITIL globally, based on a self-assessment study.

6.9   Summary and key take aways

Summary
IT Service Management is complex, and requires dedicated resources and leadership to implement effectively. It helps to transition an organization from chaos to order, from a reactive to a proactive environment, from firefighting (most of the time) to a planned environment (with firefighting some of the time), and from random service efforts to predictable and more cost

Environment & Drivers	Approach

• Annual revenue range - $45 to 55 bn
• Number of Employees – 200,000+
• Number of IT employees – 3,500 – 5,000
• IT spend as a % of revenue – 1.1 to 2.5%
• Conservative management, very financially focused
• Brand management driven
• Decentralized on a regional (geographic) basis
• Think globally, act locally
• Technology used primarily to increase efficiency, reduce costs with limited focus on growth
• Company has primarily grown through acquisitions
• CIOs (corporate and regional) report to CFOs and are not part of the Senior Executive Management Team
• Industry is consolidating both on markets (fewer and larger customers/channels) and manufacturing
	• External assessment of IT maturity was completed with mixed results for each IT governance component (range from beginning of Level 1 to Level 3 in some regions)
	• Regional Business/IT Executive Steering Group – Approves major IT investments across all companies (e.g. >$1.0million) in region to optimize strategy and alignment
	• Each major program/project is steered and monitored by a Program/Project Steering Committee, comprised of Business/IT folks with decision-making rights
	• Corporate and regional CIOs is developing IT policies for adoption and deployment by regional teams to improve effectiveness, efficiency and better control of compliance:
	  – Project Management Policy & process (using PMI's PMBOK and Prince2). Global training is required., but regional have enforcement flexibility
	  – ITIL policies and processes are being developed and deployed in IT Operations on a consistent basis globally, with an initial focus on 6 process areas
	  – IT architecture and security is consistent applied global
	  – People skills, competency & career choices model in-process

Issues and/or Problems	**Results – Alignment**
• Consolidate data centers by region to further reduce costs • Balance investments to support growth while integrating and streamlining the back office IT operational resources • Two levels of steering (regional and business unit) is being simplified to one to simplify one face to customer • Lack of consistent IT policies, practices and standards • Limited compliance documentation and limited sustainability	• IT/Business Investment Steering Committee significantly improved closer alignment • Established Single Point of Contact between IT and Business Units for Requirements and Priorities • Alignment has improved significantly, but requirements seem to be always greater than available resources (resource management allocation is being addressed organizationally and being enables with technology)
Results - Program/Project Management	**Results – Performance Management**

• PM training for all IT folks was mandated by the Corporate CIO
• While a consistent and uniform PM policy and process was developed based on industry standards, each region is empowered to implement based on their environment and culture – some regions are more disciplined than others.
• Major project metrics monitored include schedule, cost, quality, number of open issues and customer satisfaction
	• Key performance indicators for IT are:
	  – Costs and headcount for IT budget (pressure to constantly reduce is continuous)
	  – Major projects, which represent 50-70% of the IT resources are tracked closely based on cost, schedule, resources and high risks. Minor projects are much less rigorously managed
	  – IT Service Management uses several tools to track and report a variety of dashboard & key performance indicators (e.g. SLAs, asset utilization, men time to repair incidents, etc.)

Figure 6.7   Case study - global manufacturing company

Results - IT Service Management & Delivery	Critical Success Factors
• ITIL is being adopted as the process standard for IT operations and infrastructure. • Six ITIL processes have been implemented (e.g. change mgt., configuration mgt., service level mgt., release mgt., incident mgt. & problem mgt.) • Corporate and regional 'Centers of Excellence' have been formed to develop, adopt, train and deploy ITIL within their region. • The initiative was launched has been a success	• Global CIO sponsorship of consistent global processes and term definitions for Project Management, ITIL and Security, which are deployed with regional and local flexibility • Clearly defined roles and responsibilities for global and regional IT organizations • Mandated education and training in these areas • Sponsor and reward applicable industry certifications • Use outside consultants to fill gaps and get started
Lessons Learned	
• Management style in each region will determine the level and degree of IT governance enforcement • Conduct an assessment of IT maturity levels, based on industry best practices, for each governance area, identify gaps and develop a plan to fill gaps • Large, complex and highly visible programs and projects are tightly controlled, while others are controlled based on the discretion of the Project Board and project Manager for the project • Conduct a detailed post-mortem on completed or challenged projects and record lesson learned.	

Figure 6.7   Case study - global manufacturing company (Cont'd)

effective service quality. An IT Service Management initiative does not end after the framework has been implemented. IT must be continually monitored, maintained and improved. ITIL consists of a repository of five books of best practices that can guide an organization's people, processes and technology towards a common objective of delivering IT service excellence.

ITIL, much as any other IT governance framework, represents a journey that is based on a combination of formal life cycle phases, processes and checklists, combined with common sense and managing change proactively. Each organization can tailor ITIL to fit its environment, culture, resources and level of maturity.

Key take aways

• IT Service Management puts a heavy emphasis on the importance of the Service Lifecycle, and the implementation and improvement of key process areas.
• It is important to identify priorities and critical success factors.
• Processes should be well defined, documented, define organizational interfaces, and be scalable, flexible and measurable.
• Roles and responsibilities should be well defined with respect to each ITSM function and process.
• Leverage tools should support and enable the efficient management of ITSM processes.
• It is important to measure and communicate life cycle and process refinement progress, as well as financial and service improvement benefits.

7 Strategic sourcing, outsourcing and vendor management excellence

"It is not the strongest among the species that survive, nor is it the most intelligent. It's those that are most adaptive to change."

- Charles Darwin

"US firms have begun to ship millions of knowledge jobs to foreign shores, where labor is an irresistible bargain and will probably remain so for a generation or probably longer."

- Doug Brown and Scott Wilson, 2005

7.1 What is covered in this chapter?

This chapter:
- discusses major strategic sourcing and outsourcing definitions, trends, opportunities, issues and challenges
- reviews the strategic sourcing business case process and contents, and identifies build versus buy criteria
- describes the outsourcing end-to-end life cycle process, stages, key deliverables and 'go/no-go' criteria and identifies why and what organization's outsource
- describes the vendor selection, evaluation, contract negotiations and award process
- discusses how to manage the outsourcing relationship, governance process, key metrics, and escalation model
- identifies steps in making outsourcing real

7.2 Overview

According to James Brian Quinn of Dartmouth College, *"outsourcing is one of the greatest organizational and industry structure shifts of the 21st century"* (Quinn, 2000).

Strategic IT sourcing, outsourcing and vendor management is part of execution management, and, due to its growth, has become a critical component of IT governance. Halvey and Melby, stated in their book on IT outsourcing, *"virtually every Fortune 500 company in this country, and an increasing number of companies throughout the world, outsource some significant portion of their IT services"* (Halvey and Melby, 2005).

According to a blend of International Data Corporation and Gartner estimates, the IT outsourcing business will exceed $1.0 trillion by 2008-09. This does not include other outsourcing services, such as business process outsourcing, legal, accounting, manufacturing, customer services, medical, administrative services and many others.

Again, it is not the intention of this chapter to rehash what has already been published, but rather to provide a blend of pragmatic and actionable checklists, techniques, lessons learned and critical success factors, based on current and emerging outsourcing best practices, to help organizations plan, negotiate, deploy and manage successful outsourcing deals and relationships.

Strategic sourcing and outsourcing definitions

According to the International Association of Outsourcing Professionals (IAOP) outsourcing is a long-term, results-oriented business relationship with a specialized third party services provider that can be strategic and transformational or tactical or both (IAOP, May, 2007):

- **Strategic or transformational sourcing** – assets and processes are transferred to service providers and/or core competencies are supplemented by service providers' centers of excellence (eg R & D, Product Design/Development, etc.). This represents a business focus, and is all about creating value; it aligns with the business processes that change in line with strategic business goals and objectives, and is based on the creation of a 'win-win' partnership between the customer and the service provider.

- **Tactical outsourcing** – can include staff supplementation and easily scalable IT services, such as additional web server or application services provider (ASP) capacity, where there are no asset transfers. These are often linked to specific problems or opportunities in a company with an operational focus, and are all about adding resources or capacity for a limited time period.

Other terms that are associated with outsourcing include:

- **Onshore (Home Country) outsourcing** – obtaining services from an external source in your home country
- **Rural outsourcing** – variation of home country outsourcing, where an organization obtains the services of an external source in a rural area of the home country, where the service is usually less expensive than in an urban part of the country
- **Near - shore outsourcing** – refers to a service provider located in a country which is near to your home country, often one that shares a border. Canada or Mexico are near – shore countries for US-based customers
- **Offshore outsourcing** – refers to contracting with a company that is geographically distant, like India, Ireland, China, Philippines, Israel and Rumania, where an ocean separates the countries
- **Best - shore outsourcing** – a recently coined term that describes the 'shore' that offers the best 'deal' for the customer

In addition to the IAOP, another excellent reference for client and service provider outsourcing best practice frameworks, processes and tools was developed by a consortium led by Carnegie Mellon University's Information Technology Services Qualification Center (ITSqc). ITSqc published two documents, one of which is the eSourcing Capability Model for Service Providers; the other is the eSourcing Capability Model for Client Organizations. Both are referenced in more detail in Chapter 2.

Major outsourcing trends and challenges

There are a number of trends and challenges associated with outsourcing. In a special report on outsourcing, *Business Week* identified two of the major trends: the modular corporation and outsourcing 'going global'. Figure 7.1 identifies the modular corporation and estimates the dollar value of the largest outsourcing areas that organizations have outsourced in 2005 (Business Week, January 30, 2006). At that time, the largest outsourcing segments were in manufacturing, logistics and information technology.

Leading to What Some Have Called the Modular Corporation, the Estimated Value of the Outsourced Functions = $546 bn+ in 2005.

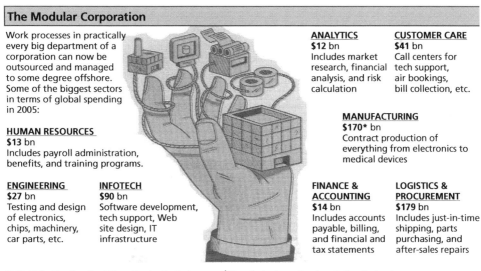

The Modular Corporation

Work processes in practically every big department of a corporation can now be outsourced and managed to some degree offshore. Some of the biggest sectors in terms of global spending in 2005:

HUMAN RESOURCES
$13 bn
Includes payroll administration, benefits, and training programs.

ENGINEERING
$27 bn
Testing and design of electronics, chips, machinery, car parts, etc.

INFOTECH
$90 bn
Software development, tech support, Web site design, IT infrastructure

ANALYTICS
$12 bn
Includes market research, financial analysis, and risk calculation

CUSTOMER CARE
$41 bn
Call centers for tech support, air bookings, bill collection, etc.

MANUFACTURING
$170* bn
Contract production of everything from electronics to medical devices

FINANCE & ACCOUNTING
$14 bn
Includes accounts payable, billing, and financial and tax statements

LOGISTICS & PROCUREMENT
$179 bn
Includes just-in-time shipping, parts purchasing, and after-sales repairs

Data: IDC estimates. Analytics estimates by Evalueserve *Manufacturing estimate only for electronics
January 30, 2006 | **Business Week** | 55

Figure 7.1   The modular corporation

The *Business Week* article goes on to suggest that the outsourcing industry has become global, with India still in the lead in the offshore services area, and other regions and countries becoming much more active in gaining entry in the industry. Figure 7.2 provides examples of these regions, select countries and service providers.

Other major outsourcing trends and challenges include:

- Market trends in contracting are changing - total contract value and duration is trending lower, based on traditional outsourcing contracts, and is spread across a limited number of preferred service providers by customers.
- Customers are increasingly going with strategic sourcing specialists such as IT, business process outsourcing, human resources, finance and accounting.
- Business process and knowledge management outsourcing is growing faster than IT.
- Customers are placing increased pressure on service providers to be certified or licensed (eg ISO 9000, SEI's CMMI, PMI's PMP, ITIL, CPA, ISO 17799, CSSP, etc.).

Outsourcing Goes Global			
India still dominates services offshoring, with three-fifths of total industry revenues, but other countries around the world are trying to hone in on the lucrative work			
REGION	**CENTRAL AND EASTERN EUROPE**	**CHINA AND SOUTHEAST ASIA**	**LATIN AMERICA AND CARIBBEAN**	**MIDDLE EAST AND AFRICA**
Market Size	$3.3 bn	$3.1 bn	$2.9 bn	$425 m
Top-Ranked* Countries	Czech Republic, Bulgaria, Slovakia, Poland, Hungary	China, Malaysia, Philippines, Singapore, Thailand	Chile, Brazil, Mexico, Costa Rica, Argentina	Egypt, Jordan, United Arab Emirates, Ghana, Tunisia
Up-and-Comers	Romania, Russia, Ukraine, Belarus	Indonesia, Vietnam, Sri Lanka	Jamaica, Panama, Nicaragua, Colombia	South Africa, Israel, Turkey, Morocco
Emerging Local Providers	Luxoft (Russia), EPAM Systems (Belarus), Softline (Ukraine), DataArt (Russia)	NCS (Singapore), Bluem, Neusoft Group, BroadenGate Systems (China	Softtek (Mexico), Neoris (Mexico), Politec (Brazil), DBAccess (Venezuela)	Xceed (Egypt), Ness Technologies (Israel), Jeraisy Group (Saudi Arabia)

Data: Gartner, A.T. Keamey, Nasscom, *BusinessWeek*

*Rankings by A.T. Keamey list countries in order of attractiveness for outsourcing based on costs, people skills, and business environment (Source: A.T. Keamey Global Services Location Index 2005)

Figure 7.2   Outsourcing is a global reality

- Outsourcing can be challenging - according to a Deloitte Consulting Survey of 25 large companies, 70% have had negative experiences and have brought some outsourcing work back in-house, for the following reasons (Deloitte, December, 2005):
  - improved quality/management by in-sourcing – 65%
  - functions being outsourced became strategic/core – 44%
  - increased cost savings by in-sourcing – 33%
  - vendor inflexibility – 11%
- Additional lessons from the study included the trend that firms tend to switch from being cost-focused to being growth-focused as the economy grows, and outsourcing is increasingly becoming an issue of business strategy. Alternatives that must be evaluated are not only cost reduction benefits, but also improved innovation techniques.
- According to a recent Forrester Research report on outsourcing with over 100 organizations:
  - 53% reported that they have outsourcing challenges because their companies lacked or were weak in project management skills and competencies for managing outsourcing work
  - 58% reported that they lacked a good process for specifying the work
  - 48% said they did not have the right metrics for measuring adequate service provider performance metrics

Why do organizations outsource?

There are many reasons why organizations choose to outsource or in-source, or deploy a combination of both strategies. Figure 7.3 provides a list of outsourcing (or buy) and in-sourcing (or build) motivations.

BUY (OUTSOURCING) CRITERIA	BUILD (IN-SOURCING) CRITERIA
Cost Reduction	Competitive advantage (proprietary requirements)
Speed up time-to-market	Expertise available in-house
Assist a rapid growth situation or overflow situations	May be less expensive than buying
Aggressive Schedule	Can be completed on time
Politically correct	Opportunity costs trade-offs
Lower risk	No suitable vendors available
Improve flexibility	Core competency
Acquire new skills/resources/management	Security and control are critical
Avoid major capital investments	Strategic initiative or function or process
Improve performance	Threat to intellectual property theft
Enable innovation	

Figure 7.3   Outsourcing motivations – build versus buy

What do organizations outsource?

Today, virtually any IT functions can be outsourced such as:

- **IT architecture** – includes database management, data architecture, etc.
- **IT infrastructure** – elements of the IT infrastructure include computer center, network management and operations, help desk operations, data entry, hardware maintenance and service, etc.
- **Systems and software development and maintenance** – coding, testing, integration, maintenance, etc.
- **Web development and hosting** – e-commerce front end, middleware and backend systems
- **Training, education and certification** – IT, customer and management personnel

Examples of recent IT and other outsourcing deals demonstrate the extent to which select companies outsource both core functions and non-core functions or processes:

- Brokerage firm – outsourced data center and network operations
- Computer manufacturer – outsourced assembly of its PCs and call center
- Medical office – outsourced transcription of doctor's voice recording notes on a patient off-shore
- Bank – outsourced customer service center and IT help desk
- Pharmaceutical company – outsourced manufacture of product
- University – hired a service provider to manage its entire IT function and transferred all IT assets to the service provider
- Architecture firm – outsourced design and blueprints of buildings to eastern Europe
- Airplane manufacturer – outsourced the manufacture of different components to strategic partner vendors in different countries with large market potential
- Retail firm – outsourced their payroll and select accounting functions
- Consulting firm – outsourced the design, development and maintenance of their website
- Law firm – experimenting with outsourcing legal research off-shore for US clients

All of the above demonstrate the way in which we now operate in a global economy, and doing business in developing and emerging countries is part of the model. It is always useful to start with a business model evaluation of the outsourcing opportunity, and then an assessment of what is core and non-core to IT, and what can be supplemented by global service provider resources. As an example, a large telecommunications company uses offshore locations in India and Brazil to promote a 'follow-the-sun-model' for IT testing and production support.

Benefits of outsourcing from a customer and service provider perspective

There are many benefits to outsourcing from a customer's perspective. They include:

- enables business to focus on strategic functions
- lowers annual operating costs and capital investments
- frees up time and resources (opportunity costs) to focus on core strengths
- increases speed to market
- provides access to scarce or supplementary resources
- capital infusion (depending on what is outsourced) for assets that are transferred
- more politically acceptable in certain situations, if the in-house function does not have a good reputation
- provides scalable resources and bench strength
- enables greater innovation
- improves productivity and quality through individual or company certifications

There are also benefits and market realities from a service provider perspective, such as:

- substantial revenue stream potential and growing global market
- long-term customer relationships, with opportunities for cross-selling and up-selling other products and services
- Increasingly, customers are going with a limited number strategic sourcing specialist to develop longer term relationships and negotiate better deals

Barriers to and risks of outsourcing

While there are many good reasons to outsource, there are also barriers and risks that need to be overcome or mitigated, especially in dealing with off-shore deals. Select obstacles and risks are:

- loss of control of confidential information
- function or process is too critical to outsource
- loss of flexibility due to inflexible contracts
- negative customer reaction
- employee resistance due to job loss or transfer
- poor outsourcing process or management
- service provider failure
- lack of intellectual property protection
- differences in culture and time zones relating to offshore deals
- regulatory and legal country differences
- lack of security and data protection

- legaland arbitration adjudication and dispute settlement
- off-shordbribery or 'baksheesh'

The information technology balancing dilemma

In most companies, IT needs to balance its resources between minimizing the total cost of operations, while maximizing its use to help the companies achieve solid growth, innovation and competitive advantage. Outsourcing can facilitate this balancing act. Figure 7.4 illustrates that outsourcing can contribute, both to the cost reduction, containment and avoidance side, as well as to increasing the value of an organization, by allowing the organization to focus on core competencies, innovations and other revenue generating functions.

Outsourcing can Help to Reduce Total Cost of Operations (TCO) while Maximizing its Use to Achieve Growth and Competitive Advantage

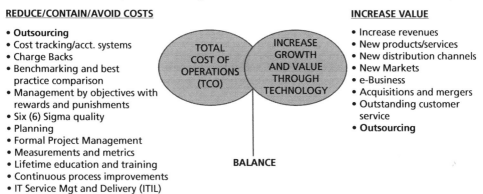

REDUCE/CONTAIN/AVOID COSTS

- **Outsourcing**
- Cost tracking/acct. systems
- Charge Backs
- Benchmarking and best practice comparison
- Management by objectives with rewards and punishments
- Six (6) Sigma quality
- Planning
- Formal Project Management
- Measurements and metrics
- Lifetime education and training
- Continuous process improvements
- IT Service Mgt and Delivery (ITIL)

INCREASE VALUE

- Increase revenues
- New products/services
- New distribution channels
- New Markets
- e-Business
- Acquisitions and mergers
- Outstanding customer service
- **Outsourcing**

Figure 7.4   The information technology balancing dilemma

7.3   Principles and practices for outsourcing excellence from a customer perspective

Even with the increased outsourcing initiatives in customer organizations, it appears that organizations continue to struggle with establishing and enforcing a more formal, consistent and repeatable outsourcing policy, process and methodology.

According to the ITsqc at Carnegie Mellon University, *"managing and meeting client expectations is a major challenge for service providers in these business relationships, and examples of failures abound"* (Hefley and Locsche, 2006).

They go on to summarize the key issues faced by customer organizations, which are also re-enforced and supplemented by the IAOP in their outsourcing body of knowledge (IAOP, 2006):

- establishingan appropriate outsourcing strategy, business case and plan
- identifyingthe appropriate outsourcing opportunities

- developing appropriate approaches and techniques for outsourcing activities
- identifying selecting and negotiating 'win-win' deal service providers
- managing service provider governance and performance management
- managing the transition from the customer to the service provider as a project (see Chapter 5)
- managing the on-going relationship

Based on an extensive review of the literature and select case studies, there are a number of best practice principles and practices that can represent a checklist, for helping companies achieve improvements and higher levels of outsourcing maturity and effectiveness in their environments.

Key principles and practices for outsourcing excellence

General:
- have a clear strategy and plan that supports the business:
  - what are you expecting to achieve and what would success look like?
  - at what cost?
- the clarity of purpose for both sides with defined roles and responsibilities
- establish key performance measures that are realistic and meaningful
- empowerment - let people do what they are suppose to do – hold them accountable, both on the service provider and customer side
- have an escalation policy and process, with clear roles and responsibilities for both sides
- periodic, formal progress reviews and reports, based on specific metrics relating to the type of outsourcing service or project
- for large initiatives, establish a high level peer outsourcing governance board for joint reviews
- assign a service provider account relationship manager as a single point of contact/interface with the customer, and establish a customer/service provider relationship model
- keep closer tabs on the relationship during first 90 days of a contract, and make any necessary adjustments fast

Customer do's:

Key customer 'to do's' should include:

- executive alignment and commitment to outsourcing that creates a favorable outsourcing culture within the organization
- create a well defined and realistic business case process and case
- establish a consistent and formal process for service provider selection and contract negotiations
- develop an outsourcing transition plan from pilot to full implementation provision, for either re-deployment or termination of displaced resources
- build key performance indicators into the contract performance evaluation system, with both rewards for extra-ordinary performance and penalties for poor performance
- make KPIs relevant, simple, comparable, easy to report and focused on measurable outcomes
- develop an outsourcing communication plan, risk management and mitigation plan, policy and process

- balance stakeholder needs – companies that successfully outsource continuously 'take the pulse' of all stakeholder groups, to adjust their needs over time
- pursue stakeholder involvement on major outsourcing deals through governance boards, steering committees and working committees
- manage the expectations of all stakeholders well – deliver what you promise; do not over-promise things you or the outsourcing service provider cannot deliver – credibility is a fleeting attribute that if lost, is extremely difficult or almost impossible to regain
- experience matters – governance groups can rapidly fill their experience deficit through subject matter expert coaching or outside consulting support
- SLAs are not enough – service-level agreements are extremely important and should be continuously refined and improved over the life of the contract; however, they must be augmented by other methods to ensure customer satisfaction (eg formal and/or informal surveys, listening to the voice of the customer, etc.)
- develop disengagement options and conditions as part of the contract that includes renegotiations options
- make sure that a disaster prevention and recovery plan with contingencies is in place

"The buyer needs a hundred eyes, the seller not one."

- Jacula Prudentum, Circa 1500

Avoiding the major sins of outsourcing

For every 'do', there is a 'don't'. These include the following:

- lack of executive management commitment
- lack of an outsourcing communications plan
- minimum knowledge of outsourcing processes and techniques
- failure to recognize outsourcing risks
- failure to obtain assistance from outside outsourcing experts and professionals
- not dedicating the best and brightest internal resources
- rushing through the outsourcing requirements, scope, RFP and vendor selection and contract phases
- not recognizing the impact of cultural differences
- underestimating what it will take to get the vendor to become productive
- no formal outsourcing governance program
- do not put all of your eggs in one service provider's basket; split the work or designate a primary and secondary service provider for back-up purposes
- do not de-skill by outsourcing all of an organizations knowledge and experience in particular areas, so that one becomes overly or dangerously dependent on the service provider

Customer's outsourcing planning checklist

It is always useful to have a checklist as a reminder of the activities that should be considered. The following provides such a checklist for outsourcing:

- executive sponsor (s)
- charter define boundaries

- appoint an outsourcing project team and manager – pre – outsourcing stage and post-outsourcing stage (if outsourcing is pursued)
- project scope and requirements
- assumptions, obstacles and constraints
- core and non-core competencies
- critical success factors
- business case (cost/benefit analysis, including impact on current employees and unions, where applicable)
- communications plan
- work breakdown structure
- roles and responsibilities – customer and service provider
- resource plan
- risk management and contingency plan
- procurement and contracting plan
- service provider selection and evaluation criteria, with a consistent weighting scheme
- quality plan
- governance plan, escalation and key metrics
- project or service schedule and deliverables
- change management plan
- implementation, conversion and transition plan
- disengagement plan
- develop a list of qualified service providers for consideration

Outsourcing life cycle

Outsourcing initiatives, like projects, have life cycles with phases or stages or both. The following examples are provided by the IAOP and the ITesq respectively.

Stages of outsourcing life cycle and 'go/go no' criteria

As part of their Outsourcing Professional Body of Knowledge (OPBOK®), the IAOP has defined five stages of outsourcing as follows (IAOP, 2006):

- **Idea stage** - which outsourcing opportunities are appropriate in support of the organization's business strategy?
- **Assessment and planning stage** - with the development of the business case and of the provider marketplace, are the anticipated benefits, indeed, real?
- **Implementation stage** - can we reach agreement on a deal with one or more of the service providers?
- **Transition stage** - can we execute successfully?
- **Management (operating) stage** - with the transition complete, are we ready to operate under the new agreement? Are the benefits being realized?

Figure 7.5 illustrates the five stages.

Figure 7.6 summarizes the key deliverable and 'go/no' go criteria, by outsourcing stage.

The five stages of outsourcing include: idea, assessment and planning, implementation, transitions and management (ongoing).

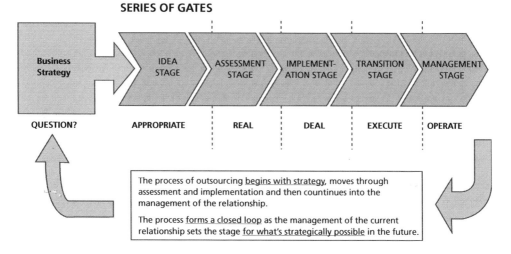

Source: IAOP

Figure 7.5   Five stages of outsourcing

Stage	Idea	Assessment & Planning	Implementation	Transition	Management
Deliverables	• Develop Concept • Perform High Level Review of Operations • Identify corporate direction • Perform Situation Analysis & Identify Outsourcing Opportunity • Get executive sponsor • Assign Steering Comm.	• Analyze current processes & functions • Define proposed processes & functions • Define user needs • Perform risk analysis • Develop business case (with plan)	• Issue RFP • Finalize deal structure and terms • Develop and negotiate contract • Develop human resource and asset transfer plan • Communications Plan • Governance plan	• Detailed transition plan (with pilot) • Implement new organization structure • Transfer people, assets, functions and/or processes • Develop training plan • Outplacement plan and arrangements of personnel	• Perform daily management activities • Monitor performance • Implement relationship management process • Institute change management process
Go/No Go Criteria	Appropriate? • Alignment with business strategy? • Core competency? • High level cost/benefit acceptable? • Acceptable risk? • Competitive advantage? • Legal, ethical, etc.?	Real? • Acceptable business case? • Acceptable risk? • Acceptable reward/ risk analysis?	Deal? • Approved/ signed contract?	Execute? • Approved transition plan? • Approved pilot? • Monitor progress during transition and fix issues as necessary • Defined roles and responsibilities for all transition tasks	Operate? • Governance and Metrics Being Met? • Renew, Expand, or Disengage?

Figure 7.6   Key deliverables and 'go/no go' decision criteria by outsourcing stage

Sourcing life cycle

Another outsourcing life cycle alternative has been developed and documented by the ITesq. A summary of the life cycle phases include:

- **On-going management phase** - spans the entire outsourcing life cycle
- **Initiation phase** – includes business case, vendor selection, negotiation, contracting and deployment planning
- **Delivery phase** - involves the transition to the service provider or provision of the service provider's deliverables
- **Completion phase** – extends the contract or re-insources the functions, processes or services

Steps in making outsourcing real

The following steps will help to make outsourcing deals real:

- identify executive champion and multi-disciplinary team
- do your homework – educate yourself on current and emerging best practices
- understand current state of organization's level of outsourcing maturity and gaps
- use a formal procurement process with Requests for Information (RFIs), Requests for Quote (RFQs) and Requests for Proposal (RFPs)
- determine the critical factors to be used for service provider selection and evaluation
- negotiate a fair contract for both parties
- develop a transition plan with clear roles and responsibilities
- appoint a senior manager accountable for the results:
  - manage relationship
  - manage contract
  - manage governance, risk and issues escalation
- monitor key performance indicators and resolve issues quickly on a regular basis
- treat the outsourcing work package as part of your company's IT services or projects, and manage the work accordingly

7.4   Vendor selection, contract negotiations and governance process

Steps in vendor selection and RFIs, RFQs and RFPs

There are a number of steps that, if followed will facilitate the vendor selection and negotiations process. These assume that an outsourcing business case has been completed and approved.

- convene the project manager and vendor selection team
- identify appropriate and qualified vendors
- set a realistic schedule
- define vendor evaluation criteria and weights before issuing bid requests (to maintain objectivity)
- prepare requests for proposal (RFPs); if necessary or desired, an RFI and an RFQ
- evaluate the bids

- conduct a due diligence investigation on the most likely service provider(s) to be selected; visit the vendor locations and interview the people who will be doing the work
- negotiate the deal
- select a vendor
- sign the contract

Figure 7.7 identifies the vendor selection, evaluation, contract negotiations and award process flow.

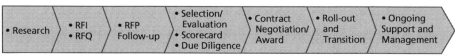

- Internal/external vendor research(assumes that business case has been approved)
- Evaluation criteria

  - RFI/RFQ/RFP focused on services, infrastructure, technology skills, processes, HR policies, governance and metrics

    - Vendor presentations; reference checks; site visits; due diligence investigation

      - Debriefing sessions; Bidder's Conference
      - Weighted Scorecard

        - Contract strategy, type & negotiations
        - Transition planning

          - Governance and metrics
          - Operating and relationship model/roles
          - Disengagement Considerations

Figure 7.7   Vendor selection, evaluation, contract negotiations and award process flow

Figure 7.8 defines the purpose and lists the major content categories for the Request for Information (RFI), Request for Quote (RFQ) and Request for Proposal (RFP):

Vendor evaluation criteria and weights

While companies may use different criteria, and assign different weights for selection criteria, it is nevertheless important that within a given organization, the criteria and weights are consistently applied on a basis which is as objective as possible. Figure 7.9 lists a number of vendor evaluation criteria, organized by four major weighted categories, including demonstrated competencies, total capabilities, fit and competitiveness of solution and relationship fit and dynamics.

Key contract negotiation pointers

The customer's negotiation team should include:

- procurement staff expert in dealing with technology vendors
- legal staff with contract expertise
- outsourcing project manager and relationship manager (if not the same)
- senior management representative
- subject area experts brought in to advise the core team as needed (financial staff, technical staff, end users)

Provide formal request for information, quotation and proposals from customer to service provider.

Request for Information (RFI)
The RFI is used to collect information (business, financial, product, service, other etc.) about companies.

Desired Information:

Company Profile
Products and Services – Current and Future Research and Development Focus and Funding
Financial Stability (Growing or Shrinking)
Plans and Direction
Customer Base and References
Key Players in Organization
Number of Locations and Strategic Alliances
Service, Support and Training Facilities and Resources
Pre-Installation and Post-Installation
Support, Maintenance and Service
+++
Provide formal request for information, quotation and proposals from customer to service provider.

Request for Quote (RFQ)
The RFQ is primarily used to solicit pricing and/or cost information from vendors.

Desired Information:

Requirements and Deliverables (from RFP or high level prior to RFP)
Contract Type, Terms and Special Conditions
Pricing and Discounts
Change Criteria and Their Impact on Pricing
Payment Terms
+++
RFPs provide formal request for information, quotation and proposals from customer to service provider.

Request for Proposal (RFP)
The RFP is used to define the buyer's requirements, scope, objectives and deliverables in order for the vendor to provide a proposal to supply the product or service for evaluation by the buyer .

Desired Information:

Background
Objectives and Scope
General/Detailed Requirements
Functions, Features and Performance Criteria
Standards and regulatory compliance
Constraints – Time, Business, Technical, Other
Governance, Reporting and Dispute Escalation
Customer/Vendor Contacts
Backup, Recovery and Contingency Plans
Vendor's quality assurance and risk mitigation plans
Detailed schedule of deliverables
Insurance
Contract Information and type
Contract Clauses – Discretionary or Mandatory clauses
Recourse, Remedies and Warranty
Pricing
Change Management
Acceptance Criteria
Disengagement Conditions and Responsibilities
+++

Figure 7.8   RFIs, RFQs and RFPs

Demonstrated Competencies – 20% (Weight)	Competitiveness of Solution – 40%
– People (Recruitment, Training, Experience) – Processes (Benchmarking, Certification, Continuous Improvement) – Technologies (Level of Investment, Leading Edge) – Experience (Functional, Industry) – Proven Performance & Certifications – Track Record of Innovation	– Solution itself (Fit to Requirements, Innovative) – Service Delivery (Quality of Processes/Tools/ Resources, Performance, Management Depth and Capabilities) – Risks and Risk Sharing – Financial Proposal (Pricing, Volume Considerations, Structure, Switching Costs) – Terms and Conditions (Commercial, Change, Dispute, Adjudication) – Human Resources Requirements (Employee Transition, Career Opportunities)
Vendor Capabilities – 10%	Relationship Dynamics – 30%
– Financial Strength and Stability – Infrastructure and Resources (Bench Strength, Weaknesses/Points of Failure) – Management Systems – Complete Suite of Services (Type and Scope, Ability to Scale, Backup, Redundancy, Security, IP protection, etc.)	– Culture – Mission and Strategy – Relationship Management (Flexibility, Partnership, Trust, Executive Presence, Governance and Reporting) – Relative Importance (Size, as a Client) – Achievement (esp. existing relationship)

Source: IAOP; Weights for each evaluation component will vary by organization.

Figure 7.9   Scoring and selecting potential vendors

There are many legal terms and conditions that are omitted from the following negotiations list. Key outsourcing contract negotiation pointers should be able to validate in writing:

- scope, requirements, deliverables and schedule
- create a mutual understanding of 'in scope'; define a process for 'out-of-scope' requests and formal charge request
- financial and legal arrangements – payments, discounts, rewards and penalties, pricing formulas and changes; insurance, taxes, foreign exchange, indemnities, liability limitations, escrow, ownership and consequential damages
- acceptance criteria - quantitative and qualitative criteria
- metrics and service criteria - volume, capacity, speed, performance, quality documentation, training, mean time to repair, schedule, budget, program/project, etc.; consider metrics in three different areas:
  - outcome and performance based metrics (eg volume, speed, scalability, etc.)
  - metrics for quality assurance (eg consistency, accuracy, satisfaction, etc.)
  - key indicator project or operational metrics (eg schedule, reliability index, help desk problem resolution time, etc.)
- governance, disputes, recourse, remedies, escalation and issues resolution
- support services - training, documentation, maintenance, service and transition
- updates, new releases, upgrades
- performance warrantees and service levels – OLAs (Operational Level Agreements), SLAs (Service Level Agreements) with incentives and penalties
- status reports, meetings, format and contents - what? when? to whom? how often?
- disengagement options – termination triggers, conditions, responsibilities, transition plan (who is responsible for what?)

- defin∉roles and responsibilities of both parties
- ownershipof hardware, software, network, data contents, software licenses, etc.
- changanagement triggers, process and approvals
- confidentialityon-disclosure and security (physical, logical) considerations
- intellectuaproperty and content protection
- contingencyback-up and disaster recovery plans, processes and resources
- identifysingle point of contact(s) for co-ordination and follow-up
- construct an agreement that contains detailed service descriptions with adequate metrics for each activity
- make the supplier fully accountable for delivering services and subject to penalties when it misses service levels; remove ambiguity from service descriptions

Equally important is a breakdown of fees, types of contract (ie fixed priced, cost plus fixed fee, time and material, gain or risk sharing, volume or transaction based, etc.), as well as both penalty and incentive provisions clearly outlined:

- amountsperiod by period
- volumeof work covered
- qualityof work to be provided
- provisionfor over- and under-performance
- guidelines for selecting specific outsourcing metrics, including aligning metrics with the business objectives of the service
- selecting metrics that enhance the ability to diagnose problems, escalate attention, and remedy performance issues
- limitinghe metrics for each service to one or two encompassing measurements
- bundlingoutsourcing services to leverage resources and lower costs

Outsourcing governance process, organization, escalation and metrics

Some best practice starting points for measuring outsourcing performance include (Accenture, 2001):
- clarifyobjectives at the start of the negotiations to align for success
- choose fewer metrics with higher stakes (and increase the rewards and penalties accordingly) in order to help focus, minimize administrative demands and improve the relationship
- shift from input to output metrics, where possible; instead of counting how many hours it took to complete each order, a photographic firm asked its outsourcer to count how many orders it completed each hour – this helped to speed up the number of orders processed per hour
- define metrics early in the relationship (as part of the contract, not after the contract is signed)
- you get what you pay for; if you demand rock-bottom pricing, do not expect a world-class SLAs

The IT Services Qualification Center (ITSqc) at Carnegie Mellon University suggests the following seven best practices for sourcing governance (ITSqc, 2006):

- **Sourcing policy** – establish and implement the organizational sourcing policy (eg purpose, organization, decision authority, support systems, processes, performance management guidelines, etc.)

- **Service provider management** – establish and implement procedures to manage service providers (eg relationship management, tracking performance, create issues, dispute and escalation process, etc.)
- **Internal stakeholder management** – establish and implement procedures to manage internal stakeholders (eg relationship model, identify liaison personnel, define communications mechanisms, track stakeholder issues and resolutions, etc.)
- **Defined sourcing process** – establish and maintain documented sourcing processes for use across the organization (eg establish sourcing process guidelines and owners of each process, determine measures to track sourcing process performance, etc.)
- **Align strategy and architectures** – align strategies and architectures to support sourcing across the organization (develop and support processes for aligning business strategies and plans with architecture strategy, align IT capability with sourced services, ensure that the business processes performed as sourced services are consistent with, and integrated with, the business processes of the organization, etc.)
- **Business process integration** – establish and implement procedures to manage the integration of business processes with those performed by service providers (eg document and support procedures and processes that enable integration, identify performance measures of the integrated business process, track status, etc.)
- **Adapt to business change** – establish and implement guidelines for reviewing and adapting to changes (eg create change management system and process, for reviewing and adapting to change, create change management and service modification requests for approved changes, etc.)

Also, ITSqc identified four best practices related to sourcing people management:

- **Assign sourcing responsibilities** – assign roles and responsibilities to sourcing personnel based on appropriate personnel competencies
- **Personnel competencies** - develop personnel competencies needed by individuals with sourcing responsibilities to perform their assignments
- **Organizational sourcing competencies** – define and manage a workforce competency focused on sourcing across the organization
- **Define roles** – define and communicate the roles and responsibilities of sourcing personnel across the organization

Figure 7.10 identifies an outsourcing governance organizational model with clear roles and responsibilities assigned to both the customer and service provider at multiple levels.

7.5   Case study - Telecommunications

Figure 7.11 shows a case study which describes an outsourcing case between Textron and AT&T which is in the public domain.

A formal outsourcing governance and review process should be established and followed with clearly defined roles, responsibilities and actions.

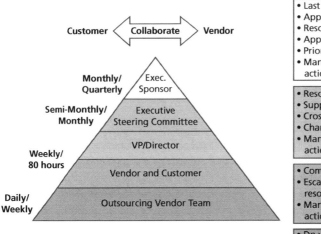

Figure 7.10   Outsourcing governance and escalation roles – customer and vendor

The Deal: AT&T to upgrade, expand and manage Textron's global communications infrastructure that services the company's 30 business units globally. **Value:** $1.1 billion over 10 years (1996-2006) **Value Proposition:** "Textron must be able to deploy telecommunications technology cost-effectively across the entire enterprise." VP & CIO, Textron **Textron:** $10+ Billion in revenues; 50,000 +employees who operate in 24 time zones in 130 countries and conduct business 24/7.	**What AT&T Brings to Textron** • Ability to build a global network in a compressed time frame and manage the network effectively • Infrastructure to provide full service networking management and technology expertise on a global basis • Alliance and partner relationships with most PTTs in many countires • AT&T Program Manager and team on sight at Textron
Textron Corporate Objectives: • Aggressive growth via acquisitions and new product development (product and innovation centric) • Global expansion and diversity • Productivity enhancement and agility • Operational excellence (cost-centric)	**Benefits of Outsourcing to Textron:** • Ability to scale easily and meet the demand for growth o the business • Reduce Operating cost – over $125Million in 10 years • Ability to implement new technologies efficiently and effectively • Clause in contract allowed Textron to re-evaluate deal every three years.

AT& T to Perform the following:
• Acquire and consolidate Textron's current network (and transition 35 employees to AT&T)
• Optimize current service levels
• Manage and optimize Textron's network (voice, data and video)
• Design and deploy a next-generation network platform on a global basis
	Lessons Learned:
	• Develop strong customer/vendor relationship model
	  – Open and honest communications
	  – Formal and informal status and performance reviews
	• Allow for realistic time and schedule to transition to outsourcing vendor (business unit by business unit)

Select SLA's for AT&T: • Response time of help desk • Network Availability • Accuracy and timing of billing • Meeting scheduled due dates • 3 year re-evaluation of contract's overall performance	

Figure 7.11   Case study: Textron and AT&T

7.6 Summary steps in vendor/outsourcing selection, negotiations and management and key take aways

Summary

Figure 7.12 provides a summary checklist for developing and managing successful outsourcing deals.

• Develop a Plan and Build a Business Case
  – Baseline model
  – Requirements & scope
  – Costs (realistic)/savings
  – Contingency Plan
  – Assumptions/Constraint
  – Obstacles
  – Metrics – OLAs, SLAs, Cost, Schedule, Other
 	
• Go/No-Go
  – Communicate decision to stakeholders
 	
• RFP
  – Preparation
  – Narrow the field - RFI, RFQ
  – Invitation to Vendors
  – Vendor briefings
  – Site visits
  – Vendor proposals
 	
• Evaluation & Selection
  – Multidisciplinary team
  – Qualitative & quantitative evaluation
  – criteria
  – Cultural match/bench strength
  – Due Diligence
  – Final selection
	• Contract Negotiation/Signing
	  – It takes two to tango
	  – Contract types
	    – Fixed price (well defined)
	    – Time & material (not well defined)
	    – Cost & fixed fee
	    – Cost & variable fee
	    – Unit price contract
	  – Terms & Conditions
	  – Change and Risk Management
	  – Governance, Metrics and Escalation
	  – Contingency and Disaster Recovery Options
	  – Disengagement Options & Responsibilities
	    – Triggers and Conditions
	    – Ownership
	    – Transition Roles/Responsibilities
	
	• Transition Management, Contract Management &
	  Performance Monitoring
	    – Transition Planning, Roles, Pilot, Training &
	      Readiness Validation
	    – Assure compliance with project or service
	      objectives, scope, schedule, & deliverables
	    – Measure and evaluate delivered work
	    – Vendor governance and reporting
	    – Integrate vendor tasks and deliverables into
	      Project Plan
	    – Assign Senior Manager/Director/VP to
	      manage vendor relationship with "clout"

Figure 7.12   Summary checklist for managing successful outsourcing deals

As an example, the CIO of a major global telecommunications company suggested the following simple and pragmatic model that works within the environment:
- keep it simple: limit number of vendors on-shore or off-shore
- know who is off-shoring and to what other subs in what other off-shoring countries
- train all levels of the IT organization - managers need to mange globally, not just locally (insourced and outsourced functions)
- expect to spend time in the air; visit, visit and visit at multiple levels
- put your IT managers in India, Brazil and China (get on the ground)
- plan for turn-over (not just cheap labor)
- constantly revisit business cases and keep contracts alive
- grow beyond vendors (look at having your own presence in the countries – maximize effectiveness such as with captive subsidiaries)

Key take aways

- executivesponsorship is critical
- getthe right people involved in each stage
- knowyour current baseline and costs
- issue an RFP - contract with a primary and secondary vendor (do not put all of your eggs in one basket)
- strong relationship management - create a customer/vendor team and engagement model, with clearly defined roles and responsibilities
- communicate,communicate, communicate
- identifyand measure meaningful performance metrics
- short-versus long-term contracts, with more frequent renewable periods
- vendorcertification is better than no certification
- managethe vendor - do not let the vendor manage you

Make your peace with outsourcing now. Either get on the outsourcing train or get in front of it.

<u>There is no magic: Outsourcing is hard work!</u>

8   Performance management, management controls, risk management, business continuity and enabling technology excellence

"Those that keep score, know they are winning and have the necessary information to maintain the lead. Those that keep score, know they are losing but have the information they need to change direction. Those that don't keep score truly don't know their position and may be beyond help."

- Unknown Author

8.1   What is covered in this chapter?

This chapter:
- explains the issues, constraints and opportunities involved in improving IT performance management and measurement, management controls, compliance and business/IT continuity planning, as components of IT governance
- explains the principles and practices of achieving IT performance management excellence using Balanced Scorecard and other metrics, and linking critical success factors to leading and lagging indicators
- discusses how CoBiT and other frameworks can be used to establish the foundation for better IT management controls
- describes the key attributes and functions that should be an integral part of any enabling technologies selected to support one or more components of IT governance

8.2   Overview

As IT investments grow and become a larger share of an enterprise's capital expenditures, IT executives are being required by business executives to demonstrate the business value and alignment of their investments, as well as the reliability, availability, security, continuity and integrity of the information and supporting services. The IT performance management, control and reporting challenge is:
- to communicate from IT outwardly to management and the user community at multiple levels (eg strategic, management, knowledge and operational) and to multiple audiences (eg Board and/or executive management, middle management, knowledge)
- to inwardly direct and manage the IT organization

Figure 8.1 represents a modification of a framework originally developed by Robert Anthony that illustrates the multiple levels and audiences that must be accommodated in any IT performance management reporting and control system (Anthony, 1965).

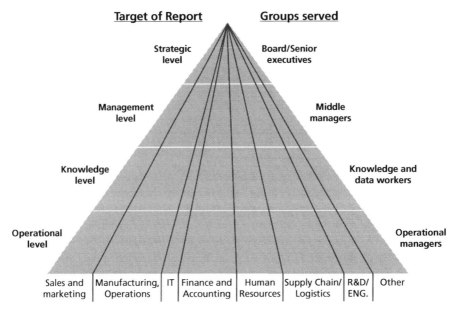

Target of Report   **Groups served**

Strategic level — Board/Senior executives

Management level — Middle managers

Knowledge level — Knowledge and data workers

Operational level — Operational managers

| Sales and marketing | Manufacturing, Operations | IT | Finance and Accounting | Human Resources | Supply Chain/ Logistics | R&D/ ENG. | Other |

Source: Modified from Anthony, R. N. , Planning and Control Systems: A Framework for Analysis, Cambridge, MA: Harvard University Press (1965)

Figure 8.1   A framework for IT performance management, analysis, control and reporting: organizational levels and groups served

Gartner's research suggests that IT must master the art of managing measures that matter to the business (such as business process measures, product/service innovation and the value of money), as well as IT performance measures from multiple perspectives (including alignment, contribution to the bottom line, innovation and transformation, project management and service levels) (Gartner, 2001).

A performance management, control, continuity and compliance plan must be developed for IT, as part of a governance initiative. The development of the plan should be a collaborative effort between the business and IT. It should be based on a number of objectives, such as strategic, financials, quality, operational and service effectiveness, which support an organization's business vision, mission, plans, objectives and financials.

There are many issues involved in measuring, monitoring and controlling IT that need to be addressed in a comprehensive manner:

- What industry frameworks would be helpful in this area?
- Who should own measurement? Control? Continuity of Service? Compliance?
- What key performance indicators should be measured?
  - business impact – revenues, costs, profits
  - workload, availability, capacity, reliability, scalability
  - agility and speed
  - alignment
  - rate of technology absorption

- – organization fluidity and synergy
  - – process innovation (internal and external)
  - – program/project management effectiveness
  - – service levels
  - – integration
  - – quality
  - – investment impact
  - – customer relationship
  - – value chain impact
  - – historic or predictive or a hybrid of both factors
- • Whatto do with the measurements?
  - – establish a report card for performance
  - – link each measure to a critical success factor, for the business or for IT, or for both
  - – create meaningful, understandable, relevant benchmarks
  - – create a set of metrics outwardly bound from IT to the organization
  - – create a set of metrics that are inwardly bound to help manage the IT organization
- • When should measurements be done? Continuously? Daily? Weekly? Monthly? Quarterly? Semi-annually? Annually?
- • What level of measurement detail should be reported and in what reporting format? To whom?

8.3 Principles for achieving performance management and control excellence

As part of improving IT governance, it is critical for an organization to establish an overall framework that includes (amongst other things) an IT enterprise strategy (which includes business capability roadmaps and Balanced Scorecard metrics), performance management, management controls and compliance components. Figure 8.2 represents such a framework for a major communications company. It is interesting to note the highlighted areas, since they specifically focus on IT strategy, compliance, life cycle and reporting.

In addition, by using industry best practice frameworks or guidelines, and their components (such as domains and checklists, such as COSO® and CobiT®), which were previously described in Chapter 2, a company can develop a more consistent and sustainable approach to making IT performance management and management controls more effective and sustainable. Of course, one needs to assign decision authority, ownership and link deliverables and performance to a reward structure, to make individuals and teams more accountable. Figure 8.3 illustrates a high level framework, linking COSO® and CobiT® with SOX (described in Chapter 1) and the Balanced Scorecard. Organizations that are not impacted by SOX can substitute whatever compliance regulations impact their environments.

Key Components for Performance Management, Compliance and Reporting Include:
IT Enterprise Strategy, Enterprise Compliance, Lifecycle and Quality and Organizational Reporting

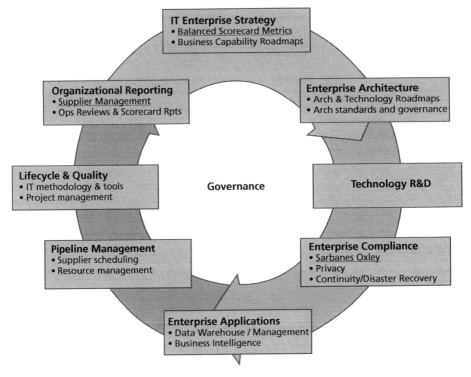

Figure 8.2   IT governance – How it works: major communications company

Other principles for achieving performance management and management control excellence include:

- identify critical success factors for the business and IT, and identify the key performance indicators (KPIs) linked to these factors
- build key performance indicators into your performance evaluation system, starting at the top and permeating to all positions that can influence those KPIs
- make KPIs relevant, simple, comparable, easy-to-report and focused on goals and objectives
- define and issue a management control policy and related procedures, which identify all of the areas requiring management controls, using CobiT as a checklist
- monitor audit and assure that IT operates in accordance with the approved controls
- develop a risk management and mitigation plan, policy and process
- develop business/IT continuity and disaster recovery plan and policy
- develop a clear performance review, escalation and issues resolution policy and process, with clear accountability and responsibilities

A well-designed framework based on industry standards and guidelines can help create more consistency for performance and compliance management and controls.

- Establish a baseline framework for measurement, reporting and control
- Optimize controls and related processes
- Integrate financial and KPI reporting and internal control processes
- Redirect efforts from risk aversion to risk intelligence
- Enhance market competitiveness
- Reduce the cost of compliance & certification
- Appoint owners to each component and link results with reward system

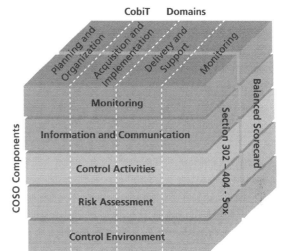

Figure 8.3   A framework for making IT performance management and management controls more consistent and sustainable

What critical success factors and key performance indicators should be tracked?

According to a corporate executive board report:

"… best practice IT organizations are increasingly adopting the Balanced Scorecard as a management tool incorporating financial, operational, talent management, project management and user satisfaction perspectives into assessments of the performance of the IT function."

- Corporate Executive Board, 2003

IT performance measures have evolved over time. Gartner and others have identified a number of limitations to current IT measurement systems and metrics such as:

- outputmeasures do not tell one how to improve
- historicmetrics do not identify issues driving current performance
- there is usually a lack of balance between leading or predictive metrics and lagging or historic metrics; there are usually many more lagging than leading indicators
- manysystems reflect a lack of external comparison against best practice organizations
- itis often difficult to measure strategic or added value
- too many metrics; a surplus of metrics overwhelms the scorecard reader and leads to suboptimal use of senior decision-makers' limited time
- no individual impact; the absence of incentives, linking individual behavior to IT Balanced Scorecard use, hampers scorecard application and achievement of targets

The execution of these plans and objectives must be monitored and measured by a combination of Balanced Scorecard key performance indicators (KPIs) as well as formal and informal status review meetings and reports (eg report cards, dashboards). The outcomes should link critical success factors to KPIs that are measurable, part of a standard reporting system and linked to a governance component. If one cannot measure it, it does not count. Remember, one gets what one measures, so it is critical to measure and control the right things.

The Balanced Scorecard system, developed by Drs. Kaplan and Norton, is a management system that provides a clear prescription as to what companies should 'measure' to clarify their vision and strategy, and translate them into actions with respect to four areas: financial, customers, internal business processes and learning and growth.

Figure 8.4 illustrates the original Balanced Scorecard concept. Figure 8.5 identifies critical success factors, based on expanded Balanced Scorecard categories, and relates them to key performance indicators, as well as describing key historic and predictive performance metric attributes that are useful for IT.

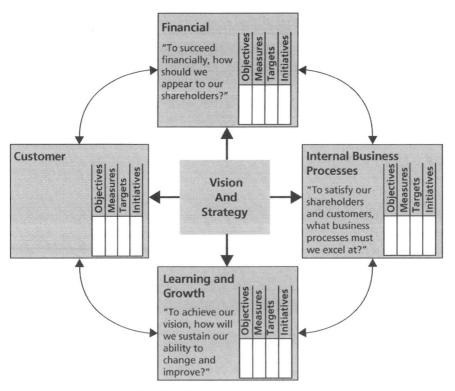

Source: www.balancescorecard.org/basics/bsc1

Figure 8.4   The Balanced Scorecard

What Key Performance Indicators Should Be Tracked for IT?
The CSFs and KPIs are best determined by the current environment, objectives and strategies of an organization. They must be measurable, comparable & reportable.

- **Critical Success Factor (CSFs) Categories:**
  - Financial*
  - Customer*
  - Employee
  - Process & Product Innovation*
  - Program/Project Innovation
  - Service Level Innovation
  - Learning and Growth*
  - * Balanced Scorecard

- **Key Performance Indicators (KPIs):**
  - Financial
  - Customer – Internal & External
  - Performance – Team & Individual
  - Program/Project Mgt.
  - Skills/Competencies
  - Service availability & readiness

- **Attributes:**
  - Performance (Historic)
    - Time
    - Cost – Reduction, Containment & Avoidance
    - Profitability – Direct or Indirect
    - Responsiveness
    - Quality
    - Availability
    - Capacity
    - Reliability
  - Predictive (Future)
    - Maturity Level
    - Capability/Skills
    - Alignment
    - Key Issues
    - Major Risks
    - Customer Satisfaction

Reality Check – Do the CSFs and KPIs...
- Translate into specific actions?
- Help align business and IT?
- Provide leverage to institute change?
- Manage end-to-end results across silos?
- Drive performance and process improvements?
- Allow for benchmarking to compare best practice performance?
- Enhance your ability to compete in the future?
- Drive learning and innovation?
- Predictors of Future Poor Performance?

Figure 8.5   CSFs, KPIs and their key attributes related to IT

Select examples of additional KPIs in support of IT governance

Each company must tailor the CSFs and KPIs of the Balanced Scorecard to its business strategies, plans and objectives. Each company must also construct a performance report card that should have two audiences – business and IT. One part should focus on key KPIs that are business-centric and are used to communicate from IT outwardly to management and the user community. These include the need for IT to link IT strategy with the business strategy, to monitor service levels, while reducing the TCO (total cost of operations), and to better illustrate the business value of IT. The second part should be IT-centric and should be used by the CIO inwardly to direct, manage and control the performance of the IT organization in terms of customer satisfaction, human capital management, outsourcing vendor management, resource allocations, project management and Service Management and delivery.

For one global communications organization, the IT Balanced Scorecard:

- supports the enterprise Balanced Scorecard
- aligns with IT customers' Balanced Scorecards
- cascades down to IT VP level Scorecards
- is directly tied to individual performance objectives

The same organization monitors performance against strategy, for each major objective that is identified in the IT plan, and for each objective it also identifies its owner, the metrics used to measure results, specific targets, reports the status of each objective on a monthly basis, and identifies any actions required. On a quarterly basis, an overall IT performance report card is issued to management. The focus includes alignment, major program/project investment management, key IT Service Management and delivery metrics, financial analysis of contributions and expenses, and asset utilization.

8.6 identifies an example of an outwardly-focused report card for a financial service organization that includes both business-centric and IT-centric metrics.

Financial:
- IT Spending/Company FTE (Full Time Employees)
- IT Spending/Company Revenue
- Keep-the-Lights On Spending/Company FTE
- Some aspects of Innovation (as measured by volume increase, speed to market increase, defect reduction, process improvement)
- Total IT Budget versus Actuals and Key IT Components (Capital, Expense, People, Hardware, Software, Network, etc.)

Non-Financial:
- IT Employee Turnover
- Quality of Management Index (Measures IT worker satisfaction with IT management)
- Engaged Employee Index (Measures IT worker motivation)
- Risk Mitigation Index (Measures degree of risk mitigation actions)
*Note: Numerous intra-IT project and service level metrics are used as well.

Figure 8.6   High level IT Balanced Scorecard metrics used as part of a monthly executive operations review for a financial services organization

Figure 8.7 provides a series of composite Balanced Scorecard metrics, collected from both case study organizations and secondary research, and decomposed into performance metrics covering financial, project management, IT Service Management and vendor performance, IT human resources and customers.

Based on a review of best practice case study companies, using some form of Balanced Scorecard for IT, several critical success factors are necessary to successfully institutionalize IT Balanced Scorecards in organizations:

- makekey performance indicators simple, intuitively obvious and focused on goals
- develop key performance indicators with balance and the 'big picture' in mind (outward from IT to the business and inward to manage IT)
- integrate key performance indicators into individual and team performance evaluation systems
- broad executive commitment – use a mix of business and IT leadership in the design, selection, review and continuous improvement of metrics
- developstandard metrics definition based on consensus

Governance calendar

To establish more consistency in tracking performance, many organizations are issuing annual governance calendars. These calendars list key IT components and their periodic governance reporting, meeting and review periods, activities and events. Figure 8.8 illustrates one such governance calendar. This can also can be developed on a more detailed and granular basis.

Financial Performance	
Most Common Metrics Total IT expenditures as a % of sales IT cost per employee Total IT spending by geography % of IT expenditures on new versus maintenance systems % of "lights on" operating costs (including break/fix, depreciation) versus total IT spend **Project and Investment Cost Performance** % of R&D investment resulting in operational applications Total value creation from IT enabled projects IT Project ROI % of key projects completed on time within budget **IT Service Management and Delivery Costs** Dollar value of technology assets still in use beyond depreciation schedule Share of discretionary spending shared by IT % reduction in maintenance cost of all systems Average network circuit cost reduction per quarter PC/laptop software maintenance cost per month per user Workstation software maintenance cost per month per workstation E-mail service: cost per month per user Infrastructure spending as a % of total IT spending Total maintenance cost % of year-over-year cost reduction per service Total cost of ownership of IT services versus external benchmarks Service unit cost	**IT Departmental Cost** IT cost per employee Total IT spending by geography Total IT spending by business unit Expenses compared to revenue per quarter Spend per portfolio category (e.g. new revenue generation, cost reduction, business transformation) Performance against IT spending performance Central IT spend as percentage of total IT spend Net present value delivered during payback period
Project Management Performance	
Most Common Metrics % of projects on time, on budget, within scope % of projects compliant with architectural standards Customer Satisfaction Index **Project Spending and Costs** Actual versus planned ROI for implementation of key initiatives % of projects with completed business case % of budget allocated to unplanned projects Earned value Cost Performance Index **Project Timeliness and Delivery** % and cost of project rework due to changed scope, poor requirements definition, etc. Average project duration % of projects with detailed project plan Dollars saved through productivity improvement and reusable code Schedule performance index % of project milestones delivered	**Project Alignment with IT Strategy** % of projects directly linked to business objectives % of applications deployed on a global basis % of infrastructure standardization projects of total project pool % of projects using common project methodology % of application failures within first 90 days of deployment % of 'at-risk' projects that adopt quality, security, and compliance standards Increase in project management maturity Project quality index

Figure 8.7   Select Scorecard metrics - financial, project management, Service Management and vendor management, IT HR management and customer satisfaction

IT Service Management and Vendor Performance	
Most Common Metrics Key applications and systems availability Help-desk first-call resolution rate	**IT Vendor Management** IT contract cost ($) IT contract cost as a % of IT spend IT project completion (on time, within budget) SLA performance (%) Customer satisfaction index (%)
User-Centric Operational Performance Average number of incidents per user per month (average number of times end user experiences global desktop availability outages per month) Consistently available and reliable IT services to users Rate of failure incidents impacting business	**Help-Desk Performance** Mean time to repair for all network and desktop outages Mean time to repair for all application systems outages less than four hours % of infrastructure service requests closed within service level agreements
Network and Systems Performance Print server availability All critical systems and infrastructure have viable business continuity plans System/application database maintained with more than 95 % accuracy E-mail transmit less than 20 seconds (all regions) Monthly average of network availability consistently more than 99.5 % Monthly average of critical systems availability consistently above 99.5 % Mean time to repair for all client outages less than two hours Network uptime PC/laptop hardware fix or replacement within 48 hours Total cost of ownership of identified products and services compared to industry standards	**Operational Strategy Adoption** Completion of service transformation with minimum business disruption All announced changes completed within advertised downtime window % of IT architectural plans approved, reviewed, and accepted by business Number of applications used by more than one line of business % of desktop PC standardized End-to-end availability for customer service IT effectiveness in resource allocation supporting business objectives Identify and manage strategic alliances with IT partners Decrease average development cost by 10 %
Information Security % of systems compliant with IT security standards Number and type of security incidents time to respond and resolve security incidents	
IT HR Skills Management	
Most Common Metrics Employee morale/satisfaction Overall IT staff retention and attrition rate	**Training and Personal Development** % of performance assessment and development plans delivered to employees % of employees with mentors % of employees with individual development plans % of individual training objectives met Employee 'business knowledge' survey performance % of managers trained in employee motivation % of staff with appropriate measures for their personal goals Share of IT training spent in business units Number of IT person-hours spent at industry events Number of training hours per employee per quarter

Figure 8.7   Select Scorecard metrics - financial, project management, Service Management and vendor management, IT HR management and customer satisfaction (cont'd)

Staffing	Marketing/ PR - Related Metrics
% of non-entry-level position filled internally	Number of awards won by company for use
Average tenure of solid performers (in years)	of IT
% of projects assignments that are cross-functional	Competitiveness of current employment offer
Ratio of skills sets needed to skills set represented	versus industry
Performance against staff diversity goals	Citation of IT organization in press
Number of candidates interviewed per open position	
IT headcount (number of full-time IT staff)	
Contractor headcount	
% of planned staffing levels	
Average years of IT experience	
% of IT staff who are certified (number of industry recognized certifications)	
Customer Satisfaction	**Customer Satisfaction**
Most Common Metrics	**Most Common Metrics**
Customer satisfaction survey – quarterly or semi-annually	Customer satisfaction survey – quarterly or semi-annually
Surveys	**Surveys**
Overall business executive satisfaction rating	Overall business executive satisfaction rating
Survey Questions	**Survey Questions**
Perceived versus actual price competitiveness of IT services	Perceived versus actual price competitiveness of IT services
Perceived ability to deliver technical/business solutions and services	Perceived ability to deliver technical/business solutions and services
Quality of communication about available services and new technologies	Quality of communication about available services and new technologies
Help-desk client satisfaction—% dissatisfied	Help-desk client satisfaction—% dissatisfied
Contribution to business process improvement and innovation	Contribution to business process improvement and innovation
Contribution to business value creation	Contribution to business value creation
Contribution to corporate business strategy	Contribution to corporate business strategy

Figure 8.7 Select Scorecard metrics - financial, project management, Service Management and vendor management, IT HR management and customer satisfaction (cont'd)

8.4 CobiT® and key management controls

CobiT® is a model for control of the IT environment. CobiT® stands for Control Objectives for Information and related Technology. CobiT® is a model designed to control and help audit the IT function. This model was originally developed by the Information Systems Audit and Control Foundation (ISACF), the research institute for the Information Systems Audit and Control Association (ISACA). CobiT® was transferred to the IT Governance Institute (ITGI), which is an independent body within ISACA. CobiT® is primarily intended for management, business users of IT and auditors.

Figure 8.9 illustrates the CobiT® framework, its four domains (eg Plan and Organize, Acquire and Implement, Deliver and Support and Monitor and Evaluate) and the IT processes (and controls) that are part of each of the domains.

More information on CobiT® is covered in Chapter 2.

A Governance Schedule should be issued annually Identifying the Key Deliverables, Reports, Review Meetings, etc.

| JAN | MARCH | MAY | JULY | AUGUST | OCT | DEC |

Strategic & Operational Plans & Budgets (Capital & Expense) PROGRAMS, PROJECTS and INFRASTRUCTURE OPERATIONS PLANS/BUDGETS/REPORTS*

- **Strategic Plan**
  - **Annual Operating Plan**
    - Investment Approvals
    - Program/Project Reports, Metrics and Reviews
    - IT Service Management & Delivery (Operations and and Infrastructure Reoprts, Metrics and Reviews

- **Program/Project Plans**
  - Charter
  - Schedule
  - Budget/Actuals
  - Deliverables

Weekly
- Projects Status Report (milestones/issues)
- Operations Status Project
- Technical Exchange Group
- Staff Meetings
- Weekly Activity/Status Report to Management

Bi-Weekly/Monthly
- Project Status Reviews (Financials, Schedule)
- Monthly Management Report
- Multiple Dashboards (Top 10 Projects + Key Service SLA's) - Green, Amber, Red Report

Bi-Montly/Quarterly
- Executive Steerting/Governance Board Reviews

Semi-Annual/Annual
- State of IT Report Card
- Performance Reviews

Figure 8.8   Governance calendar

IT performance, control and compliance framework

A growing number of organizations are using both the COSO® and CobiT® frameworks as a checklist to develop more effective and complete IT controls. Critical success steps used by several best practice companies to improve controls include:

- establish an IT governance and control framework
- establish management compliance forum
- determine Sarbanes-Oxley and/or other regulatory compliance requirements
- determine IT owners for applications and general controls
- manage performance, control and compliance issues
- VP-appointed compliance stewards
- VP-appointed applications and controls SME's (subject matter experts)
- design of IT control documentation
- review and audit of IT controls

8.5   Risk assessment, management and mitigation

Risk management objectives and definition

Risk analysis is the systematic identification of potential areas of project uncertainty or concern. There are three primary aspects of risk management to be considered:
- risk identification and analysis
- risk quantification
- risk response, mitigation and contingency plan development

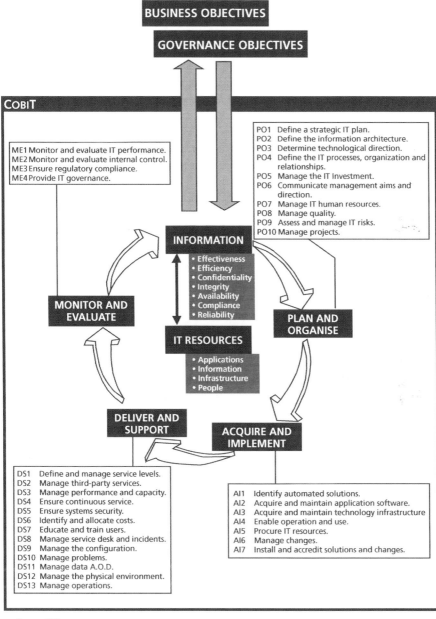

Source: ITGI

Figure 8.9   COBIT® - IT processes by domain

Risk management objectives include:
- to understand the concept of risk, and the importance of risk management in the business, functional and IT environments
- to understand the risk management methodology and framework, identify the various causes of risk, and review the activities and tasks essential to minimize, avoid or address the consequences of the risk

- to review the tools and techniques utilized in risk management to identify, analyze, quantify, prioritize and mitigate high risk areas
- to develop risk mitigation and contingency strategies and plans

Classification of risks

In order to address threats and their risk impact, each of potential threats and risks should be identified in terms of:

Causes of Risks
- manmade (eg terrorism; espionage)
- natural (eg hurricanes)
- industrial accidents (eg fire)

Business and IT continuity
- disruption of business processes and/or IT services
- loss of physical locations
- lack of or inadequate disaster prevention/recovery plans
- discontinuity of business services
- discontinuity of IT services
- loss of vital assets – physical, human, intellectual property, facilities, other
- loss of software, hardware, networks, data centers, network control centers, etc.

Security breaches
- physical
- logical
- information technology

Theft
- physical property
- intellectual property
- assets

For each potential threat or risk, ask these questions, and then assign a value of high, medium, or low:

- What are the possible triggers for this risk?
- What is the probability ($ or time) that this risk will occur?
- What would be the impact on the organization if this risk should occur?
- What can be done to mitigate the risk (eg avoid, mitigate, contingency)?

Figure 8.10 illustrates a risk analysis process flow. Figure 8.11 provides an example of a risk assessment and impact template. It helps to quantify the risk impact (eg catastrophic, critical, marginal and negligible) versus its probability of occurrence (eg near certainty versus improbably). The template can be easily tailored by organizations, to fit their requirements and environments.

For risks with high probability and high impact, develop contingency and continuity plans (see Figure 8.12).

Figure 8.12 provides a risk/threat assessment template that can facilitate the analysis of risks and their potential impact and probability of occurrence on the organization. A contingency plan should be developed for all threats that appear in the high impact, high probability quadrant, and may be developed for those threats that appear in the high impact, but low probability quadrant. This again, is a function of the management philosophy and style of an organization.

Risk management mitigation options

Responses to risks and threats generally fit into one of the following categories:

- **Avoidance** - eliminate the risk by eliminating the cause
- **Mitigation** - reduce the monetary value of the risk by reducing the probability, impact or both
- **Acceptance** - simply accept the consequences
- **Transfer** – to a third party

There are several responses to potential risks:

- **Outsourcing** - get additional products/services from outside
- **Create 'centers of excellence'** on a global basis (do not put all of your eggs in one basket)
- **Contingency planning** - define action steps that will be taken in the event the risk event occurs, and estimating the costs associated with that action
- **Alternative strategies** - consider changing the approach
- **Insurance** - may protect against financial losses associated with certain types of risk

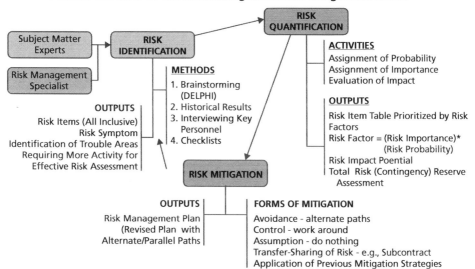

Outlines the Flow of the Risk Management and Mitigation Process

Figure 8.10   Risk analysis process flow schematic

Risk Exposure Key

- Highest (R_E = 15-20) Contingency Plan Required
- High (R_E = 9-12) Contingency Plan Highly Recommended
- Medium (R_E = 4-8) Contingency Plan Discretionary
- Low (R_E = 1-3) Contingency Plan Not Required

Criteria	Risk Impact [R_I]			
	Catastrophic (4)	**Critical (3)**	**Marginal (2)**	**Negligible (1)**
Hazard	Unrecoverable impact to environment, system, and/or personnel health *and/or*	Major damage impact to environment, system, and/or personnel health *and/or*	Minor impact to environment, system, and/or personnel health *and/or*	Negligible impact to environment, system, and/or personnel health *and/or*
Schedule	Unachievable *and/or*	Serious delay (>30% late) *and/or*	Moderate delay (10%-30% late) *and/or*	Will meet schedule but use all 'slack time' *and/or*
Cost	Major budget overrun (>50%) *and/or*	Serious budget overrun (30%-50%) *and/or*	Budget overrun (10%-30%) *and/or*	Consumption of all management financial reserves *and/or*
Support	Unsupportable system *and/or*	Major delays in systems modifications *and/or*	Minor delays in systems modifications *and/or*	Irritating and awkward maintenance *and/or*
Performance	Non-achievement of technical performance	Significant degradation of technical performance	Some reduction in technical performance	Minimal to small reduction in technical perrormance, at the detailed level

Risk Exposure (R_E) = $R_I \times R_P$

▲ Value (R_E) ▲	Catastrophic (4)	Critical (3)	Marginal (2)	Negligible (1)
Near Certain (5) 81%-99% Probability of Happening	20	15	10	5
Probable (4) 61%-80% Probability of Happening	16	12	8	4
Possible (3) 41%-60% Probability of Happening	12	9	6	3
Marginal (2) 21%-40% Probability of Happening	8	6	4	2
Improbable (1) 1%-20% Probability of Happening	4	3	2	1

Risk Probability [R_P]

Figure 8.11   Risk assessment matrix

• For each contingency plan, specify the circumstances that would trigger that plan into action.

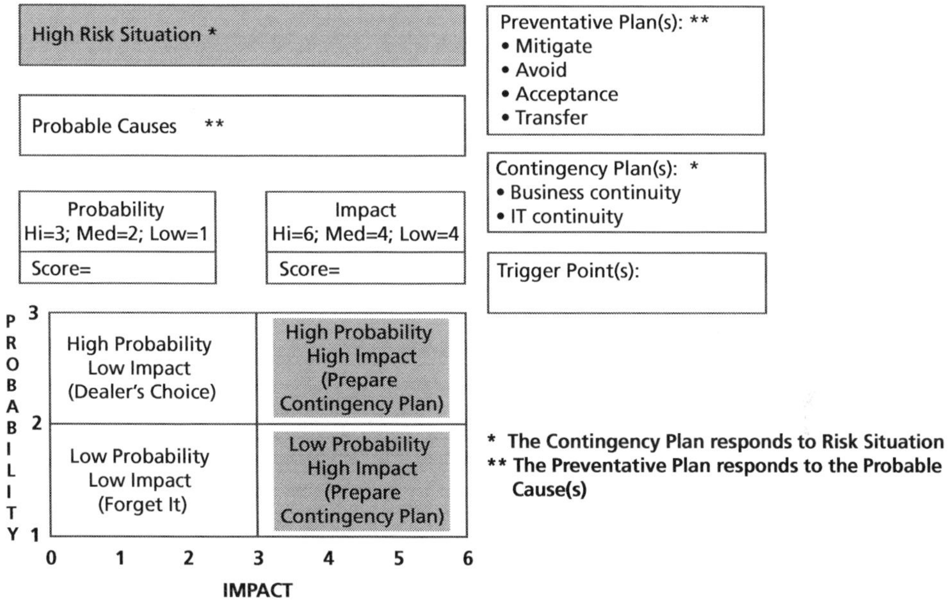

Figure 8.12   Risk management and mitigation template

In summary, a risk assessment matrix can be developed for each major component of IT governance.

8.6   Business and IT continuity and protection plan checklist

There is general consensus that there are a number of corporate governance principles and practices, which if followed, can better prepare organizations to detect, analyze and proactively mitigate and manage threats and their associated risks. These principles and practices can speed-up the recovery process, and minimize disruptions and losses. They include, but are not limited to:

• identify and classify potential threats and their risks, using intelligence systems, processes (eg data collection and analysis; threat and/or impact assessment and evaluation; information dissemination to the right individuals; triggering events for potential action, and enabling technologies)
• institute a risk management and mitigation policy and process, to assess the impact and probability of occurrence of potential catastrophes and disasters on the organization, and develop a mitigation and contingency plan
• develop a business continuity plan and a disaster recovery plan
• develop a corporate and information security plan and policy
• identify roles and responsibilities for each component of the plan

1.0	**Preparing the Plan**
2.0	**Initiating the BCPP Project**
2.1	Project Initiation Tasks
2.1.1	Review of Existing BCPP
2.1.2	Benefits of Developing a BCPP (Value Proposition and Marketing)
2.1.3	BCPP Policy Statement
2.1.4	Decision Authority and Approvals
2.1.5	Communications Plan
2.2	Project Organization
2.2.1	Charter – Objectives, Timetable, Budget, Deliverables, Scope, Authorization
2.2.2	Appoint Project Manager and Team
2.2.3	Reporting Requirements and Metrics
3.0	**Assessing Business Risk and Impact of Potential Threats and Emergencies**
3.1	Threat Assessment
3.1.1.	Environmental Disasters
3.1.2	Terrorist or Other Deliberate Disruptions
3.1.3	Loss of External Services – Supplies, Utilities, Raw Material
3.1.4	Equipment or System or Information Technology Failures
3.1.5	Serious Security Breaches
3.1.6	Other Emergencies
3.2	Business Risk Assessment
3.2.1	Major Business Processes and Locations
3.2.2	Assess Financial and Operational Impact
3.2.3	Determine Time Outage Impacts
3.2.4	Key Business Executives/Personnel and Contact Information
3.3	Information Technology
3.3.1	Determine Business and IT Dependencies
3.3.2	Major IT Systems, Networks and Data
3.3.3	Key IT Personnel and Contact Information
3.3.4	Key IT Vendors and Facilities
3.3.5	IT Recovery Policies and Procedures
3.4	Current Emergency Policies and Procedures
3.4.1	Summary of Current Policies, Procedures and Responsibilities for Handling Emergencies
3.4.2	Key Personnel and Contact Information for Business Recovery Organization (BRO), Escalation and Delegation of Authority
3.4.3	External Emergency Services and Contact Information
3.4.4	Building, Power, Information, Vital Records Back-up

4.0	**Preparing for a Possible Emergency**
4.1.	Emergency Response Procedures
4.2	Command, Control and Emergency Operations Center (Crisis Management)
4.2.1	Organization Chart
4.2.2	Key Personnel and Emergency Contact Information
4.2.3	Key Vendors and Suppliers and Emergency Contact Information
4.2.4	Manpower Recovery Strategy
4.2.5	Establish the Disaster Recovery Team
4.2.6	Establish the Business Recovery Team
4.3	**Emergency Response Linkage to Business Recovery**
4.3.1	Alternative Business Process Strategy
4.3.2	IT Systems, Networks and Data Back-up and Recovery Strategy
4.3.3	Premises and Critical Equipment and Asset Back-up
4.3.4	Customer Service and Call Center Back-up
4.3.4	Administration and Operations Back-up
4.3.5	Insurance Coverage
4.4	Key Documents and Procedures
4.4.1	Documents and Records Vital to the Business
4.4.2	Off- Site Storage and Back-up
4.4.3	Emergency Office Supplies
5.0	**Disaster Recovery**
5.1.	Mobilizing the Disaster Recovery Team, Roles, Responsibilities and Authority
5.2	Disaster Recovery Plan
5.2.1	Identification of Potential Disaster Status and Assess Extent of Damage and Business Impact
5.2.2	Notification and Reporting During Disaster Recovery Phase
5.2.3	Prepare Specific Recovery Plans – Detailed Resumption, Recovery and Restoration
5.2.4	Communicate Status of Recovery
5.2.5	Business Recovery Tasks
5.2.5.1	Power and Other Utilities
5.2.5.2	Premises, Fixtures, Furniture (Facilities Recovery Management)
5.2.5.3	IT and Communications Systems and Facilities
5.2.5.4	Production Facilities and Equipment
5.2.5.5	Operations
5.2.5.6	Distribution, Warehousing, Logistics and Supply Chain Management
5.2.5.7	Sales, Marketing and Customer Service
5.2.5.8	Engineering and Research and Development
5.2.5.9	Finance, Administration and Security
5.2.5. 10	Other +++
6.0	**Testing the Business Recover Plan and Process**
6.1	Planning the Tests
6.1.1	Test Multiple Scenarios based on Different Threats
6.1.2	Evaluate Results, Identify Gaps and Improve
7.0	**Education, Training and Plan Updating**
7.1.	Develop organizational awareness and training programs
7.2	Develop Vehicles for Dissemination Information
7.3	Develop budget and schedule for plan updates
7.4	Plan Distribution, Audits and Security

Figure 8.13   Business/IT continuity plan and checklist outline

The above can serve as a guideline for organizations to select and customize the appropriate approach applicable to their environment, prioritize actions and ensure that the right resources are available. With some astute planning and a solid understanding of business and IT vulnerabilities and risk tolerance, it is possible to develop a pragmatic and effective business protection plan that will minimize disruptions and financial losses.

A business continuity and protection policy, plan, process and related templates should be developed, disseminated (to select constituents in the organizations) and updated periodically, for all critical business units and functions. A business continuity and protection plan must contain a number of components: business impact analysis, risk assessment, mitigation and management, preparing for emergencies and business recovery processes.

A detailed business and IT continuity and protection plan outline or checklist is provided in 8.13.

8.7   Enabling technologies to improve IT governance

There are numerous software tools that enable enterprises to collect, record, analyze, track and report KPIs relating to each IT governance area, but none thus far, that address all of the areas. Several vendors are working on tools that address the enterprise governance processes.

Select technology software solution attributes necessary to support IT governance and its major components:

The following attributes, functions and features, at a minimum, should be included in software packages that support IT governance and its major components:

- **Demand and customer relationship management** – process IT requests, work flow, authorization, accommodate multiple designations (discretionary, mandatory and/or strategic; planned or unplanned; new, enhancements, maintenance and/or 'keep the lights on'), etc.
- **Portfolio management** – investment and alignment evaluation criteria, rankings vis-à-vis alternatives, priorities, approval, etc.
- **Work flow, process management, tracking and authorization** - processes, phases and templates (imbedded and/or custom designed), 'go/no go' gates, etc.
- **Planning**
  - link initiatives and track to strategic/tactical/capital/budget plans and initiatives
  - 'what if' alternative analysis
  - work breakdown structure - work package management
  - task list
  - organization breakdown structure
  - estimating and budgeting
  - resource loading
  - scheduling – multiple techniques
- **Program and project life cycle support** – phases, templates, reviews, authorization, progress

tracking and reporting; required to be updated and accessible at multiple levels; ability to link tasks to related tasks and/or projects and/or programs, and record and/or report on multiple key performance indicators – budget, schedule and actuals with variance reporting, status of deliverables, current period, prior period, next period projections, year to date, inception to date, base lining and re-base lining comparisons, etc.

- **Asset management** – inventory of assets, $ value, utilization, aging, depreciation, asset refresh planning, asset retirement and disposal tracking, etc.
- **Configuration management** - asset description, features, costs, location, protocols supported, version and release control, etc.
- **Resource management** – skills inventory, labor rates, labor hours, facilities, inventory, forecasting, level loading, etc.
- **Cost management** – labor rates, procurement rates, committed costs, overhead rates, budget versus actual by labor or procurement category for this period, last period, year to date, inception to date, cost at completion, by product/service, etc.
- **Time management** – from lowest level (activity or tasks) to highest level (project or program), time reporting, budget versus actual comparison by labor or procurement category, etc.
- **Product/service catalogue** – list of standard repetitive IT product and service solutions offered by IT with pricing and estimated deployment time, etc.
- **Financial management** – support capital and expense budgets, cost management, budget and forecasts, accommodate multiple base lines and changes, chargebacks, etc.
- **Performance management** – support and reporting of multiple Balanced Scorecard metrics - planning, project, operational and service performance dashboards, etc.
- **Service level management and support** – incident and problem reporting, tracking and resolution; help desk support; capacity and availability planning and forecasting; usage based tracking, cost allocation, quality control, security, etc.
- **Procurement, vendor, outsourcing management** – link to vendor governance and reporting, contract management, license tracking, metrics, escalation, etc.
- **Compliance management** – documentation, traceability, secure third party access, audit support, etc.

Environment & Drivers	Approach
<ul><li>Annual revenue range - 2004 - $3.0 to $6.0 bn</li><li>Number of IT personnel range –500 – 800</li><li>Major compliance issues with former executive management team (replaced by new executive management team focused on transformation and-re invigorating growth)</li><li>Former IT organization was reactive, lethargic and slow to address business needs</li><li>Lack of formalized IT policies, practices and disciplines</li><li>New CIO reports to CEO and is part of the senior executive management team</li><li>Fragmented business processes</li></ul>	<ul><li>New executive management team hired a new CIO, who brought in a new senior leadership team in IT</li><li>Reconstituted Business/IT Executive Steering Group which developed a strategy & priorities focused on: business growth, creating a performance based culture that rewards achievement of goals, accountability and innovation and building strong customer partnerships</li><li>CIO developed a transformation plan which was approved by executive management team</li><li>IT reorganized with following major functions:<ul><li>– IT Strategy and Governance (includes PMO, PR/Marketing & People Development)</li><li>– Application Development</li><li>– IT Operations & Infrastructure</li><li>– Enterprise Architecture</li></ul></li></ul>

Figure 8.14   Case Study - Leading Software Company

Issues and/or Opportunities	
• Poor IT governance, reporting and inadequate business intelligence – requires a cultural change • Poor IT customer satisfaction and unmet business needs caused business units to ramp up their own systems development functions • Inadequate and inappropriate IT skills, competencies and leadership • Challenge - Drive business process transform business for growth and greater profitability using IT • Self fund (through cost reduction programs) IT budget growth for new initiatives & keeping the lights on • Lack of business intelligence (multiple sources of inaccurate business information)	• IT hired a consulting firm to assist in developing a blueprint for IT governance framework and process • Company is moving towards a two year realistic strategic plan (from a three year plan) linked to an annual operating plan • With new IT management team in place for only six month, many initiatives are in process and key results are not yet clearly visible or measurable (they are definitely going in the right direction, but the jury is still out)
Results –Alignment	**Results -IT Service Management & Delivery**
• Business/IT Executive Steering Committee (consisting of "C"level executives) are closely co-ordinated strategy, direction, priorities, investments and periodically review progress on major IT/business transformation initiatives • Business strategic and operating plans drive IT plans • IT is in process of developing and deploying a pragmatic strategy and governance policy and process for the organization and re-centralizing IT development based on an improved relationships service with the business units	• ITIL is being deployed on a phased basis to improve customer service, satisfaction and related metrics (e.g. SLA, response and repair time to reported problems and outages, etc.)
Results -Program/Project Management	**Results -Performance Management**
• An IT PMO is being established using the Nikku software tool for Portfolio Management, Project Management, Time Reporting and Resource Management • Folks being hired into the IT PMO 'Center of Excellence' are or will be certified via Six Sigma and/or PMI's PMP • Demand Management (IT Requests for Service) will be reviewed in a consistent and uniform manner based select critical success factors and associated metrics in two categories –Discretionary and Non-Discretionary (Mandatory)	• IT is in the process of identifying key performance indicators to measure its effectiveness and progress
Critical Success Factors	
• To transform a culture and use IT to enable that transformation mandates the sponsorship and commitment of the CEO and the executive management team • Hire select competent business and IT leaders who bring in external experiences and success and who are not part of the old guard	
Lessons Learned	
• Conduct an assessment of current state of IT maturity against best practice companies and industry standards • Develop a plan and roadmap for transformation to a desired future state • Assign adequate resource to deploy a successful transition • Make sure that you have the right talent to do the job	

Figure 8.14   Case Study - Leading Software Company (cont'd)

- **Communications management** – manage expectations of customers and constituents - types and frequency of reports, graphs, comparisons, method and frequency of communications supported (e-mail, web-casts, formal reviews, other)
- **Change management** – templates, process, recording, reporting, authorization, original base line and re-base line tracking, version control, etc.
- **Release management** – ensure that all aspects of a new or revised release (eg hardware, software, documentations, checklists and roll-outs) are co-ordinated and approved by the impacted constituents (eg development, operations, client, sponsor, etc.)
- **Issues and problem management** – tracking, reporting and resolution status
- **Security** – access control and authorization data base, authentication, encryption, virus protection, etc.
- **Best practice knowledge management** – maintain a database of internal and external IT governance best practices and continuous improvement ideas and innovations; enable access for select constituents, etc.

8.8 Summary and key take aways

Summary

Each organization should adopt current and emerging industry performance management and control frameworks and models, and tailor them to fit its specific environment. Key points to remember include:

- IT should partner with finance, business and the internal auditors
- align IT objectives, strategies and initiatives with the customer, and develop a set of critical success factors required to meet those objectives – then build key performance indicators to measure performance, and monitor improvement and progress or issues toward those objectives
- identify and prioritize the IT performance management and control policies and procedures, to facilitate compliance, traceability, audit-ability, honesty, security, privacy and control
- make sure that the reward and compensation structure is linked to continuous improvement performance management programs for individuals and teams:
  - provide a link between outcomes and organizational objectives
  - communicate the impact of improvements to all of the stakeholders

Key take aways

The bottom line for each organization is to define, track and enforce those KPIs that measure the CSFs and objectives, and are relevant to the performance management practices and compensation incentives of their enterprises.

IT organizations that gain significant and sustainable improvement in their effectiveness have done so by balancing their focus between the management of IT and the application of IT in the business.

IT managers, who want to build and sustain higher levels of business impact and effectiveness, will implement 'continuous improvement programs' and report 'understandable' results through a robust performance management and control system.

9 Summary, lessons learned, critical success factors and future challenges

"For to win one hundred victories in one hundred battles is not the Acme of skill. To subdue the enemy without fighting is the Acme of skill."

- Sun Tzu
The Art of War
Oxford University Press, 1971

9.1 What is covered in this chapter?

This chapter:
- identifies the steps necessary to make IT governance real
- provides a composite master checklist (selected from all of the chapters) of activities and tasks required to implement and sustain successful IT governance
- identifies the lessons learned and critical success factors from best practice organizations
- raises future challenges to IT governance

9.2 Migration plan for making IT governance real and sustainable

IT is an integral part of the business; therefore IT governance must be an integral part of enterprise governance. The following actions are required to achieve a migration to higher levels of IT governance effectiveness and maturity:

- There must be a corporate mandate from the top - the Board and the executive team (including the CIO) are committed to implementing and sustaining a robust governance environment.
- There must be dedicated and available resources - identify executive champion and multi-disciplinary team (to focus on each IT governance component).
- Executives must do their homework – educate on past, current and emerging best practices.
- Executives must market the IT governance value propositions and benefits to the organization - develop and conduct a communications, awareness and public relations campaign.
- A tailored IT governance framework and roadmap must be developed for the organization, based on current and emerging industry best practices.
- An assessment of the 'current state' of the level of IT governance maturity, or other frameworks that relate to specific IT governance components, such as project management, maturity model (PMMM), vendor management (eSCM), performance management (Balanced Scorecard) and others, as a reference base ('where are we today?'), using a leading industry best practice framework such as CMMI or another framework, that may apply to a specific component of IT governance.

- There must be a 'future state' IT governance blueprint ('where you want to be') developed and kept it in focus.
- There should be activity to decompose the IT governance components into well defined work packages (assign an owner and champion to each process component).
- Executives must develop an IT governance action plan, identify deliverables, establish priorities, milestones, allocate resources and measure progress.
- The organization should sponsor organizational and individual certifications in the IT governance component areas, where they are available (eg PMP, ITIL, IT Security, IT Audit, BCP, Outsourcing, eSCM, COP, etc.).
- There must be activities to identify enabling technologies to support the IT governance initiative.
- There should be a 'web portal' established to access IT governance policies, processes, information, communications and provide support.
- Celebrate wins.
- Plan for and sustain IT governance process improvements, and link to a reward and incentive structure. Create a 'continuous IT governance improvement group' to sustain the framework.
- Do not focus on specific ROI as a measure of success - use TCO (Total Cost of Operations) and business innovation and transformation metrics as measures of improvement.

9.3   Composite checklist for implementing and sustaining successful IT governance in organizations

This section provides a composite checklist of select best practices identified in the chapters of the book by chapter. It is intended to remind practitioners of the 'must do's' and brings together every critical aspect relating to IT governance in one convenient checklist to help the Board, executive management and, most of all, CIO's and IT professionals, think through what has worked, what can work and how to deploy IT governance successfully.

Chapter 1: Introduction and executive overview

Summary of key strategic, value enhancing and execution questions:

Strategic questions - Is the right thing being done?
Is the investment in IT:
- inline with business vision and strategy?
- consistent with business principles, plan and direction?
- contributing to strategic objectives, sustainable competitive differentiation and business continuity support?
- providing optimum value at an acceptable level of risk?
- representing a long-term view (roadmap)
- including an architectural roadmap, based on a detailed analysis of the current state or condition of IT?

Value Questions – Are the benefits being realized?

Are they:

- delivering a clear and shared understanding and commitment to achieve the expected benefits?
- defining clear accountability, for achieving the benefits which should be linked to MBOs and incentive compensation schemes for individuals and business units or functional areas?
- basedon relevant and meaningful metrics?
- basedon a consistent benefits realization process and sign-off?

Execution Questions – Is the deployment successful and effective? How are results measured?

Are they:

- scalable, disciplined and consistent management, governance and delivery of quality processes?
- appropriate and with sufficient resources available with the right competencies, capabilities and attitudes?
- a consistent set of metrics linked to critical success factors and realistic key performance indicators (KPIs)?
- includingsuccession planning?

Purpose and scope of IT governance:

Purpose of IT governance

The purpose of IT governance is to:

- alignIT investments and priorities more closely with the business
- manage, evaluate, prioritize, fund, measure and monitor requests for IT services, and the resulting work and deliverables, in a more consistent and repeatable manner that optimize returns to the business
- providceresponsible utilization of resources and assets
- establishand clarify accountability and decision rights (clearly defines roles and authority)
- ensurethat IT delivers on its plans, budgets and commitments
- managemajor risks, threats, change and contingencies proactively
- improve IT organizational performance, compliance, maturity, staff development and outsourcing initiatives
- improve the voice of the customer (VOC), demand management and overall customer and constituent satisfaction and responsiveness
- manageand think globally, but act locally
- championinnovation within the IT function and business

Scope of IT governance

Key IT governance strategy and resource decisions must address the following topics:

- **IT principles** – high level statements about how IT is used in the business (eg scale, simplify and integrate; reduce TCO (Total Cost of Operations) and self fund by re-investing savings; invest in customer facing systems; transform business and IT through business process transformation; strategic plan directions, PMO (Project Management Office), sustain compliance and other regulatory requirements, etc.)

- **IT architecture** – organizing logic for data, applications and infrastructure captured in a set of policies, relationships, processes, standards and technical choices, to achieve desired business and technical integration and standardization
- **SOA architecture** – service-oriented architecture (SOA) is a business-centric IT architectural approach that supports the integration of the business as linked, repeatable business tasks or services. SOA helps users build composite applications that draw upon functionality from multiple sources within and beyond the enterprise to support business processes
- **IT infrastructure and security** – centrally co-ordinated, based on shared IT services that provide the foundation for the enterprise's IT capability, support and security
- **Business application needs** – specifying the business need for purchased or internally developed IT applications
- **IT investment and prioritization** – decisions about how much and where to invest in IT (eg capital and expense), including development and maintenance projects, infrastructure, security, people, etc.
- **People (human capital) development** – decisions about how to develop and maintain global IT leadership, management and technical skills and competencies (eg how much and where to spend on training and development, industry certifications, etc.)
- **IT governance policies, processes, mechanisms, tools and metrics** – decisions on composition and roles of steering groups, advisory councils, technical and architecture working committees, project teams; key performance indicators (KPIs); chargeback alternatives; performance reporting, meaningful audit process and the need to have a business owner for each project and investment

Three critical pillars of effective IT governance:
- **Leadership, organization and decision rights** - defines the organization structure, roles and responsibilities, decision rights (decision influencers and makers), a shared vision and interface/integration touch points and champions for proactive change
- **Flexible and scalable processes** - the IT governance model places heavy emphasis on the importance of process transformation and improvement (eg planning, project management, portfolio investment management, risk management, IT Service Management and delivery, performance management, vendor management, controls and audits, etc.)
- **Enabling technology** - leverage leading tools and technologies that support the major IT governance components

If any one of the above pillars is missing or ineffective, the IT governance initiative will not be effective or sustainable. In addition, over dependence on one dimension over the others will result in sub-optimal performance.

Chapter 2: Integrated IT governance framework
Grounded in industry best practice research, and required to plan, develop, deploy and sustain a cost effective approach to IT governance, the blended and integrated governance framework consists of five critical IT governance imperatives (which leverage best practice models described in the chapter and are 'must do's') and address the following work areas:

- **Business strategy, plan and objectives (demand management)** - this involves the development of the business strategy and plan which should drive the IT strategy and plan

- **IT strategy, plan and objectives (demand management)** – this should be based on the business plan and objectives, and will provide the direction and priorities of the IT functions and resources; this should also include portfolio investment management investments, a prioritization scheme and identify the decision rights (who influences decisions and who is authorized to make the decisions) on a wide variety of IT areas, including enterprise architecture; in addition, the CIO is responsible for the infrastructure investment for such items as capacity planning availability management, security management and related areas.
- **IT plan execution (execution management)** – this encompasses the processes of program and project management, IT Service Management (including ITIL – IT Infrastructure Library and ISO/IEC 20000), risk and continuity management, change management, security, contingency plans and others
- **Performance management and management controls (execution management)** – this includes such areas as the Balanced Scorecard, key performance indicators, COBIT, and regulatory compliance areas
- **Vendor management and outsourcing management (execution management)** – since companies are increasing their outsourcing spending, selecting and managing the vendors and their deliverables has become critical
- **People development, continuous process improvement and learning** - it is critical to invest in people, knowledge management and sustain continuous process improvement and innovation initiatives

An organization should leverage, adopt and tailor those models, frameworks and/or standards that address those issues, opportunities, pain points and threats most critical to the organization, and create an IT governance roadmap, with clearly defined the roles and responsibilities for IT governance development, process ownership and continuous improvement. The selection of a particular framework or combination of frameworks is largely dependent on the strategic objectives, available resources of an organization and their desired outcomes. All of the frameworks require varying degrees of managing change and cultural transformation.

Chapter 3: Business/IT alignment, strategic/operational planning and portfolio investment management

There are several strategic planning, management control and supplementary principles and practices that, when deployed well, will improve the business and IT alignment environment. They include, but are not limited to, the following:

Strategic planning practices:

This process should be a formal process developed as a partnership and contract (in the loose definition of the word) between the business and IT. It should clearly focus on defining and relating the value that IT provides in support of the business. Specific planning principles and practices should be deployed such as (Selig, 1983):

- **Strategic planning program and processes** - develop a strategic IT plan that is an integral part of the strategic business plan; the plan framework, format and process should be consistent, repeatable and similar, allowing for functional differences between the business units and functions and IT, to facilitate alignment and integration

- **Executive steering committee(s)** - involves top management in the IT/business planning process, to establish overall IT direction, investment levels and approval of major initiatives across the enterprise; each business unit and corporate staff function should have an equivalent body to focus on their respective areas to establish priorities and formalize periodic reviews
- **Investment portfolio management, capital and expense planning and budgeting** – ensures that all IT investments are evaluated, prioritized, funded, approved and monitored using a consistent, but flexible process and a common set of evaluation criteria that are linked to the strategic and annual operating plans and budgets, both capital and expense, at multiple organizational levels
- **Performance management and measurement** – monitors strategic plan outcomes based on specific Balanced Scorecard and service level measurement categories and metrics, and establishes organizational and functional accountability linked to MBO (management by objectives) performance criteria and reviews
- **Planning guidelines and requisites** – a set of general instructions describing the format, content and timing of the business and IT plans; these are general in nature, as opposed to specific standards, and should provide the business units some latitude and flexibility to accommodate local conditions

Management control practices:

These management control practices focus on the tactical and operating plans and programs, and on the day-to-day operational environment:
- **Formalize multi-level IT/business functional/operations/technology steering and governance boards** - with specific roles and decision rights in the day-to-day implementation and Service Management of the tactical IT plans, programs and services
- **Tactical/operating plans and resource allocation** – establishes annual and near term IT objectives, programs, projects and the resources to accomplish the objectives (eg application development plan, infrastructure refresh plan, etc.)
- **Budget/accounting/charge-back** – establishes budgets and monitors expenditures; charges IT costs back to the business or functional users to assure more effective involvement and ownership by the business
- **Performance management and measurement** – collects, analyzes and reports on performance of results against objectives at a more detailed and operational level than at the strategic plan level (see Chapter 8 - Performance Management); in addition, formal periodic monthly and quarterly review meetings should be held to review the status of major initiatives and the on-going performance of IT

Supplementary practices:

These programs will vary by organization that can result in improving alignment:
- **IT/customer engagement and relationship model** - establishes a customer-focused relationship model to facilitate interfaces, decisions, resolution of issues, collaborative plan development, better communications and build trust between IT and the business
- **Program management office (PMO)** – establishes the processes, tools and IT/business unit roles and responsibilities for program and project management; initially, PMOs were established by IT to help manage IT programs and projects; as organizations recognize the increased benefits that a PMO brings to an environment, PMOs are being established at the executive level by a growing number of organizations, to ensure that major corporate business

initiatives utilize the same discipline and structure as IT initiatives, to implement them within scope, on-time, within budget and to the customer's satisfaction

- **Marketing, public relations and communications program for IT** – most IT departments are terrible in promoting and marketing their accomplishments and value; developing this function to its full potential creates awareness and promotes executive, management and employee education and commitment to the value of IT, in support of the business through newsletters, websites, press releases, testimonials and other marketing and public relation events

- **IT charter** – promotes effective and definitive interaction and links between the IT and the business/functional groups they support; a charter can provide information on scope, roles and responsibilities, and provide specific program or project authority and limits to that authority

- **Standards and guidelines** – adopt and maintain best practice standards and flexible guidelines to describe and document IT alignment, investment and planning processes, policies and procedures for IT governance and other areas within IT; for example, a financial services organization developed a simple guideline for its customers entitled, *'How to Request IT Services and Get Them Approved'*, which was a major success

- **Organizational and people development, skills and competencies** – develop a proactive learning environment by encouraging and rewarding education, training and certification (where appropriate)

- **Annual/semi-annual IT management meeting** – conduct periodic IT/business management meetings, to share best practices, develop stronger relationships, address organizational wide issues and opportunities

Key principles for effective business/IT strategic plan alignment:

IT plans should be developed iteratively with the business and updated as necessary. Additional principles to strengthen plan alignment include:

- **Ownership** - CIO with involvement of IT leadership and of the executive officers and business unit leadership

- **Frequency** – IT strategic plan is written/revised/refreshed annually, although major changes may cause the plan to be updated more frequently or on an iterative basis

- **Time horizon** – IT strategic plan usually covers a three year period, with annual operating plans identifying capital and expense budget levels for the first year of the plan cycle

- **Plan process** – IT reviews the business strategic plan major objectives, themes and priorities with the business units and corporate services

- **IT interviews** – IT interviews the business units, to align and map IT objectives, initiatives and priorities with the business, using the key plan questions and discussion topics

- **New applications and services** - IT identifies major new or enhancement business application or service support initiatives, as well as significant technology refresh requirements (eg replace obsolete technology; support anticipated growth and new infrastructure requirements), using the business/IT strategic plan initiative alignment template (see Figure 3.14).

- **Business and infrastructure initiatives** - both the business-driven initiatives and the infrastructure initiatives are combined in the IT strategic plan (which includes a rough estimate of capital funding needs) and presented to the executive operating committee and SBU heads for approval

- **Communication of the IT strategic plan** – a short version (highlights) of the approved plan is posted on the IT web intranet and reviewed with the IT department and appropriate business constituents
- **Link to annual operating plan and budget plan** - the annual capital and expense budget are approved by the executive team for the initiatives identified in the plan; often, new or break-fix initiatives come up during the year (not in original plan) that require prioritization, funding and resources; a formal portfolio investment management approval process is followed for that purpose
- **Link to portfolio of projects for annual operating plan** – once the annual operating plan and budget have been approved, a project list and related business cases are prepared, prioritized and reviewed; projects charters are developed for approved projects and the appropriate implementation resources are allocated and/or committed
- **Link to annual MBOs (management by objectives), performance measurements, KPIs and rewards/incentives** – both the strategic plan and annual operating plan must be driven by measurable outcomes (eg cost, time, profit, volume, customer satisfaction, strategic competitive value, etc.) and appropriate management actions taken according to positive or negative results

Business and IT alignment will remain a major issue in some organizations until they realize that they both need each other to sustain the growth and prosperity of the enterprise.

Chapter 4: Leadership, teams and managing change

Key components of managing large scale enterprise change successfully

As organizations transition to a more mature and effective governance environment, a 'sea change' has to occur, either through incremental and/or radical change that could involve large scale change, depending on an organization's level of maturity, management philosophy and cultural readiness. The four key principles for managing large scale change successfully include (Kotter, 1996):

- engage the top and lead the change –
  - create the 'value proposition' and market the case for change
  - committed leadership
  - develop a plan and ensure consequence management
- cascade down and across the organization, and break down barriers including silos
  - create cross-functional and global teams (where appropriate)
  - compete on 'speed'
  - ensure a performance-driven approach
- mobilize the organization and create ownership
  - roll-out change initiative
  - measure results of change (pre-change versus post-change baselines)
  - embrace continuous learning, Knowledge and best practice sharing
- attributes of effective change teams and agents
  - strong and focused leader
  - credibility and authority (charter) to lead the initiative
  - 'chutzpa', persistent and change zealots

- ability to demonstrate and communicate 'early wins' to build the momentum
- create a sense of urgency and avoid stagnation
- knock obstacles out of the way, diplomatically or otherwise

By applying the above principles to facilitate the transition to a successful IT governance culture and environment, the following steps can be followed:

- **Proactively design and manage the IT governance program** – requires executive management sponsorship, an executive champion and creating a shared vision that is pragmatic, achievable, marketable, beneficial and measurable; link goals, objectives and strategies to the vision and performance evaluations
- **Mobilizing commitment, create the guiding coalition and provide the right incentives** – there is a strong commitment to the change from key senior managers, professionals and other relevant constituents; they are committed to make it happen, make it work and invest their attention and energy for the benefit of the enterprise as a whole; create a multi-disciplinary empowered 'Tiger Team' representing all key constituents to collaborate, develop, market and facilitate execution in their respective areas of influence and responsibility
- **Make tradeoffs and choices, and clarify escalation and exception decisions** – IT governance is complex, and requires trade-offs and choices, which impact resources, costs, priorities, level of detail required, who approves choices, to whom are issues escalated etc.; at the end of the day, a key question that must be answered is 'when is enough, enough?'
- **Making change last, assign ownership and accountability** – change is reinforced, supported, rewarded, communicated (the results are through the web and intranet), recognized and championed by owners who are accountable to facilitate the change, so that it endures and flourishes throughout the organization
- **Monitoring progress, common processes, technology and learning** – develop/adapt common policies, practices, processes and technologies, which are consistent across the IT governance landscape and enable (not hinder) progress, learning and best practice benchmarking; make IT governance an objective in the periodic performance evaluation system of key employees and reward significant progress
- **Establish a sense of urgency** – time is money
- **Generate short-term wins** – complete short-term wins that are communicated to the constituents, and are very effective for gaining support and sustaining the change direction
- **Consolidate gains and produce more change** – leverage increased credibility from successes, which facilitates and stimulates the introduction of more change
- **Anchor new approaches in the culture** – institutionalize the process, adapt enabling technology and tools, and link progress to performance

Best practice teams:
Key attributes of best practice teams include:

- clear purpose, common vision and accountability
- obsession with external customer
- participation and well defined roles
- civilized disagreement and style diversity – allow for workout meetings and discussions
- encourage open communications – silence is consent – voice your ideas

- encourage flexible discipline and even expulsion of non-productive team members
- blend of informality and formality
- focus both on process and end results; however, remember that results are more important than process
- acknowledgement of the need for change
- strong respect and trust between members and leaders
- single point of contact for official team progress and communications (do not feed rumor-mill)
- self-assessment of team members and adjustment
- no ideas are bad ideas; encourage no 'blame game'
- use automated tools to increase speed and communications

Chapter 5: Program and project management excellence

Key attributes of a successful program and project based environment
The following principles represent a checklist for helping companies achieve improvements in their program and project management practices and processes:

Program/project management excellence and visibility:
- the CEO (eg CIO; CFO; CMO; COO; etc.) is committed to implementing project management as a core competency to manage all types of projects
- top management must prioritize projects based on a consistent set of evaluation attributes and investment prioritization processes
- customers must approve and set priorities among projects
- implement projects successfully (eg on-time, on-budget, within scope, with high quality and to the customers satisfaction)
- successful project management must be a joint effort between customers and the project teams; but the final responsibility for success or failure lies with the customer in terms of ownership of the results
- market and communicate the benefits and positive results of good fundamental project management disciplines, through newsletters, websites, word of mouth, customer testimonials and other promotion vehicles
- develop a business case for major complex and moderate projects
- an essential element of every project is a complete project plan, based on a work break down structure, with assignable work packages, task identification, estimating, budgeting and scheduling
- planning is everything and on-going – detailed, systematic and team-involved
- what is not documented, has not been said or does not exist
- the more ridiculous the deadline, the more it costs to try to meet it
- project sponsors and constituents must be active participants – this builds relationships, communications and commitment
- use industry standards and guidelines to guide your project management direction - CMMI, PMMM, PMBOK, PRINCE2 and others

Sponsorship and accountability:

- All programs/projects must have a sponsor and/or owner and an overall program/project manager.
- Key roles and responsibilities must be formally agreed to upfront and communicated to all of the constituencies where individuals are assigned specific actions in the form of a **RACI** matrix (**R**esponsible, **A**pprove, **C**onsult, **I**nform) which becomes part of the project documentation.
- Program/project scope, requirements and deliverables should be approved upfront by the sponsor.
- Program/project costs and benefits (including non-financial benefits) should be quantified and approved by the Sponsor and charged back to the sponsor or owner.
- Fast projects have strong leaders who create a sense of urgency and speed.
- Professionalize project management, reward certification and celebrate successes.
- Project Managers must focus on five dimensions of project success
  - on time
  - within budget
  - within scope
  - with acceptable quality
  - to the customer's satisfaction
- Project life cycle with 'go/no go' gates allows for mid-course project reviews and adjustments and/or cancellations.
- A project manager's most valuable and least used word is 'no'.
- Project team members deserve a clear, written charter and guidelines as to the tasks they must perform and the time available to perform them.
- Establish project review panels consisting of key constituents, and conduct formal reviews with follow-up actions, dates and assigned responsibility.
- Use outside subject matter project management experts as needed.

Program/project management (PM) governance:

Key practices for successful and sustainable project management governance include the following:

- A formal project management governance policy should be established defining the components of the policy, and identify what is mandatory and discretionary and who has decision authority for approval, resource allocation, escalation and change authorization.
- A formal governance calendar should be published, which identifies formal project reviews, status reports (eg weekly, bi-weekly, monthly, quarterly), funding reviews, etc.
- A flexible and scalable project management process should be established and continuously improved, to accommodate different project types such as light, moderate and complex.
- A project management 'center of excellence' (PMO) should be established to develop criteria for project management competencies, encourage project management training and certification, provide expert project management help, act as project management advocates and conduct periodic health checks on select programs/projects.
- Establish a reward and recognition system to recognize project management excellence and encourage certification.

- Deliver short-term incremental project deliverables that work to establish credibility and visibility (decompose complex programs and projects into no more than 80 hour work packages with targeted deliverables, formal project reviews, etc.).
- Incorporate project management objectives into annual performance reviews.
- Consistent program and project metrics should be instituted based on time, cost, resources, quality and customer satisfaction (including earned value, where applicable). There are a number of tools that can help with estimating, resource allocation, level loading and resource utilization.
- Management must be provided with meaningful visibility into projects if suspicion and distrust are to be minimized. The ability to compare planned to actual results or base lines is essential for effective project management.
- The key to good project management is effective and honest communications.
- A formal escalation process, with clear accountability and roles should be established to resolve key program/project issues, risks and approve changes.
- A consistent methodology must be developed and applied to report the **RAG** (eg **R**ed, **A**mber or **G**reen status of programs, projects or other major tasks. Red = significant trouble; Amber = emerging trouble; Green = everything is on target).
- Reporting must be produced on a consistent basis (eg weekly, bi-weekly, monthly, other) using a consistent format (eg with allowances made for the audience of the report).
- A formal time tracking system should be in place to record how time is spent on projects.

Resource optimization, availability and commitment:
- Sponsors and program/project managers should have access to the right resources based on the project phase, and task requirements and competencies needed.
- The availability and commitment of the resources should be guaranteed by senior management once the program/project is approved and resourced.

Program/project management lessons learned:
- Lessons learned should be developed and made available to all constituencies who require them, with consideration given to security and access policies.
- Current and evolving best practice benchmarking should be tracked, adopted and continuously improved.
- Maintain a project management knowledge management system of lessons learned and lessons to be changed.
- Desirable work must be rewarded; undesirable work must be changed.

Chapter 6: IT Service Management
Based on a review of best practice companies, a number of consistent practices seem to be prevalent in these organizations, with regard to superior IT Service Management. They include:

- All steady-state operations (eg PBX, Data Center, Help Desk, Network Management, etc.) must have a primary owner and secondary (back-up) owner.
- The overall ITSM budget should be divided into a set of defined products and services, so that all IT costs can be mapped to supportable business processes, either directly or indirectly.
- All IT services should consistently achieve the desired level of efficiency, productivity, reliability and availability, as measured by the appropriate key performance indicators (eg service level agreements, customer satisfaction, costs, etc.).

- Most IT services should be described as processes that are well documented, consistently performed and repeatable to maximize their efficiency.
- Most ITSM services should be charged back to the user or customer organization to achieve a greater level of accountability.
- The use of an IT service catalogue that can define, price and provide estimated installation time for repetitive productized IT services (eg install a new computer or network connection) is growing in use. It can benefit the customer by providing an easy way to select, order and communicate to IT the required services desired by the customer. The service catalogue does not work for complex, one time initiatives that are not repetitive.
- A formal ITSM governance, reporting and escalation process should be established to resolve key operational issues, risks and conduct periodic reviews. All steady-state operations have business continuity, back-up (including one or more off-site locations), disaster recovery and security policies and procedures.
- All ITSM related processes should be documented in a consistent, repeatable and standard framework, consisting of life cycles, processes and metrics. such as ITIL (IT Infrastructure Library) or ISO/IEC 20000 and be continuously improved.
- Optimizing the utilization of IT assets and resources is critical.

IT Service Management is complex, and requires dedicated resources and leadership to implement effectively. It helps to transition an organization from chaos to order, from a reactive to a proactive environment, from firefighting (most of the time) to a planned environment (with firefighting some of the time), and from random service efforts to predictable and more cost effective service quality. ITIL, much like other IT governance frameworks, represents a journey that is based on a combination of formal life cycle phases, processes and checklists, combined with common sense and managing change proactively.

An IT Service Management initiative does not end after the framework has been implemented. It must be continually monitored, maintained and improved.

Chapter 7: Strategic sourcing, outsourcing and vendor management

Even with the increased outsourcing initiatives in customer organizations, it appears that organizations continue to struggle with establishing and enforcing a more formal, consistent and repeatable outsourcing policy, process and methodology. There are a number of best practice principles and practices that can represent a checklist for helping companies achieve sourcing and outsourcing improvements:

- establishing an appropriate outsourcing strategy, business case and plan
- identifying the appropriate (and prioritizing) the outsourcing opportunities
- developing appropriate approaches and techniques for outsourcing activities
- identifying, selecting and negotiating a 'win-win' deal for service providers
- managing service provider governance and performance management
- managing the transition from the customer to the service provider as a project
- managing the on-going relationship
- conducting periodic formal progress reviews and reports, based on specific metrics relating to the type of outsourcing service or project

- for large initiatives, establishing a high level peer outsourcing governance board for joint reviews
- assigning a service provider account relationship manager as a single point of contact/interface with the customer, and establishing a customer/service provider relationship model

Customer "to do's"
- executive alignment and commitment to outsourcing that creates a favorable outsourcing culture within the organization
- create a well defined and realistic business case process and case with alternatives
- establish a consistent and formal process for service provider selection and contract negotiations
- develop an outsourcing transition plan from pilot to full implementation, with either re-deployment or termination of displaced resources
- build key performance indicators into the contract performance evaluation system, with both rewards for extraordinary performance and penalties for poor performance
- make KPIs relevant, simple, comparable, easy to report and focused on measurable outcomes
- develop an outsourcing communication plan, risk management and mitigation plan, policy and process
- balance stakeholder needs – companies that successfully outsource continuously 'take the pulse' of all stakeholder groups to adjust their needs over time
- pursue stakeholder involvement on major outsourcing deals, through governance boards, steering committees and working committees
- manage the expectations of all stakeholders well – deliver what you promise; do not over-promise things you or the outsourcing service provider cannot deliver – credibility is a fleeting attribute that, if lost, is extremely difficult or almost impossible to regain
- experience matters – governance groups can rapidly fill their experience deficit through subject matter expert coaching or outside consulting support
- SLAs are not enough – service-level agreements are extremely important and should be continuously refined and improved over the life of the contract; however, they must be augmented by other methods to ensure customer satisfaction (eg formal and/or informal surveys, listening to the voice of the customer, etc.)
- develop disengagement options and conditions as part of the contract that includes renegotiations options; do not put all of the eggs in one basket
- make sure that a disaster prevention and recovery plan with contingencies is in place

Service provider 'do's':
- understand the expectations of the customer
- communicate your expectations of the customer to the customer
- industry and application knowledge, insight and skills are key
- must be able to scale for volume, capacity, people resources, etc.
- proven methodology, meaningful metrics and performance management reporting
- outline processes and behaviors
- communicate critical information to avoid cultural misunderstandings
- build cross-cultural relationships vital to team success
- use a relationship model with escalation considerations
- have back-up, and recovery plans and facilities

Chapter 8: Performance management and management controls

As part of improving IT governance, it is critical for an organization to establish an overall framework that includes amongst other things, an IT enterprise strategy (which includes business capability roadmaps and Balanced Scorecard metrics), performance management, management controls and compliance components. By using industry best practice frameworks or guidelines, and their components (such as COSO® and CobiT®), a company can develop a more consistent approach to making IT performance management and management controls more effective and sustainable. One needs to assign decision authority, ownership and link deliverables and performance to a reward structure, to make individuals and teams more accountable.

Principles for achieving performance management and management control excellence include:

- identify critical success factors for the business and IT, and identify the key performance indicators (KPIs) linked to these factors
- build key performance indicators into your performance evaluation system, starting at the top and permeating to all positions that can influence those KPIs
- make KPIs relevant, simple, comparable, easy-to-report and focused on goals and objectives
- define and issue a management control policy and related procedures, which identify all of the areas requiring management controls, using CobiT as a checklist
- monitor, audit and ensure that IT operates in accordance with the approved controls
- develop a risk management and mitigation plan, policy and process
- develop a business/IT continuity and disaster recovery plan and policy
- develop a clear performance review, escalation and issues resolution policy and process, with clear accountability and responsibilities
- develop key performance indicators with balance and the 'big picture' in mind (outward from IT to the business and inward to manage IT)
- integrate key performance indicators into individual and team performance evaluation systems
- broad executive commitment – use a mix of business and IT leadership in the design, selection, review and continuous improvement of metrics
- develop standard metrics definition based on consensus
- establish an IT governance and control framework
- establish a management compliance forum
- determine Sarbanes-Oxley and/or other regulatory compliance requirements
- determine IT owners for applications and general controls
- manage performance, control and compliance issues

The execution of these plans and objectives must be monitored and measured by a combination of Balanced Scorecard key performance indicators (KPIs), as well as formal and informal status review meetings and reports (eg report cards, dashboards). The outcomes should link critical success factors to KPIs that are measurable, part of a standard reporting system and linked to a governance component. If one cannot measure it, it does not count. Remember, one gets what one measures, so it is critical to measure and control the right things.

9.4   Lessons learned

IT governance is a broad and complex topic, with many parts. IT governance represents a journey. It is not a one time event, and to achieve higher levels of IT maturity, IT governance should be persistently and relentlessly pursued, both from a top-down and a bottom-up perspective. Creating and sustaining a more effective IT governance environment will take time and resources, and should be focused on achieving incremental IT governance successes in priority areas, based on their value proposition or reduction of major 'pain point' to the organization.

It is critical to break down or segment the IT governance initiative into manageable, assignable and measurable components, or work packages with targeted deliverables. It is important to define clear roles for the board, executive management and the IT governance project team, including ownership and accountability for each component and the overall initiative.

Based on the extensive research and case studies, the major lessons learned to be successful in implementing a successful IT governance initiative must:

* have corporate mandate from the top
* have dedicated and available resources
* recognize that 80 to 90% of an IT governance initiative represents a 'cultural change', and organizations must prepare for a lengthy and involved period of adjustment
* use a phased approach to implement new processes and enabling technologies
* develop and conduct a marketing, communications and awareness campaign focus on value propositions
* create a 'continuous IT governance improvement group', to sustain the momentum, be advocates, act as change agents and sustain the framework and components
* use 'total cost of operations' as a measure of improvement from the current state baseline to the future state baseline

9.5   Critical success factors

Critical success factors for achieving IT governance excellence:

* Create the right environment and culture:
  - establish the appropriate organizational mindset, culture and environment
  - obtain executive sponsorship, commitment and multi-level management buy-in and ownership
  - establish an IT executive governance steering committee and working committee with clearly defined roles and responsibilities
  - success depends on creating a sustainable foundation (eg policy, process, metrics) for managing programs and projects, and integrating results and methodologies into the culture of the organization
  - define roles and get the right people involved in phase
  - market and re-enforce (eg training, rewards, mentors, tools, flexible processes) the value and benefits of good IT governance practices

- understand the risks, constraints and obstacles and develop contingency plans and actions
- adopt a flexible and scalable IT governance process (phases, templates, repository, tools and tailor when required) to accommodate different levels of maturity and organizational styles

- Develop an IT governance implementation plan:
  - define the project's charter and boundaries including scope, objectives, requirements and deliverables
  - establish well-defined phases/tasks, 'go/no go' gates and milestones (break the job down into manageable work packages – '80 hour' rule) with realistic baselines (costs, time, resources and contingencies) based on short term incremental and visible deliverables
  - define a responsibility assignment matrix – Responsible, Inform, Consult and/or Approve
  - establish formal change management and risk management processes
  - establish and assess current baseline in terms of costs, resources, competencies, documentation, levels of maturity and identify gaps
  - define the future desired or targeted baseline

- Ensure governance and excellent communications:
  - establish a governance, control, reporting and escalation policy and process
  - manage expectations of all stakeholders proactively
  - identify, measure and track mandatory and discretionary vital signs, metrics, key issues and take necessary actions quickly – knock obstacles out of the way
  - establish frequent and open communications with stakeholders (both formal and informal review meetings) on a daily, weekly, monthly and quarterly basis depending on the project's importance and closeness to being implemented
  - ensure accurate, timely and meaningful monitoring and progress reporting

- Institutionalize and operationalize IT governance
  - create IT governance 'centers of excellence' (eg Advocacy Center, Help Desk, Education, Training, Subject Matter Expert Help, Process, Project Tracking, Certification, Website, etc.)
  - create a reward and/or recognition policy to re-enforce and sustain
  - conduct formal program/project reviews
  - develop and use consistent, flexible and scalable processes (eg fast track or light versus complex projects) and automate processes and tools (web-based)
  - capture and apply lessons learned, and focus on continuous improvement

9.6   Implications for the future and personal action plan

Implications for the future

The approach to IT governance must be consistent, but yet scalable and tailored to each organization's environment and management style, issues, opportunities, level of maturity, audit/legal requirements, available resources and cultural readiness. Remember, IT governance represents a journey towards higher levels of IT maturity and effectiveness.

There are numerous alternative models and standards for companies to help plan, deploy and manage an IT governance initiative, which focuses on reaching higher levels of IT maturity and effectiveness.

While there is no single right or best way for organizations to approach improvements in IT governance, this book proposes a comprehensive and integrated IT governance framework and roadmap, which identifies the appropriate current and emerging best practice methodologies for each of the major IT governance components that must be addressed in any approach, and is critical for companies to achieve more effective alignment and management of IT. The framework can serve as a guideline for organizations to select and customize the appropriate approach applicable to their environment, priorities, capabilities and available resources. A balanced approach, consisting of both a top-down framework and roadmap, together with bottom-up implementation is essential for success.

Personal action plan
Based on the lessons learned, the critical success factors identified in the book and your own experience regarding IT governance:

- identifyyour and your organizations' strengths, limitations and gaps
- list and prioritize the gaps in the processes, skills, techniques and tools you and your organization wants and needs to develop and/or update
- defineyour and your organizations' action plan for next steps:
  – create awareness and commitment to action
  – develop a plan with ownership, milestones and metrics
  – use, as appropriate, inside/outside subject matter experts to fill the gaps and facilitate organizational change and transformation
  – institute continuous learning and education – improve your skills, competencies and knowledge of the relevant standards, processes, tools, techniques, etc.
  – institute continuous process improvement, based on current and emerging best practices

"Now this is not the end. It is not even the beginning of the end. But it is, perhaps, the end of the beginning."

- Sir Winston Churchill,
Former British Prime Minister, 1942

Glossary

Alphabetical List

A:

Absorption Costing: A principle whereby fixed, as well as variable costs, are allotted to cost units, and total overheads are absorbed according to activity level.

Acceptance: The agreement by the customer that the deliverable meets contractual requirements.

Accomplishment: The value of work completed in accordance with the predetermined baseline value for that work. The terms "accomplishment", "earned value", and "baseline cost for work performed" are all synonymous.

Account Manager: Account Manager is the customer interface.

Accountability Matrix: See Responsibility Assignment Matrix.

Accounting Period: The period into which time is sectioned for cost accumulation, accounting, and performance measurement purposed.

Accrual: The recognition of events and conditions as they occur, rather than in the period of their incurrence, receipt, or payment.

Action Lists: Defined actions, allocated to recovery teams and individuals, within a phase of a plan. These are supported by reference data.

Activity Definition: A narrative depiction of the detail steps required to complete an activity, often including inputs and outputs (handoffs and deliverables) and responsibility assignment.

Activity Description (AD): A short phrase or label used in a project network diagram. The activity description normally describes the scope of work of the activity.

Activity Duration Estimating: Estimating the number of work periods, which will be needed to complete individual activities or tasks.

Activity: An element of work performed. An activity normally has an expected duration, an expected cost, and expected resource requirement. Activities are often synonymous with tasks.

Activity-Based Costing: Activity-based costing looks at aspects of an organization's operations and attempts to answer the very simple, but sometimes hard to answer question, 'How much does it cost to do that?' For example, how much does a company spend processing a receivable or taking a customer call? How much does it cost a city to fill a pothole? The term relates to outsourcing, in that once an organization can answer the cost question at the activity level, it can more objectively compare the cost of internal versus external sourcing for performing it.

Activity-On-Arrow (AOA): See Arrow Diagramming Method.

Activity-On-Node (AON): See Precedence Diagramming Method.

Actual Baseline Chart: A Bar (Gantt) Chart that compares the current schedule with the baseline schedule.

Actual Cost of Work Performed (ACWP): Total costs incurred (direct and indirect) in accomplishing work during a given time period. See also Earned Value.

Actual Finish Date (AF): The point in time that work actually ended on an activity or tasks. (Note in some application areas, the activity is considered "finished" when work is "substantially complete.")

Actual Progress: All activities or portions thereof occurring prior to the status date on an updated schedule or progress report. Any one of a number of methods (milestone, percent complete, remaining duration, etc.) is used to evaluate or portray status to date on in-process activities; some measure accomplishment, while others only assess time.

Actual Start Date (AS): The point in time that work actually started on an activity.

ACWP: Actual Cost of Work Performed.

Administrative Closure: Generating, gathering and disseminating information to formalize project completion.

Agreement: The written agreement (contract or statement of work) between the customer and the contractor covering the work to be performed.

Alert Phase: The first phase of a business continuity plan in which initial emergency procedures and damage assessments are activated.

Alignment: Process to ensure that IT supports the objectives and direction of the business.

Allocated Cost: A cost that can be directly identified with a business unit.

ANSI: American National Standards Institute, responsible for creating and managing US standards. See ISO.

AOA: Activity-On-Arrow.

AON: Activity-On-Node.

Application Area: Application areas are usually defined in terms of either the product of the project (ie, by similar technologies or industry sectors) or the type of customer (eg internal vs external, government vs commercial) or the function it supports (finance, manufacturing, etc...).

Apportioned Cost: A cost that is shared by a number of business units (an indirect cost). This cost must be shared out between these units on an equitable basis.

Arrow Diagramming Method (ADM): A network diagramming technique in which activities are represented by arrows. The tail of the arrow represents the start and the head represents the finish of the activity (the length of the arrow does not represent the expected duration of the activity). Activities are connected at points called nodes (usually drawn as small circles) to illustrate the sequence in which the activities are expected to be performed. See also Precedence Diagramming Method.

Arrow: The graphic presentation of an activity in ADM. See Arrow Diagramming Method.

ASPs: Application Service Providers are companies that remotely host software applications and provide access to and use of the applications over the internet or a private network. Typically, the service fee is usage based, for example, per user per month.

Assessment: Analyze or evaluate or check whether a standard or guideline is being followed and/or that efficiency, effectiveness or maturity targets are being met.

Asset: Component of a business process. Assets can include people, accommodation, computer systems, networks, paper records, fax machines, facilities, etc.

Audit: (1) An independent review for the purpose of assessing compliance with scope, requirements, specifications, baselines, standards, procedures, instructions, codes and contractual and licensing requirements. (2) An activity to determine through investigation the adequacy of and adherence to established procedures, instructions, specifications, codes, standards or regulations, and the effectiveness of implementation.

Authorized Work: That effort which has been defined and is on contract (original negotiated contract and all negotiated change orders).

Availability Management: Availability Management is the process of ensuring the appropriate deployment of resources, methods and techniques, to support the availability of IT services agreed to with customer. Availability Management addresses issues such as optimizing maintenance, design measures to minimize the number of incidents.

Availability: Ability of a component or service to perform its required function at a stated instant or over a stated period of time. It is usually expressed as the availability ratio, ie the proportion of time that the service is actually available for use by the Customers within the agreed service hours.

B:

BAC: Baseline at Completion.

Back-up: Provisions made for back-up and recovery of facilities, equipment, systems, people and other resources and/or assets.

Backward Pass: The calculation of late finish dates and late start dates for the uncompleted portions of all the network activities. Determined by working backwards through the network logic from the project's end date. The end date may be calculated in a forward pass or set by the customer or sponsor. See also Network Analysis.

Balanced Scorecard: Performance management tool that helps to breakdown key performance indicators into financial targets, internal processes, customer satisfaction and learning and growth metrics, which are used to measure an organization's effectiveness. Developed by Drs. Robert Kaplan and David Norton.

Bar Chart: A graphic display of schedule-related information. In the typical bar chart, activities or tasks and other project elements are listed down the left side of the chart, dates are shown across the top, and activity durations are shown as date-placed horizontal bars. Also called a Gantt chart.

Baseline Authorization (BA): A document which identifies the scope of work, baseline, and schedule. Once approved, the BA is a "contract" between the customer (sponsor) and project management.

Baseline Maintenance: The term used to describe control of revisions to the budgets. Baseline revisions are made as a result of contract or SOW changes, regulatory changes, or internal re-planning.

Baseline Rates: Baseline rates are established for all labor and other expense categories consistent with the methods employed to record actual costs.

Baseline: The original plan (for a project, a work package, an activity or task), plus or minus approved changes. Usually used with a modifier (eg cost baseline, schedule baseline, performance measurement baseline, people baseline). Also called a reference base.

BCWP: Budgeted (baseline) Cost for Work Performed.

BCWS: Budgeted (baseline) Cost for Work Scheduled.

Benchmark: An objective measure of performance that can be used to compare performance across organizations against best practice organizations. One can benchmark a variety of metrics, such as cost, time, quality, speed, profit etc.

Best Practice: Proven activities, methodologies, processes and/or frameworks that have been successfully used by multiple organizations.

Bid & Proposal (B&P): Effort associated with the preparation and submittal of pricing in the proposals.

Bid: To submit a price for products or services; a proposal either verbal or written, for doing work and for supplying materials, equipment, people, systems and other resources.

Bottom-Up: Data collection starting at the lowest (usually the work package) level and, through the WBS, summarized to the contract or SOW or product or systems level.

BPO: Business Process Outsourcing puts together two powerful business tools - business process management and outsourcing. Business process management uses technology to break down barriers between traditional functional silos, such as those found in finance, order processing, and call centers. Outsourcing uses skills and resources of specialized outside service providers to perform many of these critical, yet non-core activities. BPO means examining the processes that make up the business and its functional units, and streamlining them.

Brand Management: The management of a brand from its inception to its maturity and decline.

Brand: The identity of a product in the eyes of the buyer in terms of such attributes such as quality, value, durability, high technology, safety, etc.

British Standards Institution (BSI): The UK National Standards body, responsible for creating and maintaining British standards.

BS7799: The British standard for Information Security Management. This standard provides a comprehensive set of controls comprising best practices in information security.

Budget Allocation: An allocation of resources to the functional departments, measured in terms of people-hours, dollars, or other designated units, for accomplishing specific tasks.

Budget At Completion (BAC): The estimate total budgeted cost of the project when completed.

Budget: The resources (measured in dollars, people-hours, or other definitive units) which are formally assigned for the accomplishment of a specified task or group of tasks.

Budgeted Cost of Work Performed (BCWP): The value of work completed (including any overhead allocation) for activities (or portions of activities) during a given period (usually project-to-date). See also Earned Value.

Budgeted Cost of Work Scheduled (BCWS): The sum of the approved cost estimates (including any overhead allocation) for activities (or portions of activities) completed during a given period (usually project-to-date). See also Earned Value.

Business Case: The business, economic, technology and regulatory motivations for pursuing an initiative stated in terms of business, requirements, costs and benefits, resources and risk.

Business Design Phase: The period during the Systems Development Lifecycle when the development team performs system design activities requiring active customer participation and approval.

Business Function: A business unit within an organisation, eg a department, division, branch.

Business Planning: Planning that addresses such topics as the vision of the organization, the target markets, the products and services the organization will offer, how the organization will achieve and maintain a competitive advantage and financials. The process of producing a business plan.

Business Process (BP): A group of business activities undertaken by an organization in pursuit of a common goal. Typical business processes include receiving orders, marketing services, selling products, delivering services, distributing products, invoicing for services, accounting for money received. A business process usually depends upon several business functions for support, eg IT, personnel, operations. A business process rarely operates in isolation, ie other business processes will depend on it and it will depend on other processes.

Business Recovery Objective: The desired time within which business processes should be recovered, and the minimum staff, assets and services required within this time.

Business Recovery Plans: Documents describing the roles, responsibilities and actions necessary to resume business processes following a business disruption.

Business Requirements: Criteria that define a business need, opportunity and/or solution.

Business Unit: A segment of the business entity by which both revenues are received and expenditure are caused or controlled, such revenues and expenditure being used to evaluate segmental performance.

C:

Calendar Unit: The smallest unit of time used in scheduling the project. Calendar units are generally in hours, days, or weeks, but can also be in shifts or even in minutes.

Capacity Management: Capacity Management is the process of optimizing the cost, timing of acquisition, and deployment of IT resources, to support the agreements made with the customer. Capacity management addresses resource management, performance management, demand management, modeling, capacity planning, load management and application sizing. Capacity Management emphasizes planning to ensure that the agreed to Service Levels can be fulfilled.

Capital Costs: Typically those costs applying to the physical (substantial) assets of the organisation. Traditionally this was equipment necessary to produce the enterprise's product. Capital Costs are the purchase or major enhancement of fixed assets, for example computer equipment, building and plant and are often also referred to as 'one-off' costs.

Capital Investment Proposal: The process of evaluating proposed investment in initiatives or assets and the benefits to be obtained from their acquisition. The techniques used in the evaluation can be summarized as return on capital and payback period, and discounted cash flow methods.

Capitalization: The process of identifying major expenditure as Capital, whether there is a substantial asset or not, to reduce the impact on the current financial year of such expenditure. The most common item for this to be applied to is software, whether developed in-house or purchased.

Captive Center: A company-owned offshore operation. The activities are performed offshore, but they are not outsourced to another company.

Cash Flow: The net flow of dollars into or out of a project. The algebraic sum, in any time period, of all cash receipts, expenses, and investments. Also called cash proceeds or cash generated. The stream of monetary (dollar) values - costs and benefits - resulting from a project investment.

CCB: Change Control Board.

Change Analysis: The function of reviewing a change to a program or project to assess impact prior to applying the change.

Change Control Board (CCB): A formally constituted group of stakeholders responsible for approving or rejecting changes to the project baselines.

Change Control: The process by which a change is proposed, evaluated, approved or rejected, scheduled, implemented, tested and tracked.

Change in Scope: See Scope Change.

Change Log: A log of Requests for Change raised during the project, showing information on each Change, its evaluation, what decisions have been made and its current status, eg Initiated, Reviewed, Approved, Implemented, Closed.

Change Management: See Change Control.

Change Order: A formal authorization by the customer, sponsor and/or project manager for a change or variance to an existing contract.

Change: Alteration or variation to a scope of work and/or the schedule/cost for completing the work.

Chart of Accounts: Any numbering system used to monitor project costs by category (eg labor, supplies, materials). The project chart of accounts is usually based upon the corporate chart of accounts of the primary performing organization.

Charter: See Project Charter.

Claim: A written statement requesting additional time and/or money for acts or omissions during the performance of the contract. The contract must provide for collecting the facts and identifying the circumstances for which the customer is responsible to be entitled to additional compensation and/or time.

Classification: Process of formally grouping Configuration Items by type, eg software, hardware, documentation, environment, application.

Client: The customer who has contracted for services.

CMMI®: Capability Maturity Model Integrated- Developed by the Software Engineering Institute (SEI) as a phased approach to develop software or systems with a focus on quality. CMMI® is an organizational certification.

Command, Control and Communications: The processes by which an organization retains overall co-ordination of its recovery effort during deployment of business recovery plans.

Committed Costs: Costs, which have been contractually committed, but not yet used on a project (should be considered when calculating earned value).

Communications Planning: Determining the information and communications needs of the project stakeholders.

Concurrent Engineering: An approach to project staffing that, in its most general form, calls for implementers to be involved in the design phase.

Configuration Baseline: Configuration of a product or system established at a specific point in time, which captures both the structure and details of the product or system, and enables that product or system to be rebuilt at a later date.

Configuration Control: The process of evaluating, approving or disapproving, and co-ordinating changes to configuration items after final establishment of their configuration identification.

Configuration Documentation: Documents that define requirements, system design, build, production, and verification for a configuration item.

Configuration Identification: Activities that determine the product structure, the selection of Configuration Items, and the documentation of the Configuration Item's physical and functional characteristics including interfaces and subsequent Changes. It includes the allocation of identification characters or numbers to the Configuration Items and their documents. It also includes the unique numbering of configuration control forms associated with Changes and Problems.

Configuration Item (CI): Component of an infrastructure - or an item, such as a Request for Change, associated with an infrastructure - which is (or is to be) under the control of Configuration Management. CIs may vary widely in complexity, size and type - from an entire system (including all hardware, software, network and documentation) to a single module or a minor hardware component.

Configuration Management Database: A database which contains all relevant details of each CI and details of the important relationships between CIs.

Configuration Management Tool (CM Tool): A software product providing automatic support for Change, Configuration or version control.

Configuration Management: The process of identifying and defining the elements in a system, controlling the release and change of these items throughout the life cycle, recording and reporting the status of configuration items and change requests, and verifying the completeness and correctness of configuration items.

Configuration: (1) The requirements, design, and implementation that define a particular version of a product or system. (2) The functional and/or physical characteristics of a product or system.

Constraint: The logical relationship between the start and/or finish of one activity and the start and/or finish of another activity. Also, Conditions that define or restrict how project objectives are met (constraints may include policies, environment, staff, technology, budgets, regulations and schedules).

Context Diagram: The top-level diagram of a leveled set of data-flow diagrams that portrays all the net inputs and outputs of a system; also called the system interface model.

Contingencies: See Reserve, and Contingency Planning.

Contingency Allowance: See Reserve.

Contingency Planning: The development of a management plan that identifies alternative strategies and plans to be used to ensure success if specified risk events occur.

Contingency Reserve: A separately planned cushion is used to allow for future situations, which may be planned for only in part. (sometimes called "known unknowns"). For example, rework is certain, the amount of rework is not. Contingency reserves may involve cost, schedule, people, etc. Contingency reserves are intended to reduce the impact of missing cost or schedule objectives. Contingency reserves are normally included in the project's cost and schedule baselines.

Contract Administration: Managing the relationship with the seller.

Contract Change (Contract Directed Change): A revision approved by the customer in writing directing a change to the contract. Contract changes authorize a change in scope of work or schedule and normally result in a dollar change to the Total Contract Baseline.

Contract Close-out: Completion and settlement of the contract, including resolution of all outstanding items.

Contract Cost: The contract target cost (excluding profit or fee) negotiated for all authorized work defined in the Statement of Work when the contract is defined.

Contract Date: Any date specified in the contract or imposed on any project activity or event that impacts the activity/project schedule.

Contract Price/Contract Target Price: The total value, including fee, for the contract.

Contract: A contract is a mutually binding agreement, which obligates the seller to provide the specified product, and obligates the buyer to pay for it. Contracts generally fall into one of three broad categories: Fixed price or lump sum contracts - this category of contract involves a fixed total price for a well-defined product. Fixed price contracts may also include incentives for meeting or exceeding selected project objectives such as schedule targets. Cost reimbursable contracts - this category of contract involves payment (reimbursement) to the contractor for its actual costs. Costs are usually classed as direct costs (costs incurred directly by the project, such as wages for members of the project team) and indirect costs (costs allocated to the project by the performing organization as a cost of doing business, such as salaries for corporate executives). Indirect costs are usually calculated as a percentage of direct costs. Cost reimbursable contracts often include incentives for meeting or exceeding selected project objectives such as schedule targets or total cost. Unit price contracts - the contractor is paid a preset amount per unit of service (eg, $100 per hour for professional services or $2.00 per cubic yard of earth removed) and the total value of the contract is a function of the quantities needed to complete the work.

Control Charts: Control charts are a graphic display of the results, over time and against established control limits, of a process. They are used to determine if the process is "in control" or in need of adjustment.

Control: The process of comparing actual performance with planned performance, analyzing variances, evaluating possible alternatives, analyzing issues and taking appropriate corrective action as needed.

COP: Certified Outsourcing Professional. This is an individual certification issued by the international association of outsourcing professionals.

Core Competencies: The unique internal skills and knowledge sets that define an organization's competitive advantage and strengths.

Corrective Action Log: A log established to monitor action items and corrective actions.

Corrective Action: Changes made to bring expected future performance of the project into line with the plan.

Cost Benefit Analysis: Evaluation of the estimated cost to achieve project objectives against the value (benefits) of the project or phase. Uses select project investment choices using one time and recurring costs and benefits. Various financial measures may be used such as Net Present Value (NPV), Return on Investment (ROI), Payback Period and others.

Cost Budgeting: Allocating the cost estimates to individual project elements or tasks.

Cost Control: Controlling changes to the project budget.

Cost Effectiveness: Ensuring that there is a proper balance between the quality of service on the one side and expenditure on the other. Any investment that increases the costs of providing IT services should always result in enhancement to service quality or quantity.

Cost Estimate: An evaluation of all costs of the elements of a project or effort as defined by an agreed-upon scope.

Cost Estimating: Estimating the cost of the resources needed to complete project activities.

Cost Management: All the procedures, tasks and deliverables that are needed to fulfil an organisation's costing and charging requirements.

Cost of Money: Capital cost of money (cost of capital) is an imputed cost determined by applying cost-of-money rate to capital employed in contract performance. Capital employed is determined without regard to whether its source is equity or borrowed capital.

Cost of Quality: The costs incurred to ensure quality. The cost of quality includes quality planning, quality control, quality assurance, and rework.

Cost Performance Index (CPI): The ratio of budgeted costs to actual costs (BCWP/ACWP). CPI is often used to predict the magnitude of a possible cost overrun or under-run. A relative percentage indicator of cost efficiency. Values greater that 1.0 indicated efficiency is better (eg CPI =1.3 indicates work has been accomplished 30% more efficiently than baselined). Values less than 1.0 indicate efficiency is worse (eg CPI = .80 indicates work has been accomplished 20% less efficiently than baselined).

Cost Plus Fixed Fee (CPFF) Contract: A type of contract where the buyer reimburses the seller for the allowable costs (allowable costs are defined by the contract) plus a fixed amount of profit (fee).

Cost Plus Incentive Fee (CPIF) Contract: A type of contract where the buyer reimburses the seller for the seller's allowable costs (allowable costs are defined by the contract), and the seller earns its profit if it meets defined performance criteria.

Cost Proposal: An all-inclusive statement of work effort and associated cost factors, which includes, but is not limited to, equipment and human resources, software development, training, etc.

Cost Sharing: On a cost plus incentive fee (CPIF) type contract, a clause is included which defines a share ratio for cost over/underruns which normally is 80/20%. That is, the customer will reimburse the contractor 80% of the total overrun (100% of the overrun, less 20% of the overrun amount, from the fee) on underrun the contractor receives an additional 20% of the underrun amount as incentive fee.

Cost Variance (CV): (1) Any difference between the estimated cost of an activity and the actual cost of that activity. (2) In earned value, BCWP less ACWP.

Cost: Cost is a measurement, in monetary terms, of the amount of resources used for some purpose.

Countermeasure: A check or restraint on the service designed to enhance security by reducing the risk of an attack (by reducing either the threat or the vulnerability), reducing the Impact of an attack, detecting the occurrence of an attack and/or assisting in the recovery from an attack.

CPI: Cost Performance Index.

CPIF: Cost Plus Incentive Fee.

CPM: Critical Path Method.

Critical Activity (Task): Any activity (task) on a critical path. Most commonly determined by using the critical path method.

Critical Path Method (CPM): A network analysis technique used to predict project duration by analyzing which sequence of activities or tasks (which path) has the least amount of scheduling flexibility (the least amount of float). Early dates are calculated by means of a forward pass using a specified start date. Late dates are calculated by means of a backward pass starting from a specified completion date (usually the forward pass's calculated project early finish date).

Critical Path Network: A plan for executing a project that consists of activities, their durations, and their logical relationships to one another.

Critical Path: In a project network diagram, the series of activities (tasks) which determines the earliest completion of the project. The critical path will generally change from time to time as activities are completed ahead of or behind schedule. Although normally calculated for the entire project, the critical path can also be determined for a milestone or a subproject. The critical path is usually defined as those activities with float equal to zero. See Critical Path Method.

Critical Versus Core: Many operations are critical to a business's operations but do not represent a differentiating competitive capability; that is, they are not core competencies. A classic example is payroll. Processing payroll accurately and timely is critical to the success of any organization, but is a core competency of very few organizations – mainly those that provide this service to other companies as their business.

Customer Reporting Level: The lowest level of the Work Breakdown Structure at which performance data is reported to the customer.

Customer: The recipient and/or ultimate owner of the deliverable produced as a result of an agreement.

CV: Cost Variance.

D:

Data Management: The function of organizing, cataloguing, structuring, locating, storing, maintaining, retrieving, securing, and recovering data, including the processes of data modeling, data mining, data warehousing and data base administration.

Deadline: A date by which a project, activity and/or task must be finished.

Definitive Software Library (DSL): The library in which the definitive authorized versions of all software CIs are stored and protected. It is a physical library or storage repository where master copies of software versions are placed. They should be separate from development and test filestore areas. The DSL may also include a physical store to hold master copies of bought-in software, eg fire-proof safe. Only authorized software should be accepted into the DSL, strictly controlled by Change and Release Management. The DSL exists not directly because of the needs of the Configuration Management process, but as a common base for the Release Management and Configuration Management processes.

Deliverable: Any measurable, tangible, verifiable outcome, result, or item that must be produced to complete a project or part of a project.

Dependency: See Logical Relationship.

Depreciation: The loss in value of an asset due to its use and/or the passage of time. The annual depreciation charge in accounts represents the amount of capital assets used up in the accounting period. It is charged in the cost accounts to ensure that the cost of capital equipment is reflected in the unit costs of the services provided using the equipment. There are various methods of calculating depreciation.

Detail Schedule: Lowest-level method of scheduling and determining status of a work package that is contained in the Cost Account Plan or budget.

Deviation: A departure from established requirements. A deviation in the work product may be classified as an imperfection, non conformance, or defect, based on its severity in failing to meet or unnecessarily exceed the requirements.

Direct Costs: Any cost which can be identified specifically with a particular final cost objective. It consists of those costs (labor, material, etc.), that can be directly charged to the contract or product or service without distribution to an overhead unit.

Direct Labor: Any labor cost that can be specifically identified with a particular final contract objective. It consists of labor that can be directly charged to the contract or project without distribution to an overhead unit. It excludes materials, as well as overhead costs, and cost of money.

Disaster Recovery Planning: A series of processes that focus only upon the recovery processes, principally in response to physical disasters, which are contained within Business Continuity Plan.

Disaster Recovery: The process of executing a definitive plan for recovery from any act, natural or man-made, which caused the system, product or facility to fail.

Discounted Cash Flow: An evaluation of the future net cash flows generated by a project by discounting them to their present-day value.

Division/Department: A group with a common operational orientation, such as Technical, Operations, Quality Assurance, Finance or a Strategic Business Unit.

Dummy Activity: An activity (task) of zero duration used to show a logical network relationship in the arrow diagramming method. Dummy activities are used when logical relationships cannot be completely or correctly described with regular activity arrows. Dummies are shown graphically as a dashed line headed by an arrow.

Duration (DU): The number of work periods (not including holidays or other non-working periods) required to complete an activity or other project element. Usually expressed as workdays or workweeks. Sometimes incorrectly equated with elapsed time. See also Effort.

Duration Compression: Shortening the project schedule without reducing the project scope. Duration compression is not always possible and often requires an increase in project cost.

E:

EAC: Estimate at Completion.

Early Finish Date (EF): In the critical path method, the earliest possible point in time on which the uncompleted portions of an activity (or the. project) can finish based on the network logic and any schedule logical relationships. Early finish dates can change as the project progresses and changes are made to the project plan.

Early Start Date (ES): In the critical path method, the earliest possible point in time on which the unstarted portions of an activity (or the project) can start, based on the network logic and any schedule logical relationships. Early start dates can change as the project progresses and changes are made to the project plan.

Earned Value (EV): (1) A method for measuring project performance. It compares the amount of work that was planned with what was actually accomplished to determine if cost and schedule performance is as planned. See also Actual Cost of Work Performed (acwp), Budgeted Cost of Work Scheduled (bcws), Budgeted Cost of Work Performed (bcwp), Cost Variance (cv), Cost Performance Index (cpi), Schedule Variance (sc), and Schedule Performance Index (SPI). (2) The earned value cost at completion (EAC) = ACWP + Work Remaining/CPI.

EF: Early Finish Date.

Effort: The number of labor units required to complete an activity or other project element. Usually expressed as staffhours, staffdays, or staffweeks. Should not be confused with duration.

Eighty-Hour Rule: All project work should be decomposed into 80-hour periods (two weeks) when deliverables should be produced and formal project status reviews should be held. No magic to the rule. It creates discipline, and incremental deliverables - can be shorter, but should not be any longer.

End Item: The final product or service when completed and ready for release.

Engagement Model (EM): Used to develop better relationships between customers & IT built on trust, open communications, credabilites, knowledge & understanding of each other's environments. The IT Engagement Manager is the interface between the customer & the IT orgazation.

ES: Early Start Date.

eSCM®: The eSourcing capability models developed by the IT Services Qualification Center (ITsqc) at Carnegie Mellon University, to improve sourcing relationships in the internet-enabled economy. ITsqc developed the eSourcing capability models for both service providers (eSCM-SP) and for client organizations (eSCM-CL).

eSourcing Capability Model for Service Providers (eSCM-SP): A framework to help IT Service Providers develop their IT Service Management Capabilities from a Service Sourcing perspective. eSCM-SP was developed by Carnegie Mellon University.

eSourcing Model for Client Organizations (eSCM-CL): A framework to help organizations guide their analysis and decisions on sourcing models and strategies. eSCML-CL was developed by Carnegie Mellon University.

E-Sourcing: Internet-based outsourcing that takes advantage of the application service provider (ASP) delivery model. See ASP.

Estimate At Completion (EAC): The expected total cost of an activity (task), a group of activities (tasks), or the project when the defined scope of work has been completed. Most techniques for forecasting EAC include some adjustment of the original cost estimate based on project performance to date. Also shown as "estimated at completion." Often shown as EAC=Actuals-to-date+ETC. See also Earned Value and Estimate to Complete.

Estimate To Complete (ETC): The expected additional cost needed to complete an activity, a group of activities, or the project. Most techniques for forecasting ETC include some adjustment to the original estimate based on project performance to date. Also called "estimated to complete. See also Earned Value and Estimate at Completion.

Estimate: An assessment of the likely quantitative result. Usually applied to project costs and durations and should always include some indication of accuracy (eg, ± x percent). Usually used with a modifier (eg, preliminary, conceptual, feasibility). Some application areas have specific modifiers that imply particular accuracy ranges (eg, order-of-magnitude estimate, budget estimate, and definitive estimate (in engineering and construction projects). Estimating should become more accurate with each project phase and with more experience.

Estimated Work Remaining (EWR): The forecast of labor hours and costs (direct and indirect) required to complete the authorized work remaining. It is based on past performance plus knowledgeable projections of the scope of the work remaining to be accomplished.

ETC: Estimate (or Estimated) To Complete (or Completion).

EV: Earned Value.

Event-on-Node: A network diagramming technique in which events are presented by boxes (or nodes) connected by arrows to show the sequence in which the events are to occur. Used in the original Program Evaluation and Review Technique (PERT).

Exception Report: Document that includes only major variations from plan (rather than all variations).

F:

Family Tree: Hierarchical product, process or functional structure.

Fast Tracking: Compressing the project processes (schedule) by overlapping activities (tasks) that would normally be done in sequence, such as design and construction and using iterative life cycle methodologies to frequently validate the results with the sponsor or customer.

Fee: The charge for the use of one's services to the extent specified in the contract.

FF: Free Float or Finish-to-Finish.

FFP: Firm Fixed Price.

Financial Management of IT Services: One of the ITIL processes that addresses the budgeting, costs, benefits and charging methods for IT services.

Finish Date: A point in time associated with an activity's completion. Usually qualified by one of the following: actual, planned, estimated, scheduled, early, late, baseline, target or current.

Finish-to-Finish (FF): See Logical Relationship.

Finish-to-Start (FS): See Logical Relationship.

Firm Fixed Price (FFP) Contract: A type of contract where the buyer pays the seller a set amount (as defined by the contract) regardless of the seller's costs.

Fiscal Year: The grouping of twelve accounting months.

Fixed Price Contract: See Firm Fixed Price Contract.

Fixed Price Incentive Fee (FPIF) Contract: A type of contract where the buyer pays the seller a set amount (as defined by the contract), and the seller can earn an additional amount if it meets defined performance criteria.

Forward Pass: The calculation of the early start and early finish dates for the unstarted portions of all network activities. See also Network Analysis and Backward Pass.

Forward Pricing Rates: The progressively escalated rates used to develop an escalated estimate. See Forward Pricing.

Forward Pricing: Use of progressively escalated rates to develop an escalated estimate. (Contrasted with "constant dollar pricing" which uses a single unescalated set of rates to develop an unescalated estimate.)

FPIF: Fixed Price Incentive Fee.

Free Float (FF): The amount of time an activity (task) can be delayed without delaying the early start of any immediately following activities. See also Float.

FS: Finish-to-Start.

Full Cost: The total cost of all the resources used in supplying a service ie the sum of the direct costs of producing the output, a proportional share of overhead costs and any selling and distribution expenses. Both cash costs and non-cash costs should be included, including the cost of capital.

Full Risk Mitigation PM Process: Also known as classical or traditional program or project management, where the PM process is followed and no compression or short cuts are taken. See Fast Tracking.

Functional Manager: A manager responsible for activities in a specialized department or function (eg engineering, manufacturing, marketing). See Division/Department.

Functional organization: An organization structure in which staff are grouped hierarchically by specialty (eg production, marketing, engineering, and accounting at the top level; with engineering, further divided into mechanical, electrical and others).

Functional Process Outsourcing: A company's business processes end at its true customers, the people paying the bills. There are, however, many internal processes that exist to support people within the company and are often performed within a single department. Human resources, finance and accounting, travel, and facilities services are examples. When these functional processes are outsourced, along with the supporting technologies and supply chains that feed into them, it is referred to as functional process outsourcing.

Funding: Funding represents the actual dollars available for expenditure in the accomplishment of contract effort. Funds are normally issued by the customer on a fiscal year or annual basis. Actual release of funds is frequently on an incremental basis within the year. The planning of work and the time-phasing of baselines for a given period must be consistent with the known available funding.

Funds: The sum of money authorized for a specific project or contract. Funds or funding refers to the transactions of real money, which is accounted for in expenditure and commitment reports.

G:

Gain-sharing: A contract structure where both the customer and provider share financially in the value created through the relationship. One example is when a service provider receives a share of the savings it generates for its client.

Gantt Chart: See Bar Chart.

GERT: Graphical Evaluation and Review Technique.

Governance: The oversight and accountability of all aspects of a business, a function like IT or a project. It also defines rules, responsibilities and decision authority of the board, executive management team and others in an organization. Areas of focus include: strategic management, investment management, project management, business/IT alignment, regulatory compliance, performance management, operational management, risk management, ethics and integrity and others.

Graphical Evaluation and Review Technique (GERT): A network analysis technique that allows for conditional and probabilistic treatment of logical relationships (ie, some activities may not be performed).

H:

Hardware/Software Evaluation: Assessment of compatibility between existing or required hardware and new application (or operating systems or database) software that will operate in the environment.

Hierarchy: An outline structure. Any group of tasks with indented levels of detail.

Histogram: A graphic representation of resource availability and utilization levels. A histogram represents these levels by means of a series of rectangular bars above a time scale, with different sizes representing different levels.

Hybrid SDLC: Refers to a systems/software development life cycle process that combines waterfall (sequential) and spiral (iterative) methodologies. See also Waterfall and Spiral.

I:

IFB: Invitation For Bid (similar to RFI and RFP).

Impact Analysis: The identification of critical business processes, and the potential damage or loss that may be caused to the organization resulting from a disruption to those processes.

Incident : Any event which is not part of the standard operation of a service and which causes, or may cause, an interruption to, or a reduction in, the quality of that service.

Incident Management: The Incident Management process aims to resolve the incident and restore the provision of services quickly. If an incident recurs, it is considered a problem.

Indirect Costs: Costs which, because of their incurrence for common or joint objectives, are not readily assignable to a particular contract or deliverable item. Therefore, indirect costs are allocated to the products/contracts involved on some consistent basis, which is in general accord with the extent to which each product/contract has benefited from the objective for which the costs were incurred.

Information Distribution: Making needed information available to project stakeholders in a timely manner.

Information Planning: Long- and short-range goal setting and action planning with respect to a client firm's information technology activities, strategy formulation.

Initiation: Committing the organization to begin a project phase and should include such components as project charter, objectives, needs, deliverables, authorization, etc.).

Intermediate Recovery: Previously called 'warm stand-by', typically involves the re-establishment of the critical systems and services within a 24 to 72 hour period, and is used by organizations that need to recover IT facilities within a predetermined time to prevent impacts to the business process.

International Organization for Standardization (ISO): The International Organization for Standardization (ISO) is the world's largest developer of Standards. ISO is a non-governmental organization which is a network of the national standards institutes of 156 countries. Further information about ISO is available from http://www.iso.org/

Inventory: Raw materials, work in process, and finished products required for plant operation or the value of such material and other supplies.

Invitation for Bid (IFB): Generally, this term is equivalent to request for proposal (RRP). However, in some application areas, it may have a narrower or more specific meaning.

Ishikawa Diagram: A technique that helps a team to identify all the possible causes of a problem. Originally devised by Kaoru Ishikawa, the output of this technique is a diagram that looks like a fishbone.

ISO 17799: Information Security Standard.

ISO 20000: ISO Specification and Code of Practice for IT Service Management. ISO/IEC 20000 is aligned with ITIL Best Practice.

ISO 27001: ISO Specification for Information Security Management. The corresponding Code of Practice is ISO 17799.

ISO 9000: A generic term that refers to a number of international Standards and Guidelines for Quality Management Systems. See http://www.iso.org/ for more information. See ISO.

ISO 9001: The internationally accepted set of standards concerning quality management systems.

Issue: A problem (or opportunity) that should be resolved to continue progress on a task, activity or project. The number of open issues on a project should be kept to a minimum.

IT Service Continuity Management: This process addresses the preparation and planning of disaster recovery measures for IT services in the event of a business interruption. It emphasizes the links with all the measures necessary to safeguard the continuity of the customer organization in the event of a disaster (Business Continuity Management) as well as the measures to prevent such disasters. An ITIL process.

IT Service Management (ITSM): The implementation and management of Quality IT Services that meet the needs of the Business. IT Service Management is performed by IT Service Providers through an appropriate mix of people, process and information technology.

IT Service Management Forum (itSMF): The IT Service Management Forum is an independent organization dedicated to promoting a professional approach to IT Service Management. The itSMF and its membership contribute to the development of ITIL and associated IT Service Management Standards. See http://www.itsmf.com/ for more information.

Iterative SDLC: Refers to a systems/software life cycle methodology that has frequent validations by the customer and other project constituencies as the system is built to ensure frequent corrections or adjustments to the scope, requirements and in-process system development efforts. See also Spiral SDLC.

ITIL (IT Infrastructure Library): A set of best practice guidance for IT Service Management. ITIL is owned by the OGC and consists of a series of publications giving guidance on the provision of Quality IT Services, and on the processes and facilities needed to support them. ITIL focuses on operational or infrastructure IT services. It consists of twelve IT Service Management and Delivery Processes. (Incident Management, Problem Management, Configuration Management, etc.). ITIL is being revised to a more IT Service Lifecycle process approach. See http://www.itil.co.uk/ for more information.

J:

K:

Kano Model: A model developed by Noriaki Kano that is used to help understand customer preferences. The Kano model considers attributes of a product or IT Service grouped into areas such as basic factors, excitement factors, performance factors, etc.

Key Performance Indicators (KPIs): The metrics used by management to assess the performance of an organization, function, process, individuals and/or teams.

L:

Lag: A modification of a logical relationship, which directs a delay in the successor, task. For example, in a finish-to-start dependency with a ten-day lag, the successor activity cannot start until 10 days after the predecessor has finished. Depending on software capabilities, lag may be identified with a negative integer.

Late Finish Date (LF): In the critical path method, the latest possible point in time that an activity or task must be completed without delaying a specific milestone (usually the project finish date).

Late Start Date (LS): In the critical path method, the latest possible point in time that an activity or task may begin without delaying a specified milestone (usually the project finish date).

Latest Revised Estimate (LRE): The total end-point amount (forecast) which represents actual labor hours and costs (direct and indirect) to date plus the estimate of labor hours and costs (direct and indirect) for authorized work remaining. The terms "estimate at completion" and "latest revised estimate" are synonymous.

Level of Detail: A policy or expression of content of plans, schedules, and reports in accordance with the scale of the breakdown of information.

Level of Effort (LOE): Support-type activity (eg, vendor or customer liaison) that does not readily lend itself to measurement of discreet accomplishment. It is generally characterized by a uniform rate of activity over a specific period of time.

Leveling: See Resource Leveling.

LF: Late Finish Date.

Life-cycle Costing: The concept of including acquisition, operating, and disposal costs when evaluating various alternatives.

Lifecycle / life cycle: A series of states, connected by allowable transitions. The lifecycle represents an approval process for systems or infrastructure phases with going to gates.

Line Manager: (1) The manager of any group that actually makes a product or performs a service. (2) A functional manager.

LOE: Level Of Effort.

Logical Relationship: A dependency between two project activities (tasks), or between a project activity and a milestone. See also Precedence Relationship. The four possible types of logical relationships are Finish-to-finish: the" "from" activity must finish before the "to" activity can finish. Start-to start: the "from" activity must start before the "to" activity can start. Start-to-finish: the "from" activity must start before the "to" activity can finish. Finish-to-start: the predecessor activity must finish before the successor activity can start.

Loop: A network path that passes the same node twice. Loops cannot be analyzed using traditional network analysis techniques such as CPM and PERT. Loops are allowed in GERT.

LS: Late Start Date.

M:

Maintenance: Post-delivery modification of a software/hardware product to correct faults, to improve performance or other attributes, or to adapt the product to a changed environment.

Make Versus Buy: Outsourcing is often referred to as a 'make versus buy' decision on the part of the customer. The question is, "Is it in the organization's best interests to continue to (or start to) perform the activity itself using its own people, process expertise, and technology or to 'buy' the activity from the service provider marketplace?"

Management Control Systems: The systems (eg planning, scheduling, budgeting, estimating, work authorization, cost accumulation, performance measurement, etc.) used by customers and contractors to plan and control the cost and scheduling of work.

Management Reserve Budget: An amount of the total allocated budget withheld for management control purposes, rather than designated for the accomplishment of a specific task or set of tasks.

Management Reserve: A separately planned quantity used to allow for future situations, which are impossible to predict (sometimes called "unknown unknowns"). Management reserves may involve cost or schedule. Management reserves are intended to reduce the risk of missing cost or schedule objectives. Use of management reserve requires a change to the project's cost baseline.

Man-Month: The equivalent number of hours worked in a month by one person working standard time, taking into consideration the average labor loss factors.

Market-Driven Sourcing: A market-driven approach to sourcing means that the organization's sourcing decisions are in direct response to the capabilities of the marketplace of available providers. Where the organization's internal capabilities are superior to the marketplace of providers, the activity is performed internally; where they are not, the activity is performed externally.

Master Schedule: A summary-level schedule which identifies the major activities and key milestones. See also Milestone Schedule.

Material Requirements Planning (MRP): A system which uses bills of material, inventory and open order data, and master production schedule information to calculate requirements for materials. It makes recommendations to release replenishment orders for material. Further, since it is time-phased, it makes recommendations to reschedule. Open orders when due dates and need dates are not in phase.

Material: All direct costs excluding labor and other direct costs (ODC). It consists of materials (including spares) and subcontract effort.

Matrix Organization: Any organizational structure in which the project manager shares responsibility with the functional managers for assigning priorities and for directing the work of individuals assigned to the project.

Maturity Model: The degree to which an organization improves its level of effectiveness and efficiency based on an industry framework, such as SEI's CMMI (Capability Maturity Model Integrated).

Measurement: The act or process of measuring to compare results to requirements. A quantitative estimate of performance. See Key Performance Indicators (KPIs).

Metrics: Specific quantitative measures that help in monitoring and controlling the progress of a program or project (eg CPI, SPI, budget/actual cost and schedule variances, number of open issues, status of tasks on critical path, etc.) or service (service level) or function.

Milestone Schedule: A summary-level schedule which identifies the major milestones. See also Master Schedule.

Mitigation: Taking steps to lessen risk by lowering the probability of a risk event's occurrence or reducing its effect should it occur.

Modern Project Management (MPM): A term used to distinguish the current broad range of project management (scope, cost, time, quality, risk, customer satisfaction, etc.) components.

Monitoring: The collection, analysis, and reporting of project performance, usually as compared to plan through the use of metrics.

Monte Carlo Analysis: A schedule risk assessment technique that performs a project simulation many times in order to calculate a distribution of likely results.

MPM: Modern Project Management.

MPS: Master Program Schedule.

N:

Near-Critical Activity: An activity/task that has low total float.

Network Analysis: The process of identifying early and late start and finish dates for the uncompleted portions of project activities. See also Critical Path Method, Program Evaluation and Review Technique, and Graphical Evaluation and Review Technique.

Network Diagram: A schematic display of activities and logical relationships of activities/ tasks that comprise the project. Two popular drawing methods for scheduling are 'arrow' and 'precedence' diagramming methods.

Network Logic: The collection of activity/task dependencies that make up a project network diagram.

Network Planning: A broad generic term for techniques used to plan complex projects using logic diagrams (networks). Two of the most popular techniques are ADM (Arrow Diagramming Methods) and PDM (Precedence Diagramming Methods).

Network: See Project Network Diagram.

Node: One of the defining points of a network; a junction point joined to some or all of the other dependency lines. See also Arrow Diagramming Method and Precedence Diagramming Method.

O:

Objective: A predetermined result; the end toward which effort is directed.

OBS: Organization Breakdown Structure.

Offshore Outsourcing: The outsourcing of any operation, be it information technology, a business process, or manufacturing, to a firm whose principal base of operation is outside the country. Terms such as near-shore outsourcing or close-shore outsourcing are also used to indicate that while still outside the country, there is a closer proximity between the customer organization's primary operations and that of the provider. For example, for a US company, Canada might be considered near-shore, while India is offshore.

Offshoring: Performing or sourcing any part of an organization's activities at or from a location outside the company's home country. Companies create captive centers offshore, where the employees work for them, or outsource offshore, where the employees work for the outsourcing provider.

OLA (Operational Level Agreement): An internal agreement covering the delivery of services which support the IT organisation in their delivery of services.

OPBOK: The Outsourcing Professional Body of Knowledge (OPBOK) was developed by the international association of outsourcing professional as a framework for understanding what outsourcing is and how it fits within contemporary business operations.

Operating Plan: The organized collection of short-range (1 year or less) objectives and initiatives that provide direction for an organization.

Operational Costs: Those costs resulting from the day-to-day running of the IT Services section, eg staff costs, hardware maintenance and electricity, and relating to repeating payments whose effects can be measured within a short timeframe, usually less than the 12-month financial year.

Operational Planning: Planning concerned with the development of control mechanisms to assure the effective implementation of actions in the strategic or tactical plans. Operational planning provides a basis for the measurement of actual performance relative to the plan and usually has a planning horizon for one year or less.

Opportunity Cost: The value of a benefit sacrificed in favor of an alternative course of action. That is the cost of using resources in a particular operation expressed in terms of foregoing the benefit that could be derived from the best alternative use of those resources.

Order of Magnitude Estimate: See Estimate.

Organizational Breakdown Structure (OBS): A depiction of the project organization arranged so as to relate work packages to organizational units, ie Division/Department.

Organizational Planning: Identifying, documenting, and assigning project roles, responsibilities, and reporting relationships.

Organizing: The process of defining certain parameters by which a project can be effectively administered.

Original Budget: The budget established at, or near, the time the contract or project authorization was signed and based on the negotiated contract cost.

Outline: The organization of tasks into related task groups or sub-projects. An outline illustrates a hierarchy by indenting successively lower levels of detail.

Outputs: Materials or information provided to others (internal or external customers).

Outsourcing at the Customer Interface: Outsourcing where a provider assumes responsibility for direct interaction with an organization's customers. This interaction may be in person, over the telephone, via email, mail, or any other direct means.

Outsourcing Framework: The outsourcing framework is a structure for mapping all of the activities of an organization in a way that allows consistent evaluation, planning, implementation, and management of sourcing decisions.

Outsourcing Process Maturity: Use an industry best practice framework (such as CMMI) to analyze current and target state maturity levels for outsourcing.

Outsourcing Process: A repeatable, multistage, management process for identifying outsourcing opportunities and moving those opportunities from concept though implementation and ongoing management.

Outsourcing Teams: Multi-disciplinary working groups that form for specific purposes throughout the outsourcing process.

Outsourcing: A long-term, results-oriented relationship with an external service provider for activities traditionally performed within the company. Outsourcing usually applies to a business or IT process or function. It assumes a degree of managerial control and risk on the part of the provider and buyer.

Overall Change Control: Co-ordinating changes across the entire project.

Overhead (OH): Costs, which because of their incurrence for common or joint objectives are not subject readily to treatment as direct costs (eg Maintenance).

Overhead Costs: Overhead costs are a specific category of indirect costs.

Overhead Pool: Grouping of incurred cost identified with two or more cost objectives, but not identified specifically with a final cost objective. The cost within each pool has similar beneficial or causal relationships to cost objectives.

Overrun (Underrun): The value for the work performed to date minus the actual cost for that same work. When value exceeds actual cost, an underrun exists, When actual cost exceeds value, an overrun condition exists. See Earned Value.

P:

Parametric Estimating: An estimating technique that uses a statistical relationship between historical data and other variables (eg square footage in construction, lines of code in software development) to calculate an estimate.

Pareto Diagram: A histogram, ordered by frequency of occurrence, that shows how many results were generated by each identified cause.

Path Convergence: In mathematical network analysis, the tendency of parallel paths of approximately equal duration to delay the completion of the milestone where they meet.

Path Float: See Float.

Path: A set of sequentially connected activities or tasks in a project network diagram.

PC: Percent Complete.

PCL: Project Control Log.

PCs: Project Control System.

PDM: Precedence Diagramming Method.

Percent Complete (PC): An estimate, expressed as a percent, of the amount of work which has been completed on an activity or group of activities (tasks).

Performance Measurement Baseline (PMB): The time-phased baseline plan against which contract or project performance is measured. It is formed by the baselines assigned to schedules work and the applicable indirect baseline. For future effort, the performance measurement baseline also includes undistributed baselines. It equals the Total Contract baseline less Authorized Undefined Work committed (but not incurred or used yet).

Performance Measurement: The methods for measuring accomplishment on work package task(s), scheduled in accordance with achievement of higher level schedules.

Performance Reporting: Collecting and disseminating information about project performance to help ensure project progress.

Performance: The term performance is used as an attribute of the work product itself and as a general characteristic. The broad performance characteristics that are of interest to management are quality (effectiveness), cost (efficiency), and schedule. Performance is the highly effective common measurement that links the quality of the work product to efficiency and productivity.

Performance-Based Pricing: Contractual pricing mechanisms that link compensation to meeting specific performance objectives or outcomes.

Performing Organization: The enterprise whose employees are most directly involved in doing the work of the project.

PERT Chart: A specific type of project network diagram. See Program Evaluation and Review Technique.

PERT: Program Evaluation and Reviewing Technique

PF: Planned Finish Date.

Phase: See Project Phase.

Plan: A predetermined course of action over a specified period of time which represents a projected response to an anticipated environment or condition in order to accomplish a specific set of objectives and actions.

Planned Finish Date (PF): See Scheduled Finish Date.

Planned Start Date (PS): See Scheduled Start Date.

Planning: The determination of an initiative's objectives, scope, requirements and deliverables with identification of the activities/tasks to be performed, processes and resources to be used for accomplishing the tasks, assignment of responsibility and accountability, and establishment of an integrated plan to achieve completion as required. It is also a process to produce a plan (eg Business, Project, etc.).

PM: Project or Product Manager.

PMB: Performance Measurement Baseline.

PMBOK: Project Management Body Of Knowledge. Developed by PMI (Project Management Institute).

PMCS: Program or Project Management and Control System.

PMP: Project Management Professional who is certified through PMI (Project Management Institute). It is an individual certification.

Policy: A statement of principles and beliefs, or a settled course, adopted to guide the overall management of affairs in support of a stated aim or goal. It is mostly related to fundamental conduct and usually defines a general framework within which other business and management actions are carried out.

Portfolio Management: Process that ensures that IT investments are evaluated, prioritized, funded and approved in a consistent manner.

Precedence Diagramming Method (PDM): A network diagramming technique in which activities/tasks are represented by boxes (or nodes). Activities are linked by precedence relationships to show the sequence in which the activities are to be performed.

Precedence Relationship: The term used in the precedence diagramming method for a logical relationship. In current usage, however, precedence relationship, logical relationship, and dependency and constraint are widely used interchangeably regardless of the diagramming method in use.

Predecessor Activity: (1) In the arrow diagramming method, the activity which enters a node. (2) In the precedence diagramming method, any activity which is constrained to the activity in question by a logical relationship.

Price: The amount of money asked or given for a product or service (eg exchange value).

PRINCE2™: The standard UK Government method for project management.

Problem Management: Problem Management attempts to identify the underlying cause. Once the causes have been identified (known errors), a business decision is taken whether to make permanent improvements to the infrastructure to prevent new incidents.

Problem/Opportunity Analysis: Evaluation of problems and/or opportunities to determine the feasibility of developing a proposal or authorization for a project.

Problem: A question or situation proposed for solution. The result of not conforming to requirements or, in other words, a potential task resulting from the existence of defects. An unknown underlying cause of one or more incidents.

Process Control: The set of activities employed to detect and remove special causes of variation in order to maintain or restore stability of a process.

Process Enterprise: A process enterprise operates its business as a collection of end-to-end business processes where executive leadership, education, responsibilities, measurement and reward systems are all oriented to this view of the business's operations. This process orientation is in direct contrast to the traditional hierarchical view of an organization.

Process Improvement: The set of activities employed to detect and remove common causes of variation in order to improve process capability. Process improvement leads to quality improvement.

Process Management: Management approach comprising quality management and process optimization.

Process: A process is also defined as the logical organization of people, materials, energy, equipment, systems, processes and procedures into work activities designed to produce a specified end result (work product). A process is continuous (eg processing a sales order).

Procurement Planning: Determining what to procure, when, how, how much and why.

Product Development Lifecycle: The phases of a product's life cycle from concept through maturity and decline. Specific phases or stages include: idea generation and concept development; market research and validation; regulatory check (where appropriate; competitive analysis; develop product concept and prototype; test market; develop product/service; commercialize and launch product and post-launch product support.

Product Management: The dedicated management of a specific product or service to increase its profit contribution from current and potential markets accountable for all phases of the Product Development Lifecycle. (See Product Development Lifecycle)

Product Positioning: The relative positioning of the product in terms of its brand, functions, features, benefits and other criteria in comparison to competitor products.

Product Pricing: The price represents the cost of the product to the customer and revenues and profits to the supplier.

Production Environment: The hardware, software, communication links, and operating systems to be used when a system has been implemented, as determined during the Business Design Phase and established during the Implementation Phase.

Production Planning: The function of setting the overall level of manufacturing or construction output. Its prime purpose is to establish production rates that will achieve management's objective, while usually attempting to keep the production force relatively stable.

Production Support: The process of operating, maintaining, and enhancing a computer or manufacturing system.

Program Evaluation and Review Technique (PERT): An event-oriented network analysis technique used to estimate project duration when there is a high degree of uncertainty with the individual activity duration estimates. PERT applies the critical path method to a weighted average duration estimate. (Also given as Program Evaluation and Review Technique.)

Program Management Office (PMO): Focal point for helping program and project managers to develop and/or administer the project management processes, tools and techniques. Can also be involved in project governance, reporting, training, project audits and related functions. May also be a 'center of excellence' for project management competencies and skills.

Program Management: The management of a related series of projects (or one project) executed over a longer period of time, and which are designed to accomplish broad goals and objectives, to which the individual projects contribute.

Program Manager (PM): The individual who is assigned complete responsibility, authority, and control over all technical and administrative aspects of a program (project). The PM may delegate responsibilities to deputies who report to the PM.

Program: A group of inter-related projects managed in a coordinated way. Programs usually are larger, more complex, higher risk and higher value than projects.

Project Charter: A document authorized by senior management that provides the project manager with the scope, boundary and authority to apply organizational resources to project activities.

Project Communications Management: A subset of project management that includes the process required to ensure proper collection and dissemination of project status information. It consists of communications planning, information distribution, performance reporting, and administrative closure.

Project Cost Management: A subset of project management that includes the processes required to ensure that the project is completed within the approved budget. It consists of resource planning, cost estimating, cost budgeting, and cost control.

Project Human Resource Management: A subset of project management that includes the processes required to ensure that the various people related elements of the project are properly coordinated. It consists of project plan development, project plan execution, and overall change control.

Project Integration Management: A subset of project management that includes the processes required to ensure that the various elements of the project are properly coordinated. It consists of project plan development, project plan execution, and overall change control.

Project Lifecycle: A collection of generally sequential project phases whose name and number are determined by the control needs of the organization or organizations involved in the project (eg initiation, planning, executing and terminating).

Project Management (PM): The application of knowledge, skills, tools, and techniques to project activities in order to meet or exceed stakeholder needs and expectations from a project.

Project Management Body of Knowledge (PMBOK): An inclusive term that describes the sum of knowledge within the profession of project management. As with other professions such as law, medicine, and accounting, the body of knowledge rests with - the practitioners and academics that applies and advances It. The PMBOK includes proven, traditional practices, which are widely applied, as well as innovative and advanced ones, which have seen more limited use. Developed by PMI.

Project Management Professional (PMP): An individual certified as such by the Project Management Institute or a company.

Project Management Software: A class of computer applications specifically designed to aid with planning, controlling, reporting project costs, schedules and resources.

Project Management Team: The members of the project team who are directly involved in project management activities. On some smaller projects, the project management team may include virtually all of the project team members.

Project Manager (PM): The individual responsible for managing a project.

Project Network Diagram: Any schematic display of the logical relationships of project activities. Always drawn from left to right to reflect project chronology (however, not scaled to reflect elapsed time). Often incorrectly referred to as 'PERT chart'.

Project Phase: A collection of logically related project activities (tasks), usually culminating in the completion of a major deliverable.

Project Plan Development: Taking the results of other planning processes and putting them into a consistent, coherent document.

Project Plan Execution: Carrying out the project plan by performing the activities therein.

Project Plan: A formal, approved document used to guide both project execution and project control. The primary uses of the project plan are to document planning assumptions and decisions, to facilitate communication among stakeholders, and to document approved scope, cost, and schedule baselines. A project plan may be summary or detailed.

Project Planning: The development and maintenance of the project plan.

Project Procurement Management: A subset of project management that includes the processes required to acquire goods and services from outside the performing organization. It consists of procurement planning, solicitation planning, solicitation, end or selection, contract administration, and contract closeout.

Project Quality Management: A subset of project management that includes the processes required to ensure that the project would satisfy the need for which it was undertaken. It consists of quality planning, quality assurance, and quality control.

Project Risk Management: A subset of project management that includes the processes concerned with identifying, analyzing, and responding to project risk. It consists of risk identification, risk quantification, risk response development, risk response control, risk mitigation and contingency planning.

Project Schedule: The planned dates for performing activities and the planned dates for meeting milestones.

Project Scope Management: A subset of project management that includes the processes required to ensure that the project includes all of the work required, and only the work required, to complete the project successfully. It consists of initiation, scope planning, scope determination, scope verification, and scope change control.

Project Summary: A brief synopsis of the project that dearly states the project objectives, goals, constraints and deliverables.

Project Team Members: The people who report either directly or indirectly to the project manager.

Project Time Management: A subset of project management that includes the processes required to ensure timely completion of the project. It consists of activity definition, activity sequencing, activity duration estimating, schedule development, and schedule control.

Project: A one time endeavor undertaken to create a unique product or service. All projects have a start and end date and attributes such as: time, costs, benefits, resources, quality, deliverables and customer satisfaction.

Projected Organization: Any organizational structure in which the project manager has full authority to assign priorities and to direct the work of individuals assigned to the project.

Projected Staffing Plan: A plan that describes the types of resources needed, how much of each type are needed, and when they are needed. Should include dates, resources needed to be hired, and when.

Proposal Development: The process of choosing the best alternative to meet a customer's need and developing a written requirements and scope document.

Prototype: A simulated view of a proposed system using actual data together with text and illustrations or models screens.

PS: Planned Start Date.

Q:

QA: Quality Assurance.

QC: Quality Control.

Quality Assurance (QA): (1) The process of evaluating overall project performance on a regular basis to provide confidence that the project will satisfy the relevant quality standards. (2) The organizational unit that is assigned responsibility for quality assurance.

Quality Control (QC): (1) The process of monitoring specific project results to determine if they comply with relevant quality standards and identifying ways to eliminate causes of unsatisfactory performance. (2) The organizational unit that is assigned responsibility for quality control.

Quality Planning: Identifying which quality standards are relevant to the project and determining how to satisfy them.

R:

RACI: Authority matrix that identifies specific roles of individuals such as R=Responsibility, A=Authority, C=Consult and I=Inform.

RAM: Responsibility Assignment Matrix. Identifies rules and responsibilities for initiatives or tasks.

Release Management: A release is a set configuration items (CIs) that are tested and introduced into the live environment together. The objective of Release Management is to ensure the successful rollout of releases, including integration, testing and storage. Release Management is closely related to Configuration Management and Change Management activities.

Release: A collection of new and/or changed CIs which are tested and introduced into a live environment together. Release Management is the process of controlling releases.

Remaining Duration (RDU): The time needed to complete an activity/task once it has started.

Request for Change (RFC): Form, or screen, used to record details of a request for a change to any CI within an infrastructure or to procedures and items associated with the infrastructure or a change in project scope for deliverables.

Request for Information (RFI): Description of the products and/or services that a potential customer wishes to learn about from the vendors.

Request for Proposal (RFP): A document used to solicit proposals from prospective vendors of products or services, which typically requests solutions, pricing, payment terms, warranties, pre and after sales support, implementation assistance, etc.

Request for Quotation (RFQ): Generally, this term is equivalent to request for pricing only to help filter out select vendors.

Reserve: A provision in the project plan to mitigate cost and/or schedule risk. Often used with a modifier (eg management reserve, contingency reserve) to provide further detail on what types of risk are meant to be mitigated.

Resource Leveling: Any form of network analysis in which scheduling decisions (start and finish dates) are driven by resource management concerns (eg limited resource availability or difficult-to-manage changes in resource levels). The process of manipulating network data to create the resource plan which most effectively utilizes project resources subject to project constraints.

Resource Plan: A list of the resources and quantities that will be required over time to perform the project work.

Resource Planning: Determining what resources (people, equipment, materials, systems) are needed in what quantities to perform project activities.

Resource-Limited Schedule: A project schedule whose start and finish dates reflect expected resource availability. The final project schedule should always be resource limited.

Responsibility Assignment Matrix (RAM): A structure which relates the project organization structure to the work breakdown structure to help ensure that each element of the project's scope of work is assigned to a responsible individual.

Responsibility Center (RC): The number used for accumulating actual costs at the Control Account level.

Responsibility Chart: See Responsibility Assignment Matrix.

Responsibility Matrix: See Responsibility Assignment Matrix.

Responsibility: Originates when one accepts the assignment to perform assigned duties and activities. The acceptance creates a liability for which the assignee is held answerable for and to the assignor. It constitutes an obligation or accountability for performance.

Responsible Organization: A defined unit within a company structure which is assigned the responsibility for accomplishing specific tasks and to which one or more Control Accounts is assigned.

Retainage: A portion of a contract payment that is held until contract completion in order to ensure full performance of the contract terms.

Risk Analysis: The identification and assessment of the level (measure) of the risks calculated from the assessed values of assets and the assessed levels of threats to, and vulnerabilities of, those assets.

Risk Identification: Determining which risk events are likely to affect the project, business or IT.

Risk Management: The process of identifying, evaluating, quantifying, mitigating and tracking risk items.

Risk Quantification: Evaluating the probability of risk event occurrence and effect.

Risk Reduction Measure: Measures taken to reduce the likelihood or consequences of disruption occurring (as opposed to planning to recover after a disruption).

Risk Response Control: Responding to changes in risk over the course of the project.

Risk Response Development: Defining enhancement steps for opportunities and mitigation steps for threats.

Risk: A measure of the exposure to which an organisation may be subjected. This is a combination of the likelihood of a business disruption occurring and the possible loss that may result from such business disruption.

Root Cause: Original reason for non conformance within a process. When the root cause is removed or corrected, the non conformance will be eliminated.

S:

Schedule Analysis: See Network Analysis.

Schedule Compression: See Duration Compression.

Schedule Control: Controlling changes to the project schedule.

Schedule Development: Analyzing activity/task sequences, activity durations, and resource requirements to create the project schedule.

Schedule Performance Index (SPI): The ratio of work performed to work scheduled (BCWP/BCWS). See Earned Value.

Schedule Variance (SV): (1) Any difference between the scheduled completion of an activity and the actual completion of that activity. (2) In earned value, BCWP less BCWS.

Schedule: See Project Schedule.

Scheduled Finish Date (SF): The point in time work is scheduled to finish on an activity. The scheduled finish date is normally within the range of dates delimited by the early finish date and the late finish date.

Scheduled Start Date (SS): The point in time work is scheduled to start on an activity. The scheduled start date is normally within the range of dates delimited by the early start date and the late start date.

Scheduled Start Date (SS): The point in time work was scheduled to start on an activity. The scheduled start date is normally within the range of dates delimited by the early start date and the late start date.

Scheduling: The assignment of desired start and finish times to each activity/task in the project within the overall time cycle required for completion according to plan.

Scope Baseline: See Baseline.

Scope Change Control: Controlling changes to the project scope.

Scope Change: Any change to the project scope. A scope change almost always requires an adjustment to the project cost or schedule.

Scope Definition: Decomposing the major deliverables into smaller, more manageable components to provide better control.

Scope of Services: The services provided under an outsourcing agreement.

Scope Planning: Developing a written scope statement that includes the project justification, the major deliverables, and the project objectives.

Scope Verification: Ensuring that all identified project deliverables have been completed satisfactorily.

Scope: The sum of the products and services to be provided as a project.

Security Management: The objective of Security Management is to protect the IT, organization and resources against unauthorized use or penetration.

Security: The protection of products, systems, facilities and people from accidental or malicious harm, access, use, modification, destruction, or disclosure. Security also pertains to personnel data, communications, and the physical protection of facilities, files, etc.

Sequential SDLC: See Waterfall SDLC.

Service achievement: The actual service levels delivered by the IT organization to a customer within a defined life-span.

Service Catalogue: Written statement of IT services, pricing, descriptions and options. It is used to describe repetitive IT services to ordering by the customer.

Service Desk: The Service Desk is the initial point of contact with the IT organization for users. The major task of the Service Desk is to record, resolve and monitor problems. A Service Desk can carry out activities belonging to several processes.

Service Desk: The single point of contact within the IT organization for users of IT services.

Service Improvement Program: A formal project undertaken within an organization to identify and introduce measurable improvements within a specified work area or work process.

Service Level Agreement (SLA): The service level agreement, or SLA, defines the intended or expected level of service. For example, how quickly a service will be performed, what availability, quality and cost targets will be met, what level of customer satisfaction will be achieved, etc.

Service Level Management: The process of defining, agreeing, documenting, measuring and managing the levels of customer IT service, that are required and cost justified.

Service Provider: A company that provides outsourcing services. Terms such as provider, vendor, and partner are often used interchangeably each carrying a slightly different connotation intended by the user.

Service Quality Plan: The written plan and specification of internal targets designed to guarantee the agreed service levels.

Service Request: Every Incident not being a failure in the IT Infrastructure or operation.

Service: One or more IT systems which enable a business or IT process.

SF: Scheduled Finish Date or Start-to-Finish

Shared Services (Shared Services Centers): Shared services are common activities that are used by more than one division or unit within the company. When these services are combined into a central operation they are often referred to as shared services centers.

Significant Variance: The differences between planned and actual cost and/or schedule performance which require further review, analysis or action by the CAM and are addressed in the monthly VAR. Appropriate thresholds are established as to the magnitude of variances which will be considered "significant".

Slack: Term used in PERT for float.

SMART: An acronym that helps to remember that plans should be Specific, Measurable, Achievable, Relevant and Timely.

Software Library: A controlled collection of SCIs designated to keep those with like status and type together and distinctly segregated, to aid in development, operation and maintenance.

Solicitation: Obtaining quotations, bids, offers, or proposals as appropriate. Solicitation Planning Documenting product requirements and identifying potential sources.

Sourcing: Sourcing is generally the broadest term used in the field. It reflects the simple but essential point that everything the organization does has to be 'sourced' in some way – internally, externally, or a mix of the two.

SOW: Statement of Work.

Specification: A document containing a detailed description or enumeration of particulars. Formal description of a work product and the intended manner of providing it.

SPI: Scheduled Performance Index.

Spiral SDLC: See Iterative SDLC.

SS: Scheduled Start date or Start-to-Start.

Staff Acquisition: Getting the human resources needed assigned to and working on the project.

Stakeholder: Individuals and organizations that are involved in or may be affected by project activities.

Standard cost: A pre-determined calculation of how much costs should be under specified working conditions. Its main purposes are to provide bases for control through variance accounting, for the valuation of work in progress and for fixing selling prices.

Standard costing: A technique which uses standards for costs and revenues for the purposes of control through variance analysis.

Start Date: A point in time associated with an activities start, usually qualified by one of the following actual, planned, estimated, scheduled, early, late, target, baseline, or current.

Start-to-Finish: See Logical Relationship.

Start-to-Start: See Logical Relationship.

Statement of Work (SOW): A narrative description of products or services to be supplied under contract.

Status Date: The calendar date, which separates actual (historical) data from, forecasted data.

Status: The condition or progress of the project at a specified point in time.

Strategic Planning: The process of developing an organization's mission, vision, objectives, goals, strategies, and long range initiatives.

Strawman: A preliminary concept or plan that is presented to a group as a basis for discussion. The work 'strawman' is used to emphasize that the plan can be 'kicked around' without fear of damage to its authors; that is, the individuals who present the strawman should do so fully expecting, and welcoming, additions, deletions, and/or changes to the strawman.

Subcontract: A subcontract is a procurement from another corporate plant or from a non-corporate subcontractor requiring a Statement of Work, specifications, and design and/or manufacturing engineering effort on the part of the supplier as opposed to the procurement of 'off-the-shelf' items or items made to a drawing/specification/formula not requiring design/manufacturing engineering by the supplier.

Successor Activity: (1) In the arrow diagramming method, the activity which departs a node. (2) In the precedence diagramming method, the 'to' activity.

Summary Level: Any level of the WBS higher than the bottom level. So named because each WBS level can be summarized into the next higher level.

Supply Chain: The interlinked chain of contractors and subcontractors that provide components, subcomponents, and services that become part of the company's deliverable to its customers. Typically used to refer to the chain of suppliers in a manufacturing company's operation, but is also used more generally in regard to any product or service.

SV: Schedule Variance.

System: An integrated composite that consists of one or more of the processes, hardware, software, network, facilities and people, which provides a capability to satisfy a stated need or objective.

Systems Development Lifecycle: The use of any of several structured methodologies to plan, design, procure, test and implement a system (eg Waterfall (Sequential), Spiral (Iterative), Hybrid, etc.).

T:

Tactical Planning: Planning concerned with the effective deployment of an organization's resources in order to accomplish the objectives laid out in the strategic business plan. The planning horizon is typically shorter than a strategic plan.

Target Completion Date (TC): An imposed date which constrains or otherwise modifies the network analysis.

Target Finish Date (TF): The date work is planned (targeted) to finish on an activity.

Target Schedule: See Baseline.

Target Start Date (TS): The date work is planned (targeted) to start on an activity.

Task: See Activity.

Team Development: Developing individual and group skills to enhance project performance.

Team Members: See Project Team Members.

Template: A standardized document, developed to address redundant requirements. The document is developed once, saved in a library or repository, and used repeatedly within the system.

TF: Total Float or Target Finish Date

Third-Party Supplier: An enterprise or group, external to the Customer's enterprise, which provides services and/or products to that Customer's enterprise.

Threshold: See Variance Threshold.

Time-Scaled CPM: A plotted or drawn representation of a CPM network, where the length of the activities indicates the duration of the activity as drawn to a calendar scale.

Time-Scaled Network Diagram: Any project network diagram drawn in such a way that the positioning and length of the activity represents Its duration. Essentially, it is a bar chart that includes network logic.

Total Contract Baseline: The negotiated contract cost.

Total Cost Of Ownership: Calculated including depreciation, maintenance, staff costs, facilities, and planned renewal.

Total Float (TF): See Float.

Total Quality Management (TOM): A common approach to implementing a quality improvement program within an organization.

TQM: Total Quality Management.

Tree Diagram: A graphical representation of an outline or WBS structure which shows work elements as boxes and subsequent levels of detail broken down in levels of boxes below it. An element or task can roll up into only one higher level box.

TS: Target Start Date.

U:

UB: Undistributed Baseline.

Unit Cost: Total costs for one unit of production (ie one part, one end item, etc.).

Update: To revise project activity data to reflect the most current information on the project.

V:

Value Proposition: What value is the organization looking to gain from a system, product or outsourcing arrangement.

VAR: Variance Analysis Report.

Variance Analysis Report (VAR): A report from Control Accounts or summary WBS levels that exceed the variance thresholds. The report/notice is completed by the responsible individual who must 1) explain the cause of the problem, 2) determine the impact on the immediate task and on the total program or project, and 3) describe any corrective actions to be taken.

Variance Analysis: Evaluation of variances and narrative description of the causes of the difference between BCWP and BCWS or ACWP, and between BAC and EAC in terms of Cost and Schedule at levels where the work is performed, or at various Functional Organization, WBS, or reporting summary levels, as required. Includes determination of the nature, scope and potential impact of the problem, assignment of responsibility for corrective action, and the monitoring of results of the corrective action.

Variance Threshold: Internal and external tolerances established by management direction or through negotiations with the customer. Variance conditions outside the threshold values must be addressed formally. See Variance Analysis Report.

Variance: The difference by which cost and schedule vary from plan. Negative variances are unfavorable indicators (ie behind schedule or over cost) while positive variances are favorable indicators (ie ahead of schedule or under cost). See also specific items such as Cost Variance, Schedule Variance, etc.

Vendor: A supplier of products and/or services.

Version Identifier: A version number; version date; or version date and time stamp.

Version: An identified instance of a Configuration Item within a product breakdown structure or configuration structure for the purpose of tracking and auditing change history. Also used for software Configuration Items to define a specific identification released in development for drafting, review or modification, test or production.

Vulnerability: A weakness of the system and its assets, which could be exploited by threats.

W:

Waterfall SDLC: Refers to a systems/software lifecycle methodology that has frequent validations by the customer and other project constituencies as the system is built to ensure frequent corrections or adjustments to the scope, requirements and in-process system development efforts. See also Spiral SDLC.

WBS Dictionary: The Dictionary will describe the technical and cost content of every WBS element or task. It will describe what the element is and efforts associated with the WBS element (such as design, development, and manufacturing). For the WBS elements specified elsewhere for cost reporting, The WBS Dictionary definitions will also include the exact narrative of the directly associated work statement paragraphs, or a reference to The SOW paragraph or other document describing the work.

WBS: Work Breakdown Structure.

Work Breakdown Structure (WBS): A deliverable-oriented grouping of project elements or tasks which organizes and defines the total scope of the project. Each descending level represents an increasingly detailed definition of a project component. Project components may be products, services processes or functions. Decomposes complex programs or projects into assignable work packages.

Work Day: A unit expressing duration. Only those days when work is performed are counted. Holidays, weekends, and vacation days may or may not count.

Work Item: See Activity or Task.

Work: Any and all obligations, duties, responsibilities, labor, materials, equipment, temporary facilities and incidentals, and the furnishing thereof necessary to complete the contract deliverable which are assigned to, or undertaken by the contractor, pursuant to the contract documents. Also, the entire completed contract deliverable or the various separately identifiable parts thereof required to be furnished under the contract documents. Work is the result of performing services, furnishing labor, and furnishing and incorporating materials and equipment into the contract deliverable, all as required by the contract documents.

Workaround: A response to a negative risk event. Distinguished from contingency plan in that a workaround is not planned in advance of the occurrence of the risk event. Method of avoiding an incident or problem.

Work-around: Method of avoiding an Incident or Problem, either by a temporary fix or by a technique that means the Customer is not reliant on a particular aspect of the service that is known to have a problem.

Work-in-Progress (WIP): Product in various stages of completion throughout the factory, including raw material that has been released for initial processing and completely processes material awaiting final inspection and acceptance as finished product or shipment of a customer. Many accounting systems also include semi-finished stock and components in this category.

Workloads: The resources required to deliver a project or service deliverable and can be segmented by skills, functions and experience levels.

WP: Work Package.

X:

Y:

Z:

References

Alphabetical List

Ahern, Dennise, Clouse, Aaron and Torner, Richard, *CMMI™ Distiller - A practical to integrated Process Improvement,* Second Edition, Addison-Wesley. 2004.

Akker, Rolf , "Generic Framework for Information Management", Program for Information Research, University of Amsterdam, 1992.

Anand, S., *Sarbanes-Oxley Guide,* Second Edition, J. Wiley and Sons, New York, 2006

Anthony, Robert N. , *Planning and Control Systems: A Framework for Analysis,* Harvard University Press, Cambridge, MA, 1965

Avison, D., Jones, J., Powell, P. and Wilson, D., "Using and validating the strategic alignment model." Journal of Strategic Information Systems Volume 13, 2004.

Baggili, J., "Business-IT Alignment", http://web.ics.purdue.edu/~baggili/Portal/B_IT_Alignment.html

Barkley, Brucet, Sr., *Integrated Project Management,* McGraw Hill, NY, 2006.

Beckman, Sara L. and Rosenfield, Donald B., *Operating Strategy,* McGraw-Hill, NY, 2008.

Benson, R. J., T. L. Bugnitz, et al. *From Business Strategy to IT Action: Right Decisions for a Better Bottom Line.* Hoboken, N.J., Wiley, 2004.

Betz, Frederick, *Managing Technological Innovation: Competitive Advantage from Change.* New York: John Wiley, 2003.

Bhatia, Mohan, "IT Merger Due Diligence: A Blueprint", Information Systems Control Journal, Volume 1, 2007

BMC Software, *Sarbanes-Oxley Section 404*, White Paper, May, 2004.

Board Effectiveness Partners, "A Roadmap: Strengthening Corporate Governance", Insights, Chapter 1, Version 2.0, January 2004.

Boardman, Bruce, *Get Framed Compliance Policy Development (ISO, ITIL/ISMD & COBIT),* Network Computing Conf., Sept. 28, 2006

Bossidy, Larry and Charan, Ram, *Execution - The Discipline of Getting things Done*, Crown Business, 2002.

Boston Consulting Group, *Perspectives on Experience*, 1974.

Bragg, Steven M., *Outsourcing,* Second Edition, J. Wiley & Sons, NY, 2006.

Breyfogle, F., Cupello, J., Meadows, Becki, *Managing Six Sigma*, Wiley, 2001.

Bridges, William, *Managing Transitions*, 2nd Edition, Da Capo Press, Cambridge, Ma, 1991.

Broadbent, Marianne and Kitzis, Ellen, *The New CIO Leader*, HBR Press, 2005.

Brown, Doug and Wilson, Scott, *The Black Book of Outsourcing*, John Wiley & Sons, 2005.

Burkholder, Nicholas C., *Outsourcing,* J. Wiley & Sons, NY, 2006.

Burn, Jack and Moran, Linda, *The New Self Directed Work Teams*, McGraw-Hill, New York, 2000.

Business Continuity Planning Guidelines, http://www.yourwindow.to/business-continuity/contents.htm

Business Continuity Planning Model, http://www.drj.com/new2dr/model/bcmodel.htm

Business Week, *Special Report on Outsourcing*, January 30, 2006

Carmel, Erran and Tjia, Paul, *Offshoring Information Technology*, Cambridge University Press, UK, 2005.

Carr, N., "IT doesn't matter anymore." Harvard Business Review (5), 41-49, 2003.

Casale, Frank, "Darwin and Outsourcing", <u>Outsourcing Essentials</u>, Vol.2, No. 3 Winter 2004, The Outsourcing Institute.

Catucci, Bill, "A New Governance Model", <u>Balanced Scorecard</u>, January 15, 2005.

Catucci, Bill, "Ten Lessons for Implementing the Balanced Scorecard", <u>Balanced Scorecard</u>, January 15, 2003.

CCTA, Prince2 – *Managing Successful Projects with Prince 2, Central Computer and Telecommunications Agency*, The Stationery Office, 1998.

Center for Technology Governance and Compliance, <u>Raising the Bar for Governance and Compliance,</u> Sun Microsystems and Deloitte Consulting LLP White Paper, February, 2006

Chrissis, M., Konrad, M. and Shrum, S., *CMMI – Guidelines for Process Integration and Product Improvement*, Addison Wesley, 2003.

Ciborra, C., "De Profundis? Deconstructing the Concept of Strategic Alignment," <u>Scandinavian Journal of Information Systems</u> Volume 9, 67-82, 1997.

Clemons, E. K., Row, M. C., and Redi, S. P., "The Impact of IT on the Organization of Economic Activity", <u>Journal of Management Information Systems</u>, Vol. 9, No. 2, Fall 2002.

Click, Rick L. and Dvening, Thomas N., N., *Business Process Outsourcing*, J. Wiley & Sons, NY, 2005.

Cohen, Beth, TACtical Research SmartTip – *Rethinking Internet Forum and Collaboration Tools*, The Advisory Council (TAC), December, 2006

Colley, J., Doyle, J., Logan, G., Stettinius, W., *What is Corporate Governance?* , McGraw-Hill, December 2004

Cooper, R.G., Edgett, S.J. and Kleinschmidt, E.J., *Portfolio Management for New Products,* Addison-Wesley, Reading, MA, 1998.

Corbett, Michael F., "Outsourcing 2000: Value-Driven Customer-Focused", <u>Fortune</u>, May 29, 2000, p. S36

Corbett, Michael, *The Outsourcing Revolution*, Dearbon Trade Publication, Chicago, Il, 2004

Cordite, James, *Best Practices in Information Technology*, Prentice Hall, Upper Saddle River, NJ, 1998.

Corporate Executive Board, "IT Balanced Scorecards - End-to-End Performance Measurement for the Corporate IT Function, " Working Council for Chief Information Officers Report, 2003.

Corporate Governance: http://www.corpgov.net

Coughlan, J., Lycett, M. and Macredie, R.D., "Understanding the business-IT relationship." <u>International Journal of Information Management</u> Volume 25, 303-319, 2005.

Covey, Stephen, *Seven Habits of Highly Effective People,* Simon and Schuster, 1989.

Crawford, Ken, *Project Management Maturity Model*, Marcel Decker, Inc., 2002.

Crow, Ken, *Customer Focused Development with QFD*, DRM Associates, 2002.

Cybercan Technology Solutions, ITIL (Information Technology Infrastructure Library) Foundation Workshop, 2005.

Dalal, Jagdish, *Off-shore Outsourcing*, The Outsourcing Research Council, Raleigh, NC, October 23, 2002, p. 11, 13.

Davenport, T. H., *Mission Critical: Realizing the Promise of the Enterprise Systems,* Boston, MA: HBS Press, 2000.

Degraff, Jeff and Quinn, Shawn, *Leading Innovation,* McGrawHill, NY, 2007.

Deloitte Development, LLC, "Eliminating Roadblocks to IT and Business Alignment", <u>CIO Magazine Supplement</u>, 2004.

Deloitte, Consulting Report, "Calling a Change in the Outsourcing Model, Deloitte Consulting", December, 2005.

Doran, G.T., "There's a Smart Way to Write Management Goals and Objectives", Management Review, November 1981, pp. 35-36.

Drucker, Peter, *Managing in a Time of Great Change,* Butterworth-Heinemann, 1997.

Drucker, Peter, *Post-Capitalist Society*, Harper Business, 1993.

Duffy, Jan, "Alignment:Delivering Results", www.cio.com

Edwards, John, Dream Catalogue, CFO Magazine, September, 2005.

Ellis, James E., McDonnell Douglas, "Unfasten the Seat Belts", BusinessWeek, February 14, 1994, p. 36.

Engardio, Pete et al., "The New Global Job Shift", BusinessWeek, February 3, 2003

Erickson – Harris, Lisa, *IT Governance: Round Em Up!* Intelligent Enterprise Conf., August, 2006, p. 10-14.

Ernst and Young, *48 Questions You Need to Answer for Sarbanes-Oxley Compliance*, Tech Republic, CNET Networks, 2005.

European Corporate Governance Institute: http://www.ecgi.org

Fabian, Robert, "Interdependence of COBIT and ITIL", Information Systems Control Journal, Volume 1, 2007

Federal Financial Institutions Examination Council (FFIEC), Business Continuity Planning, March 2003, http://www.ffiec.gov/ffiecinfobase/booklets/bcp/bus_continuity_plan.pdf

Forrester Research, *Sarbanes-Oxley Solutions- Invest or Pay Later: Hybrid Applications Emerge for Internal Controls Compliance,* Forrester Research Report, March11, 2004.

Foundations of IT Service Management - An Introduction, Van Haren Publishing, The Netherlands, 2007

Friedman, Debbie, *Demystifying Outsourcing,* J. Wiley & Sons, 2006.

Gartner, "Building an IT Performance Management Program, " Gartner Measurement Presentation, July 24, 2001.

Gartner, "ITSM and ITIL Study," 2005.

General Accounting Office, *Information Technology Investment Management Model: A Framework for Assessing and Improving Process Maturity*, GAO Report # 04-394G, Version 1.1, March 2004.

General Electric Corp., *Six Sigma Training Workshop for Vendors*, GE, 2002.

General information on ITIL and parts to ITIL Team Quest: http://www.teamquest.com/solutions-products/solutions/itil/service-delivery/index.htm

General information on ITIL http://www.itil-itsm-world.com/delivery.htm

Gilbert, George and Sood, Rahul, Outsourcing's Offshore Myth, December 15, 2003, retrieved from http://www.cnetnews.com on December 17, 2003.

Graedel, Thomas, *Streamlined Life-Cycle Assessment: Englewood Cliffs*, NJ: Prentice Hall. 1998.

Gray, Clifford and Larson, Erik, *Project Management - The Management Process,* Fourth Edition, McGraw Hill, NY, 2008.

Haeckel, S. H., *Adaptive Enterprise: Creating and Leading Sense-and-Respond Organizations.* Boston, MA: Harvard Business School Press, 1999.

Hale, Judith, *Outsourcing Training and Development,* J. Wiley & Sons, NY, 2006.

Halvey, John K. and Melby, Barbara M., *Business Process Outsourcing,* J. Wiley & Sons, NY, 2007.

Halvey, John K. and Melby, Barbara M., *Informatiom Technology Outsourcing Transactions*, Second Edition, J. Wiley & Sons, NY, 2005.

Hamaker, Stacey, "Enterprise Governance & The Role of IT", Information Systems Control Journal, Volume 6, 2005.

Hamel, Gary, *Leading the Revolution*, Harvard Business School Press, 2000.

Hamm, Steve, *Bangalore Tiger*, McGraw-Hill, New York, 2007.

Hand, Anthony, Applying the Kano Model to User Experience Design, UPA Boston mini-Conference, May, 2004. www.hadnweb.com/anthony/portfolio/kanoa-hand_kano-model_boston_may-12-2004.pdf

Hardy, G., "Guidance on Aligning COBIT ITIL and ISO 17799", Journal Online, ISACA, 2006.

Hardy, G., and Goldentops, E., "COBIT 4.0: The New Face of COBIT", Information Systems Control Journal, Volume 6, 2005.

Hefley, William E. and Locsche, Ethel A., *The eSCM-CL v1.1: Model Overview*, Part 1, ITSQC, Carnegie Mellon University, 2006.

Hefley, William E. and Locsche, Ethel A., *The eSCM-CL v1.1: Model Overview*, Part 2, ITSQC, Carnegie Mellon University, 2006.

Henderson, J., and N. Venkatraman, N., "Strategic Alignment: Leveraging Information Technology for Transforming Organizations", IBM Systems Journal, Vol. 38, Nos. 2 and 3, 1999.

Henderson, J., and Venkatraman, Strategic Alignment: A Model for Organizational Transformation via Information Technology, Working Paper 3223-90, Cambridge, MA: Sloan School of Management, Massachusetts Institute of Technology, 1990.

Hitt, M., et al, *Strategic Management – Competitiveness and Globalization*, 6th Edition, Thomson-South Western, 2005.

Holub, E., Mingay, S., Brittain, K., Govekar, M. and Bittinger, S., "ITIL v3 Services Guidelines Expand Audience Through Update,"Gartner Research, June 5, 2007.

HP: The Reference Model (Hp white papers) http://www.hp.com/large/itsm

Hyder, Elaine B., Heston, Keith M., and Mark, C., *The eSCM-SP v2.01: Model Overview*, Part 1, ITSQC, Carnegie Mellon University, 2006.

Hyder, Elaine B., Heston, Keith M., and Mark, C., *The eSCM-SP v2.01: Model Overview*, Part 2, ITSQC, Carnegie Mellon University, 2006.

IBM, Business Systems Planning, Planning Guide, GE20-0527, White Plains, NY: IBM Corporation, 1981.

Institute of Internal Auditors, "Putting COSO's Theory into Practice", Tone at the Top, Issue 28, November 2005.

International Association of Outsourcing Professionals "COP Master Class Workshop", On-line Course Material, Syracuse University, May, 2007.

International Association of Outsourcing Professionals, *Outsourcing Professional Body of Knowledge,* Version 6, IAOP, 2006.

IT Governance Institute and Office of Government Commerce, Aligning COBIT, ITIL, and ISO 17799, A Management Report, 2005.

IT Governance Institute, *Board Briefing on IT Governance Report*, Second Edition, ITGI, Rolling Meadows, Il, 2003.

IT Governance Institute, COBIT 4.0, 2006.

IT Governance Institute, Enterprise Value: Governance of IT Investments, 2006.

IT Governance Institute, <u>Information Security Governance</u>, 2nd Edition, Report on Guidance for Boards of Directors and Executive Management, 2005.

IT Governance Institute, <u>The CEO's Guide to IT Value & Risk</u>, 2006.

IT Infrastructure Library: http://www.itil.co.uk

IT Service Management - Based on ITIL v3 - An Introduction, Van Haren Publishing, The Netherlands, 2007

IT Service Management Forum, Van Bon, J. *IT Service Management: An Introduction.* Van Haren Publishing, 2002.

ITIL Certification and Other Information: EXIN - http://www.exin-exams.com; ISEB – http://bcs.org.uk.iseb/ism2.htm; OGC (Office of Government Commerce-UK) – http://www.ogc.gov.uk/ogc/isie.nsf/default.html; ITSMF (IT Service Management Forum) – http://www.itsmf.org

ITSMF, Introduction to IT Governance, <u>ITSMF USA Advisory Board Paper</u>, Version 1.0.3, July 13th, 2005.

Janszen, F., *The Age of Innovation: Making Business Creativity a Competence, not a Coincidence,* London: Prentice Hall, 2000.

Johnson, Carla, *Creating Virtual Teams,* HR Magazine, June 2002.

Kano Model, http://www.betterproductdesign.net/tools/definition/kano.htm

Kaplan, J. D., *Strategic IT Portfolio Management: Governing Enterprise Transformation.* United States, Pittiglio Rabin Todd & McGrath Inc., 2005.

Kaplan, R. and Norton, D., *The Strategy Focused Company,* Harvard Business School Press, 2001.

Kaplan, R., S. and Norton, D., P., *Using the Balanced Scorecard as a Strategic Management System,* Harvard Business Review, Jan – Feb pp75-85, 1996

Kaplan, Robert and David, Norton, *Strategy Maps: Converting Intangible Assets into Tangible Outcomes.* Boston, MA: Harvard Business School Press, 2004

Kaplan, Robert and David, Norton, *The Strategy-Focused Organization: How Balanced Scorecard Companies Thrive in the New Business Environment.* Boston, MA: Harvard Business School Press, 2001

Kaplan, Robert and Norton, David, <u>The Balanced Scorecard</u>, HBR Press, Cambridge, MA, 1996.

Kapur, G., *Project Management for Information, Technology. Business and Certification*, Pearson Prentice Hall, 2005.

Katzenback, Jon and Smith, Doug, *The Discipline of Teams,* John Wiley, New York, 2001.

Keen, J. and Digrius, B., *Making Technology Investments Profitable,* J. Wiley and Sons, 2003.

Keen, Jack, "Solidifying Business-IT Alignment", <u>The Advisory Council Research Smart Tip</u>, August, 2006.

Kerzner, H., *Project Management – A Systems Approach to Planning, Scheduling and Controlling,* 9th Edition, J. Wiley & Sons, 2006.

Kotter, John P., *Leading Change,* HBR Press, Cambridge, MA 1996.

Kripalani, Manjeet and Engardio, Pete, "The Rise of India", <u>BusinessWeek,</u> December 8, 2003, p. 66-78

Kuhn, Janet, "Transitioning to ITIL v3," DITY Weekly Newsletter, Vol. 3.29, July 24, 2007.

Lambeth, John, "Using COBIT as a Tool to Lead Enterprise IT Organizations", <u>Information Systems Control Journal,</u> Volume 1, 2007

Leganza, Gene, "Overcoming Obstacles to the Alignment of IT and the Business", Giga

Research Paper, June 24, 2003.

Lohr, Steve, "IBM Showing That Giants Can Be Nimble", New York Times, July 18, 2007

Lonsdale, Derek, Clark, W. and Udvadia, B., *ITIL in a Complex World*, Journal Online, ISACA, 2006.

Luftman, Jerry, *Managing the Information Technology Resource*, Pearson Prentice Hall, Upper Saddle River, NJ, 2004.

Luftman, Jerry, Papp, Raymond and Brier, Tom, "Enablers and Inhibitors of Business-IT Alignment", Communications of the Association for Information Systems, Volume 1, Article 11, March 1999.

Lutchen, M., *Managing IT as a Business: a Survival Guide for CEOs*. Hoboken, N.J., J. Wiley, 2004

Marchand, D. A., Kettinger W.J. and Rollins, J.D., *Information orientation: the Link to Business Performance,* New York/Oxford: Oxford University Press, 2001.

Mayle, David, *Managing Innovation and Change,* Sage Publications, 2006.

McCauley, C. and Van Velsor, Ellen, Editors, *Handbook of Leadership Development*, 2nd Edition, The Center for Creative Leadership, Jossey Bass, 2004.

McCelland, David, "The Leadership Profile for Winning," Presentation on Leadership, MIT Seminar, 1995.

McDermott, Lynda, Brawley, Nolan and Waite, William, *World Class Teams*, John Wiley, New York, 1998

McFarlan, W. and Cash. J., *Strategic Planning for Information Systems*, Wiley, 1990.

McIvor, Ronan, *The Outsourcing Process,* Cambridge University Press, NY, 2006.

McNurlin, Barbara and Sprague, Ralph, Information Systems in Practice, 7th Edition, Pearson Education, Upper Saddle River, NJ, 2006.

Melnicoff, Richard, Shearer, Sandy and Goyal, Deepak, "Is There a Smarter Way to Approach IT Governance?", Outlook, 2005, Accenture, Number 1.

Monnoyer, Eric and Willmott, Paul, "What IT Leaders Do", The Mckinsey Quarterly, August, 2005.

Mosimann, Roland, Mosimann, Patrick and Dussault, Meg, *The Performance Manager,* Cognos, 2007.

National Association of Corporate Directors (USA): http://www.nacdonline.org

Nolan, R. and F., W., McFarlan, *Information Technology and the Board of Directors*, Harvard Business Review, October 2005.

Nolan, Richard and Koot, William, *Nolan's Stage Theory Today*, Holland Management Review, Number 31, 1992.

Office of Government Commerce (OGC), *ITIL v3 Life Cycle Publication Suite,* OGC, The Stationery Office, Great Britain, 2007.

Office of Government Commerce, Business Perspective: The IS View on Delivering Services to the Business. OGC, ITIL© Managing IT Services (IT Infrastructure Library). London, The Stationery Office, 2004.

Office of Government Commerce. ITIL Refresh Statement. Retrieved February 13, 2006. http://www.itil.co.uk/refresh.htm

Oltsik, Jon, "IT Governance: Is IT Governance the Answer?", Tech Republic, January 13, 2003.

Overby, Stephanie, "Simple Successful Outsourcing", CIO Magazine - Business Technology Leadership, October, 2005, pp. 51-62.

Overby, Stephanie, *The New IT Department*, www.cio.com, December 15, 2005 / January 1, 2005.

Palvia, Shailendra, *Off Shore Outsourcing – Creating a World of Difference*, Proceeding of the Second Annual International Outsourcing Conference, Center for Global Outsourcing, New York, July, 2003.

Papp, R., "Alignment of Business and Information Technology Strategy: How and Why?", Information Management(11), 3/4, pp. 6-11, 1998.

Parks, Hugh, "Shifting Governance Roles & Responsibilities", Information Systems Control Journal, Volume 5, 2006.

Paulk, Mark C., *Measurement & the eSourcing Capability Model for Service Providers v2*, ITSQC, Carnegie Mellon University, CMU-ISRI-04-128, February, 2005.

Popper, Charles, "Holistic Framework for IT Governance", Center for Information Policy Research, Harvard University, January 2000.

Porter, Michael, *Competitive Advantage: Creating and Sustaining Superior Performance*, Free Press, 1985.

Prahaland, C. and Hamel, G., *The Core Competence of the Corporation*, Harvard Business Review, March/April 1990.

Praxiom Research Group, Ltd. , "ISO/ IEC 27001 Overview," http://www.praxiom.com/iso-27001-intro.htm

Prentice, Robert, Sarbanes-Oxley Act- Student Guide, Thomson Publishing, 2005.

Prewitt, Edward and Ware, Lorraine C., The State of the CIO'06, www.cio.com/ archieve/010106/JAN1SOC.pdf , 2006.

PRINCE2 Document: http://www.ogc.gov.uk/sdtoolkit/reference/documentation/index.html

Proctivity, *Frequently Asked Questions,* Guide to the Sarbanes-Oxley Act: IT Risks and Controls, December 2003.

Project Management Institute, *A Guide to the Project Management Book of Knowledge*, 3rd Edition, PMI, Newtown Square, PA, 2004.

Project Management Institute, *OPM3 – Organizational Project Management Maturity Model*, PMI, Newtown Square, PA, 2004.

Project Management Institute, *TheStandard for Portfoli Management,* PMI, Newtown Square, PA, 2006.

Puccio, Gerard, Murdock, Mary and Mance, Marie, *Creative Leadership,* Sage Publications, 2007.

Pultorak, David and Kerrigan, Jim, *Conformance Performance and Rapport: A Framework for Corporate and IT Governance*, NACD – Directors Monthly, February 2005.

Quinn, James Brian, *Outsourcing Innovation: The New Engine of Growth*, Sloan Management Review, Summer, 2000, pp. 13-27.

Rafeq, A., "Using COBIT for IT Control Health Check Up", Information Systems Control Journal Health, Volume 5, 2005.

Robinson, Nick, "The Many Faces of IT Governance", Information Systems Control Journal, Volume 1, 2007

Rockart, J., Earl, M. and Ross, "Eight Imperatives for the New IT Organization", Sloan Management Review, Fall pp. 43-55, 1996.

Rockart, John, "Chief Executives Define Their Own Data Needs", Harvard Business Review, March-April, 1979.

Sauer, C. and Burn, J.M., The Pathology of Strategic Alignment, In: C. Sauer, P.Y. Yetton and Associates, *Steps to the Future - Fresh Thinking on the Management of IT-based Organizational Transformation,* Jossey-Bass, San Francisco, 1997.

Selig, Gad J. and Waterhouse, Peter, *IT Governance - An Integrated Framework and Roadmap: How to Plan, Deploy and Sustain for Competitive Advantage,* Computer Associates Sponsored White Paper, March 2006.

Selig, Gad J., "Best Practices for IT Project Management in Fast Track Mode," paper published in Proceedings of Project World, Fall 2004, Washington, DC, September, 2004.

Selig, Gad J., *Creating, Sustaining and Leading High Performance Co-Located and Virtual Teams and Team Leaders - Why, What and How?,* Proceedings of Southern New England Chapter of the Project Management Institute - First Annual Conference, Hartford Conference Center, Hartford, CT, May 23, 2006.

Selig, Gad J., *How to Win Deals in the Rapidly Changing World of Outsourcing - Critical Success Factors for Vendor/Customer Collaboration and Innovation to Grow Revenues,* The 2007 Outsourcing World Summit, February 18-21, 2007, Loews Hotel, Lake Las Vegas, Las Vegas, Nevada.

Selig, Gad J., *IT Governance - A Best Practice Roadmap,* ISACA (Information Systems Audit and Control Associations) - Greater Hartford Chapter Workshop, Marriott Hotel, Rocky Hill, CT, March 15, 2006.

Selig, Gad J., *Strategic Planning for Information Resource Management – A Multinational Perspective,* UMI Press, 1983.

Selig, Gad J., *Successful Business/IT Alignment, Execution & Governance Best Practices,* Society for Information Management Presentation, SIM Fairfield/Westchester Chapter Meeting, March 15, 2007, Doral Arrowwood Conf. Center, NY.

Senge, Peter M., *The Fifth Discipline: the Art and Practise of the Learning Organization.* New York: Currency/Doubleday, 1990.

Shaw, Melissa, "Management Strategies," Network Management Newsletter, 11/7/01.

Sibbet, David, *75 years of Management Ideas and Practice 1922-1997,* Harvard Business Review, Sep/Oct 1997, Supplement Vol. 75, Issue 5.

Singh-Latulipe, Rob, "Val IT: From the Vantage Point of the COBIT 4.0 Pentagon Model for IT Governance", Information Systems Control Journal, Volume 1, 2007

Situation Leadership Model, http://www.chimaeraconsulting.com/sitleader.htm, 2006.

Snyder, Bill, Teams That Span Time Zones Face New Work Rules, May 2003, http://gsb.stanford.edu/news/bmag/sbsm0305/feature_virtual_teams.shtml

Software Engineering Institute, *Capabilities Maturity Model Integrated – Staged and Continuous Model* – Version 1.l, Document Numbers CMU/SEI-2005-TR-011, CMU? SEI-2002-TR-028, CMU/SEI 2002-TR-029SEI, Carnegie Mellon University, 2002 and 2005.

Stewart, W.E., "Balanced Scorecard for Projects," Project Management Journal, Vol. 32, No. 1, March 2001, pp. 38-47.

Summary of Sarbanes-Oxley Act of 2002 AICPA: http://www.aicpa.org/info/sarbanes_oxley_summary.htm

Sun Microsystems and Deloitte, "Raising the Bar for Governance and Compliance", White paper, February, 2006.

Symons, Craig, "IT and Business Alignment, Are We There Yet?", CIO Magazine, April 13, 2005.

Tech Republic, *Forty Eight Questions You Need to Answer for Sarbanes-Oxley Compliance,* Ernst

& Young, CNET Networks, Inc., 2005.

The Business Continuity Plan and Guide, http://www.bcpgenerator.com

Treacy, Michael and Wirsema, Fred, *The Discipline of Market Leaders*, Perseus Books, 1995.

Treacy, Michael, *Double Digit Growth*, Penguin Group, 2003.

Tzu, Sun, *The Art of War*, Oxford University Press, 1971.

Van Grembergen W., *Strategies for Information technology Governance*, IDEA Group Publishing, 2004.

Violino, Bob, "IT Directions", CFO , January 2006.

Wailgum, Thomas, "Toyota's Big Fix: An IS Department Turnaround", www.cio.com, April 15, 2005.

Wailgum, Thomas, *The Rules of IT*, CIO Magazine - Business Technology Leadership, October 1, 2005, pp. 90-100

Watts, S. and Henderson, J.C., "Innovative IT Climates: CIO perspectives," Journal of Strategic Information Systems *Volume* 15, 125-151, 2006.

Weill, Peter and Broadbend, Marianne, *Leveraging the New Infrastructure: How Market Leaders Capitalize on Information Technology*, Harvard Business School Press, 1998.

Weill, Peter and Ross, Jeanne, *IT Governance: How Top Performers Manage IT Decision Rights Results*, Harvard Business Press, Cambridge, MA. 2004.

Wilcox, M. and Rush, S., *The CCL Guide to Leadership in Action*, Center for Creative Leadership, Jossey Bass, 2004.

Womack, James P. and Jones, Daniel T., *Lean Thinking: Banish Waste and Create Wealth in Your Corporation*, Revised and Updated, Harper Business, 2003.

References

Topic List
A. Strategic Planning, IT/Business Alignment and Portfolio Investment Management

Akker, Rolf , "Generic Framework for Information Management", Program for Information Research, University of Amsterdam, 1992.

Anthony, Robert N. , *Planning and Control Systems: A Framework for Analysis,* Harvard University Press, Cambridge, MA, 1965

Avison, D., Jones, J., Powell, P. and Wilson, D., "Using and validating the strategic alignment model." Journal of Strategic Information Systems Volume 13, 2004.

Baggili, J., "Business-IT Alignment", http://web.ics.purdue.edu/~baggili/Portal/B_IT_Alignment.html

Benson, R. J., T. L. Bugnitz, et al. *From Business Strategy to IT Action: Right Decisions for a Better Bottom Line.* Hoboken, N.J., Wiley, 2004.

Bossidy, Larry and Charan, Ram, *Execution – The Discipline of Getting things Done*, Crown Business, 2002.

Boston Consulting Group, *Perspectives on Experience*, 1974.

Carr, N., "IT doesn't matter anymore." Harvard Business Review (5), 41-49, 2003.

Ciborra, C., "De Profundis? Deconstructing the Concept of Strategic Alignment," Scandinavian Journal of Information Systems Volume 9, 67-82, 1997.

Clemons, E. K., Row, M. C., and Redi, S. P., "The Impact of IT on the Organization of Economic Activity", Journal of Management Information Systems, Vol. 9, No. 2, Fall 2002.

Cooper, R.G., Edgett, S.J. and Kleinschmidt, E.J., *Portfolio Management for New Products,* Addison-Wesley, Reading, MA, 1998.

Cordite, James, *Best Practices in Information Technology*, Prentice Hall, Upper Saddle River, NJ, 1998.

Coughlan, J., Lycett, M. and Macredie, R.D., "Understanding the business-IT relationship." International Journal of Information Management Volume 25, 303-319, 2005.

Covey, Stephen, *Seven Habits of Highly Effective People,* Simon and Schuster, 1989.

Crow, Ken, *Customer Focused Development with QFD*, DRM Associates, 2002.

Davenport, T. H., *Mission Critical: Realizing the Promise of the Enterprise Systems,* Boston, MA: HBS Press, 2000.

Degraff, Jeff and Quinn, Shawn, *Leading Innovation,* McGrawHill, NY, 2007.

Deloitte Development, LLC, "Eliminating Roadblocks to IT and Business Alignment", CIO Magazine Supplement, 2004.

Doran, G.T., "There's a Smart Way to Write Management Goals and Objectives", Management Review, November 1981, pp. 35-36.

Drucker, Peter, *Post-Capitalist Society*, Harper Business, 1993.

Duffy, Jan, "Alignment:Delivering Results", www.cio.com

General Accounting Office, *Information Technology Investment Management Model: A Framework for Assessing and Improving Process Maturity*, GAO Report # 04-394G, Version 1.1, March 2004.

Gilbert, George and Sood, Rahul, Outsourcing's Offshore Myth, December 15, 2003, retrieved from http://www.cnetnews.com on December 17, 2003.

Graedel, Thomas, *Streamlined Life-Cycle Assessment: Englewood Cliffs*, NJ: Prentice Hall. 1998.

Hamel, Gary, *Leading the Revolution*, Harvard Business School Press, 2000.

Hand, Anthony, Applying the Kano Model to User Experience Design, UPA Boston mini-Conference, May, 2004. www.hadnweb.com/anthony/portfolio/kanoa-hand_kano-model_boston_may-12-2004.pdf

Henderson, J., and N. Venkatraman, N., "Strategic Alignment: Leveraging Information Technology for Transforming Organizations", <u>IBM Systems Journal</u>, Vol. 38, Nos. 2 and 3, 1999.

Henderson, J., and Venkatraman, Strategic Alignment: A Model for Organizational Transformation via Information Technology, <u>Working Paper 3223-90</u>, Cambridge, MA: Sloan School of Management, Massachusetts Institute of Technology, 1990.

Hitt, M., et al, *Strategic Management – Competitiveness and Globalization*, 6th Edition, Thomson-South Western, 2005.

IBM, Business Systems Planning, Planning Guide, GE20-0527, White Plains, NY: IBM Corporation, 1981.

Kano Model, http://www.betterproductdesign.net/tools/definition/kano.htm

Kaplan, J. D., *Strategic IT Portfolio Management: Governing Enterprise Transformation*. United States, Pittiglio Rabin Todd & McGrath Inc., 2005.

Kaplan, R. and Norton, D., *The Strategy Focused Company*, Harvard Business School Press, 2001.

Keen, J. and Digrius, B., *Making Technology Investments Profitable*, J. Wiley and Sons, 2003.

Keen, Jack, "Solidifying Business-IT Alignment", <u>The Advisory Council Research Smart Tip</u>, August, 2006.

Leganza, Gene, "Overcoming Obstacles to the Alignment of IT and the Business", Giga Research Paper, June 24, 2003.

Lohr, Steve, "IBM Showing That Giants Can Be Nimble", New York Times, July 18, 2007

Luftman, Jerry, *Managing the Information Technology Resource*, Pearson Prentice Hall, Upper Saddle River, NJ, 2004.

Luftman, Jerry, Papp, Raymond and Brier, Tom, "Enablers and Inhibitors of Business-IT Alignment", <u>Communications of the Association for Information Systems</u>, Volume 1, Article 11, March 1999.

McFarlan, W. and Cash. J., *Strategic Planning for Information Systems*, Wiley, 1990.

Nolan, Richard and Koot, William, *Nolan's Stage Theory Today*, Holland Management Review, Number 31, 1992.

Overby, Stephanie, *The New IT Department*, www.cio.com, December 15, 2005 / January 1, 2005.

Papp, R., "Alignment of Business and Information Technology Strategy: How and Why?", Information Management(11), 3/4, pp. 6-11, 1998.

Porter, Michael, *Competitive Advantage: Creating and Sustaining Superior Performance*, Free Press, 1985.

Prahaland, C. and Hamel, G., *The Core Competence of the Corporation*, Harvard Business Review, March/April 1990.

Project Management Institute, *TheStandard for Portfolio Management*, PMI, Newtown Square, PA, 2006.

Rockart, J., Earl, M. and Ross, "Eight Imperatives for the New IT Organization", Sloan Management Review, Fall pp. 43-55, 1996.

Rockart, John, "Chief Executives Define Their Own Data Needs", <u>Harvard Business Review</u>,

March-April, 1979.

Sauer, C. and Burn, J.M., The Pathology of Strategic Alignment, In: C. Sauer, P.Y. Yetton and Associates, *Steps to the Future - Fresh Thinking on the Management of IT-based Organizational Transformation,* Jossey-Bass, San Francisco, 1997.

Selig, Gad J., *Strategic Planning for Information Resource Management – A Multinational Perspective*, UMI Press, 1983.

Selig, Gad J., *Successful Business/IT Alignment, Execution & Governance Best Practices,* Society for Information Management Presentation, SIM Fairfield/Westchester Chapter Meeting, March 15, 2007, Doral Arrowwood Conf. Center, NY.

Sibbet, David, *75 years of Management Ideas and Practice 1922-1997*, Harvard Business Review, Sep/Oct 1997, Supplement Vol. 75, Issue 5.

Symons, Craig, "IT and Business Alignment, Are We There Yet?", CIO Magazine, April 13, 2005.

Treacy, Michael and Wirsema, Fred, *The Discipline of Market Leaders*, Perseus Books, 1995.

Treacy, Michael, *Double Digit Growth*, Penguin Group, 2003.

Wailgum, Thomas, "Toyota's Big Fix: An IS Department Turnaround", www.cio.com, April 15, 2005.

Watts, S. and Henderson, J.C., "Innovative IT Climates: CIO perspectives," Journal of Strategic Information Systems *Volume* 15, 125-151, 2006.

Weill, Peter and Broadbend, Marianne, *Leveraging the New Infrastructure: How Market Leaders Capitalize on Information Technology*, Harvard Business School Press, 1998.

B. Program/Project Management and SDLC

Barkley, Brucet, Sr., *Integrated Project Management,* McGraw Hill, NY, 2006.

CCTA, Prince2 – *Managing Successful Projects with Prince 2, Central Computer and Telecommunications Agency*, Crown Publishers, 1998.

Chrissis, M., Konrad, M. and Shrum, S., *CMMI – Guidelines for Process Integration and Product Improvement*, Addison Wesley, 2003.

Crawford, Ken, *Project Management Maturity Model*, Marcel Decker, Inc., 2002.

Gray, Clifford and Larson, Erik, *Project Management - The Management Process,* Fourth Edition, McGraw Hill, NY, 2008.

Kapur, G., *Project Management for Information, Technology. Business and Certification*, Pearson Prentice Hall, 2005.

Kerzner, H., *Project Management – A Systems Approach to Planning, Scheduling and Controlling*, 9th Edition, J. Wiley & Sons, 2006.

Project Management Institute, *A Guide to the Project Management Book of Knowledge*, 3rd Edition, PMI, Newtown Square, PA, 2004.

Project Management Institute, *OPM3 – Organizational Project Management Maturity Model*, PMI, Newtown Square, PA, 2004.

Selig, Gad J., "Best Practices for IT Project Management in Fast Track Mode," paper published in Proceedings of Project World, Fall 2004, Washington, DC, September, 2004.

Shaw, Melissa, "Management Strategies," Network Management Newsletter, 11/7/01.

Software Engineering Institute, *Capabilities Maturity Model Integrated – Staged and Continuous Model* – Version 1.l, Document Numbers CMU/SEI-2005-TR-011, CMU? SEI-2002-TR-028, CMU/SEI 2002-TR-029SEI, Carnegie Mellon University, 2002 and 2005.

C. Governance, Performance Management, Management Controls, Quality & Risk

Ahern, Dennise, Clouse, Aaron and Torner, Richard, *CMMI™ Distiller - A practical to integrated Process Improvement,* Second Edition, Addison-Wesley. 2004.

Anand, S., *Sarbanes-Oxley Guide,* Second Edition, J. Wiley and Sons, New York, 2006

Bhatia, Mohan, "IT Merger Due Diligence: A Blueprint", Information Systems Control Journal, Volume 1, 2007

BMC Software, *Sarbanes-Oxley Section 404,* White Paper, May, 2004.

Board Effectiveness Partners, "A Roadmap: Strengthening Corporate Governance", Insights, Chapter 1, Version 2.0, January 2004.

Boardman, Bruce, *Get Framed Compliance Policy Development (ISO, ITIL/ISMD & COBIT),* Network Computing Conf., Sept. 28, 2006

Business Continuity Planning Guidelines, http://www.yourwindow.to/business-continuity/contents.htm

Business Continuity Planning Model, http://www.drj.com/new2dr/model/bcmodel.htm

Catucci, Bill, "A New Governance Model", Balanced Scorecard, January 15, 2005.

Catucci, Bill, "Ten Lessons for Implementing the Balanced Scorecard", Balanced Scorecard, January 15, 2003.

Center for Technology Governance and Compliance, Raising the Bar for Governance and Compliance, Sun Microsystems and Deloitte Consulting LLP White Paper, February, 2006

Colley, J., Doyle, J., Logan, G., Stettinius, W., *What is Corporate Governance?* , McGraw-Hill, December 2004

Corporate Executive Board, "IT Balanced Scorecards - End-to-End Performance Measurement for the Corporate IT Function, " Working Council for Chief Information Officers Report, 2003.

Erickson – Harris, Lisa, *IT Governance: Round Em Up!* Intelligent Enterprise Conf., August, 2006, p. 10-14.

Ernst and Young, *48 Questions You Need to Answer for Sarbanes-Oxley Compliance*, Tech Republic, CNET Networks, 2005.

Fabian, Robert, "Interdependence of COBIT and ITIL", Information Systems Control Journal, Volume 1, 2007

Federal Financial Institutions Examination Council (FFIEC), Business Continuity Planning, March 2003, http://www.ffiec.gov/ffiecinfobase/booklets/bcp/bus_continuity_plan.pdf

Forrester Research, *Sarbanes-Oxley Solutions- Invest or Pay Later: Hybrid Applications Emerge for Internal Controls Compliance,* Forrester Research Report, March11, 2004.

Gartner, "Building an IT Performance Management Program, " Gartner Measurement Presentation, July 24, 2001.

Hamaker, Stacey, "Enterprise Governance & The Role of IT", Information Systems Control Journal, Volume 6, 2005.

Hardy, G., "Guidance on Aligning COBIT ITIL and ISO 17799", Journal Online, ISACA, 2006.

Hardy, G., and Goldentops, E., "COBIT 4.0: The New Face of COBIT", Information Systems Control Journal, Volume 6, 2005.

Institute of Internal Auditors, "Putting COSO's Theory into Practice", Tone at the Top, Issue 28, November 2005.

IT Governance Institute and Office of Government Commerce, <u>Aligning CobiT, ITIL, and ISO 17799</u>, A Management Report, 2005.

IT Governance Institute, *Board Briefing on IT Governance Report*, Second Edition, ITGI, Rolling Meadows, Il, 2003.

IT Governance Institute, COBIT 4.0, 2006.

IT Governance Institute, <u>Enterprise Value: Governance of IT Investments</u>, 2006.

IT Governance Institute, <u>Information Security Governance</u>, 2nd Edition, Report on Guidance for Boards of Directors and Executive Management, 2005.

IT Governance Institute, <u>The CEO's Guide to IT Value & Risk</u>, 2006.

Kaplan, R., S. and Norton, D., P., *Using the Balanced Scorecard as a Strategic Management System*, Harvard Business Review, Jan – Feb pp75-85, 1996

Kaplan, Robert and David, Norton, *Strategy Maps: Converting Intangible Assets into Tangible Outcomes*. Boston, MA: Harvard Business School Press, 2004

Kaplan, Robert and David, Norton, *The Strategy-Focused Organization: How Balanced Scorecard Companies Thrive in the New Business Environment*. Boston, MA: Harvard Business School Press, 2001

Kaplan, Robert and Norton, David, <u>The Balanced Scorecard</u>, HBR Press, Cambridge, MA, 1996.

Lambeth, John, "Using COBIT as a Tool to Lead Enterprise IT Organizations", <u>Information Systems Control Journal</u>, Volume 1, 2007

Lutchen, M., *Managing IT as a Business: a Survival Guide for CEOs*. Hoboken, N.J., J. Wiley, 2004

Marchand, D. A., Kettinger W.J. and Rollins, J.D., *Information orientation: the Link to Business Performance*, New York/Oxford: Oxford University Press, 2001.

McNurlin, Barbara and Sprague, Ralph, <u>Information Systems in Practice</u>, 7th Edition, Pearson Education, Upper Saddle River, NJ, 2006.

Melnicoff, Richard, Shearer, Sandy and Goyal, Deepak, "Is There a Smarter Way to Approach IT Governance?", <u>Outlook, 2005</u>, Accenture, Number 1.

Monnoyer, Eric and Willmott, Paul, "What IT Leaders Do", <u>The Mckinsey Quarterly</u>, August, 2005.

Nolan, R. and F., W., McFarlan, *Information Technology and the Board of Directors*, Harvard Business Review, October 2005.

Oltsik, Jon, "IT Governance: Is IT Governance the Answer?", <u>Tech Republic</u>, January 13, 2003.

Parks, Hugh, "Shifting Governance Roles & Responsibilities", <u>Information Systems Control Journal</u>, Volume 5, 2006.

Popper, Charles, "Holistic Framework for IT Governance", <u>Center for Information Policy Research</u>, Harvard University, January 2000.

Prentice, Robert, <u>Sarbanes-Oxley Act- Student Guide</u>, Thomson Publishing, 2005.

Proctivity, *Frequently Asked Questions,* Guide to the Sarbanes-Oxley Act: IT Risks and Controls, December 2003.

Pultorak, David and Kerrigan, Jim, *Conformance Performance and Rapport: A Framework for Corporate and IT Governance*, <u>NACD – Directors Monthly</u>, February 2005.

Rafeq, A., "Using CobiT for IT Control Health Check Up", <u>Information Systems Control Journal Health</u>, Volume 5, 2005.

Robinson, Nick, "The Many Faces of IT Governance", Information Systems Control Journal, Volume 1, 2007

Selig, Gad J. and Waterhouse, Peter, *IT Governance - An Integrated Framework and Roadmap: How to Plan, Deploy and Sustain for Competitive Advantage,* Computer Associates Sponsored White Paper, March 2006.

Selig, Gad J., *IT Governance - A Best Practice Roadmap,* ISACA (Information Systems Audit and Control Associations) - Greater Hartford Chapter Workshop, Marriott Hotel, Rocky Hill, CT, March 15, 2006.

Singh-Latulipe, Rob, "Val IT: From the Vantage Point of the COBIT 4.0 Pentagon Model for IT Governance", Information Systems Control Journal, Volume 1, 2007

Stewart, W.E., "Balanced Scorecard for Projects," Project Management Journal, Vol. 32, No. 1, March 2001, pp. 38-47.

Sun Microsystems and Deloitte, "Raising the Bar for Governance and Compliance", White paper, February, 2006.

Tech Republic, *Forty Eight Questions You Need to Answer for Sarbanes-Oxley Compliance,* Ernst & Young, CNET Networks, Inc., 2005.

The Business Continuity Plan and Guide, http://www.bcpgenerator.com

Van Grembergen W., *Strategies for Information technology Governance*, IDEA Group Publishing, 2004.

Violino, Bob, "IT Directions", CFO , January 2006.

Weill, Peter and Ross, Jeanne, *IT Governance: How Top Performers Manage IT Decision Rights Results*, Harvard Business Press, Cambridge, MA. 2004.

Womack, James P. and Jones, Daniel T., *Lean Thinking: Banish Waste and Create Wealth in Your Corporation*, Revised and Updated, Harper Business, 2003.

D. IT Service Management (inlcuding IT Infrastructure Library)

Breyfogle, F., Cupello, J., Meadows, Becki, *Managing Six Sigma*, Wiley, 2001.

Cybercan Technology Solutions, ITIL (Information Technology Infrastructure Library) Foundation Workshop, 2005.

Edwards, John, Dream Catalogue, CFO Magazine, September, 2005.

Foundations of IT Service Management - An Introduction, Van Haren Publishing, The Netherlands, 2007

Gartner, "ITSM and ITIL Study," 2005.

General Electric Corp., *Six Sigma Training Workshop for Vendors*, GE, 2002.

General information on ITIL and parts to ITIL Team Quest: http://www.teamquest.com/solutions-products/solutions/itil/service-delivery/index.htm

General information on ITIL http://www.itil-itsm-world.com/delivery.htm

Hamm, Steve, *Bangalore Tiger*, McGraw-Hill, New York, 2007.

Holub, E., Mingay, S., Brittain, K., Govekar, M. and Bittinger, S., "ITIL v3 Services Guidelines Expand Audience Through Update,"Gartner Research, June 5, 2007.

HP: The Reference Model (Hp white papers) http://www.hp.com/large/itsm

IT Service Management - Based on ITIL v3 - An Introduction, Van Haren Publishing, The Netherlands, 2007

IT Service Management Forum, Van Bon, J. *IT Service Management: An Introduction.* Van Haren Publishing, 2002.

ITIL Certification and Other Information: EXIN - http://www.exin-exams.com; ISEB – http://bcs.org.uk.iseb/ism2.htm; OGC (Office of Government Commerce-UK) – http://www.ogc.gov.uk/ogc/isie.nsf/default.html; ITSMF (IT Service Management Forum) – http://www.itsmf.org

ITSMF, Introduction to IT Governance, <u>ITSMF USA Advisory Board Paper</u>, Version 1.0.3, July 13th, 2005.

Kuhn, Janet, "Transitioning to ITIL v3," DITY Weekly Newsletter, Vol. 3.29, July 24, 2007.

Lonsdale, Derek, Clark, W. and Udvadia, B., *ITIL in a Complex World*, <u>Journal Online</u>, ISACA, 2006.

Office of Government Commerce (OGC), *ITIL v3 Life Cycle Publication Suite,*OGC, Great Britain, 2007.

Office of Government Commerce, Business Perspective: The IS View on Delivering Services to the Business. OGC, ITIL© Managing IT Services (IT Infrastructure Library). London, The Stationery Office, 2004.

Office of Government Commerce. ITIL Refresh Statement. Retrieved February 13, 2006. http://www.itil.co.uk/refresh.htm

Praxiom Research Group, Ltd. , "ISO/ IEC 27001 Overview," http://www.praxiom.com/iso-27001-intro.htm

E. Strategic Sourcing, Outsourcing and Vendor Management

Beckman, Sara L. and Rosenfield, Donald B., *Operating Strategy,* McGraw-Hill, NY, 2008.

Bragg, Steven M., *Outsourcing,* Second Edition, J. Wiley & Sons, NY, 2006.

Brown, Doug and Wilson, Scott, *The Black Book of Outsourcing*, John Wiley & Sons, 2005.

Burkholder, Nicholas C., *Outsourcing,* J. Wiley & Sons, NY, 2006.

Business Week, *Special Report on Outsourcing*, January 30, 2006

Carmel, Erran and Tjia, Paul, *Offshoring Information Technology*, Cambridge University Press, UK, 2005.

Casale, Frank, "Darwin and Outsourcing", <u>Outsourcing Essentials</u>, Vol.2, No. 3 Winter 2004, The Outsourcing Institute.

Click, Rick L. and Dvening, Thomas N., N., *Business Process Outsourcing,* J. Wiley & Sons, NY, 2005.

Corbett, Michael F., "Outsourcing 2000: Value-Driven Customer-Focused", <u>Fortune</u>, May 29, 2000, p. S36

Corbett, Michael, *The Outsourcing Revolution*, Dearbon Trade Publication, Chicago, Il, 2004

Dalal, Jagdish, *Off-shore Outsourcing*, The Outsourcing Research Council, Raleigh, NC, October 23, 2002, p. 11, 13.

Deloitte, Consulting Report, "Calling a Change in the Outsourcing Model, Deloitte Consulting", December, 2005.

Ellis, James E., McDonnell Douglas, "Unfasten the Seat Belts", <u>BusinessWeek</u>, February 14, 1994, p. 36.

Engardio, Pete et al., "The New Global Job Shift", <u>BusinessWeek</u>, February 3, 2003

Friedman, Debbie, *Demystifying Outsourcing,* J. Wiley & Sons, 2006.

Hale, Judith, *Outsourcing Training and Development,* J. Wiley & Sons, NY, 2006.

Halvey, John K. and Melby, Barbara M., *Business Process Outsourcing,* J. Wiley & Sons, NY, 2007.

Halvey, John K. and Melby, Barbara M., *Informatiom Technology Outsourcing Transactions*,

Second Edition, J. Wiley & Sons, NY, 2005.

Hefley, William E. and Locsche, Ethel A., *The eSCM-CL v1.1: Model Overview,* Part 1, ITSQC, Carnegie Mellon University, 2006.

Hefley, William E. and Locsche, Ethel A., *The eSCM-CL v1.1: Model Overview,* Part 2, ITSQC, Carnegie Mellon University, 2006.

Hyder, Elaine B., Heston, Keith M., and Mark, C., *The eSCM-SP v2.01: Model Overview*, Part 1, ITSQC, Carnegie Mellon University, 2006.

Hyder, Elaine B., Heston, Keith M., and Mark, C., *The eSCM-SP v2.01: Model Overview*, Part 2, ITSQC, Carnegie Mellon University, 2006.

International Association of Outsourcing Professionals, *Outsourcing Professional Body of Knowledge,* Version 6, IAOP, 2006.

Kripalani, Manjeet and Engardio, Pete, "The Rise of India", BusinessWeek, December 8, 2003, p. 66-78

McIvor, Ronan, *The Outsourcing Process,* Cambridge University Press, NY, 2006.

Overby, Stephanie, "Simple Successful Outsourcing", CIO Magazine - Business Technology Leadership, October, 2005, pp. 51-62.

Palvia, Shailendra, *Off Shore Outsourcing – Creating a World of Difference*, Proceeding of the Second Annual International Outsourcing Conference, Center for Global Outsourcing, New York, July, 2003.

Paulk, Mark C., *Measurement & the eSourcing Capability Model for Service Providers v2,* ITSQC, Carnegie Mellon University, CMU-ISRI-04-128, February, 2005.

Quinn, James Brian, *Outsourcing Innovation: The New Engine of Growth*, Sloan Management Review, Summer, 2000, pp. 13-27.

Selig, Gad J., *How to Win Deals in the Rapidly Changing World of Outsourcing - Critical Success Factors for Vendor/Customer Collaboration and Innovation to Grow Revenues,* The 2007 Outsourcing World Summit, February 18-21, 2007, Loews Hotel, Lake Las Vegas, Las Vegas, Nevada.

F. Leadership, Teams, Managing Change & Innovation

Betz, Frederick, *Managing Technological Innovation: Competitive Advantage from Change*. New York: John Wiley, 2003.

Bridges, William, *Managing Transitions*, 2nd Edition, Da Capo Press, Cambridge, Ma, 1991.

Broadbent, Marianne and Kitzis, Ellen, *The New CIO Leader*, HBR Press, 2005.

Burn, Jack and Moran, Linda, *The New Self Directed Work Teams*, McGraw-Hill, New York, 2000.

Cohen, Beth, TACtical Research SmartTip – *Rethinking Internet Forum and Collaboration Tools*, The Advisory Council (TAC), December, 2006

Drucker, Peter, *Managing in a Time of Great Change,* Butterworth-Heinemann, 1997.

Haeckel, S. H., *Adaptive Enterprise: Creating and Leading Sense-and-Respond Organizations*. Boston, MA: Harvard Business School Press, 1999.

Janszen, F., *The Age of Innovation: Making Business Creativity a Competence, not a Coincidence,* London: Prentice Hall, 2000.

Johnson, Carla, *Creating Virtual Teams*, HR Magazine, June 2002.

Katzenback, Jon and Smith, Doug, *The Discipline of Teams*, John Wiley, New York, 2001.

Kotter, John P., *Leading Change*, HBR Press, Cambridge, MA 1996.

Mayle, David, *Managing Innovation and Change,* Sage Publications, 2006.

McCauley, C. and Van Velsor, Ellen, Editors, *Handbook of Leadership Development*, 2nd Edition, The Center for Creative Leadership, Jossey Bass, 2004.

McCelland, David, "The Leadership Profile for Winning," Presentation on Leadership, MIT Seminar, 1995.

McDermott, Lynda, Brawley, Nolan and Waite, William, *World Class Teams*, John Wiley, New York, 1998

Mosimann, Roland, Mosimann, Patrick and Dussault, Meg, *The Performance Manager*, Cognos, 2007.

Prewitt, Edward and Ware, Lorraine C., The State of the CIO'06, www.cio.com/archieve/010106/JAN1SOC.pdf , 2006.

Puccio, Gerard, Murdock, Mary and Mance, Marie, *Creative Leadership*, Sage Publications, 2007.

Selig, Gad J., *Creating, Sustaining and Leading High Performance Co-Located and Virtual Teams and Team Leaders - Why, What and How?*, Proceedings of Southern New England Chapter of the Project Management Institute - First Annual Conference, Hartford Conference Center, Hartford, CT, May 23, 2006.

Senge, Peter M., *The Fifth Discipline: the Art and Practise of the Learning Organization*. New York: Currency/Doubleday, 1990.

Situation Leadership Model, http://www.chimaeraconsulting.com/sitleader.htm, 2006.

Snyder, Bill, Teams That Span Time Zones Face New Work Rules, May 2003, http://gsb.stanford.edu/news/bmag/sbsm0305/feature_virtual_teams.shtml

Tzu, Sun, *The Art of War*, Oxford University Press, 1971.

Wailgum, Thomas, *The Rules of IT*, CIO Magazine - Business Technology Leadership, October 1, 2005, pp. 90-100

Wilcox, M. and Rush, S., *The CCL Guide to Leadership in Action*, Center for Creative Leadership, Jossey Bass, 2004.

G. External Links

Corporate Governance: http://www.corpgov.net

European Corporate Governance Institute: http://www.ecgi.org

International Association of Outsourcing Professionals "COP Master Class Workshop", On-line Course Material, Syracuse University, May, 2007.

IT Infrastructure Library: http://www.itil.co.uk

National Association of Corporate Directors (USA): http://www.nacdonline.org

PRINCE2 Document: http://www.ogc.gov.uk/sdtoolkit/reference/documentation/index.html

Summary of Sarbanes-Oxley Act of 2002 AICPA: http://www.aicpa.org/info/sarbanes_oxley_summary.htm

Appendix 1 – Sarbanes Oxley

Appendix 1 Sarbanes-Oxley Controls Template for a Manufacturing Company (Illustrative Example)		Control Activities	Completeness	Existence	Valuation	Rights & Obligations	Presentation & Disclosure	Control Type (FOC)	Frequency of Occurrence (Q,M,W,D)	Control Type 2 (Preventive / Detective)	Aerospace Operational
			(Purpose of Control Activities)								
Cycle	VIII.	Information Technology									
Sub-Cycle	VIII.1	System Development Life Cycle									
Control Objective	VIII.1	Controls provide reasonable assurance that systems and applications are designed and modified to adhere to business requirements, are properly authorized, tested, and approved prior to migration to the production environment. (Implementation of financia									
Control Activities	VIII. 1.1	A formal systems development methodology is in place to guide the organization through the systems development life cycle.						F			
	VIII. 1.2	Business unit management and users are involved in the review and approval of all business system requirements prior to development. Authorization and written approval is required for business systems requirements. (I.e. a passport steering committee or						F			
	VIII. 1.3	Formal and documented unit, integration, and user acceptance testing is required prior to implementation.						F			
	VIII. 1.4	Individuals responsible for development or coding changes are separate from those who test and migrate the change into production. For smaller locations, mitigating controls are in place.				X		F			

Appendix 1
Sarbanes-Oxley Controls Template for a Manufacturing Company (Illustrative Example)

	Control Activities	Purpose of Control Activities					Control Type		Frequency of Occurrence	Control Type 2	Aerospace Operational
		Completeness	Existence	Valuation	Rights & Obligations	Presentation & Disclosure	FOC		Q,M,W,D	Preventive / Detective	
VIII. 1.5	Management approval of the readiness of the business requirements and corresponding test results and data conversion (if applicable) is required prior to implementation.				X		F				
VIII. 1.6	Program change management tools (such as Visual Source Save or Excel logs) are utilized to track software changes and to segregate the development and production environments.						F				
VIII. 2	Change Management										
VIII. 2	Controls provide reasonable assurance that minor modifications are designed and modified to adhere to business requirements, are properly authorized, tested, and approved prior to migration to the production environment. (Report generation, patches, fun										
VIII. 2.1	A change control process is in place to ensure production changes are documented and implemented only after proper approval. This process should require user/management involvement.						F				
VIII. 2.2	Formal and documented unit, integration, and user acceptance testing is required and must be approved by Mgt prior to implementation.						F				

Appendix 1
Sarbanes-Oxley Controls Template for a Manufacturing Company (Illustrative Example)

	Control Activities	Completeness	Existence	Valuation	Rights & Obligations	Presentation & Disclosure	FOC		Q,M,W,D	Preventive / Detective	Aerospace Operational
		Purpose of Control Activities					Control Type		Frequency of Occurrence	Control Type 2	
VIII. 2.3	Individuals responsible for development or coding changes are separate from those who test and migrate the change into production. For smaller locations, mitigating controls are in place.				X		F				
VIII. 2.4	Program change management tools (such as Visual Source Save or Excel logs) are utilized to track software changes and to segregate the development and production environments.						F				
VIII. 3	Data and Systems Backup and Recovery										
VIII. 3	Controls provide reasonable assurance that programs and data files are regularly backed up and data is available for restoration in the event of processing errors and/or unexpected interruptions.	X									
VIII. 3.1	Backups of critical programs and data files are scheduled, managed, and backup media tracked by a tape management system. Daily backup status and backup reports are reviewed to ensure successful completion.						F				
VIII. 3.2	Backup media are rotated to an approved offsite storage location at predetermined rotation schedules. Formal policies and procedures exist for logging when Media are sent to and received back from the offsite location.						F				

Appendix 1
Sarbanes-Oxley Controls Template for a Manufacturing Company (Illustrative Example)

	Control Activities	Purpose of Control Activities					Control Type (FOC)		Frequency of Occurrence (Q,M,W,D)	Control Type 2 (Preventive / Detective)	Aerospace Operational
		Completeness	Existence	Valuation	Rights & Obligations	Presentation & Disclosure					
VIII. 3.3	Access to backup media are restricted to authorized personnel.				X		F				
VIII. 3.4	Testing of data restoration procedures is performed on a periodic basis.	X					F				
VIII. 4	Data and Systems Backup and Recovery										
VIII. 4	Controls provide reasonable assurance that data centers are adequately protected from environmental hazards.										
VIII. 4.1	Environmental factors such as temperature, humidity, and water leaks are monitored by automated monitoring tools which alert the appropriate individuals of problems.	X				'	O				
VIII. 4.2	Fire suppression sensors and systems are installed within the data centers.	X					O				
VIII. 4.3	Uninterruptible Power Supply (UPS) or emergency generators are in place and automatically start in the event of a power outage.	X					O				
VIII. 4.4	Preventive maintenance of environmental control systems is performed.						O				
VIII. 5	Data and Systems Backup and Recovery										
VIII. 5	Controls provide reasonable assurance that formal plans exists to recover critical IT services and applications in accordance with established business requirements.										

Appendix 1
Sarbanes-Oxley Controls Template for a Manufacturing Company (Illustrative Example)

	Control Activities	Completeness	Existence	Valuation	Rights & Obligations	Presentation & Disclosure	Control Type (FOC)	Frequency of Occurrence (Q,M,W,D)	Control Type 2 (Preventive / Detective)	Aerospace Operational
		Purpose of Control Activities								
VIII. 5.1	A disaster recovery planning process is in place to identify potential disaster risks and document formal recovery procedures and prioritization.	X					O			
VIII. 5.2	Management periodically reviews and formally approves the plan.						O			
VIII. 5.3	The plan identifies and prioritizes critical applications to be recovered, and timeframes for recovery have been documented.				X		O			
VIII. 5.4	The plan includes the equipment requirements and configuration standards needed to support the recovery of critical applications and data.						O			
VIII. 5.5	The plan includes formal identification of key personnel and specific functions to be performed by management, IT personnel and external vendors.				X		O			
VIII. 5.6	The disaster recovery plan is tested periodically for critical systems and that external vendors were included in the plan.	X			X		O			
VIII. 6	Logical Access									
VIII. 6	Controls provide reasonable assurance that logical access to production applications and data files is restricted to appropriately authorized personnel.									
VIII. 6.1	User, developer and Security Administrator access to business systems is determined based on job roles, responsibilities and written management approval for adding and/or modifying user access.	X	X	X	X		F			

Appendix 1
Sarbanes-Oxley Controls Template for a Manufacturing Company (Illustrative Example)

	Control Activities	Purpose of Control Activities					Control Type (FOC)	Frequency of Occurrence (Q,M,W,D)	Control Type 2 (Preventive / Detective)	Aerospace Operational
		Completeness	Existence	Valuation	Rights & Obligations	Presentation & Disclosure				
VIII. 6.2	Users are required to have a unique user id and password in order to access production business systems. Passwords are periodically forced to expire, follow strict password composition rules, and are encrypted to prevent viewing.	X	X	X	X		F			
VIII. 6.3	Users are allowed a limited number of invalid access attempts before being locked out. Security violations and remote access attempts are logged, maintained, periodically reviewed and reported to management.	X	X	X	X		F			
VIII. 6.4	HR distributes termination and transfer lists to IT and security administration to facilitate the access review process and if necessary, removal of terminated user accounts.						F			
VIII. 6.5	Networks have installed UTC approved and managed barriers (i.e. firewalls) to prevent unauthorized outside penetration.						F			
VIII. 6.6	Wide Area Networks are monitored and potential security issues are identified and investigated to resolution.						F			
VIII. 6.7	Adequate safeguards exist to ensure that data that is deemed to be critical or sensitive and that is transmitted externally is protected from unauthorized access by encryption or dedicated connections.	X					F			

Appendix 1
Sarbanes-Oxley Controls Template for a Manufacturing Company (Illustrative Example)

	Control Activities	Completeness	Existence	Valuation	Rights & Obligations	Presentation & Disclosure	Control Type (FOC)	Frequency of Occurrence (Q,M,W,D)	Control Type 2 (Preventive / Detective)	Aerospace Operational
				Purpose of Control Activities						
VIII. 6.8	Procedures for remote operations are in place to ensure that access is properly secured and managed.						F			
VIII. 6.9	A process exists to ensure that all critical software is appropriately licensed.						O			
VIII. 7	Physical Access									
VIII. 7	Controls provide reasonable assurance that physical access to computer equipment and storage media is limited to appropriately authorized personnel.						F			
VIII. 7.1	Access to computer operations and data center facilities is physically secured and logs (electronic or paper based) of user access exist.	X	X	X	X		F			
VIII. 7.2	Access is granted only upon receipt of a formal request from an authorized approver. A list of authorized approvers is maintained.	X	X	X	X		F			
VIII. 7.3	Server terminals automatically lock or logoff a user after a period of inactivity.	X	X	X	X		F			
VIII. 7.4	Periodic reviews of all individuals with access to data center facilities are performed.	X	X	X	X		O			
VIII. 7.5	Facilities are alarmed and monitored.						O			
VIII. 8	Production/Batch Processing									
VIII. 8	Controls provide reasonable assurance that production processing is appropriately scheduled, and deviations from scheduled processing are identified and resolved timely.						F			

Appendix 1
Sarbanes-Oxley Controls Template for a Manufacturing Company (Illustrative Example)

	Control Activities	Purpose of Control Activities					Control Type		Frequency of Occurrence	Control Type 2	Aerospace Operational
		Completeness	Existence	Valuation	Rights & Obligations	Presentation & Disclosure	FOC		Q,M,W,D	Preventive / Detective	
VIII. 8.1	System capacity and performance is monitored to ensure system availability and application response times are consistent with the business requirements.	X					O				
VIII. 8.2	A process exists to inform the appropriate individuals when a processing problem occurred and that the functional owner provides written notice that the output of the rescheduled jobs are correct.	X		X			F				
VIII. 8.3	Changes to production processing/job schedules are required to go through a change management process and should be authorized by the functional owner.	X		X			F				
VIII. 8.4	Formal policies and emergency access controls are utilized when migrating non scheduled changes to production programs/data.						F				
VIII. 9	Organization and management										
VIII. 9	Appropriate IT governance exists to ensure management and oversight of IT initiatives are aligned to the business needs.										
VIII. 9.1	A steering committee, comprised of IT and business area management, is in place to prioritize and monitor IT planning and significant projects.						O				
VIII. 9.2	An IT strategic planning process exist to support the business units medium and long-term goals.						O				

Appendix 1
Sarbanes-Oxley Controls Template for a Manufacturing Company (Illustrative Example)

	Control Activities	Purpose of Control Activities						Control Type (FOC)		Frequency of Occurrence (Q,M,W,D)	Control Type 2 (Preventive / Detective)	Aerospace Operational
		Completeness	Existence	Valuation	Rights & Obligations	Presentation & Disclosure						
VIII. 9.3	Appropriate expense budgeting and monitoring for IT expenditures is reviewed by management.							O				
VIII. 10	Organization and management											
VIII. 10	Controls provide reasonable assurance that outsourced resources maintain adequate levels of IT controls and service levels. (UTC will Cover CSC)											
VIII. 10.1	Formal contracts with each third-party/outsourcing service provider exists and are in written accordance with business unit or corporate standards and guidelines.							O				
VIII. 10.2	Contracts clearly define the responsibilities and obligations of both the Business Unit and the third party service provider.							O				
VIII. 10.3	A business area manager is responsible for managing the service provider and monitoring the performance of the third party against their contractual obligations.							O				
VIII. 10.4	IT Management obtains and reviews periodic reporting of key performance indicators or service level agreements (SLA's) and formally addresses service issues and monitors through to resolution.							O				

Appendix 2 – Select IT governance and other frameworks and standards

(In general, the models, frameworks and standards referenced in the table are vendor independent & often only address one or more components that must be part of a comprehensive IT Governance Framework solution)

Model Focus	Model Name	Author	Use
IT Governance –General	COBIT; Decisions Rights; Generic Framework for Information Management	IT Governance Institute, 2003; Weil and Ross, 2004; University of Holland,	A framework which links IT processes to four domains (plan/organize; acquire/implement; delivery; support); Who influences and makes IT decisions
Project Management (PM)	PMBOK – PM Book of Knowledge	Project Management Institute, 2004	Defines 9 knowledge & 5 process areas of PM
	OPM3(Organizational PM Maturity Model)		Tool to help organizations self assess their PM Maturity
	PMMM – PM Maturity Model	Crawford, 2002	Maps SEI's CMMI (see below) model to PMBOK to provide a PM maturity roadmap based on stages of maturity
	Prince2	CCTA (Central Computer & Telecomm. Agency (UK Government), 199.8 (Now known as OGC – Office of Government Commerce)	A PM methodology that focuses on the business case
	IT investment Management	General Accounting Office (U.S. Federal Government)	Helps to evaluate, select and prioritize IT investments
Systems/Software Development	CMMI (Capabilities Maturity Model – Integrated)	Software Engineering Institute (SEI) – Carnegie Mellon, 2002 and 2005	Used to analyze 5 stages of maturity for achieving process improvements in systems & software development
	SSADM (Structured Systems & Design Method)	CCTA (Central Computer & Telecomm. Agency. Now (UK Government - OGC)	Structured methodology to develop systems
	DSDM (Dynamic Systems Development Method	The DSDM Consortium	Used as a RAD (Rapid Application Development) Methodology
Quality & Security	Six Sigma; Lean; Baldrige Quality Award	Motorola with GE popularizing the concept; Breyfogle, et. al.	Framework used to continuously improve processes and reduce errors or defects (can be applied to any process)

Model Focus	Model Name	Author	Use
	ISO 9001 (Quality)	International Standards Organization	Focus on quality management policies and practices of an enterprise
	ISO 17799 and 27001	International Standards Organization	IT security frameworks and models
IT Operations & Infrastructure	ITIL (IT Infrastructure Library) v2 and v3;	Originated by CCTA (Central Computer & Telecomm. Agency, now OGC. (UK Government); Currently ITIL is licensed to and maintained by APMG, which also is responsible for accreditation.	A framework of 10 processes and functions focused on improving IT service management.
	ISO/ IEC 20000 – IT Service Management	Currently owned and maintained by ITSMF	
Human Resources	P-CMM (People -Capability Maturity Model)	Software Engineering Institute (SEI) – Carnegie Mellon University	Model for advancing people and their competencies
Performance Measurement	Balanced Scorecard; Critical Success Factors	Kaplan & Norton; Cattuci; Rockhart	Method for strategy focused measures of success
Regulatory Compliance	Sarbanes Oxley Act (SOX) of 2002 – All public US companies	US Congress – HR 3763	SOX - Law that identifies public company Board and Executive Officers' responsibilities regarding audits, controls, oversight and related matters. Used as a guideline to assist in Public Company compliance, which includes IT.
	FDA, FDIC, HIPPA, SEC Others	Various government agencies that apply to either all or select industries	
Outsourcing and Vendor Management	Outsourcing Frameworks – OPBOK; eSCM (eSourcing Cabability Models for service providers and client organizations)	Palvia; Casale; Brown, et. al. eSCM, IAOP	Various frameworks and guidelines on how to outsource IT and manage vendors.
Voice of the Customer VOC)	Kano	Kano	Frameworks to capture VOC and customer requirements

Appendix 3 – Managing accelerating change and transformation

Critical Success Enablers for Managing Change, Accelerating Change and Cultural Transformation – are segmented into the following categories:

- **Change Acceleration Framework** – Overall pre-requisites for effecting accelerating change and transformation
  - **People, Organization Architecture and Leadership**
  - **Scalable and Flexible Process**
  - **Enabling Technology**

- **Six Prerequisites for Managing Change**
  - **Creating a shared need** – the reason for change is instilled within the organization – widely understood, motivational, pragmatic, achievable and embraced. The felt need (and benefits of the change) for the change must exceed the (natural) resistances.
  - **Shaping a vision** – the desired outcomes of the change are clear, widely understood and shared. Individuals can envision the impacts and opportunities of the change for themselves (Demonstrate and sell the benefits of the vision as it evolves and materializes. Link goals, objectives and strategies to vision).
  - **Mobilizing commitment** – There is a strong commitment to the change from key constituents. They are committed to make it happen, make it work and invest their attention and energy.
  - **Making change last** – Change is reinforced, supported and refreshed so that it endures and flourishes throughout the organization.
  - **Monitoring progress and learning** - Progress is real (needs a baseline). Measurement systems are established, benchmarks are set and realized. **Learnings** are shared throughout the organization. **Current and evolving best practices** (both internal and external) are used as a basis fro continuous improvement
  - **Changing systems, structures, capabilities and attitudes** – Develop policies, practices and processes which facilitate, support and sustain change.

People/Organization Architecture & Leadership
- Obtain **executive sponsorship** and champion(s) – Need "Leadership" at highest levels
- **Get the right people** involved at the right time (phases)
  - Know the skills and competencies of your people
  - Develop and maintain a current database
  - Define roles and responsibilities
  - Co–location
- **Create peer pressure** that forces behavior change based on:
  - Value propositions
  - Speed
  - Acceptable attitude about taking prudent risks and making mistakes (learn from them)
  - Balance risk with appropriate rewards
  - Define optimum individual performance objectives & measure progress:
    - Energy – How much energy you demonstrate on your job?
    - Energize – How effective are you in influencing others?
    - Edge – Do you know and take advantage of your core competencies?
    - Execution – How effectively do you implement?
    - Ethics – Honesty and Integrity
    - Excellence – 'Be All That You Can Be'
- Set **bold cycle time** reduction objectives –
  - Establish current state base line
  - Establish desired state baseline
  - Define transitional approach
  - Time sensitive performance metrics and vital signs
- Embrace **speed and excellence**
  - Establish 'speed' incentives and rewards (balance with quality, risk and customer involvement)
  - Incentivize employees to challenge the norms **(think and do out-of-the box; dare to be different)**
  - Recognize people and teams for a superior job
  - Continuous reinforcement of a job well done
  - Make decisions locally and in real time

Most organizations grossly underestimate the amount of and strength of resistance to change — it comes in many forms – overt, covert, conscious and unconscious.

- Create **'speed' teams**
  - Fast teams have strong leaders (well trained)
  - Keep team focused
  - Knock obstacles out of the way or neutralize them
  - Best-in-class talent
  - Establish ultra-clear priorities, roles and responsibilities
  - Reduce/eliminate job fragmentation **(do what you do best – do not sub-optimize)**
  - Fast electronic communications (24 by 7) –Cell, Teleconferencing, Videoconferencing
  - Make fast adjustments
  - Leapfrog & compete on speed
  - Act within the spirit of the process (not strictly by the process)
  - Rotate 'high potential team members' (at end of project) as change agents (to other initiatives) and incent them
  - Leverage the same Project Manager across similar type projects
- Conduct **fast team meetings**
  - Do your homework
  - Don't mind your manners
  - Stand up meetings make meetings short (no coffee or doughnuts)
  - Focus fast and keep focused
  - Encourage fast follow up
  - Make fast work out of peripheral issues
  - Bump up, not down (for meeting attendees)
  - Stand up meeting speed things up
  - Turn off cell phones
  - No side conversation – listen when someone else is talking
- Create **flatter, smaller and nimbler organizations based on effective teams**
  - Increase span of control – virtual organization with access to **global brains**
  - Change fast
  - Multifunctional and team based
  - Work on **building effective teams** – Forming, Storming, Norming and Performing
  - Real-time communication amongst team members

- **70/30% Decision Process** – it is an attitude about how sure you have to be to make a decision that provides permission to speed things up by not working harder, but smarter:
  - Complete consensus not required
  - **Time box scope and deliverables**
  - Use your judgment and previous experience – **odds are you are right**
  - Set time constraints on decisions
  - Make decisions and then move on - no rehash
  - Mistakes are acceptable – **but fix them fast**
  - Frequent customer validations
  - Take informed risks – **no pain, no gain**
  - Encourage continuous improvement
  - Learn how much you need to engage others to be 70% certain of your decision
  - Learn how much information is required to be 70% certain of your decision
  - Champion the 70% solution
  - Less stress
  - Encourage all to support and commit – it's an attitude that affects behavior change

- Create and sustain a continuous learning environment
  - Know skills sets of employees **(skills database)**
  - Establish minimum competencies for various positions
  - Know gaps
  - Encourage personal development, education and training programs and subsidize
  - Invest in continuous education and training (set minimum requirements per employee per year)
  - Design training and education offerings to fit 'speed' criteria (e.g. Webcasts, Video Conferencing, 3 hour focused modules, etc.)
  - Encourage regular (senior to junior) and reverse (junior to senior) mentoring programs
  - Establish **Knowledge Management** process to capture and access **Lessons learned**

- **Best practice benchmarking**
  - Form peer (external) group to share best practices
  - Continuously monitor, improve and adopt
  - Ensure that the organization develops as a learning system

Scalable and Flexible Process

- Develop **scalable, flexible and tailored business, project and innovation processes (e.g. ideation process)**
- Define **Mandatory (Minimum) and Discretionary** Phases, Components, Templates, Procedures, etc.
  - Accommodate **multiple program/project/process types** (e.g. new, enhancements, operational software, infrastructure, product, etc.) & **complexity - size/value/reach/integration/funding/etc.**
  - Accommodate **outsourcing, in-sourcing and hybrid models**
  - Accommodate **fast track and full risk mitigation** initiatives
- Define Business Process Models (How the business should operate), streamline and then automate

- Establish and enforce a well defined **governance process** with simple clear metrics, reporting guidelines and escalation processes:
  - **Clear roles and responsibilities**
  - **Issues management**
  - **Change management**
  - Employ **multiple communications techniques and frequencies** (especially prior to due dates for deliverables, milestones, meetings, etc- 60 day, 30 day, 15 day, 7, day, 2 day, 1 day reminder notices)
  - Use **meaningful dashboards, metrics and graphs** (color coded) to convey successes and show laggards
  - **Escalate sooner** than later
- Institute a **Portfolio Investment Management process** –formalize the selection, evaluation prioritization and funding of initiatives based on business criteria
  - Reprioritize active projects on an on-going basis
  - Do not classify each project as a priority
- **Time Box Scope**
  - Smallest and clearest scope possible
  - Decompose large initiatives into programs and/or interrelated projects with time boxing
  - Chunk scope into time slots (no individual initiative exceeds 3 months, but interrelated projects can be longer as a group)
- **Time Box Deliverables**
  - Short term incremental deliverables (80 hour rule)
  - Frequent iterations with constituencies, customer(s), team, etc.
  - Acceptance criteria
- **Outsource** (non-core initiatives or tasks, domestically or internationally) with a limited number of qualified (and certified) vendors
  - Have a vendor selection and RFP process in place
  - Have a vendor management, escalation. and metrics process in place
- Create **knowledge management cafes and repositories (capture intellectual capital for reuse)**
  - Lessons learned, best of breed processes, training for junior and senior folks
  - Leverage process experience to create templates, etc. for reuse Enabling Technology

Enabling Technology

- Streamline the work flow before automation
- Encourage collaborative tools (Share documents, Central Repository for Projects, Groupware, etc.)
- Automate, automate, automate – Web and sub-webs , tools, templates, PM software, lessons learned repository, knowledge management,
- Easy to use, easy to locate
- Use expert systems and knowledge management to capture and re-use best practices and change poor practices
- Fast electronic communications (24 by 7)

Made in the USA
Lexington, KY
21 September 2013